Is a core-periphery cleavage tearing the European Union apart? This timely book critically examines the transformation of political conflict in Europe in the wake of the Eurocrisis. José Magone, Brigid Laffan and Christian Schweiger have assembled a leading group of theoretical and empirical scholars to apply the core-periphery lens on the Eurocrisis. The collection provides a compelling explanation for the intensity of conflict, coalitional patterns, and declining policy effectiveness in the contemporary European Union. It shows how the Eurocrisis has exacerbated – rather than created – old core-periphery tensions, and how the EU institutions' inability to diffuse these tensions is hastening Europe's geopolitical decline. This path-breaking study will change our understanding of European governance. It is also a wake-up call for Europe's leaders.

Liesbet Hooghe, *University of North Carolina at Chapel Hill, USA*

Core-periphery Relations in the European Union

Successive enlargements to the European Union membership have transformed it into an economically, politically and culturally heterogeneous body with distinct vulnerabilities in its multi-level governance.

This book analyses core–periphery relations to highlight the growing cleavage, and potential conflict, between the core and peripheral member states of the Union in the face of the devastating consequences of the Eurozone crisis. Taking a comparative and theoretical approach and using a variety of case studies, it examines how the crisis has both exacerbated tensions in centre–periphery relations within and outside the Eurozone and how the European Union's economic and political status is declining globally.

This text will be of key interest to students and scholars of European Union studies, European integration, political economy, public policy and comparative politics.

José M. Magone is Professor of Regional and Global Governance at the Berlin School of Economics and Law.

Brigid Laffan is Director and Professor at the Robert Schuman Centre for Advanced Studies and Director of the Global Governance Programme, European University Institute (EUI), Florence.

Christian Schweiger is Senior Lecturer in the School of Government and International Affairs at Durham University.

Routledge/UACES Contemporary European Studies

Edited by Federica Bicchi, London School of Economics and Political Science, Tanja Börzel, Free University of Berlin, and Mark Pollack, Temple University, on behalf of the University Association for Contemporary European Studies

The primary objective of the new Contemporary European Studies series is to provide a research outlet for scholars of European Studies from all disciplines. The series publishes important scholarly works and aims to forge for itself an international reputation.

1. The EU and Conflict Resolution
Promoting peace in the backyard
Nathalie Tocci

2. Central Banking Governance in the European Union
A comparative analysis
Lucia Quaglia

3. New Security Issues in Northern Europe
The Nordic and Baltic states and the ESDP
Edited by Clive Archer

4. The European Union and International Development
The politics of foreign aid
Maurizio Carbone

5. The End of European Integration
Anti-Europeanism examined
Paul Taylor

6. The European Union and the Asia-Pacific
Media, public and elite perceptions of the EU
Edited by Natalia Chaban and Martin Holland

7. The History of the European Union
Origins of a trans- and supranational polity 1950–72
Edited by Wolfram Kaiser, Brigitte Leucht and Morten Rasmussen

8. International Actors, Democratization and the Rule of Law
Anchoring democracy?
Edited by Amichai Magen and Leonardo Morlino

9. Minority Nationalist Parties and European Integration
A comparative study
Anwen Elias

10. European Union Intergovernmental Conferences
Domestic preference formation, transgovernmental networks and the dynamics of compromise
Paul W. Thurner and Franz Urban Pappi

11. The Political Economy of State-Business Relations in Europe
Interest mediation, capitalism and EU policy making
Rainer Eising

12. Governing Financial Services in the European Union
Banking, securities and post-trading
Lucia Quaglia

13. European Union Governance
Efficiency and legitimacy in European commission committees
Karen Heard-Lauréote

14. European Governmentality
The liberal drift of multilevel governance
Richard Münch

15. The European Union as a Leader in International Climate Change Politics
Edited by Rüdiger K. W. Wurzel and James Connelly

16. Diversity in Europe
Dilemmas of differential treatment in theory and practice
Edited by Gideon Calder and Emanuela Ceva

17. EU Conflict Prevention and Crisis Management
Roles, institutions and policies
Edited by Eva Gross and Ana E. Juncos

18. The European Parliament's Committees
National party influence and legislative empowerment
Richard Whitaker

19. The European Union, Civil Society and Conflict
Nathalie Tocci

20. European Foreign Policy and the Challenges of Balkan Accession
Sovereignty contested
Gergana Noutcheva

21. The European Union and South East Europe
The dynamics of Europeanization and multilevel governance
Andrew Taylor, Andrew Geddes and Charles Lees

22. Bureaucrats as Law-Makers
Committee decision-making in the EU Council of Ministers
Frank M. Häge

23. Europeanization and the European Economic Area
Iceland's participation in the EU's policy process
Johanna Jonsdottir

24. The Cultural Politics of Europe
European capitals of culture and the European Union since 1980
Kiran Klaus Patel

25. European Integration and Transformation in the Western Balkans
Europeanization or business as usual?
Arolda Elbasani

26. European Union Constitutionalism in Crisis
Nicole Scicluna

27. Transnationalization and Regulatory Change in the EU's Eastern Neighbourhood
Julia Langbein

28. Lobbying in EU Foreign Policy-making
The case of the Israeli–Palestinian conflict
Benedetta Voltolini

29. War and Intervention in the Transnational Public Sphere
Problem-solving and European identity-formation
Cathleen Kantner

30. The European Union's Foreign Policy in Comparative Perspective
Evaluating and generating hypotheses on 'actorness and power'
Edited by Ingo Peters

31. The Formulation of EU Foreign Policy
Socialization, negotiations and disaggregation of the state
Nicola Chelotti

32. Core-periphery Relations in the European Union
Power and conflict in a dualist political economy
José M. Magone, Brigid Laffan and Christian Schweiger

Core-periphery Relations in the European Union

Power and conflict in a dualist political economy

Edited by
José M. Magone, Brigid Laffan and Christian Schweiger

Routledge
Taylor & Francis Group
LONDON AND NEW YORK

First published 2016
by Routledge
2 Park Square, Milton Park, Abingdon, Oxon OX14 4RN

and by Routledge
711 Third Avenue, New York, NY 10017

First issued in paperback 2017

Routledge is an imprint of the Taylor & Francis Group, an informa business

British Library Cataloguing in Publication Data
A catalogue record for this book is available from the British Library

Library of Congress Cataloging in Publication Data
Names: Magone, Josâe M. (Josâe Marâia), 1962- editor. | Laffan, Brigid, editor. | Schweiger, Christian, 1972- editor.
Title: Core-periphery relations in the European Union : power and conflict in a dualist political economy / edited by Josâe M. Magone, Brigid Laffan, Christian Schweiger.
Description: New York, NY : Routledge, 2016. | Series: Routledge/UACES contemporary European studies ; 32 | Includes bibliographical references and index.
Identifiers: LCCN 2015037386| ISBN 9781138889316 (hardback) | ISBN 9781315712994 (ebook)
Subjects: LCSH: European federation. | European Union countries–Politics and government–21st century. | Financial crises–Political aspects–European Union countries. | European Union countries–Economic conditions–Regional disparities. | European Union–Membership.
Classification: LCC JN15 .C619 2016 | DDC 341.242/2–dc23
LC record available at http://lccn.loc.gov/2015037386

ISBN 13: 978-1-138-48731-4 (pbk)
ISBN 13: 978-1-138-88931-6 (hbk)

Typeset in Baskerville
by Taylor & Francis Books

To Jacques Delors and his visionary leadership in the European Union

Contents

List of illustrations

Figures

Tables

List of contributors

Attila Ágh is Professor in the Political Science Department at Budapest Corvinus University. He was visiting professor at many universities from Aarhus to Los Angeles. His major research interest is comparative politics, especially EU developments in the new member states. He has published about twenty books and a hundred papers, mostly in English. He has substantial experience in major political science projects at EU, Central European and Hungarian level. His latest book is *10 Years After: Multi-level Governance and Differentiated Integration in the EU* (2014). Other recent publications: 'Decline of democracy in East-Central Europe: The last decade as the lost decade in democratization', *Journal of Comparative Politics*, vol. 7, no. 2 (2014), pp. 4–33; 'The fall of the Berlin Wall and European politics: Perspectives of new Europe in the early twenty-first century', pp. 116–31, in Magone, José (ed.) *Routledge Handbook of European Politics*, London: Routledge (2014); 'The roller-coaster ride of the Hungarian administrative elite: Politico-administrative relations in East-Central Europe', *Revue Francaise D'Administration Publique (RFAP)*, nos 151/2 (2014), pp. 663–80.

Stefan Auer is Director and Associate Professor of European Studies at the University of Hong Kong. Prior to this, he worked at La Trobe University in Melbourne, where he held the Jean Monnet Chair in EU Interdisciplinary Studies. His book *Liberal Nationalism in Central Europe* (Routledge, 2004) won Best Book in European Studies (2005) from the University Association for Contemporary European Studies. Recent publications include *Whose Liberty is it Anyway? Europe at the Crossroads* (Seagull, 2012), 'The end of the European dream', *Transit: Europäische Revue* (no. 44, 2013; appeared also in Bulgarian, German, Russian and Slovenian) and 'Carl Schmitt in the Kremlin: the Ukraine crisis and the return of geopolitics', *International Affairs*, vol. 91, no. 5 (2015). He also writes occasional opinion pieces for *The South China Morning Post* and *The Australian* and comments on European politics in the media – for instance ABC News 24 (based in Melbourne), CNBC and RTHK (based in Hong Kong).

Marco Brunazzo is Assistant Professor of Political Science at the University of Trento. His research focuses on the European Union policy-making and on relations between Italy and the EU.

Bernadette Connaughton is a Lecturer in Public Administration and Head of Department at the Department of Politics and Public Administration, University of Limerick. Her teaching and research interests include environmental policy, Europeanisation, the Irish public policy process and political-administrative relations. Her publications include *Europeanisation and New Patterns of Governance in Ireland* (co-authored with Brid Quinn and Nicholas Rees, 2010). She has also published in a range of international journals including *Public Administration, Irish Political Studies*, *Federal and Regional Studies*, *Halduskultuur*, *Administration*, *International Journal of Public Administration* and *Journal of Environmental Policy and Planning*.

Vincent Della Sala teaches political science at the University of Trento and is Adjunct Professor at the Bologna Center of the John Hopkins School of Advanced International Studies. His research focuses on the impact of the European Union on domestic policies, especially macroeconomic policy, and on the ways in which legitimacy of the EU is generated through social practices. His published work has looked at Italy and the EU as well as political myth and legitimacy in the EU.

Maciej Duszczyk is Deputy Director of the Institute of Social Policy and Board Member of the Centre of Migration Research, University of Warsaw. From 2008 to 2011 he was on the Board of Strategic Advisers to the Prime Minister of Poland. Currently he is a member of the Science Policy Committee, Ministry of Science and Higher Education and an external collaborator for the International Labour Organization, European Commission and International Organization for Migration. He has received scholarships from the Jean Monnet Project, Carl Duisburg Gesellschaft and the Polish Committee for Scientific Research. Duszczyk specialises in topics within the labour market, social policy and economic migration.

Béla Galgóczi has been Senior Research Officer at the European Trade Union Institute, Brussels since April 2003. He was born in Budapest, Hungary, and graduated in electrical engineering (1982) at the Technical University of Budapest, then in sociology and philosophy (1986) at the Eötvös Lóránd University of Sciences, Budapest, postgraduate studies in political sciences at the University of Amsterdam (1990), PhD in Economics 1994 (Hungarian Academy of Sciences). His field of research includes the social impact of the economic transformation in Eastern Europe; labour market research, industrial relations, collective bargaining; capital and labour mobility in an enlarged Europe in the global environment; restructuring, managing change and location competition; green transition and its impact on industrial jobs in Europe.

Olivér Kovács obtained his PhD in Economics at the University of Debrecen, Doctoral School of Economics. He is currently a Research Fellow at the ICEG European Center, Budapest. His research embraces the issues of sustainable development, fiscal sustainability and innovation policy. His articles have appeared in journals such as *Acta Oeconomica*, *Competitio*, *Economic Review*, *Eastern*

Journal of European Studies and the *TIGER Working Paper* series. He has also produced two policy briefs on services innovation and public sector innovation at the European Commission, published by Finland Futures Research Centre and the Columbia Center on Sustainable Investment, Columbia University. (E-mail: okovacs@icegec.hu, Web: www.oliverkovacs.com.)

Thorsten Kruse holds a PhD in Political Science from the University of Münster. He is a Research Associate of the Institute for Interdisciplinary Cypriot Studies and Lecturer at the Department of History (International Relations) at the University of Münster. His research activities focus on the modern history of Cyprus and Greece and on the history of Germany between 1945 and 1990. In addition, he takes an interest in recent political and economic developments in the Eastern Mediterranean. Among his publications in German are: *Bonn – Nikosia – Ostberlin: German Feuds on Foreign Soil 1960–1974* (Ruhpolding: Rutzen, 2013); 'The Forsthoff affair: The young Republic of Cyprus and its German president of the Constitutional Court', *Thetis*, no. 19 (2012), pp. 207–16; 'Cyprus and the financial crisis', *Hellenika* (Neue Folge), vol. 9 (2014), pp. 37–58; 'Cyprus and the modern Law of the Sea: A further facet in the conflict', *Thetis*, nos 16/17 (2010), pp. 141–7. Publications in English include: 'Cyprus and the two German states: 'Class struggle' in the Eastern Mediterranean', *The Cyprus Review*, vol. 24, no. 1 (2012), pp. 55–69.

Brigid Laffan is Director and Professor at the Robert Schuman Centre for Advanced Studies, European University Institute (EUI), Florence. In September 2014 Professor Laffan was awarded the UACES Lifetime Achievement Award. In 2012 she was awarded the THESEUS Award for outstanding research on European Integration. Recent publications include 'Testing times: the growing primacy of responsibility in the Euro area', *West European Politics*, vol. 37, no. 2 (2014), pp. 270–87; 'In the shadow of austerity: Ireland's seventh presidency of the European Union', *Journal of Common Market Studies*, vol. 52, no. 1 (2014), pp. 90–8; and 'Framing the crisis, defining the problems: decoding the Euro area crisis', *Perspectives on European Politics and Society*, vol. 15, no. 3 (2014), pp. 266–80.

José M. Magone is Professor of Regional and Global Governance at the Berlin School of Economics and Law. He has published 13 books, over 48 chapters in edited books and 14 journal articles on European politics, particularly on southern Europe and European integration. Among his latest publications are the single-authored books *The New World Architecture: The Role of the European Union in the Making of Global Governance* (Transaction, 2006); *Contemporary Spanish Politics*, second edition (Routledge 2009); *Contemporary European Politics* (Routledge, 2011); *The Politics of Contemporary Portugal; Evolving Democracy* (Lynne Rienner, 2014); and the edited volume *Routledge Handbook of European Politics* (Routledge, 2015).

Ignacio Paredero Huerta is a PhD candidate at the University of Salamanca funded by the Spanish Ministry of Education. A sociologist, he earned an MA at the University of Salamanca and another (on leadership in political management) at the Universidad Autónoma de Barcelona. He is writing his PhD on 'North, South and East sociopolitical divisions in the European Union'. He specialises in the European Union and euro crisis and has spent some months working in Brussels institutions to advance the qualitative work of his thesis. Other academic interests are social movements, LGBT studies and political economy. He also recently wrote the chapter, 'The Electoral Behaviour of the Province of Salamanca (1976–2011)' with Manuel Alcántara and Patricia Marenghi for the book *Historia de Salamanca V,* Centro de Estudios Salmantinos [in Spanish].

Carolin Rüger studied Political Science, Sociology and German Language and Literature. She holds a PhD in Political Science from the University of Würzburg where she lectures in International Relations and European Studies. She lectured as a visiting scholar at the University of Lucerne, Switzerland. She published various articles in journals and edited volumes on the reform process of the EU and on the EU as a global actor. In her PhD thesis she analysed public and media opinion on the EU foreign and security policy. She co-edited the volume, *The High Representative for the EU Foreign and Security Policy: Review and Prospects.* Her most recent publication on EU foreign policy is the co-authored title *Die Aussenpolitik der EU* (De Gruyter Oldenbourg, 2015). Rüger is a member of Team Europe, the European Commission's panel of independent expert speakers.

Christian Schweiger is Senior Lecturer in the School of Government and International Affairs at Durham University. His research interests concentrate on the institutions, policies and the member states of the European Union (particularly the UK, Germany and the CEE countries), the political economy of the EU Single Market, economic globalisation and transatlantic relations. He coordinates the UACES collaborative research network, the EU Single Market in the Global Economy, and is Associate Fellow at the Central European Policy Institute in Bratislava, Slovakia. He is the author of two monographs on the EU: *Britain, Germany and the Future of the European Union* (Palgrave, 2007) and *The EU and the Global Financial Crisis: New Varieties of Capitalism* (Edward Elgar, 2014). His most recent publications in the journals *Perspectives on European Politics and Society* and *Europe-Asia Studies* focus on the EU's internal developments in the aftermath of the global financial crisis.

Angelos Sepos is Assistant Professor in European Politics at Al Akhawayn University, Ifrane, Morocco. Following the completion of his PhD in International Studies at the University of Cambridge (2003), he was a Jean Monnet Fellow (2003–2004) at the Robert Schuman Centre for Advanced Studies at the European University Institute in Florence. He subsequently held lectureship (Assistant Professor) positions in International and European Politics at the European University Cyprus (2004–2005), University of Cyprus (2005–2006), University of Newcastle (2006–2008) and University of Manchester (2009–2010). He is the author of the book *The Europeanization of Cyprus: Polity, Policies and*

Politics (Palgrave Macmillan, 2008) and the co-editor (with Kenneth Dyson) of the book *Which Europe? The Politics of Differentiated Integration* (Palgrave Macmillan, 2010). He has also published articles in various edited volumes and leading scientific journals such as the *Journal of Political Power*, *Journal of European Integration*, *Journal of Southern Europe and the Balkans* and *Regional and Federal Studies*.

Anna Visvizi, PhD, is a political analyst and economist, editor and research consultant with extensive experience in academia and the think-tank sector. Dr Visvizi has presented her work in many forums across Europe and the US, including Capitol Hill. Former DAAD and Marie Curie Fellow, Dr Visvizi's expertise includes (a) the political economy of the crisis in Greece, (b) global safety and security, including transatlantic relations and global governance structures, (c) security, economy and politics in East-Central Europe and the post-Soviet space, (d) theoretical dimensions of these processes, including ethics in international affairs. She has recently published: 'From Grexit to Grecovery: the paradox of the Troika's engagement with Greece', *Perspectives on European Politics and Society*, vol. 15, no. 3 (2014), pp. 335–45; 'Poland's winding road to the Euro area: from cost-benefit analysis to risk aversion' (with P. Tokarski), *Polish Quarterly of International Affairs*, vol. 40, no. 4 (2015); 'Slovenia's role in the V4: a view from Poland', *European Perspectives of the Western Balkans*, vol. 7, no. 2 (13) (2015), pp. 87–113; 'Safety, risk, governance and the Eurozone crisis: rethinking the conceptual merits of "global safety governance"', in Kłosińska-Dąbrowska, P. (ed.) *Essays on Global Safety Governance: Challenges and Solutions*, Warsaw: Centre for Europe, University of Warsaw, ASPRA-JR (2015), pp. 21-40.

Edward Yencken is a PhD candidate in the School of Social and Political Sciences, University of Melbourne. He received a BA (Hons) from the University of Melbourne in 2010 having also spent a semester studying at University College, Dublin. As part of his PhD research Edward spent time as Visiting Scholar at Universität Trier, Germany, in 2012. In 2013 Edward was a Visiting Fellow at Freie Universität Berlin, Germany, attached to the NFG (Nachwuchsforschergruppe) Research Project, 'Asian Perceptions of the EU: External views on the EU as a Civilian Power'. His current PhD thesis explores relations between Australia and the EU and the extent to which they have improved over the past two decades. In particular, the thesis is seeking to analyse EU–Australian relations within the broader framework of Australian foreign policy and its formulation. Edward's other research interests include EU politics, Western European politics, EU–Asia relations and Asia–Pacific regionalism.

Preface

The European Union has been a successful enterprise. After decades of division during the Cold War, the European continent is now united, the original community of six member states having grown to one of 28. Many institutional adjustments and changes have been made over the decades in order to cope with several enlargements; nevertheless, the EU remains an attractive supranational organisation. In eastern Europe as well as in the Balkans, countries such as Ukraine, Georgia, Moldavia, Serbia, Albania, Macedonia and Montenegro are engaged in processes of further European integration.

However, the successive enlargements have created a radically heterogeneous European Union. The Eurocrisis between 2007 and 2013 has shown that most countries and populations still think in terms of national interests instead of adopting a common European perspective. This is particularly evident in the relationship between the richer and poorer member states. Our purpose in this book is to examine the growing divergence in national interests, the establishment of power structures and emergent conflict between a core and a periphery in the European Union. The core countries are situated in the northwestern part of Europe, comprising Germany, France, the United Kingdom, the Netherlands, Belgium, Luxembourg, Denmark, Sweden, Finland and Austria. The periphery countries are located in southern, central and eastern Europe, comprising Portugal, Spain, Greece, Malta, Cyprus, Hungary, Poland, the Czech Republic, Slovakia, Slovenia, Croatia, Bulgaria, Romania, Estonia, Latvia and Lithuania. Ireland and Italy are at the perimeter of the core, with stronger economies than most countries of the periphery. The Eurocrisis has demonstrated that if a small country like Ireland makes a mistake, it may lose its status as a core country and quickly join the periphery. The same applies to the larger country of Italy, which in times of growth can be regarded as a country of the core despite the internal dualism between its dynamic northern and stagnant southern economies, but in times of crisis may become a country of the periphery. In this sense, we do not categorise countries as strictly belonging to the core or periphery. On the contrary, this dualism is a dynamic process and such differences may eventually fade away if the right policies are implemented.

Our main thesis is that the heterogeneity of national political and economic systems has created this conflict between the northwestern core and the southern, central and eastern periphery. This categorisation may be objectively verifiable through the use of several statistical indicators, but it is primarily a heuristic device to understand the problems of political, economic, social and cultural governance that the European Union is experiencing in the present and will be subject to in the future. Due to the low level of resources available in relation to the ambitions of the European Union, the supranational organisation may have reached its limits in terms of multilevel governance.

Throughout, we follow the question Brigid Laffan asks in chapter 2: 'Is core-periphery conflict leading to a cleavage in the European Union?' The management of the Eurocrisis through power instruments such as the Troika has exhibited elements of a 'coercive Europeanisation' exerted by the richer Eurozone members on the ailing economies of southern Europe and Ireland through the sometimes misguided bailout efforts. Although a core–periphery cleavage may potentially emerge, the book seeks to raise awareness of the fact that, objectively speaking, the European Union features a dualist economy: core economies in the northwest and peripheral economies in the south, centre and east of the Union. The variety of national interests at work in this dualist economy can lead to power struggles and eventually conflict. The emergence of social movements and political parties such as the Coalition of the Radical Left (*Syriza*) in Greece and the Alternative for Germany (*Alternative für Deutschland*-AfD) are reactions to this perceived divide. Moreover, they represent different models of capitalism and society. All this is thoroughly discussed in the book.

In this volume we focus mainly on the core–periphery divide during the Eurocrisis as a case study for the exploration of national interests, power struggles and conflict. A group of 16 scholars reflect on different perspectives of this core–periphery divide. Most of the contributions were presented in a previous version at a conference entitled 'Core-periphery relations in the European Union as an emerging cleavage of European politics and public policy? Empirical studies of differentiated integration', which took place at the Berlin School of Economics and Law (BSEL) on 11–12 October 2013. The conference was generously funded by the Fritz Thyssen Foundation. Additional funding came from the University Association of Contemporary European Studies (UACES) and the BSEL. We thank these institutions for making it possible to organise the meeting. In this context, I would like to express my gratitude to the Director of BSEL, Prof. Dr. Bernd Reissert, and the Dean of the Faculty of Business and Economics, Prof. Dr. Otto von Campenhausen, who have been very enthusiastic about and supportive of the project since it was first proposed in 2013.

A first volume of the project was published in September 2014 as a special issue under the title 'The effects of the Eurozone sovereign debt crisis: Differentiated integration between centre and the new peripheries of the EU' in *Perspectives in European Politics and Societies*, vol. 15, no. 3. A book on the same topic edited by Christian Schweiger and José M. Magone was published by Routledge in 2015.

This second volume complements the first one; however, it focuses less on the Eurozone and more on core–periphery relations and the implications for

European integration. It consists of five parts dedicated to theoretical perspectives, comparative approaches, country studies on the impact of the Troika regime on southern European countries and Ireland, case studies on non-Eurozone member states (Hungary and Poland), and finally an examination of how the divide and crisis in Europe has affected the EU's position in global politics and the world economy.

We would like to thank Senior Editor Andrew Taylor and Editorial Assistants Charlotte Endersby and Sophie Iddamalgoda for their collaboration on this project. Andrew has been supportive of the project from the very beginning, Charlotte and Sophie played a major role in getting the manuscript ready through their emails and encouragement. It is always a great pleasure to work with the Routledge team.

We would also like to take the opportunity to thank Claire Bacher for doing such an excellent job in terms of language editing before the manuscript's final submission. Many of the authors are very grateful for her comments and suggestions for improvements in language. It is not the first time that Claire has been an indispensable and excellent source of inspiration in the process of finalising a manuscript. Last but not least, we express our gratitude to the excellent work of Copyeditor Gill Gairdner and Production Editor Ruth Bradley.

Abbreviations

AfD	Alternative für Deutschland –Alternative for Germany
AKEL	Anorthotiko Komma Ergazomenou Laou – Progressive Party of the Working People (Greece)
ANA	Aeroportos de Portugal –Airports of Portugal
BE	Bloco da Esquerda-Block of Left
BPN	Banco Português dos Negócios – Portuguese Bank of Business
CDS	Credit Default Swap
CDS-PP	Centro Democratico Social-Partido – Popular Democratic Social Centre-People's Party (Portugal)
CDU/CSU	Christlich-Demokratische Partei/Christlich-Soziale Partei – Christian Democratic Party/Christian Social Party (Germany)
CEE	Central and Eastern Europe
CEECs	Central and Eastern European countries
CETA	Comprehensive Economic and Trade Agreement
CFSP	Common Foreign and Security Policy
CGTP-In	Confederação Geral dos Trabalhadores Portugueses-Intersindical/ General Confederation of Portuguese Workers-Intersindical
DFAT	Department of Foreign Affairs and Trade (Australia)
DI	Differentiated Integration
DISY	Dimokratikos Synagermos – Democratic Rally (Cyprus)
EAP	Economic Adjustment Programme
EBA	European Banking Authority
EC	European Community
EC	European Commission
ECB	European Central Bank
ECCL	Enhanced Conditions Credit Line
ECFR	European Council on Foreign Relations
Ecofin	Economy and Finance Council of Ministers
ECSC	European Coal and Steel Community
ECJ	European Court of Justice
ECU	European Currency Unit
EdP	Energias de Portugal – Energy of Portugal
EDP	Excessive Deficit Procedure

EEAS	European External Action Service
EEC	European Economic Community
EFSF	European Financial Stability Facility
EFTA	European Free Trade Area
ESAME	Missão de Acompanhamento aos Memorandos – Special unit on monitoring the memorandums (Portugal)
ELA	Emergency Liquidity Assistance
EMU	Economic and Monetary Union
EMS	European Monetary System
EMC	Economic Management Council
EP	European Parliament
EPCU	External Programme Compliance Unit
ERM	Exchange Rate Mechanism
ESCB	European System of Central Banks
ESDP	European Security and Defence Policy
ESM	European Stability Mechanism
E3	Germany, France and UK
EUR	Euro
EU27	European Union member states without Croatia
EU28	European Union member states
ETA	Euskadi ta Askatasuma – Basque Country and Freedom (Spain)
FIE	Foreign Investment Enterprise
FDI	Foreign Direct Investment
FDP	Freiheitliche Demokratische Partei – Liberal Democratic Party (Germany)
FLA	Fondo de Liquidad Autonomo
FTA	Free Trade Area
GCC	German Constitutional Court – Bundesverfassungsgericht
GDP	Gross Domestic Product
G8/7	Regular meetings of eight/seven most important economies or powerful countries
GNP	Gross National Product
GIIPS	Greece, Italy, Ireland, Portugal and Spain
G20	Meetings of 20 strongest economies in the world
HRS	Hypo Real Estate (German bank)
HUF	Hungarian Forint
ICO	Instituto de Crédito Oficial – Institute of Official Credit (Spain)
IGCP	Agência de Gestão de Tesouraria e Divida Pública – Agency for the Management of the Treasury and Public Debt (Portugal)
IIF	Institute of International Finance
ILO	International Labour Organization
IMF	International Monetary Fund
IU	Izquierda Unida – United Left (Spain)
LI	Liberal Intergovernmentalism
MEP	Member of European Parliament

MoU	Memorandum of Understanding
M5S	Movimento Cinque Stelle – Five Star Movement (Italy)
MRA	Mutual Recognition Agreement
MTFS	Medium Term Fiscal Strategy
NAMA	National Asset Management Agency
ND	Nea Dimokratia – New Democracy (Greece)
NMS	New Member States
NATO	North Atlantic Treaty Organization
NULC	Nominal Unit of Labour Costs
OECD	Organization for Economic Cooperation and Development
OMC	Open Method of Coordination
OMT	Outright Monetary Transaction
OPEC	Organization of Petroleum Exporting Countries
PCP-PEV	Partido Comunista Português/Partido Os Verdes – Portuguese Communist Party/Green Party (Portugal)
PD	Partido Democratico – Democratic Party (Italy)
PEC	Pacto de Estabilidade e Crescimento – Stability and Growth Pact (Portugal)
PASOK	Panellinio Sosialistiko Kinima-Panhellenic Socialist Movement
PEGIDA	Patriotische Europäer gegen die Islamisierung des Abendlandes-Patriotic European against the Islamisation of the West (Germany)
PIIGS	Portugal, Italy, Ireland, Greece and Spain
PP	Partido Popular – People's Party
PPP	Power Purchasing Parity
PPS	Purchasing Power Standard
PREMAC	Programa para a Reforma do Estado e Melhoria da Administração do Estado – Programme for State Reform and the Improvement of State Administration
PS	Partido Socialista – Socialist Party (Portugal)
PSD	Partido Social Democrata-Social democratic Party (PSD)
PSOE	Partido Socialista Obrero Español-Spanish Socialist Workers' Party (Spain)
PSI	Private Sector Involvement
QMV	Qualified Majority Voting
R&D	Research and Development
SBA	Stand by Arrangement
SEA	Single European Act
SGP	Stability and Growth Pact
SITC	Standard International Trade Classification
SME	Small and Medium-sized enterprise
SOE	State-Owned Enterprise
SPD	Sozialdemokratische Partei Deutschlands – Social Democratic Party of Germany

Syriza	Synaspismos Rizospastikis Aristeras – Coalition of the Radical Right
TAP	Transportes Aéreos Portugueses – Air Portugal
TEU	Treaty of the European Union
TFEU	Treaty of the Functioning of the European Union
TTIP	Transatlantic Trade and Investment Partnership
UGT	União Geral dos Trabalhadores – General Union of Workers (UGT)
UK	United Kingdom
USA	United States of America
UNCTAD	United Nations Conference on Trade and Development
VAT	Value Added Tax
Visegrad 4	Czech Republic, Hungary, Poland and Slovakia
WEF	World Economic Forum
WTO	World Trade Organization

1 The European Union as a dualist political economy

Understanding core–periphery relations

José M. Magone, Brigid Laffan and Christian Schweiger

Conceptualising core–periphery relations in the European Union

The rapid expansion of the EC/EU since 1973 has created a more heterogeneous and diverse supranational organisation in ways that are negatively affecting its multilevel governance capability (Magone, 2008). This is a major worry among policy-makers and high-ranking officials in Brussels (Maystadt, 2011; Piris, 2012).

The main argument of this volume is that the process of enlargement has created a core–periphery cleavage or divide in the European Union that has considerable implications for perceptions of power relations, influence and leverage among member states. The European Union is not a homogenous economy, but rather a dualist one. It consists of a core economic Europe and a peripheral one – or, as argued by Bela Galgóczi in this volume, several peripheries. A conflict among various perceptions of the European Union has led to tensions between core and periphery countries in the Eurozone with repercussions for the European Union as a whole.

Conceptually, we identify as 'core' the highly developed economies of western and northern Europe (Germany, France, the UK, Austria, Denmark, Sweden, Finland, the Netherlands, Belgium and Luxembourg) and as 'periphery' the less developed economies of the European south (Portugal, Spain, Greece, Malta and Cyprus), centre (Hungary, the Czech Republic, Slovenia, Slovakia and Poland), east (Bulgaria, Romania and Croatia) and the Baltics (Estonia, Latvia and Lithuania). However, there are three cases that fall on the perimeter between the core and the periphery: France due to its stagnating economy, Italy due to the dualism of north and south, and Ireland due to its dynamism and strong investment in research and development (see Figure 1.1).

Our focus will be mainly on the internal dimension of the European political economy using theoretical, comparative and case studies. This centrality of the internal dynamics of the European political economy is analysed through the lens of core–periphery relations (see Figure 1.2).

Nevertheless, internal and external dimensions of the present and future prospects of the European political economy are intertwined and influence each other. Without an internally integrated, competitive, 'even' economy it will be

CORE COUNTRIES				PERIPHERY COUNTRIES			
	GDP/per capita (basis EU28 average = 100) 2013	Social benefits per capita in € 2012	Sustainable Governance Indicators Policy Performance 2014 Ranking	Country	GDP/ per capita(basis EU28 average= 100) 2013	Social benefits € 2012	Sustainable Governance Indicators Policy Performance 2014 Ranking
Luxembourg	257	16,316.60	8	Ireland	130	11,639.42	23
Netherlands	131	10,703.92	10	Italy	99	6,884.20	36
Austria	128	9,464.06	19	Spain	94	4,852.16	35
Sweden	127	10,855.15	1	Cyprus	89	3,968.93	39
Denmark	124	12,994.98	5	Malta	86	2,724.98	34
Germany	122	8,862.09	6	Czech Republic	82	2,249.95	15
Finland	113	9,394.98	4	Slovenia	82	3,678.28	25
UK	109	8,466.25	8	Portugal	79	3,768.91	31
Belgium	109	8,887.97	15	Slovakia	75	1,549.10	27
France	107	9,483.91	14	Greece	73	4,484.56	41
				Estonia	73	1,496.99	7
				Lithuania	73	1,301.12	11
				Poland	67	1,506.71	24
				Hungary	66	1,790.84	37
				Latvia	64	1,029.55	18
				Croatia	61	1,758.82	29
				Romania	55	861.92	30
				Bulgaria	45	695.64	31

Figure 1.1 Map of core–periphery Europe
Note: Ireland and Italy are on perimeter of the core but simplification aligns them at the periphery in the figure.
Source: Eurostat and Bertelsmann Foundation Sustainable Governance Indicators (SGI).

INTERNAL DIMENSION (Between EU Member States)		
ASPECTS	**CORE**	**PERIPHERY**
RULES	Rule Makers	Rule Takers
EU BUDGET	Net Payers	Net Receivers
EUROZONE	Creditors In Eurozone	Debtors or macro-economically considerably constrained in Eurozone
INNOVATION UNION (see Table 1.2.)	Innovation Leader or Follower	Moderate innovators and innovation laggards
DESCRIPTION	The dominant categories of European Integration (values, working approaches, behaviour) are shaped by the core countries particularly in political and socioeconomic terms:	The dominant categories of European Integration are coercively Europeanised and integrated logics of political And socioeconomic terms

EXTERNAL DIMENSION
internal core-periphery relations
are weakening economically core position of European Union in the world

CONTRIBUTING FACTORS:

Demographic change
Rise of BRICS (Brazil, Russia, India, China, South Africa)
Political indecisiveness
Low growth dualist economy
Technological lag
Erosion of European social model
Military weakness
Lack of control over neighbouring regions (Post-Soviet Space, Mediterranean)

Figure 1.2 Conceptualising core–periphery relations in the European Union

quite difficult for the European Union to project its European social market economy model onto the world economy. In the context of the declining power of global Europe, our volume is a major original contribution to study of the changing internal politics of the European Union.

This chapter sets out the context for the study of core–periphery relations in the European Union's dualist economy. Following this introduction, the chapter is divided into five further sections. In the next section we expand our conceptualisation of core–periphery relations. This is followed by a section on the emergence of the Troika as a power instrument of asymmetrical relations between core and periphery countries. The third section briefly discusses the implications of this divide or cleavage for the position of the European Union in world politics and the global economy. The penultimate section reviews the chapters in the volume, and finally some conclusions are drawn.

Recognising the European Union's dualist economy

The recognition of the socio-economic heterogeneity of the European Union is not a new idea (Höpner, Schäfer, 2008, 2015). In this book, we go beyond the mere recognition of the socio-economic heterogeneity in the European Union by reconceptualising it as a core–periphery cleavage with profound implications for the political and economic relations between member states.

Although studies of core–periphery relations have always been a part of European integration studies (e.g. Leonardi, 1993; Bachtler et al., 2014), the usual perspective has focused on convergence rather than divergence as a cleavage or divide. Moreover, the tendency has been to examine core–periphery relations within member states, not in the European Union as a whole (see Wright, Mény 1985; Jones, Keating, 1995; Le Galés, Lequesne, 1998). Studies applying a more pan-European approach to core–periphery relations have thus far been quite rare (see Cole, Cole, 1997; Hudson, Williams, 1999; Magone, 2006: 192–199).

Most of the gains in GDP convergence have been lost over the past few years due to the financial crisis. Portugal, Spain, Greece, Italy and Ireland all had to deal with decreases in their GDPs, and all have experienced high levels of unemployment. Between 2008 and 2013, GDP in Greece declined by 26.2 per cent, compared to 8.9 per cent in Italy, 7.6 per cent in Ireland, 6.9 per cent in Portugal and 5.8 per cent in Spain (Eurostat, 2014a).

National selfishness was quite prominent during the Eurocrisis, demonstrating that solidarity between member states still cannot be taken for granted (see the chapter by Stefan Auer). This indicates that the European Union is presently in a process of transition from methodological nationalism to methodological Europeanism. The recent re-emergence of methodological nationalism in dealing with the Eurozone's problems is a clear sign that such a transition is underway. 'More Europe' would have been a better and cheaper way to solve the Eurocrisis; instead, intergovernmental solutions like the European Stability Mechanism (ESM) were developed. As Helen Callaghan asserts, the European integration process has been eroding national versions of capitalism, replacing them with a hybridisation in the context of European multilevel governance. This hybridisation signifies a move towards a liberal market economy. Notably, it is becoming more difficult for socially homogenous blocs to control this changing reality (Callaghan, 2010: 578–595).

The social sciences in particular are still predominantly framed in a national perspective, not a European one. According to Andreas Wimmer and Nina Glicker Schiller, the methodological nationalism assumption is 'the assumption that the nation/state/society is the natural social and political form of the modern world' (2002: 302). The authors show that the framing of the world since the second half of the nineteenth century has been shaped by social sciences based on the perspective of different nation-states. As Antoine Vauchez argues, methodological Europeanism is part of a reframing process acting through the *acquis* and equipment of the European Union that can only represent a long-term transition to a new European frame of mind. The move towards methodological Europeanism is thus dependent on what the European Union wants to be in the future (Vauchez, 2015). Either it wants to keep the status quo by muddling through or rather become a superpower shaping the categories of power in the world towards a more social and environmentally friendly capitalism.

Although always existent in the background, core–periphery relations were brought to the fore by the Euro- and sovereign debt crises. The debate over this divide then became a 'domestic' European discussion that was predominantly conducted within the Eurozone. Rosenau characterises the growing interdependence of analytically diverse domestic and international fields of action as 'intermestic' (Rosenau, 1990, 2000). We can identify a similar process of interdependence between the supranational and national levels in the European Union, which (paraphrasing Rosenau) may be characterised as 'Euromestic', a term coined by Janerik Gidlund (2000: 254).

This is not the place to present all of the indicators that map this socio-economic core–periphery divide (see Magone, 2011, 2013). Most of the chapters in this volume will address this aspect in greater detail. Here, it suffices to illustrate the lag in terms of research and development between the core (advanced) and the peripheral (less developed) economies (Eurostat, 2014b). Figure 1.3 clearly shows a considerable gap between core and periphery, although there are some outliers (such as Slovenia and Estonia).

The innovation union recently established in the context of the Europe 2020 strategy merely confirms this divide. The so-called 'innovation score board' for 2014 still depicts a variety of research cultures among the member states, reconfirming the socio-economic core–periphery cleavage (European Commission 2010a, b; European Commission, 2014) (see Table 1.1).

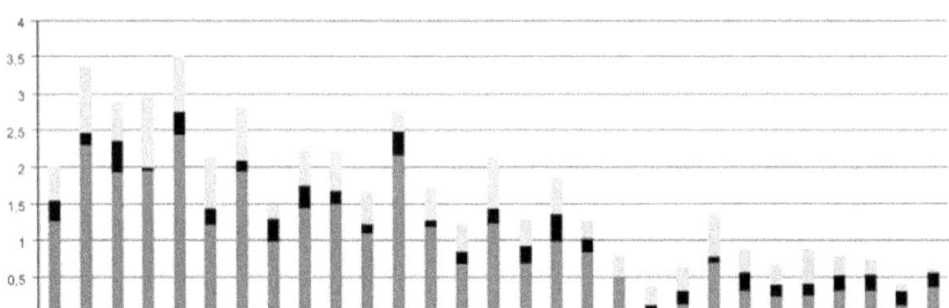

	EU 28	S	D	DK	FIN	NL	A	L	F	B	UK
		CORE									
Higher Education	0,49	0,92	0,53	0,95	0,77	0,7	0,73	0,19	0,47	0,52	0,46
Government	0,26	0,16	0,43	0,05	0,32	0,23	0,15	0,3	0,31	0,18	0,14
Business Enterprise	1,3	2,31	1,95	1,96	2,44	1,22	1,95	1	1,45	1,52	1,09

	SI	IRL	I	EE	E	CZ	HU	M	CY	LV	P	PL	GR	LT	SK	CR	ROM	BG
	PERIPHERY																	
Higher Education	0,29	0,45	0,36	0,7	0,36	0,52	0,24	0,3	0,26	0,33	0,58	0,31	0,28	0,48	0,28	0,2	0,1	0,05
Government	0,34	0,08	0,17	0,2	0,25	0,35	0,19	0,03	0,08	0,18	0,1	0,25	0,17	0,18	0,2	0,21	0,2	0,19
Business Enterprise	2,16	1,2	0,69	1,25	0,69	1,01	0,85	0,5	0,06	0,15	0,7	0,33	0,24	0,24	0,34	0,34	0,12	0,39

Figure 1.3 Research and development expenditure in the European Union, 2012
Source: Eurostat, 2014b.

Table 1.1 EU member states' innovation performance index, 2014

Core countries		*Periphery countries*	
Innovation leaders above 0.700	*Innovation followers between 0.700 and 0.500*	*Moderate innovators between 0.500 and 0.300*	*Modest innovators below 0.300*
Sweden	Luxembourg	Italy*	Romania
Denmark	Netherlands	Czech Republic	Latvia
Germany	Belgium	Spain	Bulgaria
Finland	United Kingdom	Portugal	
	Ireland *	Greece	
	Austria	Hungary	
	France	Slovakia	
	Slovenia*	Malta	
	Estonia*	Croatia	
	Cyprus *	Lithuania	
		Poland	

Note: *Countries on the perimeter of the core.
Source: European Commission, 2014: 11.

This selection of indicators makes a case for the dualist nature of the European economy. In socio-economic terms, one can also refer to other indicators (productivity per working hour, quality of the welfare state, nature of flexicurity, job quality, industrial relations, gender and social equality) that further corroborate the core–periphery divide. In many ways, one could characterise the cleavage or divide in terms of core efficient national governance and peripheral less efficient one. In some cases, this lack of efficiency degenerated to 'bad' governance like in the case of Greece (see Figure 1.1.)

In sum, the dualist economy of the European Union is an important factor that should be considered when analysing further European integration. This dualism can be observed not only in socio-economic indicators but also in 'Euromestic' politics.

The end of the benevolent European Union: the invention of the Troika

Conflicts over the EU budget have erupted regularly over the past fifteen years, especially since the Berlin European Council of 1999. The European Union neglected to provide adequate resources for the mega-enlargement of the EU after 2004. The EU budgets for the periods 2000–2006, 2007–2013 and now 2014–2020 have not included any increase in resources; recently, there has even been a reduction of the budget to about €960 billion for a six-year period. At least seven countries have organised themselves in an attempt to prevent any increase in the budget: the United Kingdom, Germany, France, Finland, Sweden, Austria and the Netherlands, a group that has been labelled the 'friends of better spending'. At the same time, a group called the 'friends of cohesion' (comprising the southern, central and eastern European countries as well as Ireland and Belgium) formed a lobby to keep structural policy funds at the highest level possible (EUInside 2012; Euractiv, 2014a; Euractiv 2014b; Magone 2014: 41–46).

For the southern, central and eastern European peripheries, the European Union is often regarded as a means to achieve more democratic accountability and transparency within their own countries. The perception of the European Union as a *vincolo esterno* ('external link') has been accompanied by idealised benevolent associations (Italian term taken from Dyson, Featherstone, 1996). However, this was the first crisis in which the Eurozone was affected. In this context, the Greek crisis was intrinsically linked to the survival of the euro as a currency. Consequently, the perceived 'benevolent' approach towards periphery economies changed overnight to one of strict conditionality, the main strategy employed to convince the markets that the Eurozone would be able to sort out its problems. This change in approach felt sudden for the southern periphery but had already been internalised in most central and eastern European countries, which had experienced a tougher, conditionality-driven European Union during their process of European integration. For these countries, the EU had introduced annual screening and progress reports to assess whether the required reforms – so-called 'anticipatory Europeanisation' – were being successfully implemented. In the process, the central and eastern European countries and the Mediterranean islands had to incorporate 80,000 pages of *acquis communautaire* into their national laws (Magone, 2008; see Auer on solidarity in this volume).

Resolving the unprecedented Greek situation before it led to the contagion of other weak Eurozone economies was a matter of urgency. In this period of uncertainty, the Franco-German alliance between the German Chancellor Angela Merkel and the French President Nicolás Sarkozy led to the establishment of new principles based on austerity. This duo became known as 'Merkozy' due to the public consensus between the two leaders (Hinz, 2013; Schwarzer, 2013). Previously, President Sarkozy and Chancellor Merkel had had considerable disagreements on the nature and the scale of the EU's collective response to the crisis. After several meetings, the two leaders were eventually able to achieve a compromise acceptable to their different views on the crisis (Crespy and Schmidt, 2014).

The Troika emerges as the symbol of the conditionality-driven policy of 'coercive Europeanisation' employed when everything else fails (term taken from Angelos Sepos in chapter 3 in this volume).

Klaus Armingeon and Lucio Baccaro argue that Ireland and countries in southern Europe are being forced to follow the German model of internal devaluation, which is clearly intended to keep inflation low. Price and wage stability are essential elements of this policy. However, without the economic development level of Germany and without a generous welfare state, such policies are quite costly and dangerous, potentially leading to a cycle of permanent austerity and pauperisation (Armingeon, Baccaro, 2012: 261–269; on the 'German stability culture' see Howarth, Rommerskirchen, 2013).

At first against it, Chancellor Angela Merkel and her finance minister Wolfgang Schäuble changed their minds when the Troika was endowed with strong monitoring powers. Schäuble wanted most of all to make sure that conditions for fiscal consolidation in the crisis countries would not be determined by the IMF alone.This point was also supported by the Netherlands (see also Hinz, 2013; Schwarzer, 2013; for a constructive discourse approach, see Crespy, Schmidt, 2014). The IMF was the model to be followed, and the European Commission therefore had to learn the institution's programme methodology in order to achieve a high level of coordination (Pisani-Ferry et al., 2013: 25).

The Troika nominally consists of the IMF, the European Commission and the European Central Bank (ECB); however, in practice the IMF and the European Commission dominate. The ECB was merely added as an advisory partner, explaining why only the IMF and the European Commission write reports during the process. The ECB was included mainly due to its interest in assessing the systemic risks to the balance sheet of the supranational institution, but also because it is trusted by the member states (Pisani-Ferry et al., 2013: 25).

The Economic and Financial Committee of the European Parliament produced a critical report on the workings of the Troika that was adopted on 28 February 2014. The Economic and Financial Committee also criticised the lack of openness and transparency regarding how the member states concerned could or could not shape negotiations with the Troika (European Parliament, 2014: 5).

According to the report, one of the major problems in the Troika's construction is that its principal is the Eurogroup (consisting of the finance ministers of the Eurozone), a non-accountable and non-transparent actor in the process. Although the European Commission is an independent supranational institution of the EU, it became an agent of the Eurogroup in the Troika's design. This has been regarded as a major flaw in construction, as the European Commission thereby compromises its independent position (European Parliament, 2014: 17). Another criticism has focused on the role of the ECB as a creditor but simultaneously as an advisor. Although it was welcomed to join the Troika, the ECB has exhibited certain conflicts of interest when exerting pressure on decision-makers on questions of liquidity (European Parliament, 2014: 17). Moreover, the national parliaments were only given the choice to accept the Troika's offer or to default on the nation's debt, a restriction that clearly contributes to the democratic deficit (European Parliament, 2014: 17).

After a victory in the early legislative elections of 25 January 2015, the new Alexis Tsipras coalition government consisting of a radical left-wing party Coalition of the Radical Left (Synaspismos Rizospastikis Aristeras – Syriza) and the right-wing Independent Greeks (Anexartitoi Ellines – ANEL) created huge expectations about changing the nature of the relationship between debtor state and the creditors. It wanted to restore national sovereignty, although in this situation of dependency of funding is quite difficult. One first step was to get rid of the informal label 'troika' that summarised the work of the IMF, European Commission and European Central Bank. After eight months a second legislative election within the year took place on 20 September confirming again almost the same result as the early election. However, now Alexis Tsipras' Syriza asked the electorate to support a new bailout programme with even more tougher conditions. Clearly, in the end the new Greek government had to submit to the demands of the creditors. This shows the lack of manoeuvrability for countries in a bailout programme.

Although a stability culture in the Eurozone and in the wider European Union is a desirable goal, it should be renegotiated, taking into account the level of the economies of the periphery. This is what former European commissioner Loukas Tsoukalis calls the 'grand bargain' that needs to be offered by the strongest economies (Tsoukalis, 2014: 66), preferably by a 'cooperative hegemony' of France and Germany (concept developed by Thomas Pedersen, quoted in Patterson, 2011: 72).

Apart from potential Greek exit of EMU (Grexit) there is also can the potential threat of British exit (Brexit). The UK's growing difficulties with its membership has further accentuated the internal differentiation of the EU. Conservative prime minister David Cameron consequently came under intense domestic pressure from within his own party, the increasingly popular UK Independence Party (UKIP) and the media to renegotiate Britain's EU membership terms and to put the result of these negotiations to the British public in a referendum. Franco-German plans to move from the strengthening of national policy coordination and supervision for all 28 member states under the *European Semester* towards full political union in the Eurozone resulted in Cameron calling for the determination of clear safeguards against further political integration for eurozone outsiders in his 2013 Bloomberg speech (HM Government 2013). The UK's demands for renegotiation remain vague as the re-elected Cameron prepares for the domestic campaign in the run-up to the public referendum on EU membership which will be held before the end of 2017.

Connected to the British case, the growing differentiated integration in the European Union is a further element that is exacerbating this core–periphery cleavage. Richer countries such as the UK, Sweden and Denmark commit themselves only to those policies that are in their interest, undermining any solidarity in the union (for more detail see Dyson, Sepos, 2010; Leuffen et. al., 2013)

In sum, the German model of a social market economy that can be found in most core countries (apart from the UK and Ireland) could be, with adjustments, a way to overcome the European core–periphery cleavage. For this to happen, the EMU would have to be re-conceptualised in a more inclusive manner, taking into account not only the needs of the core countries but also those of periphery countries.

The international dimension of the core–periphery divide in the European Union

The past forty years have seen the rise of China as a major player in the world system. A mode of state capitalism thereby emerged that was not linked to any form of liberalism; on the contrary, the authoritarian/totalitarian one-party state has created an alternative state-capitalist system without any liberal democratic foundations (Jacques, 2013). China is now identifying and opening new markets across the globe, including in the European Union. It seems that Chinese enterprises have recognised the advantages of the internal market much faster than most Europeans. The crisis in the southern European states led to a massive investment in the periphery by Chinese enterprises. For example, in Greece, the Chinese enterprise Closco Pacific invested heavily in the Piraeus port, which it will have a right to use for the next 35 years. Meanwhile, an agreement with Serbia and Hungary will lead to the construction of a Balkan rail link from Belgrade to Budapest in order to transport Chinese goods to central and eastern European countries more rapidly. In the long term, this will connect the port of Piraeus to an extended rail link from Athens to Budapest. In this sense, China views the periphery of the EU as an important strategic asset that will allow it to gain economic and possibly also political influence (Euractiv, 2014c, d).

A hegemonic war over the Asia-Pacific rim is currently being waged between China and the United States. In this context of growing antagonism between China and the US, the strong interdependency between the two countries (the so-called 'Chimerica') has contributed to the shift in the core of the world economy to the Asia-Pacific Rim. The rise of Chimerica means that the United States owes a considerable amount of money to China; China, in turn, is still highly dependent on continuing investment from the US, particularly from high-tech enterprises (Ferguson, Schularick, 2007). However, Niall Ferguson and Moritz Schularick argue that 'Chimerica' could come to an end due to the growing tensions and increasing imbalances between the two superpowers. More competition over resources and markets may be expected in the next decade or so (Ferguson, Schularick, 2009).

Another problematic issue was identified by a study conducted in 2006 by the Bertelsmann Foundation in various regions of the world. The study asked respondents about the global influence of the European Union, China and the US in 2006 and 2020. The overall expectation was that the US will decline in influence as China rises to the level of the US, while the European Union will stagnate or even decline (Bertelsmann Foundation, 2006; Fioramonti, Lucarelli, 2008: 199). This finding was confirmed by a survey by the Pew Institute that predicted that the future global balance of power will be shared between the United States and China; the European Union was not even considered to be a superpower. In the Institute's 2014 Global Attitudes Survey, 60 per cent of Europeans felt that China replaced already or will replace the US as the leading economic power (Pew Research Center, 2014: 33). Moreover, in the 2012 US defence strategy entitled 'Sustaining US Global Leadership: Priorities for 21st Century Defense', China is regarded as the main rival of the US for global leadership. All other powers are viewed as regional and insignificant. The European Union is not even mentioned as a separate world power; rather, Europe is presented as a peripheral regional area of engagement for the United States. The North Atlantic Treaty Organisation (NATO) is a key piece of the US security strategy (United States Department of Defence, 2012: 3; see also Katzenstein, 2005: 2–3).

The potential establishment of a Transatlantic Trade and Investment Partnership (TTIP) between the US and the European Union might reinforce the growing bipolarisation of the world in economic, political and military terms. The more dynamic and integrated economy of the United States may over time manage to erode the unevenly established social market economy in the European Union, a system that is quite weak in many of the southern, central and eastern European countries. The consequence could be the peripheralisation of the European Union in the new global order: the EU might be downgraded to a mere free-trade area considered to be an extension of the US market. This is the potential scenario that Mario Telò has forecast if the European Union is unable to become more integrated and project its socio-economic model (Telò, 2005: 166). George Friedman, a prominent US strategy expert, is already predicting the collapse of the EU and a return to the normal European condition of multiple competing nation-states. (Friedman, 2013; see also Friedman, 2015). Another possible scenario could involve a similar peripheralisation of Russia in relation to China, thus creating a bipolar world of macro-regions (Trenin, 2014).

The EU must therefore return to its central integration project: the internal market. At the moment, it remains incomplete, fragmented (due to national interests in various policy areas such as telecom and energy) and uneven (due to the existing core–periphery cleavage). As long as the sustainable, dynamic, European (i.e. not nationally fragmented) single market is not complete, it will be difficult to ensure spill-over effects on external policies or to mitigate the declining influence of the EU on the world stage (OECD, 2014). A survey conducted by the Bertelsmann Foundation on the internal market after 20 years of integration shows that the southern, central and eastern European countries have been losers in this process of integration, while the winners have been the countries of northern Europe, in particular Germany and Denmark. This clearly demonstrates that the internal market in its present form is simply reinforcing the socio-economic cleavage (Bertelsmann Foundation, 2014).

In sum, without delving deeper into all the aspects of the international dimension of the core–periphery cleavage in the European Union it may hamper to successfully promote a third form of capitalism based on the European social model as an alternative to the dominant neo-liberal model linked to the US and the rising state-led model practiced by China.

The structure of the book

In this volume, we present chapters that examine socio-economic centre–periphery relations from a variety of angles, including the international dimension. The book is divided into five main parts.

The first part deals with theoretical perspectives and includes two important chapters contextualising the book. In Chapter 2, Brigid Laffan analyses how the Eurocrisis was framed in terms of a centre–periphery morality tale, which led to the emergence of a cleavage between creditor and debtor states. This is followed by a more extensive chapter by Angelos Sepos, who explores alternative theoretical explanations to the Eurocrisis.

The second part is dedicated to several comparative perspectives on core–periphery relations. In Chapter 4, Christian Schweiger presents comparative insights on how the Big Three (Germany, France and Britain) perceive their national interests in the European Union. He focuses on their different strategies in the context of the Eurocrisis, describing how these core countries positioned themselves economically and politically during the crisis. This is followed by a chapter by Stefan Auer linking core and periphery countries. He critically assesses the discourses in Germany, Ireland and Slovakia during this period. In Chapter 6, José Magone concentrates on the main features of southern Europe as the periphery within the European Union. This is complemented by Chapter 7 by Ignacio Paredero Huertas, who analyses the discourses of southern European insiders in the European Union institutions. This study is based on interviews conducted by the author and allows unique insight into how southern European elites at supranational level perceive the Eurocrisis and the changing political and economic landscape in the European Union. The subsequent chapter by Attila Ágh focuses on a comparative analysis of the central and eastern European periphery. Bela Galgoczi rounds out this section with his comparison of southern, central and eastern European peripheries.

The third part presents case studies on the countries that were most severely affected by the Euro- and sovereign debt crises. Chapter 10 by Anna Visvizi analyses the impact of the Greek sovereign debt crisis on the Eurozone and how relations evolved over time. In Chapter 11, Bernadette Connaughton gives a detailed account of how Ireland won its bailout and how it coped with the strict supervision of the Troika for three years. This is followed by a chapter on Portugal by José Magone, in which he argues that the intervention of the Troika was a case of 'coercive Europeanization'. In Chapter 13, Thorsten Kruse analyses the intervention of the Troika. The subsequent two chapters deal with Spain by José Magone and Italy by Marco Brunazzo and Vincent della Sala. The fourth part includes two chapters on Hungary and Poland as examples of periphery countries outside the Eurozone written by Oliver Kovács and Maciej Duszczyk respectively.

The fifth and final part concentrates on the global dimension of the core–periphery cleavage. Carolin Rüger discusses the political impact of the Eurocrisis on European foreign and security policy. This is complemented by a chapter by Edward Yencken presents a case study on the relations between the European Union and Australia during the Eurocrisis. The rationale for enclosing these two chapters was to give on one hand a broader view of the impact of the core–periphery cleavage on the ability of the European Union to play an important role globally or not. On the other hand, the case study by Edward Yencken who got a UACES grant to give his paper at the Berlin conference on 11/12 October 2013, highlights the external perceptions of Australia, an important like-minded OECD country in relation to the management of the sovereign debt and Eurocrisis.

Conclusions: the centrality of core–periphery relations in the European Union

This introductory chapter has attempted to set the stage for the subsequent chapters of the book. The main research focus is on core–periphery relations in the European Union. We interpret core–periphery relations in socio-economic and political terms. The uneven socio-economic development of the internal market is affecting the performance of the European Union considerably, both internally and externally.

References

Armingeon, Klaus and Lucio Baccaro (2012) 'Political Economy of the Sovereign Debt Crisis: The Limits of Internal Devaluation,' *Industrial Law Journal* 41(3): 254–275.

Bachtler, John, Carlos Mendez and Fiona Wishlade (eds) (2014) *EU Cohesion Policy and European Integration: The Dynamics of EU Budget and Regional Policy Reform*. Aldershot: Ashgate.

Bertelsmann Foundation (2006) 'World Powers in the Twenty-first Century: The Results of a Representative Survey in Brazil, China, France, Germany, India, Japan, Russia, the United Kingdom and the United States,' Berlin, 2 June. Available at: www.cap.lmu.de/download/2006/2006_GPC_Survey_Results.pdf (accessed 4 November 2015).

Bertelsmann Foundation (2014) '20 Jahre Binnenmarkt. Wachstumseffekte der zunehmenden europäischen Integration,' Policy Brief no. 2014/02. Available at: www.ged-project.de/uploads/tx_uandiproducts/files/20JBinnenmarkt_2014_final.pdf (accessed 23 December 2014).

Callaghan, Helen (2010) 'Beyond methodological nationalism: how multilevel governance affects the clash of capitalisms,' *Journal of European Public Policy* 17(4): 564–580.

Cole, John and Cole, Francis (1997) *A Geography of the European Union*, 2nd edition. London: Routledge.

Crespy, Amandine and Vivien Schmidt (2014) 'The clash of Titans: France, Germany and the discursive double game of EMU reform,' *Journal of European Public Policy* 21(8): 1085–1101.

Dyson, Kenneth and Kevin Featherstone (1996) 'Italy and EMU as a *vincolo esterno*: empowering the technocrats, transforming the state', *South European Society and Politics* 1(2): 272–299.

Dyson, Kenneth and Angelos Sepos (eds) (2010) *Which Europe: The Politics of Differentiated Integration*. Basingstroke: Palgrave.

EUinside (2012) 'Friendly fire during the EU negotiations on the EU 2014–2020 Budget'. Available at: www.euinside.eu/en/analyses/friendly-fire-in-the-negotiations-on-the-eu-2014-2020-budget (accessed 19 January 2015).

EurActiv (2014a), 'EU budget talks stalled, as net payers want their money back,' 21 November. Available at: www.euractiv.com/sections/eu-priorities-2020/eu-budget-talks-stalled-net-payers-want-their-money-back-310114 (accessed 20 January 2015).

EurActiv (2014b), 'The EU negotiators strike a budget deal,' 9 December. Available at: www.euractiv.com/sections/eu-priorities-2020/eu-negotiators-strike-deal-2015-budget-310676 (accessed 19 January 2015).

EurActiv (2014c), 'Balkan Railway part of Chinese 'express lane' to Europe,' 18 December. Available at: www.euractiv.com/sections/transport/balkan-railway-part-chinese-express-lane-europe-310940 (accessed 19 January 2015).

EurActiv (2014d), 'China seeks gateway to EU via cash-strapped Balkans,' 16 December. Available at: www.euractiv.com/sections/global-europe/china-seeks-gateway-eu-cash-strapped-balkans-310839 (accessed 19 January 2015).

European Commission (2010a), 'Turning Europe into a true innovation union,' Memo 10/473, Brussels, 6 October. Available at: http://europa.eu/rapid/press-release_MEMO-10-473_en.htm?locale=en (accessed 9 December 2010).

European Commission (2010b), 'Europe 2020 Flagship Initiative: Innovation Union,' SEC(2010) 1161, Brussels, 6 October. Available at: http://ec.europa.eu/research/innovation-union/pdf/innovation-union-communication_en.pdf#view=fit&pagemode=none (accessed 9 December 2010).

European Commission (2014) 'Innovation Union Score Board 2014'. Luxembourg: Office of Publications of the European Communities. Available at: www.file:///C:/Users/Jos%C3%A9/Documents/BOOK%20CORE-PERIPHERY%20RELATIONS%20IN%20EU/MATERIAL/INNOVATION%20UNION%20SCOREBOARD.pdf (accessed 9 December 2014).

European Parliament (2014) 'Report on the enquiry of the role and operations of the Troika (European Commission,European Central Bank and International Monetary Fund),' Committee on Economic and Monetary Affairs, rapporteurs Othmar Karas and Liem Hoang Ngoc, A7–0149/2014, 28 February. Available at: www.europarl.europa.eu/sides/getDoc.do?pubRef=-//EP//NONSGML+REPORT+A7-2014-0149+0+DOC+PDF+V0//EN (accessed 30 December 2014).

Eurostat (2014a), 'Real GDP growth rate volume'. Available at: http://epp.eurostat.ec.europa.eu/tgm/table.do?tab=table&init=1&plugin=1&language=en&pcode=tec00115 (accessed 9 December 2014).

Eurostat (2014b), 'Gross domestic expenditure on R&D by sector 2007 and 2012 (per cent of GDP)'. Available at: http://epp.eurostat.ec.europa.eu/statistics_explained/index.php/File:Gross_domestic_expenditure_on_R%26D_by_sector,_2007_and_2012_(%25_of_GDP)_YB14.png (accessed 9 December 2014).

Ferguson, Niall and Moritz Schularick (2007) 'Chimerica and the global asset market boom,' *International Finance* 10(3): 215–239.

Ferguson, Niall and Moritz Schularick (2009) 'The End of Chimerica,' Working Paper 10–037, Harvard Business School, Boston.

Fioramonti, Lorenzo and Sonia Lucarelli (2008) 'How the Others See Us? European Political Identity and the External Image of the EU,' in Furio Cerutti and Sonia Lucarelli (eds) *The Search for a European Identity: Values, Policies and Legitimacy of the European Union.* London: Routledge, pp. 193–210.

Friedman, George (2013) 'Beyond the Post-Cold War World.' *Geopolitical Weekly*, 2 April. Available at: www.stratfor.com/weekly/beyond-post-cold-war-world#axzz3PM8lfVkJ (accessed 19 January 2015).

Friedman, George (2015) *Flashpoints: The Emerging Crisis in Europe.* New York: Doubleday.

Gidlund, Janerik (2000) 'Nordic Bifurcation in Postwall World,' in Janerik Gidlund and Magnus Jerneck (eds) (2000) *Local and Regional Governance in Nordic Europe: Evidence from the Nordic Regions.* Cheltenham: Edward Elgar Publishing, pp. 231–263.

Hinz, Wolfram (2013) 'Von "Merkozy" zu "Merkollande"?,' *Aus Politik und Zeitgeschichte* (1/3): 23–29.

Howarth, David and Charlotte Rommerskirchen (2013) 'A panacea for all times? The German stability culture as strategic political resource,' *West European Politics* 36(4): 750–770.

HM Government (2013) Prime Minister David Cameron's EU speech at Bloomberg, 23 January. Available at: www.gov.uk/government/speeches/eu-speech-at-bloomberg (accessed 2 November 2015).

Höpner, Martin and Armin Schäfer (2008) 'Grundzüge einer politisch-önonomischen Perspektive auf die europäische Integration,' in Martin Höpner and Armin Schäfer (eds) *Politische Ökonomie der europäischen Integration*. Frankfurt a. M.: Campus, pp. 11–44.

Höpner, Martin and Armin Schäfer (2015) 'Integration among Unequals: How the Heterogeneity of European Varieties of Capitalism Shapes the Social and Democratic Potential of Europe,' in José M. Magone (ed.) *Routledge Handbook of European Politics*. London: Routledge, pp. 725–745.

Hudson, Ray and Allan Williams (eds) (1999) *Divided Europe: Society and Territory*. London: Sage Publications.

InsideEurope (2012) 'Friends of Cohesion: joint declaration on the multiannual financial framework 2014–2020,' 8 October. Available at: http://insideurope.eu/node/247 (accessed 19 January 2015).

Jacques, Martin (2013) 'The Implications of the Rise of China,' in Andrew Gamble and David Lane (eds) *The European Union and World Politics*. London: Routledge, pp. 79–94.

Jones, Barry and Michael Keating (eds) (1995) *The European Union and the Regions*. Oxford: Clarendon Press.

Katzenstein, Peter A. (2005) *A World of Regions: Asia and Europe in the American Imperium*. Ithaca, NY and London: Cornell University Press.

Laffan, Brigid and Jane O'Mahony (2008) *Ireland and the European Union*. Basingstoke: Palgrave.

Le Galès, Patrick and Christian Lequesne (eds) (1998) *Regions in Europe*. London: Routledge.

Leonardi, Robert (1993) *The Regions and the European Community: The Regional Response to the Single European Market*. Oxford: Oxford University Press.

Leuffen, Dirk, Berthold Rittberger and Frank Schimmelfennig, (2013) *Differentiated Integration: Explaining Variation in the European Union*. Basingstoke: Palgrave.

Magone, José M. (2006) *The New World Architecture. The Role of the European Union in the Making of Global Governance*. Piscataway, NJ: Transaction.

Magone, José M. (2008) 'Leaderless Enlargement? The Difficult Reform of the New Pan-European Political System,' in Jack Hayward (ed.) *Leaderless Europe*. Oxford: Oxford University Press, pp. 188–207.

Magone, José M. (2011) 'Centre–Periphery conflict in the European Union? Europe 2020, the Southern European Model and the Euro-crisis,' in A. Attila (ed.) *European Union at the crossroads: The European Perspectives after the Global Crisis*. Budapest: Budapest College of Communication, Business and Arts, pp. 71–122.

Magone, José M. (2013) 'Living with the Crisis in Southern Europe,' in A. Agh and L. Voss (eds) *European Futures: The Perspectives of the New Member-States in the New Europe*. Budapest: Budapest College of Communication, Business and Arts, pp. 69–138.

Magone, José M. (2014) 'Divided Europe? Euroscepticism in Central, Eastern and Southern Europe,' in Kyriakos N. Demetriou (ed.) *The European Union in Crisis. Explorations in Representation and Democratic Legitimacy*. Heidelberg: Springer, pp. 33–56.

Maystadt, Philippe (2011) *Europe: Le continent perdu?* Waterloo: Avant-propos.

Organisation for Economic Cooperation and Development (OECD) (2014) *Reinvigorating the EU Single Market*. Paris: OECD. Available at: www.oecd-ilibrary.org/economics/oecd-economic-surveys-european-union-2014/reinvigorating-the-eu-single-market_eco_surveys-eur-2014-4-en (accessed 23 December 2014).

Patterson, William E. (2011) 'The "reluctant hegemon"? Germany moves centre stage in the European Union', *Journal of Common Market Studies* 49(S): 57–75.

Pew Research Center (2014), 'Global Opposition to US Surveillance and Drones, but Limited Harm to America's Image,' *Global Attitudes and Trends*, 14 July. Available at: www.pewglobal.org/files/2014/07/2014-07-14-Balance-of-Power.pdf (accessed 23 December 2014).

Piris, Jean Claude (2012) *The Future of Europe: Towards a Two-Speed EU?* Cambridge: Cambridge University Press.

Pisani-Ferry, Jean, André Sapir and Guntram B. Wolff (2013) *EU-IMF Assistance to Euro-area Countries: An Early Assessment*. Brussels: Bruegel.

Rosenau, James A. (1990) *Turbulence in World Politics: A Theory of Change and Continuity*. Princeton, NJ: Princeton University Press.

Rosenau, James N. (2000) 'Governance, Order and Change in World Politics,' in James N. Rosenau and Ernst Otto Czempiel (eds) *Governance Without Government: Order and Change in World Politics*. Cambridge: Cambridge University Press, pp. 1–29.

Schweiger, Christian (2014) *The EU and the Global Financial Crisis: New Varieties of Capitalism*. Cheltenham: Edward Elgar.

Schweiger, Christian and Magone, José M. (2014) 'The effects of the Eurozone sovereign debt crisis: differentiated integration between the centre and the new peripheries of the EU,' Special issue of *Perspectives in European Politics and Societies* 15(3).

Schwarzer, Daniela (2013) 'Deutschland und Frankreich und die Krise im Euro-rau,' *Aus Politik und Zeitgeschichte* (1/3): 30–36.

Telò, Mario (2005) *Europe: A Civilian Power? European Union, Global Governance, World Order*. Basingstoke: Palgrave.

Trenin, Dmitri (2014) 'Russia's growing China connection,' *China Daily*, 13 October. Reprinted on Carnegie Endowment for Democracy website. Available at: http://carnegieendowment.org/2014/10/13/russia-s-growing-china-connection (accessed 23 December 2014).

Tsoukalis, Loukas (2014) *The Unhappy State of the Union. Europe Needs a New Grand Bargain*. London: Policy Network. Available at: www.policy-network.net/publications/4602/The-Unhappy-State-of-the-Union (accessed 19 January 2015).

United States Defence Department (2012) 'Sustaining US Global Leadership: Priorities for Twentieth-Century Defense,' Washington, DC. Available at: www.defense.gov/news/Defense_Strategic_Guidance.pdf (accessed 20 December 2014).

Vauchez, Antoine (2015), 'Methodological Europeanism at the cradle: eur-lex, the Acquis and the making of Europe's cognitive equipment,' *Journal of European Public Policy* 37(2): 193–210.

Wimmer, Andreas and Nina Glicker Schiller (2002) 'Methodological nationalism and beyond: the nation state building, migration and social sciences,' *Global Networks* 2(4): 301–334.

Wright, Vincent and Yves Mény (eds) (1985) *Centre–Periphery Relations in Western Europe*. London: Allen and Unwin.

Part I

Theoretical perspectives

2 Core–Periphery dynamics in the Euro area

From conflict to cleavage?

Brigid Laffan

Introduction

The concepts of core and periphery are spatial and relational. The identification of a core implies the presence of a periphery. Historically, core periphery dynamics played a central role in processes of economic development and state formation in Europe. The significance of 'germinal' or core areas in the organic development of European states is emphasised by many historians of the medieval period (Pounds and Ball, 1964, Jones, 2003). According to Karl W. Deutsch, the growth of political communities was driven by the fact that 'larger, stronger, more politically, administratively, economically and educationally advanced political units were found to form the *cores of strength* around which in most cases the integrative process developed' (Deutsch et al., 1957). The concept of core, prevalent in political geography, tends to be used in two different ways: (a) from a historical perspective to identify those areas that formed the nucleus around which states were formed, and (b) in a contemporary sense to describe the area which is economically and politically dominant within a state (Whittlesey, 1939; Burghardt, 1969). The relational dimension of core–periphery dynamics emerged in Lipset and Rokkan's seminal work on state formation; they identified centre–periphery cleavages as a fundamental factor in the process of centre-formation (Lipset and Rokkan, 1967). Later in 1983, Rokkan and Urwin addressed the question of territorial politics in Europe's peripheries (Rokkan and Urwin, 1983). According to their definition, peripheral regions shared three characteristics – namely, they were geographically distant, culturally different and economically dependent on the core regions (Rokkan and Urwin, 1983, 13).

Economic modernisation and the process of centre-formation were intertwined not just within individual European states but across the continent. At the regional level, scholars of the European Union have been attentive to core–periphery dynamics within the Union and the problem of uneven development was present in the original preamble to the Rome Treaty which stated that the signatories to the treaty were committed to 'harmonious development by reducing the differences existing between the various regions and the backwardness of the less-favoured regions' (Preamble, Rome Treaty, 1957). A 1990 study of the dynamics of European integration identified the EU's core in the following terms: 'Germany and its neighbours in the Rhine Valley and across the Alpine passes constitute the contemporary core of Europe, in terms of economic interaction, social interchange and security focus. Historical "Europes" have largely revolved around the same broadly defined area' (Wallace, 1990, 14). Successive enlargements have accentuated the importance of core and for European integration as all enlargements apart from the European Free Trade Area (EFTA) enlargement of the 1990s involved the accession of economically less-developed states.

The aim of this paper is to analyse the core periphery dimension of the framing and legacy of the Eurozone crisis and to ask if relations between core and periphery have moved beyond conflict to become a cleavage in the Union. The Union developed a set of policy instruments and governance mechanisms to address economic divergence in an incremental but cumulative manner beginning with the European Coal and Steel Community (ECSC) and culminating in the Union's Cohesion Policy. Cohesion policy was and remains an expression of 'EU's solidarity with less developed countries and regions' (EU Commission, 2014). All major EU initiatives were accompanied by a distributive component such as the CAP, the structural funds and the multi-annual financial perspectives. Interestingly, although economic divergence and imbalances were identified as potential risks to the operation of a single currency, the design of the euro did not include measures to respond to asymmetric shocks and was not accompanied by a distributive component. Rather the primacy of monetary policy accompanied by weak economic policy coordination and a heterogeneous membership led to the build up of major risks within the Eurozone, risks that threatened its very existence from 2009 onwards. The question is whether the core–periphery divide that manifested itself in the Eurozone is a conflict or has become an embedded cleavage. Conflict is endemic in politics –conflict about the underlying values of a polity, the rules of the game, procedures, policy and the distributions of gains and losses. The preferences and interests of different actors may diverge which in turn may result in conflict about process and preferred outcomes. Cleavages structure conflict but are more structural and encompassing than political conflict. According to Mair, cleavage is a multidimensional social science concept that consists of three elements: (1) a social division that distinguishes among groups of citizens, (2) a sense of collective identity, and (3) organisational expression of the cleavage (Mair, 2014, 78–79). This definition will be revisited following the analysis of the framing and legacy of the Eurozone crisis.

Economic and Monetary Union (EMU)

The title of a Commission report published as agreement on EMU was secured, *Stable Money and Sound Finances* (1993) captures the core of the Euro paradigm. The euro was designed around the twin goals of stable money and sound finances enshrined in the Treaty on European Union (TEU), the Maastricht Treaty, and the 1997 Stability and Growth Pact (SGP). Underpinning the single currency was a policy consensus that privileged low inflation (McNamara, 1998). Monetary policy was characterised by a single centre of authority, the European Central

Bank (ECB) buttressed by the national central banks in the European System of Central banks (ESCB). The ECB was given treaty-based guarantees of its independence in what was to be an ECB-centric Eurozone (Dyson, 2000, 12). The treaty was definitive on the key goal and responsibility of monetary policy as laid out in TEU: 'The primary objective of the ESCB shall be to maintain price stability' (Article 105, TEU). The power of the ECB was buttressed by the fact that it was responsible for defining what price stability was and did so in a 'hawkish' manner from the outset by agreeing an inflation objective of below 2 per cent (Dyson, 2000, 12; ECB, 1999). A strong and independent ECB was accompanied by a 'no bailout 'clause which specified that neither the Community nor a member-state government would become liable for the commitments of another member state. The ECB in turn was prohibited from directly buying debt instruments (Article 104).

The centralised and unified monetary pillar was supplemented by a significantly weaker economic pillar, thereby creating an asymmetrical EMU from the outset. Although the interdependence between the two pillars was evident in the TEU, the means of ensuring an equally strong economic policy pillar were absent. The difficulty of specifying the 'economic' in EMU was not just because of the 'high politics' of ECB independence but also because economic policy can be 'varied, nuanced and phased to a much greater degree than monetary union' (Laffan et al., 1999, 144). Two dimensions of economic policy were covered by the treaty – policy coordination in budgetary and fiscal matters. The treaty provisions on economic policy established that member states would regard their 'economic policies as a matter of common concern and shall coordinate them within the Council' (Article 103). Provision was made for the establishment of Broad Economic Guidelines and a response if those guidelines were not met. In addition, member states were required to 'avoid excessive government deficits' (Article 104c); a protocol on the handling of excessive deficits was appended to the TEU. In the lead-up to the establishment of the currency in the mid-1990s there was considerable pressure from Germany to further strengthen the rules on budgetary surveillance, which led to agreement on the Stability and Growth Pact (SGP), a mechanism designed to ensure that fiscal profligacy would be contained. The creation of a stability community was to deliver the 'Sound Finances' component of the economic paradigm.

The Delors Report on economic and monetary union submitted in 1989 established in broad outline a road map for the creation of a single currency. The report did not ignore the presence of economic divergence and the problems that such divergence might generate. This is captured in the following conclusion:

> Despite a marked downward trend in the average rate of price and wage inflation, considerable national differences remain. There are also still notable divergences in budgetary positions and external imbalances have become markedly greater in the recent past. The existence of these disequilibria indicates that there are areas where economic performances will have to be made more convergent.
>
> (Delors Report, 1989, 11)

The report, however, did not conclude that economic union would require the development of instruments to deal with economic shocks. Rather it relied on the then Community's regional and structural funds rather than fiscal federalism. It did acknowledge that 'If sufficient consideration were not given to regional imbalances, the economic union would be faced with grave economic and political risks' (Delors Report, 1989, 18). The first decade of the single currency did in fact give rise to regional imbalances and the system of economic coordination, the Growth and Stability Pact, was undermined by the actions of the two leading economics in the Eurozone, Germany and France. The economic and political risks materialised with the onset of the global financial crisis.

Framing the Euro crisis

The euro area faced its first major challenge when the global financial crisis mutated into a crisis of the euro area, or to put it another way, the global crisis took on a distinctive euro-area character in autumn 2009, when the Greek government identified a serious 'fiscal gap' following the October election that saw George Papandreou return to power. Crises generate pressures for change as the status quo usually becomes untenable. During a crisis, political actors develop and present understandings of the events they encounter and the nature and extent of the challenges they face (Widmaier and Blyth, 2007; Blyth, 2007). Political actors when responding to a crisis frame a crisis narrative and discourse (Hay, 1996, 255, Schmidt 2002, 2008). In addition to a meta-narrative about the crisis, political actors diagnose the attendant problems which in turn become the problem frame. Cobb and Elder argue that 'Policy problems are not simply givens, nor are they matters of the facts of the situation, they are matters of interpretation and social definition' (Cobb and Elder, 1983, 172). The manner in which the Eurozone crisis was framed had a pronounced centre-periphery dimension which in turn had an impact on the policy instruments that were adopted to respond to it.

In the period October 2009 to May 2010, when Eurozone political actors made their first major policy intervention in the euro crisis, a meta-narrative about the euro crisis emerged and a series of attendant problems were identified. The problems in the euro area were Europeanised, although at the outset there were serious reservations about the desirability of Eurozone intervention and resistance to using financial power to rescue Greece. The European Council held in December 2009 made no reference to the Greek problem, but by 11 February 2010 the euro area was at the top of the agenda and remained there for several years. The February 2010 European Council Statement set out in fewer than 200 words the key elements of what was to become the dominant crisis frame (Laffan 2014). Four elements of the statement capture the emerging frame:

1 The shared responsibility of the each member state for the economic and financial stability of the euro area was emphasised by underlining the importance of sound national policy within agreed rules;

2 The above was linked directly to Greece's responsibility to implement the ambitious targets of its stability programme that aimed to reduce its budget deficit to 4 per cent in 2010.
3 The Commission and ECB were called on to propose additional measures to Greece and to monitor its performance;
4 There was a commitment that euro area would take determined and coordinated action to protect the financial stability of the euro area as a whole, *if necessary* (European Council, 11 February 2010, italics added).

The problem frame consisted of a series of attendant problems summarised in Figure 2.1.

The central focus was on Greece and its fiscal deficit and public debt was highlighted as the core problem to be addressed. Greece was asked to meet targets that were impossible given the recalculation of its budget 2009 deficit from 6.7 per cent to 12.7 per cent. The latter figure was subsequently raised by Eurostat to over 13 per cent in April 2010. The deficit was so high that Greece struggled to stay in the markets and thus on 23 April, the Greek prime minister finally requested the activation of bilateral loans. In April, Eco-Fin and the Eurogroup focused on agreeing a package for Greece that was enlarged by IMF participation. By 2 May an EU/IMF rescue package amounting to 110 billion euro in emergency loans was agreed and Greece became the first Euro state to become a 'programme' country. The three-year rescue package came with strong conditionality, high interest rates and a commitment to a further 30 billion euro in budget cuts. The age of rescue and retrenchment in the Eurozone had arrived (Scharpf, 2011).

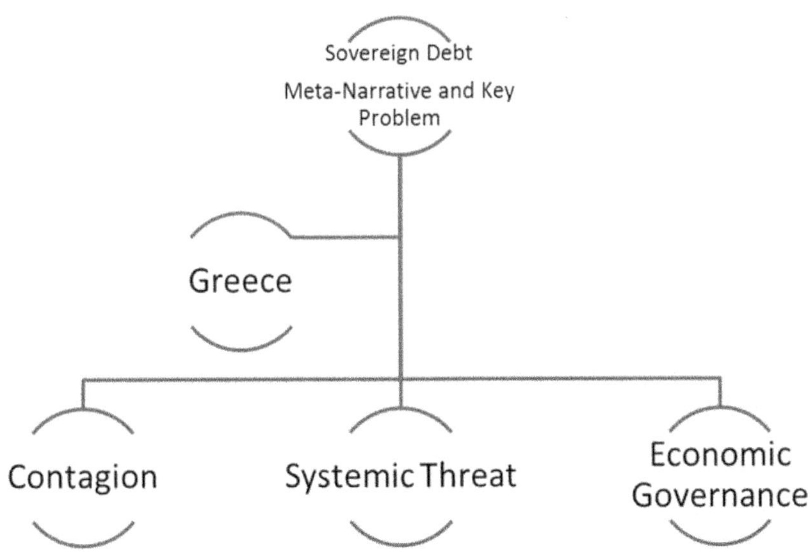

Figure 2.1 Eurozone crisis frame

Although the epicentre of the crisis was in Greece, the focus began to mutate from a problem in one country to concern about contagion to other Euro member states. The prospect of contagion which could undermine the 'macro-financial stability of the EU as a whole' was a crucial issue from May 2010 onwards and was one of the core challenges identified by EU institutions. Investors, analysts and rating agencies identified the euro states that were vulnerable to contagion as the so-called PIIGS (Portugal, Ireland/Italy, Greece and Spain), or GIIPS, all on the periphery of the EU. See Figure 2.2, which highlights interest rate divergence. The centre–periphery divergence was evident in the risk associated with sovereign bonds from the vulnerable countries.

In providing a rationale for the Greek package in May, the EU commissioner for economic and monetary affairs, Olli Rehn, argued that 'It is absolutely essential to contain the bush fire in Greece so that it will not become a forest fire and a threat to financial stability for the European Union and its economy as a whole' (Rehn, 2012).

In an interview with *Der Spiegel* (2010c), ECB president Jean-Claude Trichet expressed his concern about contagion when saying: 'In the market, there is always a danger of contagion – like the contagion we saw among the private

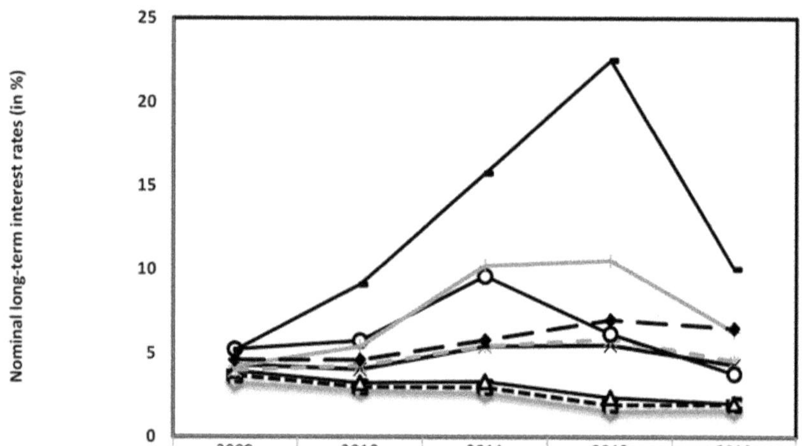

	2009	2010	2011	2012	2013
Germany	3.22	2.74	2.61	1.5	1.57
Netherlands	3.69	2.99	2.99	1.93	1.96
Austria	3.94	3.23	3.32	2.37	2.01
Italy	4.31	4.04	5.42	5.49	4.32
Spain	3.98	4.25	5.44	5.85	4.56
Ireland	5.23	5.74	9.6	6.17	3.79
Portugal	4.21	5.4	10.24	10.55	6.29
Greece	5.17	9.09	15.75	22.5	10.05
•Cyprus	4.6	4.6	5.79	7	6.5

Figure 2.2 Interest rate divergence in the Eurozone
Source: AMECO database, DG ECFIN and EUROSTAT (for the year 2013).

institutions in 2008. And it can occur quickly. Sometimes it is a question of half days.' By May evidence of the potential for contagion was apparent. The process of downgrades, which had contributed to the closing of market access to Greece, began to affect others. Ireland and Portugal were entering the vicious cycle of nervous markets, widening spreads, a rise in the cost of borrowing, further downgrades, all of which contributed to a downward spiral into a funding crisis. Ireland lost market access in November 2010 and Portugal by April 2011. The focus then returned to Greece as it became apparent that its programme was not working and the prospect of a Greek default returned to the agenda.

From the time that the threat of contagion was first identified, the situation of Spain and Italy was to the fore. These countries represented a significant proportion of the Euro economy and were both considered 'too big to bail' but also 'too big to fail'. If either of these countries could not access the markets, the problems facing the euro would deepen dramatically. There was tangible evidence of that risk in July and August 2011 as Italian and Spanish spreads widened. By 7 August, the ECB president announced steps to reassure the markets by saying that the ECB would 'actively implement its Securities Market Programme'. In that week, the ECB bought Italian and Spanish bonds on the secondary market for the first time. The ECB injected one trillion euros into the European financial system in two tranches (December 2011 and January 2012) to maintain liquidity and to lower the cost of borrowing in Spain and Italy. It achieved its goal for a short time but by May both Spain and Italy were again under severe market pressure with their borrowing costs rising to levels that triggered bailouts in the smaller euro states. By June 2012, Spain acknowledged that it required assistance to recapitalise its banks, although it avoided a full programme, but Cyprus had to request assistance. Serious contagion from the euro crisis was contained however uneasily to the four small peripheral Euro states, Greece, Ireland, Portugal and Cyprus, with the Spanish programme focussing on its financial system.

A single story line dominated the packaging of the issues associated with the crisis. The story line identified fiscal profligacy as the underlying cause, attributed blame to the peripheral states, particularly Greece, and assigned primary responsibility to the euro states themselves. In response to the systemic threat arising from contagion, responsibility was elevated to a shared one within the Eurozone, albeit based on an asymmetric relationship between creditors and debtors. This story line was characterised by a strong emphasis on core/periphery and north/south divergence of economic and fiscal performance; Club Med profligacy in contrast to northern prudence. The morality tale was captured by Tilford and Whyte in the following:

> Ever since the Eurozone crisis broke out, the North European interpretation of it has prevailed. It essentially portrayed the crisis "as a morality tale, pitting those who sinned against those who stuck to the path of virtue.
>
> (Tilford and Whyte, 2011)

The future lay with redemption and prevention. If the cause of the crisis was fiscal profligacy, then the cure was fiscal balance and consolidation. Responsibility for redemption was assigned to individual euro states encased in a set of institutions and rules that would sanction the transgressors.

Given the weakness of the programme countries and those under pressure from the markets, the dominant actors in the Eurozone crisis were the creditor states, the AAA countries. As the largest euro area economy, Germany was central to both powering and puzzling as the crisis unfolded. Together with the ECB, Germany, personified by its chancellor, played a key role in framing the crisis and in developing policies and instruments to respond to it. Its views were shared by a group of small countries that formed part of the hard core of the euro, the Netherlands, Finland and Austria. Germany represented the largest economy in the euro zone and was the major contributor of capital to the ECB. Those facts alone, however, do not account for the role Germany played in framing the crisis and in developing the policy response. Its influence stemmed not just from its structural power but also from the performance of its economy in the post-war era. It was and remains the most successful economy in the EU. In addition, German actors and institutions operated on the basis of a deeply embedded policy paradigm, Ordoliberalism, about economic, fiscal and monetary policy. This paradigm limited the range of policy options that were deemed acceptable and legitimate. Moreover, the design of EMU with ECB independence and sound money at its core was modelled on a German paradigm. From the 1970s onwards, Germany largely set the rules for European monetary collaboration. Germany had effective veto power over the timing and content of any rescue and was the pivotal state in crisis management. The German chancellor defended her policy approach of short-term rescue, long-term reforms and 'strict austerity programmes for Greece and other countries' (Merkel, 2010). She attributed responsibility in the following terms: 'to insist that countries which caused such a crisis will have to take action themselves in the future and, on the other hand, to make clear that we bear a shared European responsibility' (Merkel, 2010). Shared responsibility was to the stability of the Eurozone but domestic adjustment fell on those states with serious fiscal deficits.

The manner in which the Eurozone crisis was framed masked other issues to the disadvantage of the periphery. The crisis was never just about sovereign debt. In the case of Spain and Ireland, it was severe stress in their banking sectors that put the sovereign signature under pressure. For every debtor there was a lender and in the case of Europe's periphery, the lenders included banks in the core. German and French banks were very exposed to the Greek banking sector and to the banking sectors in the rest of the Eurozone periphery. Their exposure to Greece alone was approximately $119 billion (*Wall Street Journal*, 17 February 2010).

The German finance ministry was alerted to the potential impact of a Greek default on the German banking system in spring 2010. A letter to the German Finance Ministry from Jochen Sanio, the president of Germany's Federal Financial Supervisory Authority (BaFin) warned that a Greek default could trigger for another Lehman Brothers-type event for German banks. The Authority identified a number of banks that held large amounts of Greek debt, notably the nationalised Hypo Real Estate (HRS) with €9.1 billion exposure and the partially nationalised Commerzbank with €4.6 billion euros of Greek debt (*Der Spiegel*, 22 February 2010). Following the Greek bailout in May 2010, former Bundesbank chief, Karl Otto Pohl, concluded that the rescue

> was about protecting German banks, but especially the French banks, from debt write offs. On the day that the rescue package was agreed on, shares of French banks rose by up to 24 per cent. Looking at that, you can see what this was really about – namely, rescuing the banks and the rich Greeks.
>
> (*Der Spiegel*, 18 May 2011)

Banks owe primary responsibility to their shareholders not to taxpayers either of creditor or debtor states. Like all commercial organisations, banks did not want to face losses and if losses could be offloaded, they would protect their balance sheets. Governments in Europe had just come through a phase, following Lehman Brothers, of injecting significant capital into troubled banks. This was deeply unpopular with their citizens and they did not want to face another period of recapitalising banks. Moreover, the core countries could shift some of the burden of maintaining their financial systems and banks to the taxpayers on the periphery. The strategy was to buy time in the hope that the banking problem could be contained and that their banks would get sufficient time to strengthen capital reserves and balance sheets. The extent of the problems in the European banking system was disguised in two rounds of limited stress tests (summer 2010 and 2011). In February 2011, Barry Eichengreen, amongst others, warned of the problems in the European Banking system. Although the crisis was presented as a crisis of public finances and hence the policy response was to rescue stressed sovereigns, the objective of the French and German governments was to protect their banks that had lent large sums of money to Greece (*Der Spiegel*, 3 February 2011)

Yet there were two token rounds of stress tests of European banks. It took until the rescue of Dexia in September 2011, which had passed a stress test in July 2011, for the banking problems to become part of the overt rather than hidden agenda.

The second issue that was masked was the significance of the current account imbalances that had developed, particularly since the creation of the euro, within the Eurozone (Lapavitsas, et al., 2010; Pérez-Caldentey and Vernengo, 2012). Current account imbalances had deep structural roots but this struggled for attention as the crisis unfolded. The one indicator that distinguished the vulnerable countries was the presence of a current account deficit (see Figure 2.3).

Christine Lagarde, then French finance minister, raised the issue of current account balances in a *Financial Times* interview in March 2010. She asked, "Could those with surpluses do a little something?' and went on to say, 'When you look at unit labour costs in Germany, they have done a tremendous job in that respect. I'm not sure it is a sustainable model for the long term and for the whole of the group. Clearly we need better convergence' (*Financial Times*, 15 March 2010). She

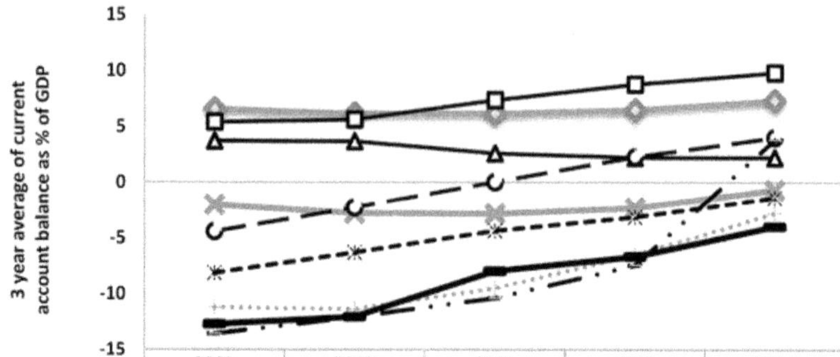

	2009	2010	2011	2012	2013
Germany	6.540495	6.141364	6.129992	6.463281	7.3
Netherlands	5.394886	5.615573	7.349059	8.76595	9.8
Austria	3.695434	3.663845	2.58794	2.21974	2.2
Italy	-2.039144	-2.782941	-2.850748	-2.316685	-0.7
Spain	-8.148499	-6.313917	-4.373852	-3.137824	-1.4
Ireland	-4.432843	-2.277749	0.013207	2.268806	4
Portugal	-11.219949	-11.379684	-9.505687	-6.537245	-2.8
Greece	-13.567437	-12.073914	-10.39738	-7.466331	3.8
Cyprus	-12.707973	-12.057404	-7.97312	-6.684614	-4

Figure 2.3 Current account imbalances in the Eurozone
Source: AMECO database, DG ECFIN and EUROSTAT (for the year 2013).

reiterated this in a radio interview later that week when she argued that an increase in German consumption would assist other countries in the Euro (*Der Spiegel*, 17 March 2010). Her attempt to widen the frame was met with implacable opposition from Germany. Current account imbalances were and are particularly problematic in the euro area because of the design of the single currency. The absence of fiscal federalism and the elimination of the policy tool of devaluation greatly narrowed the range of options available to countries in current account deficit. Regaining competitiveness had to come through internal adjustment which is politically very difficult and takes a considerable amount of time. Hence the cost of adjustment was borne by the peripheral states; it was not shared between the surplus and deficit countries and there was no fiscal compensation available in the absence of a fiscal union.

The legacy of the crisis

The legacy of the crisis is evident in a deep divergence between the economies of the core and periphery and a weakening of trust both in the EU and in national institutions among citizens in the peripheral euro states. During the good years, the peripheral states built up current account deficits that could not be funded once there was a sudden stop in financial flows from core to periphery. The peripheral states were dependent on a rescue by the core that controlled the terms of

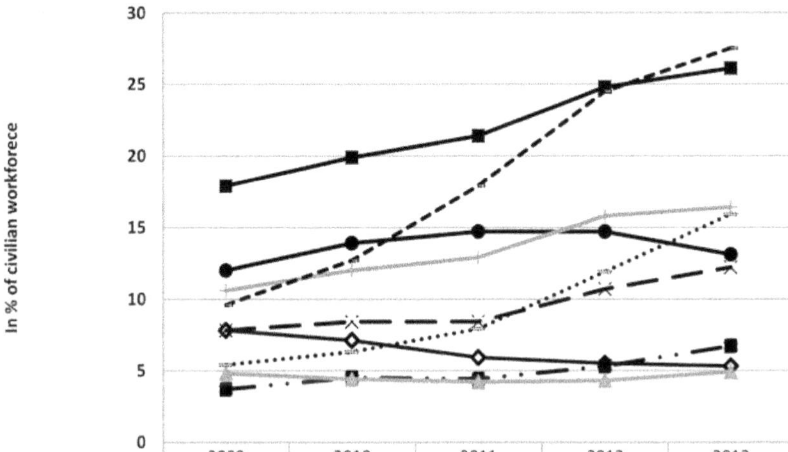

	2009	2010	2011	2012	2013
Germany	7.8	7.1	5.9	5.5	5.3
Netherlands	3.7	4.5	4.4	5.3	6.7
Austria	4.8	4.4	4.2	4.3	4.9
Italy	7.8	8.4	8.4	10.7	12.2
Spain	17.9	19.9	21.4	24.8	26.1
Ireland	12	13.9	14.7	14.7	13.1
Portugal	10.6	12	12.9	15.8	16.4
Greece	9.6	12.7	17.9	24.5	27.5
Cyprus	5.4	6.3	7.9	11.9	15.9

Figure 2.4 Unemployment in the Eurozone
Source: AMECO database, DG ECFIN and EUROSTAT (for the year 2013).

the bailouts. Those terms involved rescue in return for severe fiscal retrenchment and a policy of austerity. The peripheral states bore the weight of adjustment through internal devaluation, which drove down wages and prices, with a policy mix that led them into prolonged recession and weak recovery. The economic, social and political costs of the dominant crisis response and the profound asymmetry between core and periphery were and remain immense. Unemployment because of its consequences for individuals, families and society, is perhaps, the most compelling indicator of all (see Figure 2.4).

At the end of 2013, the gap in the average unemployment rate between the two best performing Eurozone states (Austria and Germany 5 per cent) and the two worst (Greece and Spain 26 per cent) was 21 per cent and the gap for youth unemployment was almost 50 per cent (Laffan, 2015). A debt overhang from the bubble and prolonged recession has left the peripheral states with debt levels (see Figure 2.5) that are perhaps unsustainable in the longer term notwithstanding the severity of their efforts at fiscal retrenchment (De Grauwe and Yuemei, 2014).

Although the legacy of the crisis is most clearly seen in the economies of the peripheral countries, the longer-term impact will also be felt in the political

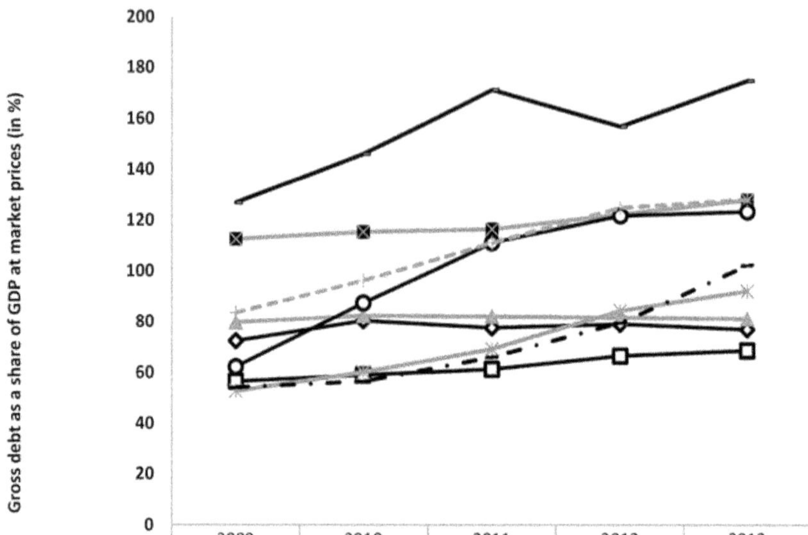

	2009	2010	2011	2012	2013
Germany	72.4	80.3	77.6	79	76.9
Netherlands	56.5	59	61.3	66.5	68.6
Austria	79.7	82.4	82.1	81.7	81.2
Italy	112.5	115.3	116.4	122.2	127.9
Spain	52.7	60.1	69.2	84.4	92.1
Ireland	62.2	87.4	111.1	121.7	123.3
Portugal	83.6	96.2	111.1	124.8	128
Greece	126.8	146	171.3	156.9	174.9
Cyprus	54.1	56.5	66	79.5	102.2

Figure 2.5 Debt levels in the Eurozone
Source: AMECO database, DG ECFIN and on EUROSTAT (for the year 2013).

realm. The countries of the periphery were traditionally very favourable towards the European Union, which was regarded as a framework for modernisation and a substitute for weak state capacity at domestic level. The severity and sustained nature of the crisis has increased political volatility in these countries and led to a marked reduction in their trust in both EU and domestic governance. The emergence of Syriza in Greece, the Five Star Movement in Italy and Podemos in Spain point to the growth of anti-establishment challenger parties in these countries. Trust in national government has displayed a marked deterioration particularly in Greece, Spain and Cyprus but has declined significantly in the other countries as well (see Figure 2.6).

Trust in the EU, which remains higher, has also declined significantly in all of the peripheral Eurozone states (see Figure 2.7).

Yet these are the states that are under most pressure to engage in deep-rooted structural reform at a time when the capacity of governments to do so is limited.

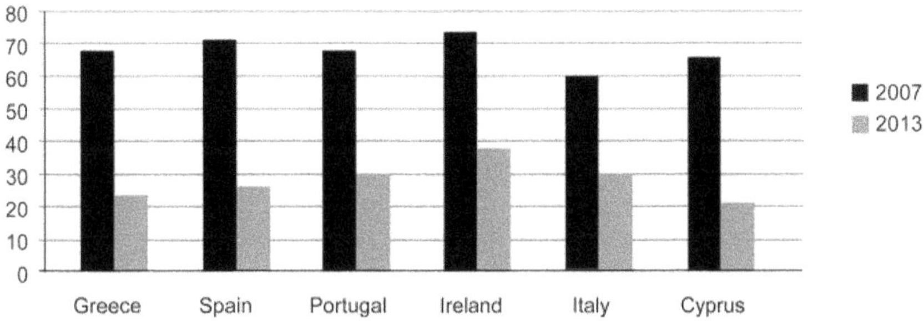

Figure 2.6 Trust in European Union in Greece, Ireland, Portugal, Spain and Cyprus
Source: Eurobarometer, 2007 (no. 68) and 2013 (no. 80). Available at: http://ec.europa.eu/public_opinion/archives/eb_arch_en.htm.

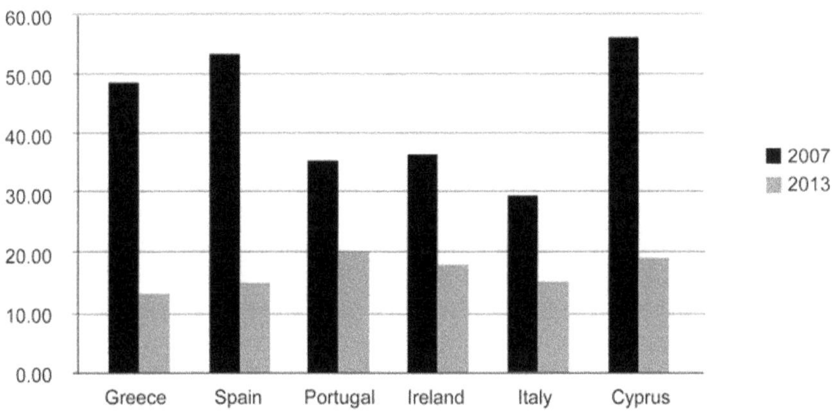

Figure 2.7 Trust in national government in Greece, Ireland, Italy, Portugal, Spain and Cyprus
Source: Eurobarometer, 2007 (no. 68) and 2013 (no. 80). Available at: http://ec.europa.eu/public_opinion/archives/eb_arch_en.htm.

The political centre has held in all of these states but the political strain in parties, party systems and in governments should not be underestimated. Top-down demands for reform will not work unless there is a reservoir of political and state capacity at domestic level. Given the widespread volatility in European politics, the resilience of politics in the peripheral states should not be taken for granted.

Conclusion: Conflict or Cleavage?

Since 2010 the Eurozone was characterised by profound conflict between creditor and debtor states which in essence was a conflict between the Eurozone core and periphery. Although the crisis was a crisis of interdependence, the framing of the crisis, the divergence of economic performance between the core and the periphery and the manner in which the crisis affected different Eurozone countries, led to a major divide within the Eurozone between the strong performing economics and the vulnerable ones. The divergent trends in spreads graphically illustrated in coloured charts became the dominant news emblem of the crisis. During the crisis, the creditor states deployed their power to address the problems on their terms and in their interests. That power was used to keep certain policy options off the agenda, such as mutualisation, and to impose high levels of conditionality on the peripheral states. The troubled countries were too weak to alter the crisis frame and draw attention to the banking problems or the question of surplus countries. The European institutions effectively sided with the creditor states as the crisis unfolded. The rescue and the imposition of austerity underlined the dependency of the troubled countries.

The concept of cleavage has been mainly used in the analysis of party systems and electoral behaviour. Applied to these phenomena, a cleavage consists of a distinctive social group within a society with a collective identity, and an organisational expression of the cleavage. The peripheral states in the Eurozone represent distinctive social groups with a shared identity contained within the organisational expression of a member state. Moreover, the development of current account imbalances during the first ten years of the euro had a distinctive geographical expression, as has the subsequent economic divergence between the core and periphery. On all economic indicators, the fall-out from the 2008 induced recession was most severe in Europe's peripheral countries and they continue to experience the legacy of the crisis in the form of high unemployment and a debt overhang. To date the creditor countries, led by Germany, have not been willing to alter in any significant manner the underlying crisis management strategy and policy package. The asymmetry of power between core and periphery has made it very difficult for the peripheral states to garner sufficient political capacity to secure an alternative policy mix. The danger of prolonged low inflation in the Eurozone and the prospect of stagnation may in time force change given the underlying interdependence between core and periphery and their mutual vulnerability.

References

AMECO database is the source of all figures in this chapter. AMECO is the annual macro-economic database of the European Commission's Directorate General for Economic and Financial Affairs (DG ECFIN).

Blyth, M. (2007) 'Powering, puzzling, or persuading? The mechanisms of building institutional orders,' *International Studies Quarterly* 51(4): 761–777.

Bomberg, Elizabeth and John Peterson (1998)'European Union decision-making: The role of sub-national authorities,' *Political Studies* 46(2): 219–235.

Burghardt, Andrew (1969) 'The core concept in political geography: A definition of terms,' *The Canadian Geographer/Le Géographe canadien* 13(4): 349–353.

Chen, R., G. M. Milesi-Ferretti and T. Thierry (2012) 'External Imbalances in the Euro Area,' IMF Working Paper, WP/12/236.

Cobb, R. W. and C. D. Elder (1983) *Participation in American Politics: The Dynamics of Agenda Building*. Baltimore, MD: Johns Hopkins University Press.

De Grauwe, P. and J. Yuemei (2014) 'The end of the Eurocrisis? Mauno Koivisto lecture 2013,' *Research on Finnish Society* 7: 71–83.

Delors Report (1989) 'Report on Economic and Monetary Union in the European Community,' 17 April. Available at: http://aei.pitt.edu/1007/1/monetary_delors.pdf (accessed 4 January 2015).

Der Spiegel (2010a) 'Währungen: Spiel mit dem höchsten Risiko,' 2 February. Available at: http://magazin.spiegel.de/EpubDelivery/spiegel/pdf/69174839 (accessed 30 August 2010 (English version)).

Der Spiegel (2010b) 'Tension in the Euro Zone: France, Germany Bicker over export surplus,' 17 March. Available at: www.spiegel.de/international/europe/tension-in-the-euro-zone-france-germany-bicker-over-export-surplus-a-684185.html (accessed 30 August 2015).

Der Spiegel (2010c) 'European Central Bank president Jean-Claude Trichet: A "quantum leap" in governance of the Euro Zone is needed,' 15 May. Available at: www.spiegel.de/international/europe/european-central-bank-president-jean-claude-trichet-a-quantum-leap-in-governance-of-the-euro-zone-is-needed-a-694960-2.html (accessed 30 August 2010).

Der Spiegel (2010d) 'Former Central Bank head Karl Otto Pöhl: Bailout plan is all about rescuing banks and rich Greeks,' 18 May. Available at: www.spiegel.de/international/germany/former-central-bank-head-karl-otto-poehl-bailout-plan-is-all-about-rescuing-banks-and-rich-greeks-a-695245.html (accessed 30 August 2015).

Der Spiegel (2011a) 'Interview with US economist Eichengreen: "Europe's banks are in far greater danger than people realize",' 2 March. Available at: www.spiegel.de/international/world/interview-with-us-economist-eichengreen-europe-s-banks-are-in-far-greater-danger-than-people-realize-a-748239.html (accessed 30 August 2015).

Deutsch, K. W., S. A. Burrell, R. A. Kann, M. J. R. Lee, M. Lichterman, R. E. Lindgren, F. L., Loewenheim and R. W. Van Wagenen (1957) *Political Community and the North Atlantic Area: International Organization in the Light of Historical Experience*. Princeton, NJ: Princeton University Press.

Dyson, K. (2000) *The Politics of the Euro-Zone: Stability or Breakdown*. Oxford: Oxford University Press.

European Central Bank (ECB) (2000) 'ECB Annual Report 1999'. Available at: www.ecb.europa.eu/pub/pdf/annrep/ar1999en.pdf?dfdb2de21e43bab7035e0fa18b9e1b9a (accessed 30 October 2015).

European Central Bank (ECB) (2011) 'Statement by the president of the ECB,' Press release. 7 August. Available at: www.ecb.europa.eu/press/pr/date/2011/html/pr110807.en.html (accessed 30 October 2015).

European Commission (1993) 'Stable Money and Sound Finances,' *European Economy*, no. 53. Available at: http://ec.europa.eu/economy_finance/publications/publication7524_en.pdf (accessed 4 January 2014).

European Commission (2014) European regional policy website. Available at: http://ec.europa.eu/regional_policy/what/index_en.cfm.

Financial Times (2010) 'Transcript of interview with Christine Lagarde,' 15 March. Available at: www.ft.com/intl/cms/s/0/78648e1a-3019-11df-8734-00144feabdc0.html#axzz3kKrgz3sj (accessed 30 August 2015).

Fuhrmanns, Vanessa and Sebastian Mofett (2010) 'Exposure to Greece weighs on French, German banks,' *Wall Street Journal*, 17 February. Available at: www.wsj.com/articles/SB10001424052748703798904575069712153415820 (accessed 5 May 2015).

Gamble, A. (2009) *The Spectre at the Feast: Capitalist Crisis and the Politics of Recession*. London: Palgrave Macmillan.

Hay, C. (1996) 'Narrating crisis: The discursive construction of the "Winter of Discontent",' *Sociology* 30(2): 253–277.

Jones, E., (2003) *The European Miracle*, 3rd edition. Cambridge: Cambridge University Press.

Keating, M. (2008) 'Thirty years of territorial politics,' *West European Politics* 31(1–2): 60–81.

Laffan, B. (2014) 'Testing times: The growing primacy of responsibility in the euro area,' *West European Politics* 37(2): 270–287.

Laffan, B. (2015) 'The state of our unsettled union,' *International Journal of Constitutional Law* 12(4): 853–863.

Laffan, B., R. O'Donnell and M. Smith (1999) *Europe's Experimental Union*. London: Routledge.

Lapavitsas, C., A. Kaltenbrunner, D. Lindo, J. Michell, J. P. Painceira, E. Pires and N. Teles (2010) 'Eurozone crisis: beggar thyself and thy neighbour,' *Journal of Balkan and Near Eastern Studies* 12(4): 321–373.

Lipset, S. M. and S. Rokkan (1967) 'Cleavage Structures, Party Systems, and Voter Alignments: An Introduction,' in S. M. Lipset and S. Rokkan (eds) *Party Systems and Voter Alignments: Cross-national Perspectives*. New York: Free Press, pp. 1–64.

Mair, P. (2014) *On parties, party systems and democracy*. Colchester: ECPR Press.

McNamara, K. (1998) *The Currency of Ideas: Monetary Politics in the European Union*. Ithaca, NY: Cornell University Press.

Merkel, A. (2010) Speech by Federal Chancellor at the opening ceremony of the 61st academic year of the College of Europe in Bruges, 2 November. Available at: file:///C:/Users/blaffan/Downloads/europakolleg_brugge_mitschrift_englisch.pdf.

Mongelli, F. P. (2013) *The Mutating EURO Area Crisis: Is The Balance Between "Sceptics" and "Advocates" Shifting?* European Central Bank, Occasional Paper Series, no. 144, February.

Pérez-Caldentey, E. and M. Vernengo (2012) 'The Euro Imbalances and Financial Deregulation: A Post-Keynesian Interpretation of the European Debt Crisis,' Working Paper no. 702, Levy Economics Institute, Bard College.

Pounds, N. J. G. and S. Simons Ball (1964) 'Core areas and the development of the European states system,' *Annals of the Association of American Geographers* 54(1): 24–40.

Rehn, Olli (2010) 'Update 1-Greek Bushfire must be contained,' *Reuters*, 5 May. Available at: www.reuters.com/article/2010/05/05/eurozone-greece-eu-idUSLDE6440Z720100505 (accessed 30 October 2015).

Rokkan, Stein and Derek W. Urwin (1983) *Economy, Territory, Identity: Politics of West European Peripheries*. London: Sage.

Scharpf, F. W. (2011) 'Monetary Union, Fiscal Crisis and the Pre-emption of Democracy,' MPIfG Discussion Paper 11/11. Cologne: Max Planck Institute for the Study of Societies.

Schmidt, V. (2002) 'Does discourse matter in the politics of welfare state adjustment?,' *Comparative Political Studies* 35(2): 168–193.

Schmidt, V. (2008) 'Discursive institutionalism: The explanatory power of ideas and discourse,' *Annual Review of Political Science* 11: 303–326.

Tilford, P. and P. Whyte (2011) 'Why stricter rules threaten the Eurozone,' Center for European Reform. Available at: www.cer.org.uk/sites/default/files/publications/attachments/pdf/2011/essay_eurozone_9nov11-4084.pdf (accessed 30 April 2015).

Wallace, William (1990) *The Transformation of Western Europe*. London: Pinter.

Wall Street Journal (2010) 'Exposure to Greece weighs on French, German banks,' 17 February. Available at: www.wsj.com/articles/SB10001424052748703798904575069712153415820 (accessed 22 October 2015).

Whittlesey, D. (1939) *The Earth and the State: A Study in Political Geography*. New York: Holt.

Widmaier, W. W. and M. Blyth (2007) 'Exogenous shocks or endogenous constructions? The meanings of wars and crises,' *International Studies Quarterly* 51(4): 747–775.

3 The centre–periphery divide in the Eurocrisis

A theoretical approach

Angelos Sepos

Introduction

The long and ongoing euro (and global) financial crisis has reignited debates regarding the value, viability and morality of capitalism as an economic (and political) system by highlighting its susceptibility and inherent structural propensity for crises and financial meltdowns with dramatic political, economic and social-cultural consequences, including social revolutions in disadvantaged regions of the world, the collapse of international, national and subnational financial and political institutions and increasing divisions and asymmetries between haves and have-nots, rich and poor people and nations across the world. In Europe, this crisis has rekindled arguments about the potential longevity and nature of the European political, economic and social integration project, calling into question founding notions such as the 'ever-closer union', 'unity in diversity' and 'peace and prosperity' and raising doubts about its level and strength of integration, democracy, social justice, solidarity, efficiency-effectiveness and identity. It has also introduced uncertainty regarding degrees of belonging, ownership and influence and the direction of the European project. These issues have been particularly evident in the growing divide and inequality between the centre and periphery *among* European nations – north vs south – but also the centre and periphery *within* European nations – rich vs poor, with the periphery (between and within nations) clearly experiencing significantly greater levels of hardship, suffering and misery than the centre as a result of the financial crisis that began in 2008. This chapter will examine the historical, institutional, political, economic and social factors behind this asymmetric effect of the crisis on the nations and peoples of Europe. One key question it will investigate is whether the rise of 'finance-capital' (or 'financialization') and ultimately capitalism is linked with the growing centre–periphery divide in Europe. It will also examine whether the nature of the European political, economic and monetary union, along with certain conditions and policies in centre and peripheral European states, played a role in the crisis. Moreover, it will discuss the EU's policy responses to the crisis, particularly that of austerity, and will explore other potential solutions such as federalism and differentiated integration. The chapter draws on theories of capitalism and the centre–periphery perspective and employs a mixed quantitative and qualitative methodological approach with inductive and deductive arguments.

Theorizing the centre–periphery divide: a focus on Europe

The centre–periphery divide originates in the study of geometry and was referenced in relation to politics by Herodotus, Plato and Aristotle in terms of recognizing spatial variation as an influential political phenomenon. Plato described the port city of Atlantis as designed in concentric circles of political, economic and cultural power, and Aristotle referred to the *polis* ('city') as the centre of governance of a community. Gottmann (1980: 17) asserts that the centre–periphery divide conveys two basic ideas: a) a symbol of the systematic organization of space around the notion of 'centrality', and b) within that established order, the opposition between the dominant centre and the subordinate periphery, suggesting the possibility of confrontation (and inequalities) along political, social and economic lines. Strassoldo (1980: 37) claims that the centre–periphery metaphor entails two assumptions: a) that the centre is the locus of power and decision-making, and b) that they both belong to an encompassing system in which they are differentiated and interdependent parts. He contends that centralization is a necessary consequence of basic processes such as democratization and social egalitarianism, and that 'political centralization is also an aspect of structural processes pertaining to the operation of large-scale technological systems of production, transportation, and communication' (Strassoldo, 1980: 37) – in other words, it is the result of basic mechanisms of societal development. Interestingly, he argues (1980: 32–35) that centralization is a 'Western cultural trait' and that Western political thought has always glorified it; in fact, the West has been 'obsessed' with the centre, in his words, viewing it as 'sacred' and 'prestigious', a pole from which everything else radiates and is measured (e.g. ancient Rome and Versailles), in opposition to a negatively defined periphery. This is despite the fact that the builders of many of these glorified empire-centres actually originated from the marginal periphery: Alexander the Great came from Macedonia, Napoleon from Corsica, Stalin from Georgia and Hitler from Austria. Some more contemporary leaders of the EU Empire have comparable origins, including Robert Schuman (from Alsace) and Konrad Adenauer (from Rhineland) – people who arguably also strove to integrate the centres and peripheries of Europe (Strassoldo, 1980: 50). In modern political science, Lipset and Rokkan (1967) conceptualized this divide or cleavage as 'the division between elites in urban areas, and those in more outlying, rural areas' (554), identifying it as one of four basic cleavages[1] determining the emergence and content of European parties. In his structural economic theory of imperialism, Galtung (1971: 83) conceptualizes the centre as having 'power over' the periphery, which brings about a 'disharmony of interests' between them. He also observes a 'harmony of interest' between the elites of the centre and the elites of the periphery, with the latter acting as a 'bridgehead' to ensure the former's dominance. There is also a disharmony of interests and an inequality gap between elites and non-elites in both the centre and periphery (with that disharmony and inequality being greater in the periphery), as well as a disharmony of interests between the periphery in the centre and the periphery in the periphery (Figure 3.1). For Galtung (1971: 89), the 'interaction structure' of empires is vertical between the centre and the periphery and relatively absent between peripheries; in addition, the periphery's interaction with other centres is also comparatively limited.

This specific form of economic imperialism (ibid: 101–103) occurs in terms of: a) *absolute properties* (e.g. development variables such as GNP per capita and per centage of population employed in non-primary sectors) – here, the centre ranks high and the periphery low; b) *interaction relations* (i.e. trade composition index) – the centre enriches itself more than the periphery; and c) the *interaction structure* (i.e. partner and commodity concentration index) – the centre is more centrally located in the interaction network than the periphery, while the periphery is ranked higher in the concentration indices. According to Galtung (1971: 101–103), in a relationship of economic imperialism, the correlation pattern arises, whereby solid lines indicate positive relations between polities and the broken lines indicate negative relations.

Similarly, Emmanuel (1972: 91–92) theorized that in a *centre–periphery* and *hierarchical* relationship, there is an unequal exchange of products, whereby the centre predominantly provides the periphery with manufactured goods (i.e. iron, steel, textiles) including medium- and high-tech products (i.e. electronic machinery,

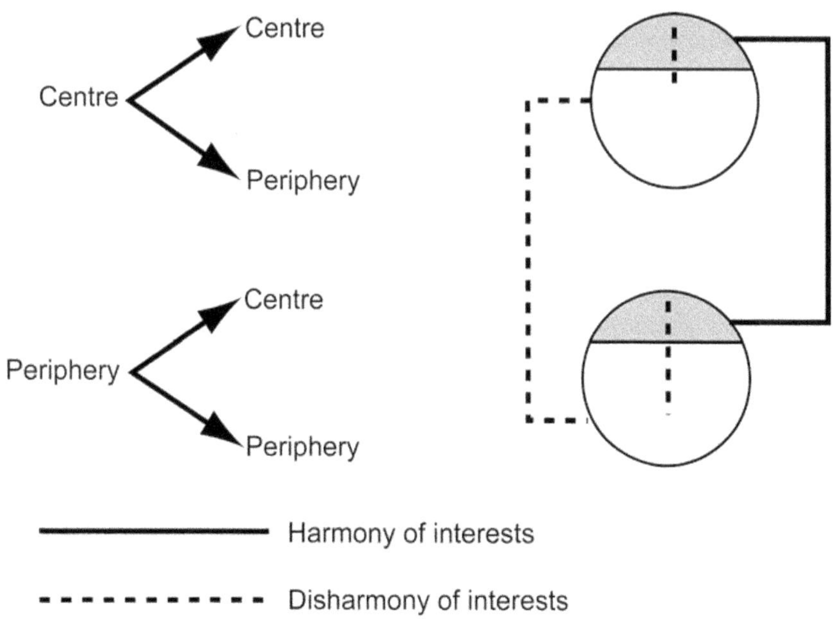

Figure 3.1 Structure of imperialism

chemicals, communications equipment) in exchange for primary goods (i.e. oil, coal, fuel, gas and agricultural products). In Europe, Rokkan (1980) and Meny and Wright (1985) identify centre–periphery structures as 'distinguished by a "privileged" territorial location characterized by a military-administrative and economic advantage as opposed to an "unprivileged" location characterized by distance, difference and dependence' (Meny and Wright, 1985). In a similar vein, other scholars have identified 'families of nations' (Castles, 1993), 'constellation' structures' (Mouritzen and Wivel, 2005), 'clusters of Europeanization' (Goetz, 2006) and 'spatial' (Keating, 2010) and other forms of 'differentiated integration' (Dyson and Sepos, 2010). Keating (2010: 57), for example, argues that while the original vision of European integration assumed that spatial economic disparities would diminish across Europe (e.g. with the help of the single market and the free movement of goods, capital, services and labour), it has now been recognized that this process has in fact exacerbated such disparities and created economic differentiation along spatial lines; this pattern is exemplified by the wealthy 'golden triangle' formed by the Ruhr, south-east England and the Paris region in relation to the poorer, more peripheral regions (i.e. the 'blue banana' metaphor). More recently, researchers have discovered that matters are more complicated: 'islands of prosperity and deprivation are scattered across Europe, in which deprivation can be found even in wealthy metropolises like Greater London (i.e. the 'mosaic' metaphor). Keating also claims that this economic differentiation is often underpinned by political-institutional and ethno-national differentiation between states and their peripheral regions, as seen, for example, in the assertion of Bavarian, Catalan, Basque, Scottish, Flemish, Silesian, Sardinian and South Tyrolean regional identities. Again, more recently, we can recognize that some peripheral regions (e.g. Bavaria, Catalonia, Flanders) have at least economically superseded their historical hegemonic centres. More broadly, Dyson and Sepos (2010) assert that a centre–periphery divide can be recognized in European integration, manifesting itself in formal and informal forms of differentiated integration such as multi-speed, variable geometry and *à la carte* integration. This can be defined in terms of the division between the big, 'strong', 'founder' member states and the smaller, weaker, newer member states: the former seek to form core, pioneer, *avant-garde* or *directoire* groups often at the exclusion of the latter. Such divisions entail a spatial recognition that not one but many Europes exist, with an identifiable centre consisting of 'Franco-German', 'Benelux' and 'Nordic' Europe versus a peripheral 'Mediterranean', 'Central' and 'Baltic' (and 'wider') Europe. In the context of the Eurocrisis, this centre–periphery divide has been defined or framed in terms of: rich (centre) vs poor (periphery), hard-working vs lazy, responsible/disciplined vs irresponsible/profligate, debtors vs creditors, surplus vs deficit, lenders vs borrowers, growth vs austerity, regulatory vs redistributive and market-opening vs market-regulating.

The centre–periphery divide in Europe is integral to those who perceive the European Union as operating as a neo-empire (Zielonka, 2006; Gravier and Parker, 2011; Sepos, 2013) in both its internal structure and external power projections. Indeed, every empire has a centre but also a periphery (Motyl, 2006) that spans its immediate borders as well as extending outside of them. For example, within the EU Empire, the centre arguably consists of the Northern European countries (i.e. Germany, France, the UK, the Netherlands, Belgium, Sweden, Finland, Denmark, Austria), and the periphery consists of the Southern countries (i.e. Portugal, Italy, Ireland, Greece, Cyprus, Spain) and the Central and Eastern European countries. The EU empire also has a periphery outside its sovereign borders; this periphery is arguably the Middle East and North Africa, the Southern Caucasus and the Eurasia region. Our focus in this chapter, however, is the centre–periphery divide *within* the EU empire.

Theorizing capitalism: 'finance-capital' and 'financialization' and their impact on the centre–periphery divide in Europe

Modern capitalism is characterized by the concept of 'financialization', i.e. the idea that the rise of finance is the main driving force in the transformation of modern capitalism, whereby financial leverage tends to override capital (equity) and financial markets tend to dominate the traditional service or industrial economy and agricultural economics. This concept originates from the early Marxist scholar Rudolf Hilferding (1910) and his seminal work *Finance Capital.* For Hilferding, as the scale of production grows, monopolistic industrial capital increasingly relies on monopolistic banks for investments and loans until the two become amalgamated, with banks as the dominant partner taking the leading role. This merged unit can be referred to as 'finance-capital'; it dominates the economy, progressively restricting competition and 'organizing' the economy to serve its interests. Hilferding's analysis provided the foundation for other Marxist scholars such as Rosa Luxemburg (1915), Vladimir Illyich Lenin, (1916), Grigory Zinoviev (1916), Nikolai Bukharin (1917) and, more recently, David Harvey (2003), all of whom linked 'finance-capital' and the 'expansion of capital' with the concept of 'imperialism'. The central argument of Marxist thinking on imperialism is the intrinsic and co-dependent relationship between capitalism and expansion, as well as the idea that capitalist expansion inevitably takes the political form of imperialism. Moreover, imperialism is viewed as critical for the survival of capitalism; the former survives through the production of space, while the latter is considered to be a certain form of production and utilization of global space.

In particular, Hilferding (1910: 25) argued that cartels export money capital to less developed countries in order to take advantage of lower wages; meanwhile, cartel tariffs provide the strongest incentive to increase capital exports and profits, uniting ruling classes in the service of finance-capital and expansion and ultimately leading to imperialism. Lenin (1916: 266) conceived of imperialism as 'the monopoly stage of capitalism' in which finance-capital is the capital of monopolistic banks and industrialists, whereas Zinoviev (1916: 23) viewed imperialism 'as the socio-economic policy of finance capital', which has the tendency to supplant free trade within the system of protective tariffs for the benefit and domination of cartels and banks. For Luxemburg (1915: 5), imperialism was 'the last chapter of the historical expansion of capital' in which capitalist states fiercely compete for non-capitalist territories, while Harvey (2003: 26) coins the notion of 'capital imperialism' as a contradictory fusion of 'the politics of state and empire' and 'the molecular processes of capital accumulation in space and time', the latter referring to ways in which economic power flows towards and away from states and regional entities through production, trade, commerce, capital flows, money transfers, labour migration, technology transfer, currency speculation and flows of information. Finally, there are others whose work echoes that of finance-capital but who do not make the specific link with imperialism. For example, Epstein (2001: 3) first used the term 'financialization' to describe 'the increasing importance of financial markets, financial motives, financial institutions and financial elites in the operations of the economy and its governing institutions, both at the national and international levels'. Similarly, for Krippner (2004: 14), financialization represents a pattern of accumulation in which profit-making increasingly occurs through financial channels rather than through trade and commodity production, whereas for Stockhammer (2004: 720), it is 'the increased activity of non-financial businesses on financial markets'.

Financialization ultimately emerged after the fall of 'embedded liberalism' at the end of the 1960s and the subsequent rise of 'neo-liberalism'; it is thus rooted in the latter movement. 'Embedded liberalism' (Ruggie, 1982), otherwise known as the post-Second World War 'social democratic Keynesian compromise' (Dumenil and Levy, 2011), signified the dawn of a new world order in the early 1950s – supposedly characterized by the conflict between capitalism and communism – marked by the creation of the Bretton Woods agreement and the establishment of international institutions (such as the United Nations, the World Bank and the IMF) intended to stabilize international relations. The free trade of goods was encouraged under a system of fixed exchange rates anchored by the US dollar. This Keynesian model of governance accepted the idea that the state, via its macroeconomic and fiscal policies, played a strong regulatory role in the market, influencing employment, growth and welfare policies such as education, health care and pensions; the state also possessed the ability to place restrictions on its foreign trade regime and capital mobility in order to allow for gradual liberalization and to protect national economic development (Harvey, 2005: 12).

Another key aspect of this compromise was the containment of financial or capitalist interests: a) the financial sector was targeted with the intention of facilitating the growth of the real economy, not to advance the 'administration' of capitalist collective interests (as in neo-liberalism), b) there was less concern for shareholders, low real interest rates and a 'not too performing' stock market, and c) higher labour costs emerged via increased wages, also leading to diminished profits (Dumenil and Levy, 2011: 16). This compromise between capital and labour was the result of an alliance between the managerial and working classes, induced by mass mobilizations of the workers' movement; while the capitalist classes were not fully excluded from the compromise, strong state interventions represented social interests that were significantly distinct from those of the capitalists (Dumenil and Levy, 2011: 17). Although these features of the post-war compromise were less accentuated in the US than in Europe, Korea and Japan, they (i.e. the limitations on capitalist interests) became an important aspect in that period for all countries of the centre. Embedded liberalism delivered high levels of economic growth in the 1950s and 1960s, but it began to stall in the 1970s – both internationally and domestically – and eventually broke down due to the onset of a serious crisis of capital accumulation, a fiscal crisis and soaring rates of unemployment and inflation. The steady growth of official and private liquid dollar claims in the hands of foreigners and the reduction in official gold holdings (especially US gold holdings), compounded by the oil embargo issued by the Organization of the Petroleum Exporting Countries (OPEC) and the subsequent shock of 1973/4, led the Bretton Woods system of fixed exchange rates to collapse (Garber, 1993: 461). One response to this global financial crisis was to further increase state control and regulation, but it was in fact the opposite solution (i.e. 'neo-liberalism') that emerged victorious as the prevailing answer to the problem (Harvey, 2005: 13): the state withdrew from regulating the economy and market forces were freed from restrictions. Along with scholars such as Milton Friedman, Ronald Reagan, Margaret Thatcher, Bill Clinton and Tony Blair were key in establishing this new orthodoxy, known as the 'Washington Consensus'. It was from this new orthodoxy that financialization ultimately arose.

The rise of neo-liberalism and financialization in the 1970s represents the second phase of financial hegemony; the first phase began in the 1890s and ended with the crisis of the Great Depression in the 1930s. According to Schumpeter (2010), these phases are a natural process in the history of capitalism, which is characterized by a 'creative destruction' in which new products and forms of distribution and organization displace older forms; according to Karl Marx, these processes are 'the dialectics of productive forces and relations of production'. Thus, neo-liberalism granted enterprises the freedom to act and promoted the 'market economy' and deregulation in every field, particularly financial mechanisms. It imposed strong macro policies aimed at the protection of lenders through the imposition of price stability and the opening of trade and capital frontiers. This dramatic social transformation could not have been achieved without an alliance of some sort; this time, however, it was between the capitalist and managerial classes (the 'neo-liberal compromise'), allowing the restoration of the hegemony of the upper classes. In this sense, neo-liberalism can be understood as a social order seeking to generate income for the upper-income classes, rather than investment in production or social progress (Dumenil and Levy, 2011: 22).

Finance-capital, financialization and neo-liberalism are important for our discussion, as they should be understood not only as one of the main causes of the American and global financial crisis (Lapavitsas, 2009; Van Treeck, 2009; Krippner, 2011) but also as a primary contributor to the Eurocrisis and the growing centre–periphery cleavage in Europe (Lapavitsas et al., 2010). According to Lapavitsas (2009), the global financial crisis that reached its peak in August 2007 can be interpreted as a crisis of 'financialized capitalism'; others view it as a crisis of 'neo-liberal capitalism' (Dumenil and Levy, 2011; Birch and Mykhnenko, 2010; Overbeek and Van Appeldoorn, 2012) that originated in the US as early as 2001. Capitalism is indeed crisis-prone due to its 'internal contradictions', according to Marx. Thus, on the one hand, the history of capitalism is one of progress, economic and social dynamism, entrepreneurship, creativity, imagination, self-invention and the extension of communication, information and entertainment; on the other, it is a history of regression, extreme inequality, insecurity, greed, social unrest and class domination (Muller, 2013). These internal contradictions have given rise to four major crises in the history of capitalism, i.e. in 1848, 1930, 1970 and 2008. Such crises almost always trigger or contribute to the advent of significant political phenomena such as waves of revolutions, democratization and war. Hence, one can argue that the 1848 crisis contributed to the European revolutions of the same year, the 1930 crisis of the Great Depression played a part in the advent of World War II, the 1970s crisis led to waves of democratization in Latin America, Asia and Southern Europe and the 2008 crisis was a factor in the onset of the Arab Spring. Scholars of revolutions such as Skocpol (1979) also support this line of reasoning, i.e. the idea the 'internationally uneven spread of capitalist economic development and nation-state formation' underlies all social revolutions (ibid.: 19). Finally, the recent crisis can also be seen as a severe form of what Marx called the 'primitive accumulation' of 'fictitious capital' (e.g. through the development of the credit system and the selling of financial products such as stocks, shares, bonds and derivatives), thereby generating immense levels of 'surplus value' and hence 'surplus labour' (Giddens, 1971: 46–55) in certain countries. More recently, this has been understood as a capitalist 'shock therapy' or 'shock doctrine' (Klein, 2007) spearheaded by capitalist international and regional institutions such as the so-called 'Troika' (i.e. the International Monetary Fund, the European Central Bank and the European Commission) and promoted in EU policies and legislation including the Lisbon Agenda (2000) and the Bolkestein (or 'Frankenstein') services directive (2006) – all operating under the watchful eye and following the lead of the US as the global economic hegemon. Paradoxically, given its post-war history, the EU has slowly become the 'new stronghold for neo-liberalism' (Dumenil and Levy, 2011: 11), an engine for free trade and deregulation 'that no longer leads the global third way between laissez-faire capitalism and managed socialism' (Newman, 2012: 3). The crisis was precipitated by housing debts among the poorest US workers and was directly related to the financialization of workers' personal income, mostly housing expenditures but also spending on education, health care, pensions and insurance. The crisis became global because of the transformation of banks and other financial institutions over the course of financialization. Commercial banks had become further removed from industrial and commercial capital while adopting investment-banking practices and turning towards individual income as a source of profits. This combination of investment banking and financialized personal income resulted in an enormous bubble in the US and elsewhere between 2001 and 2007, eventually leading to disaster (Lapavitsas, 2009: 115). The financialization of the economy has also led to the rise of a new *rentier* elite class composed of managers in financial and industrial sectors, as well as functionaries of finance such as lawyers, accountants and technical analysts. This has also brought about a change in economic policy-making institutions whereby central banks have become more influential – empowered by legal and practical independence – and have turned a blind eye to financial excesses; in fact, they have mobilized social and public resources (e.g. by cutting social welfare programmes and public sector salaries) to rescue banks and financers from the crisis. On a more social and individual level, financialization has changed the fabric, morals, ethics and mentalities of societies, making 'risk-taking' the norm, glorifying money and wealth, and encouraging greed, for example, through the transformation of housing and pensions into 'investment schemes' (commonly known as bonds, hedge funds and derivatives), thereby condemning individuals and communities to financial destruction. However, financialization has also changed the nature of modern imperialism and the dynamic of centre–periphery relations (national and regional) across the world, including in Europe. Specifically, poorer and developing countries have been forced to hold vast international reserves that have resulted in net lending by the poor to the rich. Private capital has poured into developing countries, earning high returns, but this has been more than matched by reverse flows seeking to increase the countries' reserves; these earn little interest, thus aimed at accumulating reserves by developing countries and benefiting global economic hegemons such as the US as the issuer of the international means of payment, although it also paid a price when its housing bubble burst (Lapavitsas, 2009: 116).

With regard to Europe, financialization has had an asymmetric effect and has unfolded in different ways across the centre and the periphery. Germany has largely avoided the explosion of household debt that took place in the US and peripheral Eurozone countries. Although the performance of the German economy has been mediocre for many years, great pressure has been applied to German workers' wages and conditions. The main source of growth for Germany has been its current account surplus within the Eurozone (resulting from this pressure) and the associated ability of German capital to take full advantage of cheaper labour and superior productivity in Eastern Europe. Its surplus has been recycled through foreign direct investment and German lending to peripheral European countries and beyond. Financialization in the periphery has proceeded within the framework of the monetary union and under the dominant shadow of Germany. Peripheral economies acquired entrenched current account deficits, while growth came from the expansion of consumption financed by expanding household debt or from investment bubbles characterized by real-estate speculation. There was a general rise in indebtedness for both households and corporations, and pressures were also applied to workers' wages and conditions across the periphery. The integration of peripheral countries into the Eurozone was thus precarious, leaving them vulnerable to the crisis of 2007–2009 and eventually leading to the sovereign debt crisis (Lapavitsas et al., 2010: 322). One can argue that within the framework of the 'financialization of the Eurozone', a new form of 'unequal exchange' of products (Emmanuel, 1972) and 'economic imperialism' (Galtung, 1971) developed between the European centre and the periphery, whereby the former exported financial products, credit (loans) and high-tech manufactured goods to the periphery, mainly in exchange for raw materials and agricultural products. Through this exchange, the centre enriched itself at the expense of the periphery by collecting interest (in the form of assets and income) from the peripheral countries thanks to their ever-expanding debt and by further profits resulting from the expansion of consumption in the peripheral countries (which was only made possible by loans from the centre) and the subsequent increase in purchases of centre-manufactured goods by the periphery. However, it is important to note that it was the elites (the centre) of the centre – i.e. the large commercial and central banks, state-approved cartels and quasi-monopolies, rather than the working class – that benefited the most from the profits generated from the expansion of debt and consumption in the periphery.

This crisis of 'financialized capitalism' in Europe was exacerbated by the institutional bias, malfunction and asymmetric integration within the economic, monetary and political European project. More specifically, ever since the inception in the 1970s of the idea of a common European currency, two visions of market integration have prevailed. From the start, France supported the notion that by fixing the exchange rate policies, cooperation of the respective economic policies would naturally result (the 'monetarists' camp, i.e. supporters of monetary union preceding economic union). Germany (and the Netherlands) held the opposite view, that economic policies needed to be coordinated before fixing exchange rates or introducing a single currency (the 'economists' camp, i.e. those who believed that economic union should precede monetary union) – in other words, that a common currency should be the final stage of economic integration, not the basis of it. The result was an asymmetric Franco-German compromise involving the creation of the European Monetary System (EMS) and the European Currency Unit (ECU) in 1979 by German chancellor Helmut Schmidt and French president Giscard D'Estaing. The 1992 Maastricht Treaty followed the same pattern of compromise. According to Moravscik (2012: 55), from a strictly interest-driven liberal-intergovernmentalist perspective, Germany's main motivation for a single currency was neither to aid its reunification nor to realize an idealistic federalist scheme for European political union. Rather, it was to promote its own economic welfare through open markets, a competitive exchange rate and anti-inflationary monetary policy, all supported by independent central banks and a European Central Bank (ECB) that, just like its own Bundesbank, would always prioritize low inflation over growth and employment, thus resulting in minimum Europeanization adaptation costs for Germany. In contrast, France, Italy, Spain and other peripheral countries that had traditionally weaker currencies viewed monetary union in part as a means to emulate Germany's success by committing themselves to low inflation and low interest rates, reforming the structures of their economies, and encouraging cross-border investment. However, they also saw the euro as an instrument to bring Germany closer to their own economic models, thereby relaxing external constraints and competitive pressures on their economies. These weak-currency countries had suffered many debt and exchange-rate crises in the 1970s and 1980s that were driven by the differences in prices, spending and wages between themselves and Germany. To avoid continuing this pattern, they hoped to encourage Germany to accept a

European structure that would allow for higher domestic spending, wage increases and inflation. Ultimately, their plan did not come to fruition, as Germany insisted on designing a fiercely independent ECB with policies just as anti-inflationary as those of the Bundesbank, if not more so. That basically left the other countries betting their future prosperity on their ability to adopt German standards for wage discipline, government spending and international competitiveness (Moravscik, 2012: 56); they were hoping for the creation of an 'optimal currency area' that would justify a single monetary policy, a situation that evidently never materialized. Tim Garton-Ash (2012: 7) suggests that Germany (via Chancellor Kohl) was aware of the difficulty peripheral countries would encounter in attempting to achieve such economic standards and proposed to complement the monetary union with fiscal/economic and political union so that there could be control over public spending and the coordination of economic policy. However, France opposed this proposal: 'the point was for it to gain some control over Germany's currency, not for Germany to gain control over France's budget'. The result was a compromise and the creation of a 'sickly' EMU characterized by incomplete and asymmetric economic and monetary integration, with more monetary integration (e.g. harmonization of currencies and exchange rates, ceilings on inflation, interest rates and government debt) than economic/fiscal integration (e.g. taxation, financial transactions, government expenditures) or social integration (e.g. welfare policies such as health care, education, pensions, public transportation). In addition, monetary integration was not fully implemented; in fact, the first violators of the Maastricht criteria were the core countries of France and Germany. This asymmetric integration further accentuated the centre–periphery divide, as peripheral countries could not follow the German fiscal standards without the supervision of a strong supranational economic/fiscal authority. They lost further competitiveness vis-à-vis Germany and were unable to employ two of the key instruments that had been used in the past to help them stay competitive, namely currency devaluation and domestic fiscal stimulus (inflation/deflation), as they had surrendered their currencies to ECB control. In other words, the stabilizers that had existed at the national level prior to the start of the union, such as issuing debt (printing money) in national currencies, were stripped away from the Eurozone states without being replaced at the monetary union level, thus leaving peripheral states vulnerable to national and international economic disturbances (De Grauwe, 2013: 6). Not only did the EMU dismantle the main tenets of the Keynesian social democratic compromise, it also failed to install a safety valve of supranational mechanisms of fiscal solidarity such as lender-of-last-resort functions and common debt instruments – crucial measures during a crisis, as was amply proven. As a result, following the US and British financial collapse in 2008, deficit peripheral governments immediately came under pressure from international markets: speculative domestic markets crashed, interest rates rose, external debts ballooned and growth plummeted. In contrast, Germany enjoyed an unprecedented economic boom, experiencing growth by becoming the main exporter – the 'China of Europe' – and moneylender to peripheral countries. Compounding this trend, EU institutions such as the European Commission and the

Bundesbank-modelled ECB became the main promoters and guarantors of financialization, protecting the interests of financial capital by lowering inflation, fostering liberalization and ensuring rescue operations in times of crisis, thus worsening the position of labour relative to capital (Lapavitsas, 2010: 323), facilitating the continued domination of Germany and the Eurozone and accentuating the centre–periphery divide in Europe.

Historical and structural political and socio-economic problems in the peripheral countries further undermined their ability to cope with the institutional asymmetry of the EMU and the global proliferation of financialization. These countries experienced similar problems, arguably due to their common systemic 'Mediterranean' model[2] (or syndrome) of governance, characterized by the economic development and social stratification typical of late industrialization, relatively greater reliance on agriculture and services, financial dependence on EU development aid, weak bargaining capacity and the inability to shape EU institutions and policies, deficient public administrations and poor implementation records, weak and individualistic civil societies and capital, fragmented and party-dominated policy processes, a tendency towards corruption and clientelism and a relative absence of popularly based or party Euroscepticism. At the same time, these countries are not uniform and identical, as pointed out by Heywood and McLaren (2010), who challenge the very notion of a common 'Mediterranean' model or syndrome. Indeed, the Greek crisis was for the most part the result of rent-seeking governments (Featherstone, 2011): ruling parties collaborated with media conglomerates, banks and professional trade unions in a clientelistic and corrupt manner at the expense of the population at large (Eleftheriades, 2014), with the state engaging in highly questionable fiscal policies (Marzinotto et al., 2010), including the manipulation of deficit figures to mask non-compliance with the Maastricht criteria. The Greek public allowed but also willingly engaged in rampant tax evasion, unauthorized construction, pension fraud and legislative immunity against the state's interests (Pappas, 2013). In contrast, for Spain and Ireland, domestic difficulties resulted less from state fiscal mismanagement (in 2007, Spain actually had a budget surplus) and more from market forces – that is, high volumes of capital crossing national borders, leading to credit-fueled booms in housing, tourism and construction (Marzinotto et al., 2010). However, Donovan and Murphy (2010) argue that while Ireland's crisis first began as a property market crisis, it evolved into a banking, fiscal and financial crisis for which a wide array of domestic political and economic actors were responsible, including bankers, builders, developers, economists, media outlets, political parties, financial regulators and an 'apathetic' and 'endorsing' public, suggesting that certain 'paradoxes of government' (Featherstone, 2011) and 'syndromes' experienced by Greece were also at play in the other Southern peripheral countries. These ultimately hindered their Europeanization process, their convergence with Northern economies and their effective adoption of the euro.

In contrast, not only had countries in the core like Germany shaped institutions and policies in their favour (i.e. engaged in 'uploading' Europeanization), thus reducing their euro-adoption costs, but they were further empowered by their ability to effectively handle the global and European financial crisis due to sound macroeconomic policies and strong public institutions. For example, it is a well-established fact that the design, policies and philosophy of the European Central Bank (e.g. its fierce commitment to independence and price stability) are largely modelled on the German Bundesbank, and the ECB has historically modelled European monetary policy on the economic standards and norms of Germany. A German influence was also evident in the aftermath of the economic crisis in 2008, when a German pro-austerity philosophy of fiscal discipline dominated the EU's policy response to the crisis. The rules of 'Six Pack' (2011) measures and the Fiscal Compact (2012), as well as the EU's rejection of Eurobonds and the 'transfer union' (or the 'European Banking Union') solution whereby the financial plight of debtor states would be shared, are further illustrations of German beliefs dominating EU policy (Bulmer and Patterson, 2013: 1395). At the same time, Funk (2013) asserts that the roots of Germany's economic success in handling the crisis better than other Eurozone members lie not just in its effectiveness in uploading its policies at the EU level but also in shrewd economic measures taken prior to and during the crisis. He mentions, for example, the employment- and growth-enhancing structural reforms implemented before the crisis, including labour market and welfare state incentives; Germany's production mix of capital goods, which includes advanced manufactured goods as well as consumer durables, both of which were in high demand outside the Eurozone; successful emergency management by all actors, including social partners; and the strengthening of the stability-orientated economic policy in place since 2009 under Angela Merkel's chancellorship. Funk (2014: 5) emphasizes in particular the 'courageous' economic reforms of the Social Democrat/Green Party-led government of Chancellor Gerhard Schroeder. These 'Hartz' reforms, initiated in 2003 under the name of 'Agenda 2010', significantly cut welfare benefits but also improved incentives to supply labour and increased the flexibility and competitiveness of the labour and product markets. However, Lapavitsas et al. (2010: 337) point out that these reforms and success actually came at the expense of the German working class (i.e. the periphery of the *centre*), whose wages and social welfare conditions were relentlessly squeezed in the name of increased productivity and competitiveness. Similarly, it has been the working and popular classes in the Southern countries (i.e. the periphery of the *periphery*) that have suffered the most from the crisis, with the elite upper classes even managing to increase their wealth during these globally financially dire times. This is a common pattern not only in Europe but also across other developed and developing countries of the world,[3] suggesting again that neo-liberalism and capitalism have contributed to uneven economic development and benefits both *between* nations and between classes *within* these nations.

Thus far, I have explored various factors behind the asymmetric effect of the crisis on the centre and periphery in Europe. I will now discuss some of the responses of the EU institutions and member states to the crisis. In their desperate attempts to keep the euro together, the centre countries led by Germany insisted that the periphery's 'irresponsible borrowing' was to blame for the crisis. They therefore recommended and then imposed through the Troika institutions (the ECB, the European Commission and the IMF), as a form of 'coercive Europeanization', strict budgetary fiscal reforms otherwise known as 'austerity measures' in exchange for bail-out funds to save the debt-ridden Southern economies. However, this widely unpopular austerity only made the debt problem worse, lowering demand and stifling growth; it also led to greater inequality between rich and poor, higher unemployment, higher taxes, lower wages and fewer public and social welfare services, ultimately triggering a humanitarian crisis and profound social unrest and a rupture of the social fabric of some of the most vulnerable countries in the South. Greece, for example, is experiencing its eighth year of recession and GDP contraction, with rising unemployment, poverty and other conditions signifying a growing humanitarian crisis. In particular, in October 2014, the Greek GDP marked a total decline of 33 per cent since its peak in 2007 (this is worse than the US GDP decline during the Great Depression); 25 per cent of the economy had essentially been destroyed, the adult unemployment rate stood at 26.8 per cent and youth unemployment was at 64.2 per cent – notably, of the unemployed, 90 per cent were receiving no government assistance. To the unemployed should be added the working poor, i.e. workers with such low wages that they cannot meet basic needs; at 13 per cent of the workforce, they represent the highest proportion of the working poor in the Eurozone. In addition, 31.4 per cent of the population (or 3.4 million people) were living on an income below 60 per cent of the national average of disposable income, and 27.3 per cent of the population (or 1.3 million people) were at risk of poverty; 20 per cent of Greek children were living in extreme poverty. The number of homeless people has risen to unprecedented levels for a European country, with estimates putting them at 50,000, while the proportion of Greek beneficiaries of medical services in some urban centres is 60 per cent of the total in 2013; the Church of Greece is distributing 250,000 daily food rations to vulnerable citizens. This dire situation has led, among other things, to a mass exodus and brain drain from the country: an estimated 140,000 professionals (doctors, lawyers, engineers) have left Greece since 2010.[4]

Such figures have led to Southern countries to argue that the Northern austerity policies as a remedy for debt-ridden countries are misguided and focus only on the responsibility of the borrowers, not on that of the (excessive) lenders. Indeed, there is significant truth to this, as austerity is not a politically neutral policy: it ultimately puts the burden of adjustment on debtors and workers, and all but leaves creditors and capital owners off the hook (Matthijs, 2014: 105). In economic terms, the case for solving the crisis through austerity seems to be crumbling. John Maynard Keynes clearly stated that 'the boom, not the slump, is the right time for austerity'; that is, cuts should wait until economies are stronger. According to standard textbook Keynesian economics, this is because slashing government spending reduces overall demand, which in turn leads to reduced output and employment. Krugman (2013) argues that austerity policies in the EU were prematurely imposed by the ECB, which should have waited until the Southern economies were stronger. Indeed, he provides evidence that countries such as Greece, Ireland, Portugal and Cyprus that were forced into severe austerity experienced severe contractions of their GDPs and downturns in their economies (Krugman, 2013: 8); this confirms De Grauwe and Ji's (2013: 3) conclusion that 'the deeper the austerity programme, the deeper the decline in GDP output' (i.e. a 1 per cent increase in austerity leads to a 1.4 per cent decline in GDP output). Krugman further explains that the case for austerity in Europe (and indeed the US) was promoted beginning in 2010 on the basis of two key studies by Alesina and Ardagna (2009) and Reinhart and Rogoff (2010). The former scholars showed that austerity does not have a negative impact on economic growth and might even lead to the expansion of the economy (because decisive fiscal austerity creates confidence in the private sector). The latter authors essentially showed that economies fall off a cliff once government debt exceeds 90 per cent of GDP. Both of these studies (and especially the '90 per cent' claim) were cited as the decisive argument for austerity by figures in the EU including Olli Rehn, the European Commissioner for Monetary and Economic Affairs (2004–2014), and the then president of the ECB Jean-Claude Trichet. However, following initial concerns when the studies were published, Krugman (a Nobel Laureate in Economics), along with others in the academic community, finally revealed in April 2013 that Reinhart and Rogoff's 90 per cent threshold was 'an artefact of programmatic mistakes, data omissions and peculiar statistical techniques'; this raised serious concerns about the validity of the study's methodology and conclusions. In addition, researchers at the Roosevelt Institute revealed that there were serious empirical and theoretical problems with the Alesina and Ardagna study, particularly on the measurement of fiscal policy. Krugman (2013: 12) asserts that the European elite's disregard for the warnings of the problems of the pro-austerity agenda was a combined result of 'economic irrationality' (i.e. a complete neglect of the basic Keynesian macroeconomic principle that fiscal and monetary stimulus rather than a reduction in spending is a necessary remedy to overcome economic depression, as seen in 1930), 'self-interest' (i.e. they prioritized creditors, bond holders and the top 1 per cent over the working classes) and a 'misguided moral belief'[5] deeply rooted in the tradition of countries such as Germany (i.e. the idea that a state should always have its finances in order and when in debt, it should reduce spending at all costs). All this was reinforced by the 'real-world cautionary tale' of Greece as an example of poor governance and profligacy that had to be avoided in the future. Thus, by 2013, the full-fledged austerity orthodoxy dominated both European narratives and policies and was in effect in most of Southern Europe, with subsequent disastrous consequences for the economies of these countries.

If austerity is not the answer to solving the crisis and mitigating the asymmetry between the centre and periphery, what role can federalism and differentiated integration play? Schutze (2009: 73), drawing on federal legal traditions, argues that because the EU is based on the concept of 'divided' (or 'shared') sovereignty, there should be no doubt that the Union is already a 'Federation of States'; as he puts it, it stands on a federal 'middle ground', contrary to previously established claims that the EU is *sui generis*. Schutze's thesis is strong from a legal perspective, but it arguably seemed more valid before the beginning of the Eurocrisis (when his work was written) than now. It would be inconceivable in a genuine cooperative federation for the federal government (in this case, the European Commission) to propose a bail-out financial package to indebted states (in this case, Greece, Portugal, Ireland and Cyprus) and expect them to pay back that loan through domestic financial cuts and austerity. In cooperative federations, state debts, whether they stem from financial or natural disasters (as in the cases of the US states of Michigan and New Orleans, respectively), are shared and 'communitarized' within the federation: using the federal budget, the federal government directs funds to the economically depressed states, not in the form of conditional loans but in the form of financial rescue packages. This is obviously not what happened in the EU's case, where countries such as Germany fiercely objected to such communitarization of debt in the form of a 'transfer union' (i.e. the Eurobonds proposal), and where strict austerity conditions were imposed by the Troika on bail-out packages for troubled economies. In the extreme case of Cyprus, in an attempt to salvage the country's oversized and Greek-dependent insolvent banks, the EU enforced a 40 per cent tax on all bank deposits of middle-class Cypriots, essentially raiding the bank accounts of ordinary citizens to raise 5.6 billion euros of the 10 billion euro loan requested, a measure infamously known as the 'bail-in'.[6] It is thus highly questionable whether the EU in its current structure is operating as a cooperative federation. Such a federation would *surely* require the creation of a European constitution in which the competencies of the federal government and the federated member states are clearly defined in a balanced and symmetric manner, with mechanisms in place to facilitate a cooperative rather than a confrontational decision-making environment, thus avoiding 'joint-decision traps' (Scharpf, 1988) and low-denominator policy outcomes. The creation of such a federation would also promote the symmetric integration of all policy areas of the Union (i.e. political, economic, monetary and social); this would be the key to minimizing disparities and divergence among member states. In contrast, differentiated integration initiatives such as the Euro-Plus Pact, the European Stability Mechanism (ESM) and the Fiscal Compact may possibly provide temporary solutions to the crisis but will not solve its underlying causes.

Conclusion

The proliferation of neo-liberalism and 'financialization' – the latest phase of capitalism and a new form of 'finance-capital' – along with a problematic monetary union and the lack of a political, fiscal, economic and social union, and in conjunction with domestic policy choices in both centre and peripheral countries, have arguably accentuated the already existing centre–periphery political and socio-economic divide in the EU Empire. This divide can only be bridged by 'de-imperializing' Europe, removing any overt or covert mechanisms facilitating the domination of the periphery by the centre. The creation of a full-fledged, symmetrical, cooperative EU federal model, rather than more differentiated integration, could help the Union achieve this goal and bridge the divide. Such 'grand' institutional changes (a federal constitution or an important treaty) have historically been initiated by the elites of Europe, figures such as Monnet, Adenauer, Kohl, Mitterrand, Delors and D'Estaing. Perhaps it is now time for an ambitious institutional redesign – which, as we have seen from the crisis, would clearly have a direct and profound impact on the everyday lives of European citizens – to be initiated bottom-up rather than top-down, i.e. by the people of Europe. This will of course necessitate the emergence of a strong pan-European social movement, something that has yet to occur in the entire history of European integration. The May 2006 pan-European movement 'Stop Bolkestein' (the services directive), which called for 'Another Europe, with public services for all', could be a good starting point and network for such a movement to build upon. For the movement to have any success, it would have to be larger and more diverse, united and committed than its predecessor, with broader and more ambitious demands. These might include the creation of a federal European constitution that would accommodate a symmetric political, economic, monetary/fiscal/banking and social-welfare union, thereby establishing a genuine European democratic polity whose leaders would be directly democratically elected by the European demos and that would provide equal political, civil, human and also socio-economic rights to all its citizens. This would create an egalitarian European society, eradicating all forms of political and economic domination and providing equality of opportunity for all, minimizing socio-economic disparities and inequalities and ensuring equitable, inclusive and sustainable socio-economic development for all member states and citizens. If such aims seem too idealistic, then at the least European citizens can hope and settle for another social-democratic Keynesian compromise – between labour and capital – in this latest phase of twenty-first-century capitalism.

At the time of publication of this volume, radical left-wing, anti-establishment, anti-austerity political parties in Southern Europe, such as Syriza in Greece and Podemos in Spain, have gained prominence with the electorates in these countries. In January 2015 Syriza won a snap parliamentary election and its leader Alexis Tsipras was appointed prime minister of Greece, while Podemos showed in its strong showing in the March 2013 Andalusian regional elections that it can replicate Syriza's success in Spain. At this point, these social-movements-turned-political parties, with their post-Marxist ideology, seem to represent the only genuine challenge and opposition to the capitalist neo-liberal ideology that has dominated Europe in the last three decades. Their success in managing to change Europe 'from within' and create a more social-democratic Union that serves all Europeans, will depend on whether they stay true to their pre-election promises, whether they resist the pressure from pro-capital institutions such as the Troika, and whether they manage to build broader coalitions with other similar-minded movements across Europe. Especially for the latter to occur, these movements will need to effectively communicate to European citizens that their struggle is not just against the economic inequalities that resulted from the problematic relations between capital and labour, but also against any forms of relations of oppression and inequalities in the political and social sphere.

Notes

1 The other cleavages are 'state–church', 'owner–worker' and 'land–industry'.
2 See Sepos, 2008.
3 It is indicative that between the 1980s and the mid-2000s, inequality rose in 16 out of 20 rich OECD countries, while inequality increased in all major developing countries except Brazil, Argentina and Mexico (where inequality nevertheless remains very high) (Milanovic, 2011).
4 Figures from Eurostat, IMF, World Bank, OECD and Hellenic Statistical Authority.
5 This belief is also historically paradoxical: when Germany was deep in debt following Second World War, it was not austerity and strict structural reforms but generous debt relief and stimulus packages such as the London Debt Agreement and the Marshall Plan that facilitated its economic recovery (Young, 2014: 8). In fact, German negotiators then explicitly rejected any suggestions of Anglo-Saxon austerity (Kaiser, 2013: 18).
6 'Cyprus backs painful bail-out deal', BBC News, 25 March 2013.

References

Alesina, A. and S. Ardagna (2009) 'Large Changes in Fiscal Policy: Taxes Versus Spending,' Working Paper Series, National Bureau of Economic Research.

Birch, K. and V. Mykhnenko (2010) *The Rise and Fall of Neo-Liberalism: The Collapse of an Economic Order?* London: Zed Books.

Bukharin, N. (1917) *Imperialism and World Economy*. New York: International Publishers, 1929. Available at: www.marxists.org/archive/bukharin/works/1917/imperial/ (accessed 3 April 2015).

Bulmer, S. and W. Paterson (2013) 'Germany as the EU's Reluctant Hegemon? Of Economic Strength and Political Constraints,' *Journal of European Public Policy* 20(10): 1387–1405.

Castles, F. (1993) 'Introduction' in F. Castles (ed.) *Families of Nations: Patterns of Public Policy in Western Democracies*. Aldershot: Dartmouth Publishers.

De Grauwe, P. and Yuemei Ji (2013) 'The Legacy of Austerity in the Eurozone,' Center for European Policy Studies, 4 October, 1–6.

Donovan, D. and A. Murphy (2013) *The Fall of the Celtic Tiger: Ireland and the Euro-Debt Crisis*. Oxford: Oxford University Press.

Dumenil, G. and D. Levy (2011) *Crisis of Neo-Liberalism*. Cambridge, MA: Harvard University Press.

Dyson, K. and A. Sepos (2010) 'Differentiated Integration as Design Principle and as a Tool in the Political Management of European Integration' in K. Dyson and A. Sepos (eds) *Which Europe? The Politics of Differentiated Integration*. Basingstoke: Palgrave Macmillan, pp. 3–23.

Eleftheriades, P. (2014) 'Misrule of the Few: How the Oligarchs Ruined Greece,' *Foreign Affairs* November/December: 1–7.

Emmanuel, A. (1972) *Unequal Exchange: A Study of the Imperialism of Trade*. London: New Left Books.

Epstein, G. (2001) 'Financialization, Rentier Interests and Central Bank Policy,' paper presented at the conference Financialization of the World Economy, 7–8 December, Amherst, University of Massachusetts.

Featherstone, K. (2011) 'The Greek Sovereign Debt Crisis and EMU: A Failing State in a Skewed Regime,' *Journal of Common Market Studies* 49(2): 193–217.

Funk, L. (2013) 'Germany: Sweeping Structural Reforms Can Work,' in Vít Novotný (ed.) *From Reform to Growth: Managing the Economic Crisis in Europe*, Centre for European Studies, Brussels and Delft: Eburon.

Funk, L. (2014) 'Why Has the German Job Market Done Astonishingly Well Despite the 2008–2009 "Great Recession": New Economic Miracle, Institutional Transformation or Beggar Thy Neighbour Policies?,' *Perspectives on European Politics and Society* 15(3): 1–19.

Galtung, J. (1971) 'A Structural Theory of Imperialism,' *Journal of Peace Research* 8(2): 82–83.

Garber, P. (1993) 'The Collapse of the Bretton Woods Fixed Exchange Rate System' in M. Bordo and B. Eichengreen (eds) *A Retrospective on the Bretton Woods System: Lessons for International Monetary Reform*. Chicago, IL: University of Chicago Press, pp. 461–494.

Garton-Ash, T. (2012) 'The Crisis of Europe,' *Foreign Affairs* 91(5): 2–15.

Giddens, A. (1971) *Capitalism and Modern Social Theory: An Analysis of the Writings of Marx, Durkheim and Max Weber*. Cambridge: Cambridge University Press.

Goetz, K. H. (2006) 'Territory, Temporality and Clustered Europeanization,' Political Science Series 109, Institute for Advanced Studies, University of Vienna.

Gottmann, J. (1980) 'Confronting Centre and Periphery' in J. Gottmann (ed.) *Centre and Periphery: Spatial Variation in Politics*. London: Sage, pp. 11–25.

Gravier, M. and N. Parker (2011) 'Imperial Power and the Organization of Space in Europe and North Africa,' *Journal of Political Power* 4(3): 331–336.

Harvey, D. (2005) *A Brief History of Neoliberalism*. Oxford: Oxford University Press.

Harvey, D. (2003) *The New Imperialism*. Oxford: Oxford University Press.

Heywood, P. and L. McLaren (2010) 'Mediterranean Europe' in K. Dyson and A. Sepos (eds) *Which Europe? The Politics of Differentiated Integration*. Basingstoke: Palgrave Macmillan, pp. 170–184.

Hilferding, R. (1910) *Finance Capital: A Study of the Latest Phase of Capitalist Development*; ed. Tom Bottomore (1981) London: Routledge and Kegan Paul. Available at: www.marxists.org/archive/hilferding/1910/finkap/index.htm. (accessed 17 January 2015).

Kaiser, J. (2013) 'One Made It Out of the Debt Trap: Lessons from the London Debt Agreement of 1953 for Current Debt Crises,' Department for Global Policy Development, Friedrich-Ebert-Stiftung, Berlin.

Keating, M. (2010) 'The Spatial Dimension' in K. Dyson and A. Sepos (eds) *Which Europe? The Politics of Differentiated Integration*. Basingstoke: Palgrave Macmillan, pp. 54–66.

Klein, N. (2007) *The Shock Doctrine: The Rise of Disaster Capitalism*. London: Allen Lane/Penguin.

Krippner, G. (2004) 'What is Financialization?,' mimeo, Department of Sociology, University of California, Los Angleles (UCLA).

Krippner, G. (2011) *Capitalizing on Crisis: The Political Origins of the Rise of Finance*. Cambridge, MA: Harvard University Press.

Krugman, P. (2013) 'How the Case for Austerity has Crumbled,' *New York Review of Books*, 6 June, pp. 1–14.

Lapavitsas, C., A. Kaltenbrunner, D. Lindo, J. Michell, J. P. Painceira, E. Pires, J. Powell and N. Teles (2010) 'Eurozone Crisis: Beggar Thyself and Thy Neighbour,' *Journal of Balkan and Near Eastern Studies* 12(4): 321–373.

Lapavitsas, C. (2009) 'Financialized Capitalism: Crisis and Financial Expropriation,' *Historical Materialism* 17(2): 114–148.

Lenin, V. (1916) *Imperialism: The Highest Stage of Capitalism: A Popular Outline*; introduction L. Norman and J. Malone, *Living Marxism Originals* (1996) London: Pluto Press. Available at: www.marxists.org/archive/lenin/works/1916/imp-hsc/ch07.htm (accessed 17 January 2015).

Lipset, S. M. and S. Rokkan (1967) *Party Systems and Voter Alignments: Cross-National Perspectives*. New York: Free Press.

Luxemburg, R. (1915) '*The Accumulation of Capital: An Anti-Critique*, ed. and introduction Kenneth J. Tarbuck (1972) London: Penguin. Available at: www.marxists.org/archive/luxemburg/1915/anti-critique/ (accessed 17 January 2015).

Marzinotto, B., J. Pisani-Ferry and A. Sapir (2010) 'Two Crisis, Two Responses,' Bruegel Policy Brief 1, March 1–8.

Matthijs, M. (2014) 'Mediterranean Blues: The Crisis in Southern Europe,' *Journal of Democracy* 25(1): 101–115.

Meny, Y. and V. Wright (eds) (1985) *Centre-Periphery Relations in Western Europe*. London: George Allen and Unwin.

Milanovic, B. (2011) 'More or Less: Income Inequality has Risen over the Past Quarter Century Instead of Falling as Expected,' (IMF) *Finance and Development* 48(3): 1–6.

Moravcsik, A. (2012) 'Europe After the Crisis,' *Foreign Affairs* 91(3): 54–68.

Motyl, A., (2001) *Imperial Ends: The Decay, Collapse, and Revival of Empires*. New York: Columbia University Press.

Mouritzen, H. and A. Wivel (2005) 'Constellation Theory' in H. Mouritzen and A. Wivel (eds) *The Geopolitics of Euro-Atlantic Integration*. London: Routledge.

Muller, J. Z. (2013) 'Capitalism and Inequality,' *Foreign Affairs* 92(2): 1–15.

Newman, A. (2012) 'Austerity and the End of the European Model: How Neo-Liberals Captured the Continent,' *Foreign Affairs* 91(5): 1–4.

Overbeek, H. and B. Van Appeldoorn (eds) (2012) *Neo-Liberalism in Crisis*. Basingstoke: Palgrave Macmillan.

Pappas, T. (2013) 'Why Greece Failed,' *Journal of Democracy* 24(2): 31–45.

Reinhart, C. and K. Rogoff (2010) 'Growth in a Time of Debt,' *American Economic Review Paper and Proceedings* 100(2): 573–578.

Rokkan, S. (1980) 'Territories, Centres, and Peripheries: Toward a Geoethnic-Geoeconomic-Geopolitical Model of Differentiation Within Western Europe' in J. Gottmann (ed.) *Centre and Periphery: Spatial Variation in Politics*. London: Sage, pp. 163–204.

Ruggie, J. (1982) 'International Regimes, Transactions and Change: Embedded Liberalism in the Postwar Economic Order,' *International Organization* 36(2): 379–415.

Saez, E. and G. Zucman (2014) 'Exploding Wealth Inequality in the United States,' 20 October, Washington Centre for Equitable Growth, Washington, DC.

Scharpf, F. (1988) 'The Joint-Decision Trap: Lessons from German federalism and European Integration,' *Public Administration* 66(3): 239–278.

Schumpeter, J. (2010) *Capitalism, Socialism and Democracy*. London: Routledge.

Schutze, R. (2009) *From Dual to Cooperative Federalism: The Changing Structure of European Law*. Oxford: Oxford University Press.

Sepos, A. (2013) 'Imperial Power Europe? The EU's Relations with the ACP Countries,' *Journal of Political Power* 6(2): 261–288.

Sepos, A. (2008) *The Europeanization of Cyprus: Polity, Policies and Politics*. Basingstoke: Palgrave Macmillan.

Skocpol, T. (1979) *States and Social Revolutions*. Cambridge: Cambridge University Press.

Stockhammer, E. (2004) 'Financialization and the Slowdown of Accumulation,' *Cambridge Journal of Economics* 28(5): 719–741.

Strassoldo, T. (1980) 'Centre–Periphery and System–Boundary: Culturological Perspectives' in J. Gottmann (ed.) *Centre and Periphery: Spatial Variation in Politics*. London: Sage, pp. 27–61.

Van Treeck, T. (2009) 'The Political Economy Debate on "Financialization": A Macroeconomic Perspective', *Review of International Political Economy* 16(5): 907–944.

Young, B. (2014) 'German Ordoliberalism as Agenda-Setter for the Euro-Crisis: Myth Trumps Reality,' *Journal of Contemporary European Studies* 22(3): 276–287.

Zielonka, J. (2006) *Europe as Empire: The Nature of the Enlarged European Union*. Oxford: Oxford University Press.

Zinoviev, G. (1916) 'What is Imperialism?,' *New International* 7(11): 1941 and 8(1): 1942. Available at: www.marxists.org/archive/zinoviev/works/x01/x01.htm (accessed 20 October 2015).

Part II

Comparative approaches

4 National interests and differentiated integration in the EU under crisis conditions

The cases of Germany, France and Britain

Christian Schweiger

The 2008/9 global financial crisis represents a decisive turning point in the development of the European Union, as it had profound economic and budgetary implications for a number of Eurozone countries. Despite divergent national circumstances, the crisis illustrated the strong linkage between the economies in the eurozone, mainly as a result of the close connections between national banking sectors (Kalemli-Oczan et al. 2010). The profound systemic weaknesses that the financial crisis revealed in some eurozone countries led to a rapid decline in financial market confidence in these economies, ultimately raising the risk of the demise of the eurozone should political elites fail to take action. This chapter analyses the roles played by the three largest EU member states – Germany, France and Britain – in resolving the adverse effects of the crisis under the conditions of the EU's internal *variable leadership geometry*.

Background to the crisis: lack of strategic leadership under the EU's *variable leadership geometry*

When the crisis hit the European Union, the organisation had been suffering from a notable leadership deficit for some time. With the continuing enlargement of the EU, the former Franco-German leadership duo found it increasingly difficult to continue to act as the strategic agenda-setters for the integration process.

Institutionalised regular bilateral consultations and joint initiatives between the two countries substantially drove European integration for more than four decades, beginning with the end of the Second World War (Cole 2001: 68). The Franco-German partnership was therefore frequently referred to as the leadership axis or even the 'cooperative hegemon' of the EU (Hyde-Price 2000: 194). This power structure began to change significantly in the aftermath of German reunification and the end of the Cold War. By the time the EU reached the size of 15 member states in 1995, it had become much more difficult for the two countries to determine the leadership agenda amongst a new and wider variety of national interests. Even more crucially, German reunification had fundamentally altered the power balance in the Franco-German axis, which was traditionally characterised by the smaller West German Federal Republic being content with a political role subordinate to that of France. This was an essential part of the post-war West German foreign policy tradition, whereby the country's leaders in Bonn shied away from unilateral European policy initiatives. Instead, West German European policy was exercised as a joint Franco-German project with constant close consultations, and Bonn frequently followed the general direction determined by the Elysée (Bulmer et. al. 2001: 200). The larger united Germany of more than 80 million people was substantially more powerful in terms of political influence in the EU; moreover, it was no longer able to maintain the reflexive Europeanism it had exercised before 1990. As the domestic financial and economic burdens of reunification began to increase over the course of the 1990s, German European policy became more pragmatic, with a new orientation towards rational cost-benefit analyses. This shift was reflected by the Kohl administration's demand that the creation of the euro as the single European currency be accompanied by an explicit budgetary rulebook. The negotiations for the Maastricht Treaty and the subsequent revision discussions at the May 1997 Amsterdam summit demonstrated the increasingly divergent concepts developed by France and Germany regarding the future shape of the Single European Market and the emerging eurozone. The Kohl government was under strong pressure from the German Bundesbank to ensure that the eurozone would be orientated towards monetary stability. Germany consequently demanded a binding budgetary rulebook for the eurozone in return for the abolition of its national currency, the Deutschemark, and ultimately the acceptance of the low-growth and high-deficit countries Italy and Greece into the eurozone. The result was that the design of the eurozone bore Germany's signature and may thus be characterised as an example of successful institutional export (Bulmer 1997: 74). This can be seen the institutionalised preference for monetary stability in the eurozone's Maastricht membership criteria, which strongly resembles the *Stabilitätspolitik* (stability policy) pursued by the German central bank. Moreover, the institutional independence from political authority at the heart of the design of the European Central Bank essentially replicated that of the German Bundesbank. The fact that Frankfurt was chosen as the location for the European Central Bank was merely symbolic in this context, emphasising the fact that the united Germany had begun to outgrow its long-standing role as France's junior partner (Kirchner 1996. The wording of the eurozone's stability and growth pact revealed the underlying Franco-German tensions with regard to the design of the currency area. The emphasis on the combination between stability and growth reflected the French desire to allow national governments budgetary flexibility for investment under the rules of the eurozone (Pisani-Ferry 2011: 30–31). The French were clearly keen to couple the German emphasis on monetary stability with the deeper integration of economic policies. In the run-up to the Amsterdam summit, French President Francois Mitterrand's Gaullist successor Jacques Chirac made several attempts to weaken the political independence of the emerging European Central Bank (Webber 1999: 38). At the May 1997 EU summit in Amsterdam, Chirac eventually joined forces with France's newly elected Socialist prime minister Lionel Jospin in demanding that monetary union be accompanied by the establishment of an integrated European employment policy. This was jointly opposed by German chancellor Kohl and Britain's newly elected Labour prime minister Tony Blair, who argued that employment policy should remain a predominantly national issue. As a compromise, the EU adopted employment guidelines based on overall targets that were eventually incorporated into the Lisbon Strategy (Biehler 2006: 13). The Amsterdam summit turned out to be a decisive turning point in Franco-German relations, as it laid bare the profound disagreements between the two countries on the future shape of the Single Market. France wanted the euro to be at the heart of an emerging economic union based on the increased coordination of national policies of national policies. For Germany under Kohl, the main concern was that French calls for the supranationalisation of core policy areas such as employment would most likely result in the need to increase the EU budget at a time when the domestic costs of reunification were continuing to pile up (Schweiger 2014a: 30). After 1998, Kohl's successor Gerhard Schröder was even less inclined to go along with the French desire to enhance the EU's collective responsibilities regarding economic and social policies.

Schröder displayed a fundamentally pragmatic approach towards the EU in which he prioritised subjecting EU policy proposals to strictly rational cost-benefit analyses in relation to Germany's national interests (Jeffery and Paterson 2000: 35). This brought Schröder much closer to the position of the British prime minister Tony Blair, who had adopted a similar approach. The two leaders famously published a joint position paper in March 1999 in which they branded themselves as Social Democratic modernisers. The Blair-Schröder paper explicitly favoured the streamlining of intergovernmental policy coordination on the basis of best-practice benchmarking and policy learning rather than the harmonisation of national policies (Blair and Schröder 1999). Blair and Schröder became the leading actors behind the push for the adoption of the EU's new policy mechanism, the *open method of coordination* (OMC), which became the core approach behind the Lisbon Strategy. The OMC was intended to ensure that even without policy harmonisation, national governments would achieve more consistent policy outcomes in terms of growth, employment and social cohesion (Hantrais 2007: 22; McCann 2010: 140). Kohl and Schröder's rejection of French calls for greater policy harmonisation in the context of the Single Market reflected the fact that national interests were shifting in the larger EU of 15 member states, and leadership coalitions were therefore unlikely to become a permanent feature. This explains why it was not possible for the earlier Franco-German leadership duo to develop into a permanent leadership triangle together with the UK. Despite the much more pro-active and cooperative attitude of the Blair government towards core EU policy issues during the period from 1997 until 2003 and the close relationship between Blair and Schröder, the philosophical distance between these two leaders and the French administration remained substantial (Grabbe and Münchau 2002).

France's Socialist prime minister Jospin was clearly uneasy with the intergovernmental approach endorsed by Blair and Schröder, particularly in the social policy area. Jospin therefore continued to call for the establishment of an EU social treaty in which member states would determine binding common standards in the area of employment, such as minimum wage levels and job protection requirements (Jospin 2001). President Chirac was unwilling to follow Blair and Schröder in their ambition to initiate fundamental institutional reforms (including profound changes to the Common Agricultural Policy) in preparation for the impending next wave of enlargement that would include the post-Communist countries of Central and Eastern Europe. Consequently, the three countries failed to reach an agreement on the implementation of institutional reforms at the intergovernmental conference in Nice in December 2000. This was widely considered to be a reflection of the fact that the larger EU was suffering from a leadership deficit (Finke et al. 2012: 11), primarily stemming from the inability of France and Germany to continue their traditional close consultations on EU affairs. The Schröder government was not shy about putting forward its own proposals for the future architecture of the EU, and the French reaction was predominantly one of consternation. The prime example of this was the reaction of French interior minister Jean-Pierre Chevènement to the detailed proposals regarding the future institutional architecture of the EU that Germany's foreign minister Joschka Fischer made during a speech at Humboldt University in May 2000, which Chevènement referred to as a sign that Germany had not yet overcome its Nazi past (*Le Monde* 2000).

In the absence of the Franco-German leadership axis, to a large extent the EU lost its focus, and the organisation drifted aimlessly for a considerable time. Occasionally, ad hoc leadership coalitions emerged to take the initiative in a particular policy area. Under this *variable leadership geometry* constellation, the three largest players – Germany, France and the UK – continued to play crucial roles but failed to act as a permanent leadership triangle. Instead, they engaged temporarily in alliances that shifted between various groups of countries that attempted to set the agenda in specific policy areas (Wallace 2005: 29).

In practice, it has become obvious that the new shifting leadership coalitions usually involve at least one of the three largest member states, and increasingly also one of the next three largest countries, namely Italy, Spain and Poland (Paterson 2010: 48). The role of smaller countries as supporters of initiatives has also been enhanced under these conditions. Prime examples are the development of the 2003 EU security and defence policy (ESDP) and the Rapid Reaction Force in the aftermath of the 1998/9 Kosovo crisis, as well as the establishment of the Eastern partnership under the European Neighbourhood Policy in 2009. The former initiative was heavily promoted by British prime minister Tony Blair and French president Jacques Chirac in cooperation with the governments of Germany, Belgium and Luxembourg. The Eastern partnership emerged on the basis of a joint cooperation between the Polish government and Sweden, with the strong support of the Czech Republic (Vandecasteele, Bossuyt and Orbie 2013: 3).

Under the conditions of variable leadership geometry, the national preferences of the now 28 EU member states have become a critical factor that can be decisive for coalition-building prospects. The continuing expansion of qualified majority voting (QMV) to additional policy areas has increasingly turned policy-making in the EU into a game of intergovernmental bargaining, where consensus depends on the level of correspondence between the strategic interests of groups of member states. The double majority introduced under the provisions of the Lisbon Treaty in November 2014 favours the agenda-setting role of the largest member states by mandating that a QMV decision must represent at least 65 per cent of the EU's population. At the same, the Lisbon Treaty also grants a more powerful role to smaller countries by demanding that a QMV decision be carried by at least 55 per cent of member states in the Council and a minimum of 15 member states. Thus, although larger states continue to be favoured in terms of their agenda-setting powers, the new system requires them to engage in effective coalition-building to ensure that decisions can be reached under QMV (M.O. Hosli 2008, p. 91).

In this context, Andrew Moravcsik's liberal intergovernmentalist (LI) theory remains essential for the analysis of individual member-state preferences and their impacts on the wider EU agenda. Moravcsik's application of LI two-level analysis to the intergovernmental negotiations between Helmut Kohl, Francois Mitterrand and Margaret Thatcher in cooperation with the Delors Commission in the development of the Single European Act in 1986 offers a critical perspective on how correspondence in the national interests of the larger member states can result in significant strategic policy developments (Moravcsik 1991). With regard to the developments in the EU in the aftermath of the financial crisis, Moravcsik's two-level analysis is a useful framework for attempts to explain why it was not possible to maintain the traditional Community method of uniform, single-speed integration based on sustained budgetary solidarity across all member states (Wallace 2010: 94). Moravcsik's LI analysis assumes that national member-state preferences in the EU are predominantly characterised by a rational choice approach in which national governments prioritise the consideration of the 'costs and benefits of economic interdependence' (Moravcsik 1993: 480). National governments are seen as engaged in a two-level process involving the domestic level of preference formation and the supranational level of interstate bargaining (Moravcsik 1993: 482). Most significantly, Moravcsik's application of liberal preference theory to the analysis of the domestic member state-level views the consideration of effective economic interaction as a crucial goal of domestic preference formation. Member-state governments are therefore most likely to obtain a mandate of domestic support from different societal groups for increased EU-level policy coordination or even harmonisation when such efforts are considered essential for resolving external constraints on the effective operation of national political economies (Moravcsik 1993: 495). For Moravcsik, the LI view that economic integration in the EU is predominantly driven by external events marks the essential difference between this approach and Haas's neofunctionalism, which views internal incremental spill-over processes as the main source of economic integration (Moravcsik 2005: 358). At the same time, Moravcsik accurately highlights that a substantial prerequisite for the establishment of a consensus on increased policy coordination at the EU level is a correspondence in values between member states in key policy areas such as social policy and taxation, but also immigration (Moravcsik 1997:528). When such a correspondence does not exist, it is more likely that member states will either demand an opt-out from the integration process or ultimately even decide to veto it. In summary, a lack of correspondence in national interests in core policy areas makes consensus at the EU level less likely; consequently, differentiated levels of integration become increasingly necessary. Differentiated integration thus becomes a means of resolving the threat of policy gridlock in areas in which member states exhibit low levels of correspondence in terms of national interests (Leuffen, Rittberger and Schimmelpfennig 2013: 54; Dyson and Sepos 2008).

German, French and British approaches towards the crisis: the unavoidable path towards differentiated integration

The developments that followed the unprecedented external events of the global financial crisis have re-emphasised the diversity of national political economies. Consequently, the stark differences between the strategic economic interests of member states have moved to the forefront; this is most obvious when one considers the three key strategic players: Germany, France and Britain. The crisis has accentuated the fact that in the current EU of 28 member states, the prospect of continuing down the traditional path of the Community method of uniform integration has become ever more remote. In fact, progress in developing collective solutions to address the crisis has only been possible on the basis of mechanisms that ensure the possibility of differentiated levels of integration for groups of member states. This shift is most clearly evident in the demands made by the British government under David Cameron to safeguard opt-outs from the deepening layers of policy coordination in the eurozone. However, a closer examination of the discussions surrounding the question of how the EU should respond to the mounting sovereign debt problem in selected eurozone countries also reveals a significant distance between the strategic interests of France and Germany. During the initial phase of the crisis, the move towards collective EU action seemed to emerge from a joint Franco-British initiative. British prime minister Gordon Brown joined forces with French President Nicholas Sarkozy in October 2008 to demand both an EU-wide investment programme to stimulate economic growth and a dedicated EU crisis fund programme for countries plagued by sovereign debt (Parker and Hall 2008). A few weeks later, the two leaders proposed a new Bretton Woods system of global financial regulation. Profound disagreements regarding the level of binding regulation nevertheless remained, with Gordon Brown continuing to advocate light-touch regulation for the British financial industry in the City of London (Hall and Eaglesham 2008). For both leaders, there was an indispensable need to demonstrate transnational initiative in response to the crisis. In the British case, Gordon Brown was coming under sustained domestic pressure to justify the unprecedented levels of public investment (£500 million) intended to stabilise British banks with severe liquidity problems, including Northern Rock, Lloyds TSB and the Royal Bank of Scotland. The resulting spiralling public deficit in the UK was widely portrayed by the British press and the Conservative opposition as a failure on the part of New Labour's economic policies (Gamble 2012: 39).

In order to temper the domestic debate on the failure of his government to implement effective supervisory and regulatory practices that could have prevented the crisis in the UK's financial sector, Brown tried to shift attention to the European and global levels (McCann 2014: 106). Sarkozy, in turn, viewed collective EU action to counter the crisis as a crucial response to the fact that French banks were seriously exposed to the sovereign debt crisis in Southern Europe. The exposure of French banks to public and private debt in the Southern periphery countries reached approximately €540 billion by the first quarter of 2010 – €43 billion in Greece, €336 billion in Italy, €130 billion in Spain and €33bn in Portugal (Stabe et al. 2013). This also explains why France has been more focused on resolving the plight of the sovereign debt crisis countries in Southern Europe than Germany and the United Kingdom. In practice, however, both president Sarkozy and his successor Hollande have avoided acting as the promoter of Southern European interests during and after the crisis (Paterson 2012: 244), although Hollande initially had engaged in closer consultations with Italian prime minister Monti and Spanish prime minister Rajoy than with Merkel.

While Brown supported Sarkozy in his calls for collective EU action to mitigate the effects of the financial crisis, the German chancellor Angela Merkel was extremely reluctant to act. Merkel was under substantial domestic pressure not to give in to demands for collective support for Greece, which by 2009 seemed to be trapped in a vicious circle of recession, rising unemployment, spiralling debt and a deteriorating credit rating. Merkel, who had fundamentally criticised her predecessor Gerhard Schröder's red–green coalition for having adopted a lax attitude towards the eurozone stability and growth pact, was now facing calls from within her own Christian Democratic Union-Christian Social Union (Christlich Demokratische Union-Christlich Soziale Union – CDU/CSU) and Liberal Democratic Party (Freiheitliche Demokratische Partei – FDP) coalition and from the German media to stand firm against proposals to collectivise Greek debt (Paterson 2011: 69). Both Brown and Sarkozy seemed to be taken aback by Merkel's reluctance to support collective EU action. Brown put pressure on Merkel to support the €200 billion stimulus package that EU Commission president Barroso proposed in December 2008 (Wintour 2008). Sarkozy, who had put forward his own €26 billion stimulus package for the French economy (Jamet 2013: 187), was clearly at odds with Merkel at their joint press conference at the Franco-German Council of Ministers in November 2008, where he publicly criticised the chancellor for deliberating when action was needed (Sarkozy and Merkel 2008). Until the middle of 2010, Merkel adopted the line that the countries that emerged from the financial crisis with a sovereign debt problem would have to try to resolve it on their own by implementing strict austerity measures. Domestically, Merkel faced a national election in September 2009, followed by important regional elections in which the proposals advanced by Sarkozy and other EU leaders regarding the introduction of eurobonds played a significant part. In contrast to her coalition partner the Social Democrats

(Sozialdemokratische Partei – SPD), Merkel firmly rejected these proposals, and her reluctance to heed calls for the institutionalisation of debt in the eurozone stemmed from more than simply electoral calculations. The federal government in Germany faces substantial constraints on the scope of its European policy. The large number of institutionalised veto players in the German political system, most significantly the regions represented in the Federal Council (Bundesrat), makes it essential for the ruling party to seek European policy consensus amongst opposition parties. In this system, the German Constitutional Court plays a supervisory role, and the court recently ruled that the German parliament should maintain its final say on EU budgetary matters and further integrative steps (Bulmer and Paterson 2013: 1399). Merkel was therefore wary about finding herself in a situation in which the Constitutional Court might force her to backtrack on commitments to a new EU policy initiative. She instead tried to steer towards a middle-of-the-road compromise by ceding some ground to the French demands for enhanced EU-level economic governance, under the strict condition that this step would be orientated towards strengthening the originally intended principle of developing the eurozone into a stability union. The Constitutional Court considers this concept to be an essential element of the mandate granted to Germany's federal government for participation in the monetary union (Heinemann 2014: 111).

The fact that it took Merkel until the middle of 2010, when the Greek sovereign debt crisis was threatening the very existence of the eurozone (Schweiger 2014b: 298), to act was externally regarded as a contradiction and was increasingly the subject of domestic criticism as well. The crucial question was how the leader of the country that had emerged from the financial crisis as the strongest European economy could be so reluctant to take the lead role in resolving the crisis through an effort of collective solidarity. Thus, the role of the EU's 'reluctant hegemon' (Paterson 2011) that Germany adopted under Merkel in the early phase of the eurozone crisis revealed a clear leadership deficit. By 2010, this evolved into frantic and at times seemingly uncoordinated efforts to respond to the rapid losses in market confidence in not only the crisis countries but increasingly also the eurozone as a whole. France and Germany eventually returned to closer cooperation in 2010, when Merkel and Sarkozy jointly developed the *European Financial Stability Mechanism* (EFSF) and the new annual cycle of policy coordination, the *European Semester*, under the post-Lisbon Europe 2020 Strategy. Merkel's weak initial support for the EFSF was based on the expectation that it would be a temporary institutionalised loan mechanism, offering targeted short-term financial support to Ireland and Greece in their efforts to implement budgetary austerity and boosting financial market confidence in the viability of the euro. The *European Semester*, with its monitoring of national fiscal and macroeconomic policies on the basis of Commission recommendations, peer review and agreed-upon national reform plans, was also a far cry from French plans to institute binding economic governance. Thus, the economically dominant Germany and the weakened France were finally starting to make attempts to lead the eurozone out of the crisis, albeit with 'differing views, interpretations, and also interests with regards to content and form of crisis management' (Huebner 2012:

168). Most notably, against the background of France's ailing economic performance, Sarkozy was unable to muster strong resistance against Merkel's relatively narrow focus on budgetary austerity (Schmidt 2012). Although Merkel and Sarkozy eventually managed to achieve some joint progress in managing the eurozone crisis, the persistent Franco-German disputes surrounding the post-crisis policy mechanisms once again demonstrate that the two countries have never fully reconciled their fundamentally divergent views on the principles of the eurozone. More than any other German chancellor before her, Merkel strongly advocates the *ordoliberal* tradition of the German economy at the wider EU level (Berghahn and Young 2013: 775; Funk 2014: 316). This is reflected in her attempts to instil a culture of compliance to budgetary rules in the eurozone that will support monetary stability. This attitude stands in stark contrast to the repeated (albeit flawed) efforts on the part of France to transfer the country's preferences for Keynesian policies to the eurozone's governance (Mistral 2014: 106; Guérot and Klau 2012: 2).

Merkel sought to eventually introduce the German ordoliberal culture not only into the eurozone but also the whole of the EU on the basis of the classic Community method of integration. The proposal for a collective EU treaty on economic governance in 2012 (the 'Fiscal Compact') included the demand that all signatory countries enshrine the annual structural deficit limit of 0.5 per cent of the national GDP in their constitution. This move was supported by Sarkozy on the condition that Merkel agree to the transfer of the temporary ESFSF into a permanent loan mechanism, the European Stability Mechanism (ESM), by mid-2012 (Schild 2013: 39). The Franco-German consensus on the incorporation of the treaty into the EU's existing legal *acquis* caused widespread unease amongst other EU member states, which had become increasingly discontent with the 'Merkozy' duo's push towards new layers of rule-based policy coordination (Tsebelis 2013: 1098; Vasallo 2013: 108).

The most outspoken opponent of the Merkozy Fiscal Compact endeavour has been British prime minister David Cameron. Cameron acknowledged that the eurozone needed to make sure that its budgetary rules would be effectively implemented, but rejected the extension of these rules to the rest of the EU Single Market. His concerns focused on the possibility of the Fiscal Compact becoming a mechanism by which euro outsiders would be obliged to abide by the increased policy coordination (e.g. the intended tax coordination under the 2011 Euro Plus Pact and the plans for a eurozone banking union). Cameron therefore deliberately vetoed the treaty, rejecting Merkel and Sarkozy's argument that the Fiscal Compact would be welcomed by all EU member states as part of the drive to instil a culture of budgetary self-restraint (Merkel and Sarkozy 2011). In his 2013 Bloomberg speech, he instead emphasised that differentiated integration was the only way forward to ensure that the Single Market would operate successfully in practice: 'We must not be weighed down by an insistence on a one-size-fits-all approach which implies that all countries want the same level of integration. The fact is that they don't and we shouldn't assert that they do' (Cameron 2013).

Cameron tried to forge an alliance with the conservative Czech prime minister Petr Něcas against Merkel's plans to extend binding budgetary and macroeconomic policy coordination beyond the eurozone core. Něcas joined Cameron in his refusal to sign the Fiscal Compact but it soon became clear that the Czech prime minister's opposition to the treaty was less grounded in deep-seated euroscepticism than in concerns that ratification of the treaty could fail at home due to the opposition of the deeply eurosceptic president Klaus (Král 2013). As in the cases of Germany and France, the British approach to the financial crisis has been heavily determined by the institutional culture of the national political economy. In the British case, this means a strong emphasis on ensuring domestic policy autonomy in order to maintain the perceived competitive advantage of what has been termed the UK's economic culture of 'privatised Keynesianism' (Crouch 2009). Under this policy regime, which has been the predominant feature of the British political economy since the Thatcher era, successive governments have prioritised a culture of low-level regulation in the financial industry to ensure that the British model of credit-driven growth can be maintained. The response to the crisis by both the Brown and Cameron administrations has therefore been 'paradigm-reinforcing' (Hay 2013: 23) in terms of reluctance to alter the strong reliance on the British financial industry as the national engine of growth.

Conclusions

Overall, it seems that the multiple layers of policy coordination developed by France and Germany have not been able to bridge the persistent commitment–implementation gap with regard to EU policy coordination amongst member states. The fundamentally different strategic approaches of Germany, France and Britain to the financial crisis and the subsequent divergence in their effects show that even under profound crisis conditions, national governments in the EU display tendencies to defend their national interests and the perceived competitive advantages of their domestic political economies. With Merkel continuing to prioritise austerity, the new French president Hollande displaying weak commitment to eurozone policy coordination and David Cameron demanding even more opt-outs from the EU's legal provisions, more than ever before the EU resembles a 'lowest common denominator union' (Hayward 2012: 12) with a distinctive lack of solidarity between member states. Under conditions of increasing distance between the strategic interests of the three dominant players in the EU, decisive joint leadership action between Berlin, Paris and London has become a remote prospect at a time when the EU is in desperate need of leadership. Instead, the EU seems to be on autopilot, directed towards differentiation.

References

Berghahn, V. and B. Young (2013) 'Reflections on Werner Bonefeld's "Freedom and the Strong State: On German Ordoliberalism" and the continuing importance of the ideas of ordoliberalism to understand Germany's (contested) role in resolving the Eurozone crisis,' *New Political Economy* 18(5): 768–778.

Bieler, A. (2006) *The Struggle for a Social Europe: Trade Unions and EMU in Times of Global Restructuring*. Manchester: Manchester University Press.

Blair, T. and G. Schröder (1999) *Europe: The Third Way / Die neue Mitte*. Joint paper, 8 June. Berlin and London: SPD/New Labour.

Bulmer, S. (1997) 'Shaping the Rules? The Constitutive Politics of the European Union and the German Power' in P. J. Katzenstein (ed.) *Tamed Power: Germany in Europe*. Ithaca, NY: Cornell University Press, pp. 49–79.

Bulmer, S., A. Maurer and W. E. Paterson (2001) 'The European Policy-Making Machinery in the Berlin Republic: Hindrance or Handmaiden?' in D. Webber (ed.) *New Europe, New Germany, Old Foreign Policy?* London: Frank Cass, pp. 177–206.

Bulmer, S. and W. E. Paterson (2013) 'Germany as the EU's reluctant hegemon? Of economic strength and political constraints,' *Journal of European Public Policy* 20(10): 1387–1405.

Cameron, D. (2013) EU speech at Bloomberg, 23 January. Available at: www.gov.uk/government/speeches/eu-speech-at-bloomberg (accessed 15 December 2014).

Cole, A. (2001) *Franco-German Relations*. Harlow: Pearson.

Crouch, C. (2009) 'Privatised Keynesianism: An unacknowledged policy regime,' *British Journal of Politics and International Relations* 11(3): 382–399.

Dyson, K. and A. Sepos (eds) (2008) *Which Europe? The Politics of Differentiated Integration*. Basingstoke: Palgrave MacMillan.

Finke, D., T. König, S. O. Proksch and G. Tsebelis (2012) *Reforming the European Union: Realizing the Impossible*. Princeton, NJ: Princeton University Press.

Funk, L. (2014) 'Why has the German job market done well despite the "Great Recession",' *Perspectives on European Politics and Society* 15(3): 305–321.

Gamble, A. (2012) 'The United Kingdom: The Triumph of Fiscal Realism?' in W. Grant and G. K. Wilson (eds) *The Consequences of the Global Financial Crisis: The Rhetoric of Reform and Regulation*. Oxford: Oxford University Press, pp. 34–50.

Grabbe, H. and W. Münchau (2002) *Germany and Britain: An Alliance of Necessity*. London: Centre for European Reform.

Guerot, U. and T. Klau (2012) 'After Merkozy: How France and Germany can make Europe work,' Policy Brief no. 56, May. Paris: European Council on Foreign Relations.

Hall, B. and J. Eaglesham (2008) 'Brown, Sarkozy seek "new Bretton Woods",' *Financial Times*, 2 November.

Hantrais, L. (2007) *Social Policy in the European Union*, 3rd edition. Basingstoke: Palgrave Macmillan,.

Hay, C. (2013) 'Treating the symptom not the condition: Crisis definition, deficit reduction and the search for a new British growth model,' *British Journal of Politics and International Relations* 15(1): 23–37.

Hayward, J. (2012) 'Union without Consensus' in J. Hayward and R. Wurzel (eds) *European Disunion: Between Sovereignty and Solidarity*. Basingstoke: Palgrave MacMillan, pp. 5–17.

Heinemann, F. (2014) 'Germany: Constraints in the Crisis' in K. Dervis and J. Mistral (eds) *Europe's Crisis, Europe's Future*. Washington, DC: Brookings Institution, pp. 110–132.

Hosli, M. (2008) 'Council decision rules and European constitutional design,' *Czech Economic Review* 1: 76–96.

Huebner, K. (2012) 'German crisis management and leadership: From ignorance to procrastination to action,' *Asia Europe Journal* 9(2–4): 159–177.

Hyde-Price, A. (2000) *Germany and European Order: Enlarging NATO and the EU*. Manchester: Manchester University Press.

Jamet, J. F. (2013) 'France: Lowering the Barriers to Growth' in V. Novotný (ed.) *From Reform to Growth: Managing the Economic Crisis in Europe*. Brussels: Centre for European Studies, pp. 175–200.

Jeffery, C. and W.E. Paterson (2000) *Germany's Power in Europe*, Discussion Paper no. 2000/10, Institute for German Studies, University of Birmingham.

Jospin, L. (2001) 'The Future of an Enlarged Europe,' speech at the French Ministry for Foreign Affairs, Paris, 28 May.

Kalemli-Oczan, S., E. Papaioannou and J. L. Peydro (2010) 'What lies beneath the euro's effect on financial integration? Currency risk, legal harmonisation or trade?,' *Journal of International Economics* 81(1): 75–88.

Kirchner, E. (1996) 'Germany and the European Union: From Junior to Senior Role' in G. Smith, W. E. Paterson and S. Padgett (eds) *Developments in German Politics 2*. Basingstoke: MacMillan, pp. 157–172.

Kral, D. (2013) 'Against all, with Britain forever, or just wait and see? The Czech debate on the Eurozone debt crisis,' Working Paper, January, Institute for European Policy, Prague. Available at: www.europeum.org/images/paper/wp_kral_czech_debate.pdf (accessed 5 February 2015).

Lapavitsas, C. et al. (2012) *Crisis in the Eurozone*. London: Verso.

Leuffen, D., B. Rittberger and F. Schimmelfennig (2013) *Differentiated Integration: Explaining Variation in the European Union*. Basingstoke: Palgrave MacMillan.

Le Monde (2000) 'L'Allemagne ne s'est pas encore guerie du nazisme,' 23 May.

McCann, D. (2010) *The Political Economy of the European Union*. Cambridge: Polity.

McCann, L. (2014) *International and Comparative Business: Foundations of Political Economies*. London: Sage.

Merkel, A. (2012) 'Regierungserklärung zu Stabilitätsunion, Fiskalvertrag und Europäischer Stabilitätsmechanisms,' 29 June. Available at: www.bundeskanzlerin.de/ContentArchiv/DE/Archiv17/Regierungserklaerung/2012/2012-06-29-merkel.html (accessed 15 December 2014).

Merkel, A. and N. Sarkozy (2011) Joint Press Conference, Paris, 16 August.

Mistral, J. (2014) 'France: Part of the Solution or Part of the Problem?' in K. Dervis and J. Mistral (eds) *Europe's Crisis, Europe's Future*. Washington, DC: The Brookings Institution, pp. 93–109.

Moravcsik, A. (1991) 'Negotiating the Single European Act: National interests and conventional statecraft in the European Community,' *International Organization* 45(1): 19–56.

Moravcsik, A. (1993) 'Preferences and power in the European Community: A liberal intergovernmentalist approach,' *Journal of Common Market Studies* 31(4): 473–524.

Moravcsik, A. (1997) 'Taking preferences seriously: A liberal theory of international politics,' *International Organization* 51(4): 513–553.

Moravcsik, A. (2005) 'The European constitutional compromise and the neofunctionalist legacy,' *Journal of European Public Policy* 12(2): 349–386.

Parker, G. and B. Hall (2008) 'Brown and Sarkozy seek fiscal boost,' *Financial Times*, 8 December.

Paterson, W. E. (2010) 'Does Germany still have a European vocation?' *German Politics* 19(1): 41–52.

Paterson, W. E. (2011) 'The reluctant hegemon? Germany moves centre stage in the European Union,' *Journal of Common Market Studies* 49(S1): 57–75.

Paterson, W. E. (2012) 'A Contested Franco-German Duumvirate' in J. Hayward and R. Wurzel (eds) *European Disunion: Between Sovereignty and Solidarity*. Basingstoke: Palgrave MacMillan, pp. 235–251.

Pisani-Ferry, J. (2011) *The Euro Crisis and its Aftermath*. Oxford: University Press.

Sarkozy, N. and A. Merkel (2008) Joint Press Conference at the 10th Franco-German Council of Ministers, Paris, 24 November.

Schild, J. (2013) 'Germany, France and the management of the Eurozone crisis,' *German Politics and Society* 106(31): 24–47.

Schmidt, V. A. (2014) 'What Happened to the State-Influenced Market Economies (SMEs)? France, Italy and Spain Confront the Crisis as the Good, the Bad and the Ugly,' in W. Grant and G. K. Wilson (eds) *The Consequences of the Global Financial Crisis: The Rhetoric of Reform and Regulation*. Oxford: University Press, pp. 156–186.

Schweiger, C. (2014a) *The EU and the Global Financial Crisis: New Varieties of Capitalism*. Cheltenham: Edward Elgar.

Schweiger, C. (2014b) 'The EU-25 Fiscal Compact: Differentiated spillover effects under crisis conditions,' *Perspectives on European Politics and Society* 15(3): 293–304.

Stabe, M., S. Bernard, P. Feeney and R. Minto (2013) 'Bank exposure: The eurozone risk,' *Financial Times*, 26 March. Available at: www.ft.com/cms/s/0/9686c004-fca4-11df-bfdd-00144feab49a.html#axzz3LtIX3qqu (accessed 14 December 2014).

Tsebelis, G. (2013) 'Bridging qualified majority and unanimity decisionmaking in the EU,' *Journal of European Public Policy* 20(8): 1083–1103.

Vandecasteele, B., F. Bossuyt and J. Orbie (2013) 'Unpacking the influence of the Council Presidency on European external policies: The Polish Council Presidency and the Eastern Partnership,' *European Integration online Papers (EIoP)* 1(17): 1–28.

Vasallo, F. (2013) 'Sarkozy and Merkel: The undeniable relevance of the Franco-German bilateral relationship in Europe,' *German Politics and Society* 106(31): 92–115.

Wallace, H. (2005) 'Exercising Power and Influence in the EU: The Roles of Member States' in S. Bulmer and C. Lequesne (eds) *The Member States of the European Union*. Oxford: Oxford University Press, pp. 25–44.

Wallace, H. (2010) 'An Institutional Anatomy and Five Policy Modes' in H. Wallace, M. A. Pollack and A. R. Young (eds) *Policy-Making in the European Union*. Oxford: Oxford University Press, pp. 69–106.

Webber, D. (1999) *The Franco-German Relationship in the European Union*. London: Routledge.

Wintour, P. (2008) 'Germany pressed to contribute more to EU recession fight,' *The Guardian*, 5 December.

5 Will the centre hold?

Germany, Ireland and Slovakia and the crisis of the European project

Stefan Auer

The introduction of the single European currency has brought about both more unity and more disunity. This is its basic paradox, which EU scholarship seeks to capture with the concept of differentiated integration (Schimmelfennig 2014). Integrating monetary policies while fiscal policies have remained under the control of sovereign member states has resulted in growing tensions both within and between EU member states. Even countries that have traditionally been pro-European have not been spared.

'Will the centre hold?', Brigid Laffan asked presciently (Laffan 2013). One of the key questions animating this chapter is whether *the centre of the centre* will hold. There are perhaps no better cases to test this proposition than the three countries chosen for this short comparative survey: Germany, Ireland and Slovakia. All three of these nations have experienced the European project as both empowering and liberating: Germany as it emerged from the utter devastation of Nazism in the 1950s, Ireland as it freed itself from self-imposed isolation and backwardness in the 1970s (Garvin 2005) and Slovakia after the collapse of communism in 1989 and its brief flirtation with populist authoritarianism in the 1990s (Mesežnikov 2014).

In brief, despite their differences in terms of size, length of engagement with Europe, and contrasting historical trajectories, the nations at the focus of this chapter have a credible claim to view themselves as being at the heart of the European project. Germany, for instance, was one of the founding members of the EU and has been among the most consistently pro-European. Ireland represents one of the most compelling examples of Europe's transformative power following the first enlargement in 1973. From the backward and impoverished periphery of Europe, Ireland was catapulted into its centre, both economically and politically; in the 1990s and 2000s, the small nation consistently punched above its weight. Slovakia too, at times following the Irish example, transformed itself from Europe's laggard into one of its shining stars as a result of the 2004 Big Bang enlargement.

Ten years after that momentous event, the situation was very different. Slovakia stopped catching up with its more prosperous neighbours in the west, the Celtic tiger collapsed while Irish debt continued to grow, and both countries also struggled with very high levels of unemployment. Germany appeared to be much better off economically, but was facing a serious crisis of purpose owing to its changing role in Europe. Instead of a European Germany, the euro crisis threatens to create a German Europe – a scenario that nobody seems to want, least of all the Germans themselves.

In Laffan's important question, the centre stands for the political consensus that has come to characterise post-Second World War societies in Western Europe: the shared understanding between political elites and the people that major societal challenges ought to be addressed through the instruments of liberal democracy and the rule of law. In this perspective, political radicalisation from both the left and the right was to be kept at bay by means of political and economic transformations, which would avoid past mistakes by being implemented in a piecemeal fashion designed to enable political elites to maintain popular support for their bold policies. In all three cases, Europe as both an idea and a very practical political project was integral to this endeavour. And as long as the European project itself eschewed radical steps, following Monnet's method, it offered a perfect fit for this ambition. Our three nations provide excellent illustrations of how this worked. At the time of writing, however, 'the goodness of fit' between Europe and liberal democracy can no longer be taken for granted. Indeed, in all three countries, 'Europe' is increasingly seen as a threat to economic prosperity and political stability.

The crisis brought to light and reinforced significant differences in political cultures amongst participating member states stemming from their differing historical experiences with national sovereignty, democracy and the rule of law, and the interrelationship between economics and politics. There were no value-neutral solutions to the euro crisis, and the myriad of measures and strategies adopted appear to have largely reflected the preferences and interests of Germany, the reluctance of its political elites to lead Europe notwithstanding. This is an additional reason to focus in depth on Germany here.

The tyranny of values: a case against a 'German Europe'?

Fritz Scharpf, among others, has been highly critical of German EU crisis management: 'the regime that has been established to rescue an over-extended and ill-designed monetary union is in fact jeopardizing the achievements of democratic self-government in Europe' (Scharpf 2014: 1). At the time of writing, that regime is under considerable strain. The tension between Europe's centre and its periphery was reignited by the elections in Greece in January 2015 that resulted in the victory of the populist party Coalition of the Radical Left (Syriza), which had campaigned on a pledge to defy the rescue strategies to which Greece had been subjected to since 2010. Trying to live up to its election promises, the new Greek government demanded significant concessions from Germany and other creditor states with regard to reducing the country's overall debt burden as well as softening the EU's austerity policies. The outcome of this contestation is bound to change the existing power constellation in Europe. If Germany gives in to Greek demands, other countries on the periphery, including Cyprus, Ireland and

Portugal, are likely to follow suit. This would result in the German electorate feeling overburdened and betrayed by its government, which has repeatedly promised that Europe will not become a 'transfer union'. Voters in Slovakia, one of the smaller and poorer creditor states, are bound to resent further concessions to debtors; notably, a dispute over euro rescue measures in 2011 brought down the Slovak government. If, on the other hand, no compromise can be reached and Greece is forced to leave the Eurozone, the ensuing mutual recriminations will further damage Germany's credibility abroad as a 'good European'. In such a scenario, Greece, the proverbial birthplace of European democracy, may well be seen as the victim of Germany's imperial overreach.

Well before this Greek rebellion captured newspapers headlines, commentators of all ideological persuasions had criticised the EU's handling of the crisis. They argued that the German-led policies of austerity were too demanding (Rogoff 2011, 2013) and would at any rate not bring about badly needed growth – the only sustainable way to reduce both high levels of unemployment and sovereign debt (Krugman 2013, 2014; Wolf 2014; Stiglitz 2015). Furthermore, the German government's insistence on fiscal contraction has been accompanied by the opposition of the German Bundesbank to the bolder expansionary monetary policies of the European Central Bank (ECB) that its president Mario Draghi promised at the height of the crisis in mid-2012. Although Draghi's promise to 'do whatever it takes' to rescue the Eurozone has been hailed as prudent by most observers and market participants,[1] it met with significant opposition in Germany. In fact, Draghi's policy of Outright Monetary Transactions (OMT) has been criticised as violating the EU's legal order and the Treaty of Maastricht, which explicitly ban state financing by the ECB.

The situation has become intractable for German political elites and their dual commitment to Europe and liberal democracy underpinned by the rule of law. To understand their predicament, it is instructive to turn to Carl Schmitt, the controversial German jurist who pondered the relationship between law and politics. In his polemical essay, *The Tyranny of Values*, Schmitt criticised the role of the all-powerful German Constitutional Court. His work is of the utmost relevance today owing to the growing importance of the court in the management of the Eurozone crisis. In particular, Schmitt warned against the dangers of both extremes: a purely technocratic, purportedly value-neutral approach to law, as well as its subordination to higher ideological values. 'He who talks about values wants to dominate',[2] argued Schmitt, elaborating:

> Virtues are practiced, norms are applied, orders are executed, but values are set up and enacted. Whoever asserts a value, must bring its influence to bear. Whoever maintains that it has value regardless of the influence brought to bear by any individual human being who endorses it, is simply cheating.
>
> (Schmitt 1996, 2011: 41)

The idea of the political independence of the European Central Bank, for example, is not value neutral. As we will see, it reflects a particular ideological conviction and may serve some constituencies and member states better than others. Talk about values is all too often used to disguise material and other interests.

Yet this is not an argument against values in politics *per se*. The constitutional order that emerged in West Germany after the Second World War paradoxically displays a feature that may well be described as Schmittian: namely, its explicit concern for the value of democratic order and its permanence, which is embodied in the so-called 'eternity clause' (Art. 79(3)). This is the lesson drawn from the constitutional flaws of the interwar Weimar Republic. The Weimar constitution was overburdened with provisions regulating various aspects of German society and underestimated the importance of maintaining the very political order that makes such provisions possible. This is now different. The 'eternity clause' prohibits any amendments to articles 1 and 20 of the Basic Law, which chiefly govern 'the principles of democracy, the rule of law and the constitutional state' (Preuss 1999: 166). This peculiar feature grants the German Constitutional Court a political power that was traditionally vested in sovereign rulers: the right to act as the 'guardian of the constitution'. Germans have had a good experience with this arrangement, and they tend to credit it for the political stability and economic prosperity that came to characterise the West German Federal Republic from its economic miracle in the 1950s to the present. Theirs is a 'constrained democracy' (Müller 2011) in which the political order is protected against populist, illiberal instincts that the electorate may well have continued to harbour even after the defeat of Nazi Germany.

The link between economic success and political stability is not accidental. In the German understanding, the collapse of the Weimar Republic is commonly associated with the hyperinflation of the 1920s and the ensuing lawlessness.[3] This historical memory is to a large degree responsible for the prevalence of ordoliberalism in postwar Germany, a position that envisages a free market supported by a strong regulatory state, where direct interference is kept to a minimum. Ordoliberalism informed key provisions in the Maastricht Treaty for the single European currency, such as the political independence of the ECB, strict rules about levels of public debt and deficit, and the 'no bailout' clause stipulating that each member state remains responsible for its own debt (see Joerges 2012: 12). One of the consequences of the Eurozone crisis is Germany's concern that its economic model is being undermined by those European partners who do not subscribe to ordoliberalism; meanwhile, these very partners perceive the allegedly neutral prescriptions advanced by the European Commission, the International Monetary Fund and the ECB as 'German' and profoundly destructive.

A number of Irish economists, for example, have criticised the basic architecture of the Economic and Monetary Union and the fact that 'the ECB was given the strongest degree of independence of any major central bank' (Donovan and Murphy 2013: 41). The ECB's focus on inflation and reliance on 'light touch regulation' ideology has contributed to its 'inability to assess and anticipate possible looming problems' (ibid., 98). Although they acknowledge multiple failures of domestic political and economic actors, Donal Donovan and Antoin E.

Murphy argue that 'the European institutions, by their passive attitude thus indirectly contributed to allowing fatal weakness, such as those that emerged in Ireland, to go unchecked' (ibid., 101). As the crisis unfolded, voices not just in Ireland but across the entire Eurozone and beyond (with the notable exception of Germany) were raised in support of abandoning the Maastricht Treaty's restrictions. Advocating greater pragmatism, Donovan and Murphy cited Edmund Burke: 'Nobody made a greater mistake than he who did nothing because he could only do a little' (ibid., 81).

The idea that economic crisis necessitates a more relaxed attitude to legal constraints remains anathema in the prevalent German political culture. Paul Kirchhof, a former German constitutional judge, has forcefully argued that the attempt to sacrifice legal stability for the sake of economic revival is shortsighted and profoundly misguided (Kirchhof 2012b, cf. Scicluna 2015: 86). Only a rule-based society can guarantee the stability of money, particularly when it comes to government-created *fiat* money (from the Latin for 'let it be made'); as Siekmann asserts, 'It is a creation of the legal system' (Siekmann 2011). Similarly, Kirchhof states, 'legal certainty is a precondition for monetary stability' (Kirchhof 2012a: 78). While the likes of Martin Wolf, chief economic commentator for the *Financial Times*, contemplates the virtues of 'modern monetary theory' according to which 'the government suffers from no fiscal constraint: it can always create money that residents have to accept' (Wolf 2014: 219), most German economists and legal scholars would consider this not merely bad economics but also morally wrong. Interestingly, this critical attitude has found resonance in Slovakia as well, in particular from Richard Sulík, the controversial leader of Sloboda a Solidarita [Freedom and Solidarity] and since 2014 also an MEP.

Mario Draghi as Mephistopheles

The euro was intended to be a German-type currency: hard and dependable. The initiative for the single European currency might have come from France, but its contours were originally decisively German. It remains of great symbolic importance, for example, that the seat of the European Central Bank is in Frankfurt. The location embodies the tradition of the German Bundesbank, which was instrumental in the economic success of the postwar German Federal Republic. Before being subsumed into the ECB, the Bundesbank was feared and admired by its European partners. It was this tradition that the ECB's current president, the Italian Mario Draghi, claimed as his own when he assumed office.[4] His German critics have argued that he has yet to live up to this promise. In their eyes, he can only do so by resisting the temptation of monetary easing.

Jens Weidmann, the current president of the German Bundesbank (and in this capacity also a member of the ECB's governing council), has repeatedly challenged arguments in favour of more relaxed monetary policies. In response to Draghi's promise to 'do whatever it takes' to save the euro, Weidmann invoked a passage from Goethe's *Faust* in which the ruler complains that 'there is no money' and accepts Mephisto's offer to create 'as much of it as he wants, and more'. He thus endorses Goethe's views of the dangers of modern paper-based money, which 'amounts to a continuation of alchemy by other means' (Weidmann 2012). The only way to thwart the irresistible temptation to create money out of thin air, which will inevitably lead to hyperinflation, is to ensure that the Central Bank is constrained in its actions by being politically independent and acting transparently according to strict rules.

The German proclivity to view the struggling European economy as a morality tale has led some scholars to posit 'a cultural clash view of the EU crisis' (Guiso, Herrera and Morelli 2013). Conflicting political cultures explain, they argue, why the German government tended to do too little too late in the early stages of the crisis:

> Germans and Germany's reaction to the discovery in October 2009 that the previous Greek government cooked the books, hiding half of the fiscal deficit, was to 'punish' the Greeks by 'denying timely help' when, according to various observers, early action would have contained the crisis.
>
> (Guiso, Herrera and Morelli 2013: 2)

This pattern may well be repeated in 2015, gauging from the reports that the German government is again contemplating the possibility of Greece's departure from the Eurozone (*Spiegel*, 1/2015). Cultural attitudes are difficult to measure and impossible to prove, but they do pose a real constraint on the actions of democratically elected governments. The authors provide a plethora of sources for their provocative claims. Extrapolating from the results of the European Social Survey, for example, they argue that 'Germans are significantly more willing to punish wrongdoers than the Greeks' (ibid., 7). This is corroborated by anecdotal evidence. Mario Monti, the former EU commissioner and Italian prime minister, otherwise sympathetic to structural reforms, is reported as saying that 'for Germany "economics is a branch of moral philosophy"'. Fiscal sinners had to atone, and the rightful have nothing to apologise for' (Peet and La Guardia 2014: 156). One could add that the very word for debt in German, *Schuld*, has strong moral connotations, as it is etymologically linked to guilt.[5] Thomas Wieser, an Austrian national, and President of the Euro Working Group resorted to Europe's ancient religious divides to explain Eurozone crisis conflict dynamics. He argued that in countries that are predominantly Protestant, moral standards are so demanding that 'one will never be forgiven for his sins, nor will people grant forgiveness to the sinners'. In countries influenced mainly by Catholicism, which include Italy, Spain, Portugal and Ireland, the societal expectations are such that whoever sins, can:

> always be forgiven if he/she repents and so make it into paradise. Finally, [...] Orthodox religion is so loose that in countries dominated by it – of which Greece is the leading one – if one sins there is not even a need for him/her to repent to make it into paradise.
>
> (Guiso, Herrera and Morelli 2013: 20)

Needless to say, this tongue-in-cheek account represents neither the EU's nor Germany's official position. The description of Germany as Protestant is also problematic, as is the association of Protestantism with economic success: Bavaria, one of Germany's most successful *Ländern,* is traditionally Catholic. However, the proponents of 'a cultural clash view of the EU crisis' are right to argue that 'culture can act as a conformity constraint on policy makers and this may result, in certain circumstances, in suboptimal outcomes' (ibid., 29). The authors conclude that in order to reduce the potential for a political clash between member states, a supranational fiscal union is needed, a union that would permit the replacement of 'multiple authorities subject to cultural clash [...] with a unique new authority, hence facilitating convergence, commitment, and enforcement' (ibid.). This suggestion amounts to an attempt at depoliticisation and does not convince. As we have seen, the idea of a fiscal union reflects 'German' value preferences, convictions and interests, or at any rate is perceived as such by an increasing number of people in Europe's peripheries. The rise of the populist Syriza (Coalition of the Radical Left) in Greece and Podemos (We Can) in Spain testify to the growing opposition to the German orthodoxy favouring fiscal discipline and austerity, values that are legally enshrined in the Fiscal Compact. While the German 'morality tale' of the Eurozone crisis tends to focus on reckless spending that the populations in the peripheries are asked to atone for, Greek, Spanish and Irish narratives centre on arguments about solidarity.

Law and politics in crisis

However, this is not just a dispute about morality; it is also about EU law and German constitutional law (although in the German political imagination, morality and legality seem to be interlinked). Unwittingly, the German Constitutional Court (GCC) has become one of the key actors in the management of the crisis. The Court's mandate reflects the dual commitment of the German constitution: towards European integration as well as towards democracy. Democratic self-government is guaranteed through the so-called 'eternity clause' mentioned above, while Article 23(1) 'compels German institutions to participate constructively in the development of the EU' (Scicluna 2015: 72). As the crisis worsened, reconciling these two competing demands became ever more difficult. For example, the Court had to decide on the constitutionality of the European Stability Mechanism (ESM) and the Fiscal Compact, both of which appeared to undermine the budgetary sovereignty of EU member states – one of the key areas that the GCC had previously declared indispensable for the proper functioning of democracy.[6] Similarly, the ECB's OMT programme faced legal challenges not only because of the Maastricht Treaty's explicit ban on state financing, but also owing to its consequences for German taxpayers, who might be liable for financial losses incurred by the ECB (over which the German parliament has no control). While the Court dismissed all complaints regarding the ESM and Fiscal Compact, it expressed strong reservations against the OMT and presented a series of questions on it to the European Court of Justice (ECJ). The German

Court reserved its own judgment, making it clear that it would not necessarily follow the ECJ's ruling, which is scheduled to be delivered in mid-2015.

In the midst of this legal wrangling, the euro crisis is bound to intensify as a result of the threat of deflation and the festering dispute between Germany and Greece about the handling of the latter's excessive debt. Whatever legal constraints the ECB might have, it is unlikely to refrain from the decisive actions that are expected of it by international markets as well as by governments in Europe's peripheries. This constellation has once again exposed the fallacy underpinning the single European currency – the idea that a political project of such grand ambitions could be implemented simply by technocratic and legal means. As Nicole Scicluna astutely observes in her detailed study, *EU Constitutionalism in Crisis*:

> Now, faced with the crisis-induced state of emergency, law has been found wanting and – in an ironic twist on its previous reliance on legality as substitute for legitimacy – the GCC was left with little choice but to approve of Germany's participation in the European Stability Mechanism (ESM), a pragmatic political measure of questionable legal validity and legitimacy.
> (Scicluna 2015: 81)

If the German Court ends up approving *all* of the ECB's unconventional methods, including the quantitative easing promised by the OMT announcement, it will lose a great deal of its credibility. If it rejects them, it will destroy the economic viability of the Eurozone. Well before this controversial decision is made and its legal ramifications investigated, a number of German legal scholars and observers have proclaimed the history of monetary integration to be a history of breach of contract (*Vertragsbruch*). The losses incurred through this process, they argue, go far beyond monetary sacrifices. What is vastly more consequential, according to Christian Hillgruber, 'is the loss of legal certainty and the trust on which the law is based, which – once it is lost – is very difficult to reclaim'. The pragmatic arguments about there being no alternatives to the actions taken do not convince Hillgruber: 'Only a return to law can maintain the viability of the European Union as a community of law' (Hillgruber 2013: 90).

Opposition to the argument that has dominated the management of the euro crisis between 2010 and 2015 – the reasoning that 'there is no alternative' to the euro and the policies adopted for its preservation – have found political expression even in Germany. Die Alternative für Deutschland (AfD), a new political party led by a professor of economics, Bernd Lucke, shot to prominence by objecting to the euro rescue policies, including the controversial bailout of Greece. While the party did not win seats in the German Bundestag in the 2013 elections,[7] it secured the support of 7 per cent of the electorate in the European elections in 2014 and even more in subsequent regional elections (12 per cent in Brandenburg and 11 per cent in Thuringia). In any case, within a very short period of time, the AfD has significantly changed the electoral landscape and now poses a serious threat to the German elite consensus on European integration.

Any further deterioration of the crisis, whether it be caused by the possible departure of Greece or by questions about the legality and legitimacy of the ECB's actions, is bound to increase the AfD's popularity even further. Similarly, in Slovakia, Sulík's party Freedom and Solidarity would undoubtedly benefit.

Though both parties are often dismissed by their political opponents and large parts of the mainstream media as populist, their critical stance towards the mismanagement of the euro crisis is not without merit; amongst their members are respected economists and businesspeople, such as the MEPs Joachim Starbatty and Hans-Olaf Henkel; likewise, Sulík is a trained economist and an outward-looking European fluent in both German and English (Auer 2013). More problematic is the AfD's proximity to an anti-immigration movement that emerged towards the end of 2014 in Dresden. Its name is its programme: Pegida, which stands for Patriotische Europäer gegen die Islamisierung des Abendlandes [Patriotic Europeans against the Islamisation of the West]. Though Pegida's driving force appears to be resentment towards migration, its supporters who march on the streets of Dresden in the thousands on the first Monday of every month are also expressing a sense of alienation from the mainstream political establishment, including the media. As the crisis in Europe entered a new phase, an old term made a resurgence in German political life: *Lügenpresse* [deceptive media]. One of the popular slogans of the otherwise silent marches, this is a term that historians and linguists associate with Nazi attacks on the liberal press. In fact, two key terms have thus far bookended the Eurozone crisis in Germany, both of which were declared *das Unwort des Jahres* [the 'un-word' of the year]: *alternativlos* [without alternatives] in 2010 and *Lügenpresse* in 2014. These two concepts neatly capture the growing threat to Germany's political centre.

Ireland as a 'poster child for austerity': a case for a German Europe?

Journalists from the *Economist* magazine reflected a widespread consensus when they stated that 'Only Ireland has become the German poster-child for how a bailed-out country can change itself' (Peet and La Guardia 2014: 107). This has been both the country's strength and its weakness: its strength because fiscal cuts resulted in the resumption of economic growth, which led to a reduction in unemployment and enabled the Republic of Ireland to finance itself independently of the EU and IMF support – in December 2013, Ireland became the first country to exit a Eurozone bailout programme. Paradoxically, however, this also represents a weakness, as the change was accomplished at significant social costs and huge losses to Irish taxpayers, who have yet to receive any significant concessions from their European partners.

A particular source of frustration remains the massive debt incurred by a blanket guarantee that the Irish government declared in September 2008 to secure the country's entire banking system. One month later, the then finance minister, the late Brian Lenihan, declared the step to be 'the cheapest bailout in the world so far' (Donovan and Murphy 2013: 197). In fact, it turned out to be the most expensive one to date. Citing an IMF report from 2012, Fintan O'Toole wrote in the *Irish Times*, 'there is nothing, anywhere in the developed world, anything like what was done to the Irish people' (O'Toole 2014). According to Eurostat data, for example, while the bank bailouts in the EU averaged less than €200 per capita, in Ireland the figure was almost €9,000 (O'Flynn et al. 2014: 923). Many Irish people feel that what they have been asked to pay for was not just about Ireland and its financial system but rather about the Eurozone as a whole. This argument appears to have gained some traction outside of Ireland. In late 2012, the German chancellor Angela Merkel issued a joint statement with the Irish *Taoiseach* Enda Kenny describing Ireland as a 'special case' (Quinn 2012); this raised hopes that a deal could be reached between Ireland and Germany, enabling the former to offload a significant part of its debt. However, this strategy was quietly abandoned two years later. O'Toole was scathing in his criticism of the government's change in rhetoric: 'we were not the worst victims of a euro-zone policy of rescuing all banks, however abysmal they might be. We were grand. It's all good here – the only way in which Ireland is special is in its spectacular success' (O'Toole 2014).

It is worth recalling that Ireland, unlike Greece, did not violate the Maastricht Treaty criteria and could do little on its own to prevent the crisis from happening. As Martin Wolf, amongst others, has compellingly argued, the crisis was primarily caused by structural imbalances, which are difficult to mitigate within a single-currency area and impossible to foresee: 'nobody knows what the "structural" or cyclically adjusted balance is' (Wolf 2014: 76). Particularly in Ireland, 'the underlying problem was not just fiscal profligacy, but irresponsible lending' (ibid., 84), which always requires two parties: reckless debtors need to find reckless creditors, and the latter must share some responsibility with the former.

Perhaps even more serious than the material losses for the Irish population is the damage these policies have caused to its democratic polity as well as its relationship with Europe. For Giandomenico Majone, the Troika regime imposed on Ireland was exemplary of the EU's move 'from regulatory state to a democratic default':

> For example, in 2011, the Irish budget was sent first to Germany for approval before it was even seen by the Irish parliament. [...] The paradox is that in order to satisfy its own constitutional obligations, the German parliament had to infringe a basic right of the equally sovereign parliament of a fellow Member State.
>
> (Majone 2014: 1221)

In January 2015, Ireland's hopes were directed in part towards Greece, where a contest over sovereignty and democratic legitimacy had been revived through national elections. Denis Staunton of the *Irish Times* has suggested that the 'Greek plan to write down euro-zone public debt' ought to be supported by Ireland, as it 'recognises that sovereign debt within the euro zone can no longer simply be viewed as a national issue'. The ambitious plan developed by Syriza envisages that 'the European Central Bank would buy up all debt above the 50 per cent threshold and convert it to zero-interest bonds which would be repaid by creditor governments over many decades' (Staunton 2015). Regardless of whether one views this as 'unconventional monetary policy' or 'a continuation of alchemy by other means', the proposal is bound to meet with strong German resistance. If a German government ever approved such a scheme, it would be betraying its electorate, which has been repeatedly promised that the Eurozone would not become a transfer union in which richer members would end up supporting the poorer ones on a semi-permanent basis.

Whose solidarity? For whom?

Another principle underpinning the European project that has suffered a great deal of damage is solidarity. Within and between member states, the euro rescue policies have become a travesty of fairness. *Some* bank bailouts might have been necessary for economic reasons, but their political legitimacy remains problematic. Ireland, for example, is a profoundly unequal society, and the suggestion often made by Irish officials and politicians that the crisis had no real culprits because 'we all partied' is as misguided as it is self-serving. When everybody is guilty, no one is. O'Flynn et al. (2014) convincingly demonstrate that there is a close link between elite-driven attempts to obfuscate the responsibility for the crisis and the policy of comprehensive bank-bailouts, which amounts to 'the socialisation of massive private debts' (O'Flynn et al. 2014: 931).

Even more problematic is the rhetoric of transnational solidarity as applied to Slovakia. Although it is one of the poorest members of the Eurozone, Slovakia's fiscal position has been relatively good, which makes it a creditor state with significant per capita contributions to bailout packages. This has created political controversies that have the potential to undermine strong pro-EU sentiments amongst Slovaks. The euro crisis became an important point of electoral contestation already in June 2010, when a broad coalition of pro-Western parties succeeded in defeating the populist prime minister Robert Fico, thanks in part to their opposition to the first set of credits for Greece. Once in office, the new prime minister Iveta Radičová defended the position of her government in an interview with a German weekly. She argued that describing help for Greece as an act of solidarity was misleading:

> When Slovakia faced the prospect of bankruptcy twenty years ago, it underwent painful reforms without any external assistance. 1500 companies went bust, salaries were reduced, banking sector restructured. And the Greeks – unwilling to implement these changes – are still to benefit from help? [...] I refuse solidarity with those who are irresponsible.
>
> (*Die Zeit*, 4/9/2010; Török 2014: 140–141)

Yet, a year later, the same prime minister succumbed to the pressure of her European partners and accepted the necessity of Slovak participation in the

European Financial Stability Facility (EFSF). Unable to secure the support of her junior coalition partner Freedom and Solidarity, Radičová lost her hold on power. This led to early elections in 2012, which resulted in the return to power of Robert Fico and his party, Smer. Although Fico was anxious to prove his European credentials, he had previously governed in a coalition with an extreme nationalist party (2006–2010); in addition, he showed too much sympathy towards authoritarian regimes such as Putin's Russia, undermined the independence of the judiciary and was unable to prevent serious cases of corruption in his party. In any case, Fico's success in Slovakia was not a victory for liberal democracy and the rule of law. However, more populist politics can be expected to emerge in Slovakia, particularly if its relatively high-performing economy experiences external shocks – a prospect that is not all that unlikely at the start of 2015. Surveying Slovakia's ever-changing political landscape, Tim Haughton astutely observes that the country is 'stable in its instability' (Haughton 2014: 210). But for how much longer?

Concluding remarks

This chapter is being completed in turbulent times when the unfinished project of monetary integration continues to threaten the very unity of Europe that it was meant to enhance. Advocating new approaches to the world's radically new economic challenges, Martin Wolf argues that 'the world cannot embrace its old future' (Wolf 2014: 147). This is especially applicable to Europe. As must by now be abundantly clear, the ideological project of a postnational Europe advanced by the Treaty of Maastricht, with its promise of complete freedom of movement underpinned by a single European currency and a borderless Europe, has damaged the European project. The question of 'Will the centre hold?' should thus also be raised with respect to the EU's internal geography. The centre will hold if a monetary policy is developed that is flexible enough to enable growth in struggling peripheries like Portugal and Greece without inciting German fears of a weak currency that will ultimately lead to inflation and greater instability. The centre will hold if German sensitivities about the rule of law do not prevent the effective management of the crisis by major EU actors, including the European Central Bank. The centre will hold if German, Irish, and Slovak taxpayers do not feel overburdened by obligations that they never agreed to.

Facing new challenges of a resurgent Russia and radical Islam, European unity is needed as much as it ever was. However, I believe that Europe's relentless march towards an 'ever-closer union' will continue to produce the exact opposite. I hope I will be proven wrong. As a brilliant contemporary Irish novelist tells us:

> The future is a cold mistress. You can give all your life looking to her and trying to catch a hold of her but she'll always dance away from your fingertips and laugh back at you from the distance. Them that says they know her are liars and thieves. What was ever wrote down on paper that came true, that could be checked?
>
> (Ryan 2012: 139)

Notes

1 Erik Jones, for example, declared 2012 to be *The Year the European Crisis Ended*, because 'political leaders and then the European Central Bank promised to do whatever it takes to safeguard the euro' (Jones 2014).

2 My translation, though the original statement is subtler: 'Wer Wert sagt, will geltend machen und durchsetzen' (Schmitt 2011: 41). The rest is translated by Simona Draghici: www.counter-currents.com/2014/07/the-tyranny-of-values-1959/ (Schmitt 1996).

3 Memorably depicted by the likes of Bertolt Brecht in *Die Dreigroschenoper* [Threepenny Opera] and Ödön von Horváth in *Don Juan kommt aus dem Krieg* [Don Juan returns from war]. Both plays were performed by the Berliner Ensemble in 2014/2015.

4 In a number of interviews in 2011, Draghi praised the 'German economic model', leading the *Bild* newspaper to declare him an 'honorary German' (Blome 2011). Draghi restated his admiration for Germany in 2012:

> BILD: For Germans, a central bank chief must take a strict line on inflation, be politically independent and favour a strong euro. In that light, how German are you?
>
> DRAGHI: These are indeed German virtues. But every central banker in the euro area should have them.(ECB, 2012)

5 It is telling that Dostoyevski's novel *Prestuplenije i nakasanie* (Преступление и наказание), mis-translated into English as *Crime and Punishment*, is generally translated into German as *Schuld und Sühne*: 'Guilt and Atonement'.

6 In its path-breaking Maastricht Treaty decision, it established that 'budgetary powers are a core responsibility of the parliament and a central element of democratic self-rule. The Bundestag must remain the place where "decisions are taken on its own responsibility for revenues and expenditures, including international and European debts"' (cited in Joerges 2012: 17).

7 Winning 4.7 per cent of the electorate, the AfD fell short of the 5 per cent hurdle required to secure seats in the Bundestag, but a survey in 2014 indicated that one in three German voters wanted the party to be represented in the parliament (*Die Welt*, 4/6/2014).

Bibliography

Auer, Stefan (2013) 'Richard Sulík: A Provincial or a European Slovak Politician?,' *Humanities Research* 19(1): 81–100.

Bilčík, Vladimír (2014) 'Vieme, akú EÚ chceme?,' in Grigorij Mesežnikov, Zora Bútorová and Miroslav Kollár (eds) *Desať rokov v únii: Slovenská a česká cesta.* Bratislava: Inštitút pre verejné otázky, Heinrich-Böll-Stiftung, pp. 167–174. [English: 'Do we know what kind of EU we want?', *Ten Years in the Union: The Czech and Slovak Journey.*]

Blome, Nikolaus (2011) 'So deutsch ist der neue EZB-Chef,' *Bild*, 29 April.

Die Welt (2014) 'Jeder Dritte will die AfD in den Bundestag,' 4 June. Available at: www.welt.de/politik/deutschland/article128706682/Jeder-dritte-Deutsche-will-die-AfD-im-Bundestag.html) (accessed 19 January 2014).

Donovan, Donal and Antoin E. Murphy (2013) *The Fall of the Celtic Tiger: Ireland and the Euro Debt Crisis.* Oxford: Oxford University Press.

European Central Bank (ECB) (2012) BILD interview with Mario Draghi, president of the European Central Bank, conducted by Kai Diekmann and Nikolaus Blome, 19 March. Available at: www.ecb.europa.eu/press/key/date/2012/html/sp120323.en.html (accessed 19 January 2015).

Garvin, Tom (2005) *Preventing the Future: Why Was Ireland So Poor for So Long?* Dublin: Gill & MacMillan.

Guiso, Luigi, Helios Herrera and Massimo Morelli (2013) 'A Cultural Clash View of the EU Crisis,' Centre for Economic Research Discussion Paper: 1314–1304.

Haughton, Tim (2014) 'Exit, Choice and Legacy: Explaining the Patterns of Party Politics in Post-communist Slovakia,' *East European Politics* 30(2): 210–229.

Hillgruber, Christian (2013) 'Vertrauen, Verträge, Vernunft: Auf welcher Basis gründet Europa?,' *Bonner Rechts Journal* 2: 87–91.

Joerges, Christian (2012) 'Europe's Economic Constitution in Crisis and the Emergence of a New Constitutional Constellation,' ZenTra Working Paper in Transnational Studies 6/2012.

Jones, Erik (2014) *The Year the European Crisis Ended.* Basingstoke: Palgrave Macmillan.

Kirchhof, Paul (2012a), *Deutschland im Schuldensog.* Munich: C. H. Beck.

Kirchhof, Paul (2012b), 'Verfassungsnot!,' *Frankfurter Allgemeine Zeitung*, 12 July.

Krugman, Paul (2013) 'How the Case for Austerity Has Crumbled,' *New York Review of Books*, 6 June.

Krugman, Paul (2014) 'Why Weren't Alarm Bells Ringing?,' *New York Review of Books*, 23 October.

Laffan, Brigid (2013) 'Framing the Eurocrisis and the Impact on European Integration,' paper presented at the conference Centre-periphery Relation as an Emerging Cleavage in European Politics and Policy-making? Empirical Studies on Differentiated Integration, Berlin, 11–12 October.

Majone, Giandomenico (2014) 'From Regulatory State to a Democratic Default,' *Journal of Common Market Studies* 52(6): 1216–1223.

Mesežnikov, Grigorij (2014) 'Test pre slovenskú demokraciu,' in Grigorij Mesežnikov, Zora Bútorová and Miroslav Kollár (eds) *Desat' rokov v únii: Slovenská a česká cesta.* Bratislava: Inštitút pre verejné otázky, Heinrich-Böll-Stiftung, pp. 31–42. [English 'A test for Slovak democracy'.]

Müller, Jan-Werner (2011) *Contesting Democracy: Political Thought in Twentieth-century Europe.* New Haven, CT: Yale University Press.

O'Flynn, Micheal, Lee F. Monaghan and Martin J. Power (2014) 'Scapegoating During a Time of Crisis: A Critique of Post-Celtic Tiger Ireland,' *Sociology* 48(5): 921–937.

O'Toole, Fintan (2014) 'Coalition's Seismic Shift Turns into Shifty Sidestep,' *Irish Times*, 30 December.

Peet, John and Antoin La Guardia (2014) *Unhappy Union: How the Euro Crisis – and Europe – Can Be Fixed.* London: Economist Books.

Preuss, Ulrich K. (1999) 'Political Order and Democracy: Carl Schmitt and His Influence,' in Chantal Mouffe (ed.) *The Challenge of Carl Schmitt.* London: Verso, pp. 155–179.

Quinn, Eamon (2012) 'Kenny, Merkel Say Ireland's Bank Debt Special Case,' *Wall Street Journal*, 22 October.

Rogoff, Kenneth (2011) 'The Euro's PIG-Headed Masters,' *Project Syndicate.* Available at: www.project-syndicate.org/commentary/the-euro-s-pig-headed-masters#rmJSQ208h5EqKpTM.99 (accessed 13 November 2015).

Rogoff, Kenneth (2013) 'Eurozone Crisis: Time for France to Step Up,' *The Guardian*, 23 May. Available at: www.theguardian.com/business/economics-blog/2013/may/23/eurozone-crisis-france-germany-kenneth-rogoff (accessed 13 November 2015).

Ryan, Donal (2012) *The Spinning Heart.* Dublin: Doubleday Ireland.

Scharpf, Fritz W. (2014) 'No Exit from the Euro-Rescuing Trap?,' Max Planck Institute for the Study of Sciences Discussion Paper 14/4.

Schimmelfennig, Frank (2014) 'Differentiated Integration Before and After the Crisis,' in Olaf Cramme and Sara B. Hobolt (eds) *European Union under Stress*. Oxford: Oxford University Press, pp. 120–134.

Schmitt, Carl (1996) *The Tyranny of Values*. Washington, DC: Plutarch Press.

Schmitt, Carl (2011) *Die Tyrannei der Werte*. Berlin: Duncker & Humblot.

Scicluna, Nicole (2015) *European Union Consitutionalism in Crisis*. London: Routledge.

Siekmann, Helmut (2011) 'Law and Economics of the Monetary Union,' Working Paper Series, Institute for Monetary and Financial Stability, Johann Wolfgang Goethe Universität, Frankfurt am Main.

Starbatty, Joachim (2013) *Tatort Euro: Bürger, Schützt das Recht, die Demokratie und euer Vermögen* Berlin: Europa Verlag.

Staunton, Denis (2015) 'Why Ireland Should Support Greek Plan to Write Down Euro-zone Public Debt,' *Irish Times*, January 10. Available at: www.irishtimes.com/opinion/why-ireland-should-support-greek-plan-to-write-down-euro-zone-public-debt-1.2060653 (accessed 13 November 2015).

Stiglitz, Joseph E. (2015) 'Europe's Lapse of Reason,' *Project Syndicate*, 8 January.

Török, Marián (2014) 'Tri obdobia dvoch desaťročí zahraničnej politiky Slovenskej republiky,' *Politické vedy* 3: 112–151. [English: 'Three periods of two decades of the foreign policy of the Slovak Republic'.]

Weidmann, Jens (2012) 'Traf Goethe ein Kernproblem der Geldpolitik?,' *Deutsche Bundesbank*, 18 September. Available at: www.bundesbank.de/Redaktion/DE/Reden/2012/2012_09_18_weidmann_begruessungsrede.html (accessed 19 January 2015).

Wolf, Martin (2014) *The Shifts and the Shocks: What We've Learned – and Have Still to Learn – from the Financial Crisis*. New York: Penguin.

6 From 'superficial' to 'coercive' Europeanization in southern Europe

The lack of ownership of national reforms

José M. Magone

Introduction: southern Europe as the periphery of the European Union

The recent developments in the European Union have put southern European member states in the spotlight, as the sovereign debt crisis and the Eurocrisis have led to deteriorating situations in these countries.

This chapter attempts to delineate the main patterns of Europeanization in southern European countries. To date, very few studies have compared these countries or provided a detailed overview of the characteristic nature of southern European development in the European Union.

The main thesis of this chapter is that southern European countries have an idealised image of the European Union. These countries joined the EU because there was a general belief that the very fact of being a member would resolve all the political, social and economic problems that each country was facing. Consequently, there was a marked tendency for these countries to be the passive receivers of 'democratisation' and/or 'modernisation' packages instead of being pro-active in solving their own domestic problems. In short, southern European countries have tended not to take ownership of reform processes or shape them proactively but have instead merely reacted to what the EU demands from them.

This benevolent image of the EU was sustainable until the advanced inner circle of the European Union began to evolve towards Economic and Monetary Union. However, the financial crisis originating from the USA in 2008 and subsequently the sovereign debt crisis among European states led to power struggles within the European Union that were related to the interests of national financial systems. The next section of this chapter defines the region of southern Europe and the concept of Europeanisation. Subsequently, the main features of the European integration of southern European countries are discussed. This is followed by a section assessing Europeanisation in southern Europe, including a discussion of the crisis. Finally, some brief conclusions will be offered.

Conceptualising southern Europe and Europeanisation

Although there are many definitions of southern Europe, our definition here is restricted to the southern member states of the European Union, specifically Portugal, Spain, Italy and Greece. I also include the Mediterranean islands of Cyprus and Malta. (for definitions of southern Europe, see Magone, 2003: 1–5; Malefakis, 1995: 34–36; Sapelli, 1995: 5–20). Southern European countries have been under considerable Europeanisation pressure in the past decades of European integration, particularly during and after the presidency of Jacques Delors between 1985 and 1995.

The most comprehensive definition of Europeanization was provided by Claudio Radaelli:

> Processes of (a) construction, (b) diffusion, and (c) institutionalization of formal and informal rules, procedures, policy paradigms, styles, 'ways of doing things', and shared beliefs and norms which are first defined and consolidated in the making of the EU public policy and politics and then incorporated in the logic of domestic discourse, identities, political structures and public policies.
> (Radaelli, 2003: 30; see also Ladrech, 2010; Börzel, 2005)

This describes a primarily top-down process that leads to transformations in the polities, politics and policies of the member states. Europeanized national polities, politics and policies can be measured according to what Tanja Börzel calls the 'goodfit' or 'misfit' between them and the European level. This also presupposes that each member state 'Europeanises' in a different way. The diversity of Europeanisation (so-called 'varieties' of Europeanisation) shows that despite the similarity of top-down policies, the outcomes may be quite different from the originally intended convergence of different national polities, politics and policies (Börzel, 1998). Resistance on the part of national political elites and interest groups, the misguided implementation of directives and divergent public administrative cultures may all play a role in creating 'goodfit' or 'misfit'. Börzel has developed a spectrum of potential responses to Europeanisation attempts (Börzel, 2005: 59)

In this context, the southern European countries tend superficially just to absorb and accommodate to external pressure from the supranational level.

Common features of European integration among southern European countries

There are three major features that characterise southern European integration in the European Union, all of which are interconnected and shape the peripheral position of these countries in the supranational organisation:

1 Europeanism and national democratisation;
2 a (semi-)peripheral economy and weak welfare states;
3 superficial Europeanisation.

Europeanism and the EU as a **vincolo esterno** *for national democratisation and modernisation*

One of the characteristics of European integration in all four southern European countries is the high level of support for integration among political elites. The European Community/European Union has been regarded as a panacea for all the problems that these countries faced before they joined the supranational organisation. Here, one important factor has been the significance of the EU in the consolidation of democracy in these countries. This almost blind faith in European integration as a 'millenarian' solution to all domestic problems can be called 'Europeanism'. This attitude reflects a profound faith in the power of European integration and the values that it represents in relation to the many problems that may exist domestically. This perception of the EEC/EU as an 'external link' (*vincolo esterno*) enabling passive improvements to democratic structures and lagging economies remains the major approach to European integration, not only in Italy but also in the other southern European countries (Dyson, Featherstone, 1996).

Throughout the 1980s and 1990s, all four southern European countries were keen to be at the forefront of European integration. All four countries regarded participation in the Economic and Monetary Union (EMU) as important, despite their weaker economies that were highly vulnerable to asymmetric shocks. The recent sovereign debt crisis has confirmed the warnings of critical scholars (e.g. Ardy et al., 2002).

The role of political and economic elites in these countries cannot be underestimated. A study conducted in 2008 by Nicolo Conti and his team on the attitudes of political elites shows a high level of support for European integration (over 80 per cent in Greece and 90 per cent in Portugal, Spain and Italy) and a positive assessment of the benefits of membership (over 90 per cent in all four countries; Conti et al., 2010: 123).

Similarly, the southern European populations were among the strongest supporters of European integration in the European Union until the crisis. However, the EU-imposed austerity policies and the intervention of the Troika in Greece, Portugal and Cyprus have considerably damaged support for European integration. A decline in the positive assessment of democracy in the European Union can be observed in all southern European countries. In the spring of 2014, the EU average per centage of citizens who were satisfied or very satisfied with how the EU democracy works was quite low, at 43 per cent; however, in Portugal this figure was 27 per cent, in Spain 25 per cent, in Italy 32 per cent, in Greece 25 per cent and in Cyprus 27 per cent. Only in Malta was the rating higher than average, at 56 per cent. Notably, Malta has been the only country in this southern European cluster that was able to avoid any kind of bailout or pressure to implement difficult reforms (Eurobarometer, 2014: Annex, T100). This circumstance clearly led to a fragmentation of the vote in these countries, with a shift towards Eurocritical parties, particularly in Greece and Spain. A kind of instrumental Euroscepticism related to deteriorating socioeconomic conditions (one could also refer it as a 'pauperisation process') has led to this decline in support for European integration. As long as the hardship is temporary, there is hope that support for European integration may increase again. The most problematic case is Greece, where radical parties are dominating the public debate, potentially contributing to a shift from instrumental soft to ideological hard Euroscepticism; this is due in particular to the presence of not only the left-wing radical party Syriza and the hard-Eurosceptic communists, but also the extreme right-wing party known as the Golden Dawn.

Peripheral economies and weak welfare states

The southern European countries have all peripheral inefficient economies within the European Union, however simultaneously have consumption patterns and political structures similar to those of most other developed European countries. Their political economies are still characterised by a dualism: there are certain strong economic sectors, but the overall economy is hampered by labour-intensive low-skilled sectors. This dualism also leads to a fragmentation of the labour market into protected and non-protected workers. The formal economy is paralleled by a strong informal economy of over 20 per cent of gross domestic product, with estimates varying from country to country. This allows for many invisible enterprises that tend to evade taxation (Aiginger, 2013).

Another feature of the economies of southern Europe is the excessive number of self-employed micro-businesses. This capital-poor subsistence pattern among the southern European economies marks them as the first victims of recessions and crises. Such subsistence micro-businesses can be found mainly in Portugal, Spain and Greece, but also in Italy. All four countries feature an excess of micro- and small firms (with one to nine employees) and a dearth of capital-strong enterprises; this is particularly the case for Portugal and Greece (OECD, 2014: 29, 31). Matthew Yglesias explains this by reference to the lack of a culture of cooperation and a society dominated by mistrust (Yglesias, 2012). Indeed, the European social survey regularly shows that southern Europeans exhibit rather high levels of mistrust in others, reflecting what Edward Banfield refers to as 'amoral familism', or the inability to cooperate with people outside one's family (the only people regard as trustworthy) (Magone, 2014a: 165; Banfield 1958: 89).

This peripheral situation is undoubtedly perpetuated by poor education systems. Schools play a crucial role in socialising amoral familists into moral members of society. It seems that the school systems in these countries still need to improve considerably to achieve this aim. Among the southern European countries, it seems that Portugal, Spain and Malta have the most serious problems in their education systems, in large part because of the high drop-out rate in secondary school. All three of these countries have drop-out rates of about 20 per cent; Portugal's rate is just slightly lower, while Spain and Malta have slightly higher rates (Eurostat, 2014; European Commission, 2011: 4). In these countries, many children drop out of school to go to work in order to make a contribution to the survival of their families. Moreover, these countries have poor showings in the regular Programme of International Student Assessment (PISA) studies conducted by the OECD. All Portugal, Spain, Greece and Italy are ranked below the OECD average and fall into the bottom third of nations.

The present crisis has also exposed the lack of robustness of the welfare states in southern Europe. Martin Rhodes and Maurizio Ferrera have pointed to the nature of these welfare states, which are less universal than most established systems in the more developed economies of the European Union. Particularisation through specific regimes coexists with universalising tendencies. There is also a tendency to combine elements of Anglo-Saxon and Bismarckian conservative welfare states (Rhodes, 1996; Ferrera, 1996). In addition to the fact that rudimentary welfare states emerged in southern Europe only in the 1970s, their benefit levels are among the lowest in the European Union. Only Italy is an exception, with benefit rates above the EU average, largely because it has the strongest economy in southern Europe and established its welfare policies earlier than the other three southern European countries (European Commission, 2010: 276). However, this has not contributed to the creation of a more egalitarian society. Southern European societies are among the most unequal societies in the European Union, with high levels of income distribution disparity (European Commission, 2010: 299–300). These welfare states were dismantled during the crisis, particularly in Greece, Portugal and Spain. The populations of these countries have been supported by a so-called 'welfare society', or rather 'welfare familism'. However, even welfare familism in southern Europe has come under considerable pressure due to unemployment, reductions in state benefits and wage cuts in the public sector (Santos, 2011: 73). Moreover, the role of women in society still lags behind the rest of Europe. In the 2012 Gender Equality Index of the European Gender Equality Institute, Portugal (22), Italy (24) and Greece (25) are ranked at the bottom of the index; Spain is the exception among the top ten, outperforming Germany, Austria and Luxemburg. This is without a doubt due to the long-term policies undertaken to improve the role of women in Spanish society (EIGE, 2013: 109).

Superficial Europeanisation

Southern European countries have been the absorbers of Europeanisation efforts rather than contributors in a pro-active transformation. In this sense, there has been a major contradiction between the perception of the EU as a *vincolo esterno* enabling countries to remedy their shortcomings in political, economic, social and cultural structures and the actual behaviour of political elites in allowing such transformations.

In a seminal study conducted by Tanja Börzel and her team based on a longitudinal database of compliance with EU law, it was discovered that Italy and Greece are laggards in relation to other countries. In explaining their findings, the authors argue that although Italy is a large, powerful country and Greece is one of the weakest in the EU, the two share a low government capacity that has resulted in non-compliance. In contrast, the United Kingdom and Denmark have very high government capacities. Portugal and Spain also have low government capacities, but they have been improving considerably over time. In particular, Portugal has been attempting to improve its government capacity in order to avoid the penalties for non-compliance meted out by the European Court of Justice. Of the four southern European countries, Portugal seems to fare the best, largely due to its high level of response when faced with potential penalisation (Börzel et al., 2010: 1383–1384; see also Börzel, 2001: 819). The best example of top-down superficial Europeanisation is the implementation of structural funds.

The impact of cohesion policies: a case of superficial Europeanisation

Cohesion policy accounts for about 35–40 per cent of the EU budget, almost the same level as the common agricultural policy (CAP). Structural funds unite Spain, Portugal and Greece, the so-called 'Club Med'.

All four cohesion countries (Portugal, Spain, Greece and Ireland) were quite successful in securing funding from one multiannual financial framework to the next. However, only Ireland was able to achieve major results, structurally transforming the country's political economy. The Irish formula was to invest in people, IT and networks. Ultimately, the national population became the owner of the cohesion projects (Rees et al., 2004: 391–6; Barry et al., 2001; Laffan, O'Mahony, 2008: 138–141). In contrast, smaller countries like Portugal and Greece have failed to adjust to Europeanisation efforts, instead remaining quite rigid in their relationship to the EU model of multilevel governance. In both cases, the paternalistic tendencies of a centralised state did not permit genuine involvement on the part of the population, and the private economic sector had to be subsidised to convince it to take part in projects. In the end, the outcome was the considerable governmentalisation of governance networks, with the interests of the state as the central focus. In both countries, the regional authorities handling structural funds are appointed from the centre and are therefore extended branches of the public administration. Both Portuguese and Greek policy-makers are masters at 'playing the game': instead of investing in people, most of the funding went to large prestige projects such as the Olympic Games in Greece in 2004, Expo 1998, the 2004 European Football Championship in Portugal and related infrastructure. In Portugal, this is called the 'politics of concrete' (*politica de betão)*. At the end of the funding cycle, a lack of imagination led to the construction of too many shopping centres and an exaggerated concentration of projects around the main cities (see Magone, 2004: 215–239; 231–325; Magone, 2014a; Featherstone, Kazamias, 2008; Nanetti et al., 2004; Parakesvopoulos, Leonardi, 2004; Getimis, Demotropoulou, 2004; Parakesvopoulos et al., 2009).

In contrast, the larger states of Spain and Italy moved towards a regionalised unitary model. Spain in particular has decentralised and improved relationships with its regions over time. Despite these developments, the country's weak civil society and system of capitalism allowed the central and public administrations to dictate the priorities of cohesion policy. This led to a similar pattern of concentration on infrastructure and neglect of productive enterpreneurial facilities

(Magone, 2009: 352–353; Morata, Muñoz, 1996: 208). Italy also had major difficulties in implementing EU cohesion policy. Despite the country's regionalised structure, Paolo Graziano sees a clear misfit between the policy-making structures in Italy and those of the European Union. This misfit is even more salient in the Mezzogiorno than in the northern parts of Italy (Graziano, 2003: 169–70). However, it seems that a learning process of some kind is gradually taking place. According to an excellent study conducted by Martin Bull and Jörg Baudner, implementation quality and efficiency has increased in the Mezzogiorno. The EU as an external link has allowed regional economic and social elites to join together and create a critical mass that uses the European policy-making process to reduce the traditional obstacles to further development (Bull, Baudner, 2004). Despite these improvements, Italy clearly fits into the southern European pattern of low institutional capacity and low implementation efficiency. The Italian government upgraded its monitoring and evaluation capacity at the beginning of the millennium; however, a new assessment of actual improvements has yet to be undertaken (Barca, 2006).

The impact of the Euro and sovereign debt crisis in southern Europe: the introduction of coercive Europeanisation

The worldwide financial crisis originating in the United States (the so-called 'Empire of Debt') had significant contaminating repercussions in the European Union, particularly in southern Europe. Many European countries were forced to deal with the aftermath of the toxic assets related to the US subprime market sold by Lehmann Brothers and other American institutions to banks around the world. In particular, the United Kingdom, France, Germany and Switzerland were affected by these toxic assets, leading to major bailouts of the banking sector. The consequence was a shortage of credit in the economy (Otte, 2008; Lewis, 2010).

Moreover, trust – the essential requirement for doing business – was undermined considerably. Between 2008 and 2010, the financial markets were reluctant to lend money to EU member states, particularly to southern Europe.

For decades, southern European countries could rely on a benevolent European Union. The European Union was used as a *vincolo esterno* to sort out all the problems that could not be resolved internally. The European Union was regarded as an important facilitator in achieving modernisation in the politics, economies, societies and cultures of these countries. In the long term, the sense of belonging to the regional community of democratic states led to the belief that they were economically, socially and politically at the same level as most other member states. However, the solidarity community of the 1980s had shifted considerably, resulting in a more divisive relationship between rich and poor countries and between the centre and the periphery. The sovereign debt crisis exposed this perception of the EU as an external link as no longer accurate. The benevolent attitude of the EU grew more critical and demanding, based on a mistrust in the idea that southern Europeans were capable of implementing reforms on their own. The inclusion of the International Monetary Fund (IMF) in the Troika showed that some countries (with Germany at the forefront) distrusted their own EU institutions – specifically, the European Commission and European Central Bank, presided over by the Portuguese José Manuel Durão Barroso and the French Jean Claude Trichet (and later the Italian Mario Draghi), respectively.

Even before the sovereign debt crisis broke out, southern Europe and Ireland had been characterised as the 'PIIGS' (Portugal, Italy, Ireland, Greece and Spain). This acronym was clearly intended to offend countries with major economic difficulties, and therefore many scholars (myself included) instead referred to the group as 'GIIPS'. All four southern European countries experienced considerable unit labour cost increases between 1999 and 2009, while Germany and Austria maintained their levels at 1999 rates. This meant that many southern European products were not very competitive.

This problem was exacerbated by a low level of innovation due to stagnation in research and development (see chapter 1). These countries have been forced to implement a policy of internal devaluation in order to become more competitive (Armingeon, Baccaro, 2012).

The policies of the Troika in Greece, Ireland, Portugal and Cyprus, as well as those of the European Central Bank and the European Commission with regard to Italy and Spain, could be described as imposed or 'forced' Europeanisation. After decades of benevolent Europeanization, more strictly imposed Europeanisation programmes were implemented. The so-called Memorandum of Understanding envisaged short- and medium-term economic and financial adjustments in the periphery economies, but also included a quite ambitious programme of reforms, all related to the existing obstacles to the implementation of Single European Market legislation in individual countries.

In sum, Europeanisation has been taking place, but the results have been quite mixed. Portugal and Greece tend to 'play the game'. While the smaller countries could not escape the negative effects of the Troika, the larger, more powerful countries were able to resist interventions but still had to commit themselves to drastic austerity and reform programmes. Although Portugal was able to complete the Troika austerity programme in 2014, unemployment is still at 14.1 per cent in the first quarter of 2015. The structural problems of a weak economy remain a challenge for the future. Although Spain, following the reforms of the Rajoy government, is hailed as a new motor of the European economy (along with Germany), major problems remain in low level of expenditure in research and innovation and high unemployment (Pauly, 2015). Reforms in Italy have been particularly difficult to implement, simply perpetuating a situation of economic stagnation. Last but not least, in Greece the Antonis Samaras government had achieved some reform and was almost completing the Troika programme. However, early elections brought in a new coalition government made up of the radical leftwing Syriza and the radical rightwing Independent Greeks (ANEL), which in an act of denial still cultivate the model of 'benevolent Europeanisation' against that of 'forced Europeanisation'. However, the referendum on the interrupted negotiated Memorandum in early July further increased the pressure of 'forced Europeanisation' on the Alexis Tsipras government. The new finance minister Euclid Tsakalotos had to be more cooperative in order to restore trust with the creditor countries. The new bailout negotiated by the Greek government with the Troika include worse conditions than those originally in place.

Conclusions: reforming the southern European model of capitalism

This chapter has sought to provide an overview of the relationship between the European Union and southern Europe. On balance, this relationship has been largely positive. European integration has contributed to greater stability and democratic accountability in these countries. The main pattern of Europeanization in southern Europe has utilised the EU as a *vincolo esterno* in order to modernise and democratise society. These countries also perceived the EU as a benevolent actor, but recent developments have destroyed this image. Power relationships between member states began to be salient, which took southern Europeans by surprise. They still are reacting to this new reality in the European Union.

References

Aiginger, Karl (2013) 'A New Strategy for the European Periphery,' Working Paper 443, Österreichisches Institut für Wirtschaftsforschung (WIFO), Vienna.

Ardy, Brian, Iain Begg, Waltraud Schelkle and Francisco Torres (2002) *EMU and Cohesion: Theory and Policy*. Lisbon: Principia.

Armingeon, Klaus and Lucio Baccaro (2012) 'Political economy of the sovereign debt crisis: The limits of internal devaluation,' *Industrial Law Journal* 41(3): 254–275.

Banfield, Edward (1958) *The Moral Basis of a Backward Society*. Glencoe, IL: The Free Press.

Barca, Fabrizio (2006) 'European Union evaluation between myth and reality: Reflections on the Italian experience,' *Regional Studies* 40(2): 273–276.

Barry, Frank, John Bradley and Aoife Hannan (2001) 'The Single Market, the Structural Funds and Ireland's economic growth,' *Journal of Common Market Studies* 39(3): 537–552.

Börzel, Tanja A. (1998) 'Pace-setting, foot-dragging, and fence-sitting: Member-states responses to Europeanization,' *Journal of Common Market Studies* 40(2): 193–214.

Börzel, Tanja A. (2001) 'Non-compliance in the European: Pathology or statistical artefact?,' *Journal of European Public Policy* 8(5): 803–824.

Börzel, Tanja A. (2005) 'Europeanization: How the European Union Interacts with its Member States,' in Simon Bulmer and Christian Lequesne (eds) *The Member States of the European Union*. Oxford: Oxford University Press, pp. 25–44.

Börzel, Tanja A., Tobias Hoffmann, Diana Panke and Carina Sprungk (2010) 'Obstinate and inefficient: Why member-states do not comply with EU law,' *Comparative Political Studies* 43(11): 1363–1390.

Bull, Martin and Joerg Baudner (2004) 'Europeanization and Italian policy to the Mezzogiorno,' *Journal of European Public Policy* 11(6): 1058–1076.

Conti, Nicolò, Maurizio Cotta and Pedro Tavares de Almeida (2010) 'Southern Europe: a distinctive and more pro-European region in the EU?,' *South European Society and Politics* 15(1): 121–142.

Dyson, Kenneth and Kevin Featherstone (1996) 'Italy and EMU as a *vincolo esterno*: Empowering the technocrats, transforming the state,' *South European Society and Politics* 1(2): 272–299.

Eurobarometer (2014) 'Standard Eurobarometer 82,' November. Available at: http://ec.europa.eu/public_opinion/archives/eb/eb82/eb82_en.htm (accessed 2 January 2015).

European Commission (2010) 'Social Situation in the European Union 2009'. Luxembourg: Office of Official Publications of the European Communities.

European Commission (2011) 'Tackling Early School Leaving: A Key Contribution to the Europe 2020 Strategy'. Brussels: European Commission. Available at: http://eur-lex.europa.eu/legal-content/EN/TXT/PDF/?uri=CELEX:52011SC0096&from=EN (accessed 2 January 2014).

European Institute for Gender Equality (EIGE) (2013) 'Gender Equality Index Report 2012'. Vilnius: EIGE. Available at: http://eige.europa.eu/content/document/gender-equality-index-report (accessed 25 June 2013).

Eurostat (2014) 'Early Leavers from School and Training'. Available at: http://ec.europa.eu/eurostat/tgm/table.do?tab=table&init=1&language=en&pcode=tsdsc410&plugin=1 (accessed 30 December 2014).

Featherstone, Kevin and George Kazamias (2008) *The Limits of Europeanization. Reform Capacity and Policy Conflict in Greece.* Basingstoke: Palgrave.

Ferrera, Maurizio (1996) 'The "Southern Model" of welfare in social Europe,' *Journal of European Social Policy* 6(1): 17–37.

Getimis, Panayotis and Leeda Demetropoulou (2004) 'Towards new forms of regional governance in Greece: the Southern Aegean Islands,' *Regional and Federal Studies* 14(3): 355–378.

Giannone, Diego (2014) 'Suspending Democracy? The Governance of the EU's Political and Economic Crisis as a Process of Neoliberal Restructuring,' in Kyriakos N. Demetriou (ed.) *The European Union in Crisis: Explorations in Representation and Democratic Legitimacy.* Heidelberg: Springer, pp. 101–119.

Giuliani, Marco (2001) 'Europeanization and Italy: A Bottom-Up Process?,' in Kevin Featherstone and George Kazamias (eds) *Europeanization and the Southern Periphery.* London: Frank Cass, pp. 47–72.

Graziano, Paolo (2003) 'La nuova politica regionale italiana: il ruolo dell'europeizzazione,' in Sergio Fabbrini (ed.) *L'europeizzazione dell' Italia.* Rome: Editori Laterza, pp. 80–107.

Ladrech, Robert (1994) 'Europeanization of domestic politics and institutions: The case of France,' *Journal of Common Market Studies* 32(1): 69–88.

Ladrech, Robert (2010) *Europeanization and National Politics.* Basingstoke: Palgrave.

Laffan, Brigid and Jane O'Mahony (2008) *Ireland and the European Union.* Basingstoke: Palgrave.

Lewis, Michael (2010) *The Big Short: Inside the Doomsday Machine.* New York: W. W. Norton and Company.

Magone, José M. (2003) *The Politics of Southern Europe: Integration into the EU.* Westport, CT: Praeger.

Magone, José M. (2004) *The Developing Place of Portugal in the European Union.* New Brunswick, NJ: Transaction.

Magone, José M. (2009) *Contemporary Spanish Politics.* London: Routledge.

Magone, José M. (2010) 'The Role of the EEC in the Portuguese, Spanish and Greek Transitions,' in Diego Muro and Gregorio Alonso (eds) *Politics and Memory of Democratic Transition in the Case of Spain.* London: Routledge, pp. 215–235.

Magone, José M. (2011) 'Centre-Periphery conflict in the European Union? Europe 2020, the Southern European Model and the eurocrisis,' in Attila Agh (ed.) *European Union at the crossroads: The European Perspectives after the Global Crisis*. Budapest: Budapest College of Communication, Business and Arts, pp. 71–121.

Magone, José M. (2012) 'Democrazia politica e regolazione sociale nell'Unione Europea nell' incerta transizione globale: la pressione sull' Europa meridionale,' *Sindacalismo* 20, October.

Magone, José M. (2013) 'Living with the Eurocrisis in Southern Europe,' in Attila Ágh and László Vass (eds) *European Futures: The Perspectives of the New Member States in the New Europe*. Budapest: Budapest College of Communication and Business, pp. 69–122.

Magone, José M. (2014a) *The Politics of Contemporary Portugal. Evolving Democracy*. Boulder, CO: Lynne Rienner.

Magone, José M. (2014b) 'Divided Europe? Euroscepticism in Central, Eastern and Southern Europe,' in Kyriakos N. Demetriou (eds) *The European Union in Crisis. Explorations in Representation and Democratic Legitimacy*. Heidelberg: Springer, pp. 33–53.

Malefakis, Edward (1995) 'The Political and Socioeconomic Contours of Southern European History,' in Richard Gunther, P. Nikiforos Diamandouros and Hans-Jürgen Puhle (eds) *The Politics of Democratic Consolidation: Southern Europe in Comparative Perspective*. Baltimore, MD and London: Johns Hopkins University Press, pp. 33–76.

Morata, Francesc and Xavier Muñoz (1996) 'Vying for European Funds: Territorial Restructuring in Spain,' in Liesbet Hooghe (ed.) *Cohesion Policy and European Integration: Building Multilevel Governance*. Oxford: Oxford University Press, pp. 195–218.

Nanetti, Raffaella Y., Helena Rato and Miguel Rodrigues (2004) 'Institutional capacity and reluctant decentralization in Portugal: The Lisbon and Tagus Valley Region,' *Regional and Federal Studies* 14(3): 405–429.

Organisation for Economic Cooperation and Development (OECD) (2014) *Enterpreneurship at a Glance 2014*. Paris: OECD. Available at: www.keepeek.com/Digital-Asset-Management/oecd/industry-and-services/entrepreneurship-at-a-glance-2014_entrepreneur_aag-2014-en#page1 (accessed 2 January 2014).

Otte, Max (2008) *Der Crash kommt: Die neue Weltwirtschaftskrise und wie sich darauf vorbereiten*. Berlin: Ullstein.

Paraskevopoulos, Christos J. and Robert Leonardi (2004) 'Introduction: Adaptational pressures and social learning in European regional policy cohesion (Greece, Ireland and Portugal) vs. CEE (Hungary, Poland) countries,' *Regional and Federal Studies* 14(3): 315–354.

Parakesvopoulos, Christos J., Panagiotis Getimis and Leeda Demetropoulou (2009) 'Griechenland als Gegenstand europäischer Kohäsionspolitik im Rahmen der EU-Strukturfonds,' in Björn Egner and Georgios Terizakis (eds) *Das politische System Griechenlands: Strukturen, Akteure, Politikfelder*. Baden-Baden: Nomos, pp. 229–274.

Pauly, Christopher (2015) 'Back from the brink: Spain emerges as a model for Europe,' *Der Spiegel*, 25 March. Available at: www.spiegel.de/international/europe/howspainrecoveredfromtheeconomiccrisisa1025327.html (accessed 3 April 2015).

Radaelli, Claudio M. (2003) 'The Europeanization of Public Policy,' in Kevin Featherstone and Claudio M. Radaelli (eds), *The Politics of Europeanization*. Oxford: Oxford University Press, pp. 27–56.

Rees, Nicholas, Brad Quinn and Bernadette Connaughton (2004) 'Ireland´s pragmatic adaptation to regionalization: the Mid-West Region,' *Regional and Federal Studies* 14(3): 379–404.

Rhodes, Martin (1996) 'Southern European welfare states: Identity, problems and prospects of reform,' in Martin Rhodes (ed.) Special issue – Southern European Welfare States, *South European Society and Politics* 1(3): 1–22.

Santos, Boaventura de Sousa (2011) *Portugal: Ensaio Contra A Autoflagelação*. Lisbon: Edições Almedina.

Sapelli, Giulio (1995) *Southern Europe Since 1945: Tradition and Modernity in Portugal, Spain, Italy, Greece and Turkey*. London and New York: Longman.

Yglesias, Matthew (2012) 'Southern Europe's small-business problem: Why corruption and poor regulation cause Greece, Italy and Spain to have too many workers at small firms,' *Slate*, 6 July. Available at: www.slate.com/articles/business/small_business/2012/07/the_small_business_problem_why_greece_italy_and_spain_have_too_many_small_firms_.html (accessed 3 April 2015)..

7 Sociopolitical divisions in the European Union

Discourses of southern European representatives in the European institutions[1]

Ignacio Paredero Huerta

Introduction

We are currently witnessing an intense public debate about EU economic policies (specifically, monetary policies), the institutional structure of the EU and the decisions taken to manage the euro crisis. This debate was first defined by the diagnosis of the economic crisis and later by the policies employed to confront the crisis, understood by some among the general public as the consequence of the Southern states' profligate spending and by others as the structural problems of the euro that benefit the Northern countries.

In the field of political science, diverse authors have pointed to the existence of divisions – namely, cleavages between Northern and Southern Europe in the EU's political institutions, primarily in the Council of the European Union and, by extension, in the European Council. Elgström et al. (2001), Hosli (2008), Kaeding and Selck (2005), Naurin and Lindahl (2008), Thomson and Hosli (2006) Thomson (2009, 2011), Zimmer et al. (2005) and Plechanovová (2011a, 2011b) varyingly suggest, uphold or demonstrate the existence of voting coalitions in the Council of the EU or in the negotiations of the Council among EU civil servants. Although the precise nature of the coalitions is not clear (North vs South, net receivers vs net payers, centre vs periphery, etc.), it seems evident that coalitions do exist in some form. This includes the coalitions established after the expansion of the EU in 2004 involving the new bloc of Eastern countries, as proposed by Thomson (2011) and Naurin and Lindhal (2008).

It is therefore important to confirm whether there is a real perception among EU insiders that these cleavages, divisions or coalition blocs between the North, South and East exist and influence the decision-making processes in the EU. It is also necessary to understand the possible factors (i.e. the independent variables) that activate or explain these potential divisions. To this end, an exploration of the EU insiders' discourses should be most enlightening. It would also be interesting to determine whether Germany enjoys any kind of priority in promoting its preferred public policies, whether the EU is drifting towards an intergovernmental scenario and whether informal negotiation mechanisms can ultimately explain these dynamics.

Theoretical framework

Max Weber (2001) in his classic *The Protestant Ethic and the Spirit of Capitalism* was one of the first social scientists to seek an explanation for the economic differences between Europe's North and South. Although Weber's uses of 'ideal types' are not by itself stereotypical, stereotypes inspired on his explanations continue to feed opinions and simplifications that explain the limited economic development of Southern Europe as a consequence of the lack of a work ethic, and propose solutions that are a mix of punishment, strict moral rules and austerity designed to make these profligate countries correct their excesses. The importance of these stereotypes in establishing public opinion, diagnostics, problems and solutions should not be underestimated. For example, the term 'PIIGS' (Portugal, Italy, Ireland, Greece and Spain), was presented first in *The Economist*, in its article 'A decade in the sun' (2008), and quickly, the 'PIIGS' became to some financial analysts, the weak link of the Eurozone (Dizard 2008). The acronym was used in the famous *Financial Times'* article 'Pigs in muck', (*Financial Times* 2008), which almost caused a diplomatic incident when Portugal's economy minister, Manuel Pinho, stated that he was 'shocked' and 'deeply offended' by the article, which was withdrawn from the FT.com web page soon afterwards. Knowledge of the acronym spread quickly, primarily used in the financial press, with titles like 'The PIIGS that won't fly' (The Economist 2010) or 'Grounded PIIGS' (The Economist, 2011). These articles show the existence of a substrate undercurrent of underestimation and incredulity with regard to the functioning of the economies of the South, as well as a belief in the South's profligacy and economic underdevelopment that could ultimately have self-fulfilling effects on the economy and on the policy mix.

The second theoretical pillar is outlined by Lipset and Rokkan (1967). These authors established the existence of political divisions based on profound sociological differences and marked by the historical processes that determine electoral competition and party systems. They then defined these divisions in relation to various cleavages.

On the European level, such cleavages require European public opinion, a European electoral body and a European party system; however, such a system does not truly exist in Europe, as the European parties are no more than the sum of individual national parties that attend to their domestic concerns before European concerns, as Mair asserts (2000). In addition, European elections are considered 'second order', and the European Parliament is a chamber featuring a strong consensus between the two main parties; this presents a problem for the politicisation of issues and thus for the emergence of a public opinion polarised around cleavages. Authors such as Heidar (2003), Hooghe and Marks (1997), Mair (2000), Tsebelis and Garrett (2000) and Hix (1999) have analysed and proposed different possible cleavages in the European Parliament (left–right, integration–independence), but the fact is that in the EU there are no clear-cut cleavages as there are in national elections (Heidar 2003), primarily because there is no truly European political space with its own public opinion, party system, parties or elections.

However, could sociological, economic and cultural divisions be introduced into the decision-making process through the other legislative chamber, the Council of the EU? Are there stable sociological, economic and cultural differences between European countries that could determine the common position of the Council of the EU? Diverse authors have pointed to such sociological and economic differences, including Gøsta Esping-Andersen (1990) with his classification of the three worlds of welfare capitalism. There are other economic, political and cultural issues in which these differences can also be seen, such as religious matters, trade union affiliations, education level and industrial structure (per cent of SME vs industry).

The political science literature also confirms the existence of a significant division between Europe's North and South in the Council of the European Union. One of the first specific studies on the existence of coalitions in European Union negotiations was conducted by Elgström et al. (2001). A survey of Swedish civil servants determined that 82 per cent of them consider the existence of coalitions between the North and the South in EU Council negotiations to be very common or fairly common. The study shows the ordered frequency of Swedish collaboration with other countries, a list that may well be the first empirical evidence of this North–South division: Denmark, Finland, the United Kingdom, the Netherlands, Germany, Austria, Ireland, France, Belgium, Italy, Spain, Portugal, Luxembourg and Greece. Elgström would argue that these divisions are due to geographical and cultural bonds between neighbouring countries.

Authors including Kaeding y Selck (2005), Hosli (2008), Naurin and Lindahl (2008), Thomson and Hosli (2006), Thomson (2009, 2011), Zimmer et al. (2005) and Plechanovová (2011a) all support, in one way or another, the existence of this division (under various names) through diverse methodological approaches (surveys of civil servants, utilisation of the Decision-Making on the European Union dataset, Thomson et al. (2012), analysis of Council votes), both before and after the 2004 EU enlargement. Although the final votes and the research of Arregui and Thomson (2009: 671–673) show that no specific country 'wins' in the EU Council, Thomson (2011: 65) demonstrates patterns of support between Northern and Southern countries: 36 per cent of votes are explained by these coalitions before the expansion, and 30 per cent afterwards.

However, there are intrinsic methodological problems with any research on the EU Council. EU Council negotiations cannot be comprehensively described by formal procedures alone. The experience of many researchers leads us to conclude that limiting the analysis to the formal rules (normative issues) or the votes and acts published (outputs) is highly unsatisfactory, if not methodologically incorrect, as defended by Heisenberg (2008).

An analysis based on rules in the Council has no predictive capabilities, so there must be informal rules or factors not captured by such a formal analysis. Similarly, an analysis of the actual votes (the final votes in the Council) is profoundly unsatisfactory, as in most cases, only the propositions that are sure to be approved reach the Council. In the end, the formal votes in the Council represent a collection of consensus and affirmative votes (Hosli et al. 2011; Arregui and

Thomson 2014) (with some exceptions in the form of protest votes), thanks to the tireless work of the General Secretariat of the EU Council and the informal consensual culture present in the institution. Most of the time, the General Secretariat seeks consensual, inclusive agreements that (unfortunately) overshadow the true essence of political conflict and interstate negotiations. To solve this methodological problem, some researchers have included an analysis of specific votes or states' declarations, have combined registered votes with information from interviews or, like Elgström (2001) and Naurin and Lindahl (2008), have used surveys to directly poll the civil servants working for the Council of the European Union. Such surveys entail their own problems but can ultimately reveal more clearly the real 'under-the-table' negotiations.

On top of all that, with the 2004 Eastern extension of the EU, the North–South division has become a North vs South/East division. Authors such as Naurin and Lindhal (2008), Hosli et al. (2009), Thomson (2009, 2011), Plechanovová (2011a, 2011b) and Parízek (2012) have analysed the influence of this new bloc of countries that are often allied on the basis of their common past. In fact, the extension has weakened the former North–South coalitions, although they continue to exist. According to Naurin and Lindhall (2008), the East tends to vote with Germany and Poland, in the same way that the South tends to vote with France and the North with Germany and the UK. For Thomson, the explicative capability of the North–South coalition has diminished, but it is nevertheless the most relevant explanatory factor with respect to EU Council votes. Plechanovová (2011a) and Parízek (2012) go further, questioning the 'North, South and East' terminology; they propose that the actual divisions are between the 'centre' and the 'periphery', with the centre being the countries that took advantage of the opportunity offered by the 2004 extension to capture the centrality of the decision-making process, since informal negotiations between all the country pairs on the EU Council would be impossible.

Methodology and research strategy

Taking into account this theoretical frame, we decided to use qualitative research to explore the field, with the intent to directly ask people who work for the EU whether they perceive that such divisions really do exist and affect the operations of the EU institutions. For practical reasons, we were specifically interested in the discourses of insiders from the Southern European member states. These reasons pertain to both language and accessibility: it was easier for the researcher to conduct interviews with Spanish-speaking insiders, and obtaining contacts and support from such insiders was also more straightforward.

We are primarily interested in the discourses used by insiders to affirm, justify or explain the divisions between North, South and East, if they believe that such divisions actually exist. As we have explained, public opinion on the 'North vs South' debate largely stems from the euro crisis, related public policy decisions and media. We seek to determine whether the discourses about divisions presented in the media are in fact real and exploited by insiders; in addition, we want to ascertain how these divisions affect or condition the decision-making processes of the European Union.

The main question of this preliminary research is clear:

Do divisions exist between the North, South and East in the EU, and do they affect the decision-making processes of the European Union?

Other relevant questions include:

- What macro factors at the state level or the European level might explain the existence of these divisions?
    a Are these factors cultural?
    b Are they economic factors?
- Are there discourses not previously identified that could explain these divisions?
- Has intergovernmentalism become more salient in the decision-making processes of the EU?
- Does Germany impose its policies on the EU? If so, how?
- How important are informal mechanisms in decision-making processes?

Based on the theory, we will attempt to confirm the existence of discourses on 'North–South–East' divisions. In addition, we would like to ascertain whether a discourse exists among insiders that recognises the drift toward intergovernmentalism in the EU (potentially favouring certain coalitions in the decision-making process). We also want to determine whether there is a discourse that attributes more power to Germany than the formal mechanisms allow. Finally, we seek to learn from the insiders whether the informal parts of decision-making processes are more important than the formal parts (in their opinion).

Research strategy

The research strategy involved a mix of semi-structured interviews and participant observations. To qualitatively assess the EU institutions and insiders, we applied for an internship period in the European Parliament. This internship took place between May and July 2013. During this period, I conducted most of the field research, in Brussels. The research tools were semi-structured interviews using a list of key issues we wanted answers to but not a list of questions. This method was chosen due to the time constraints of the insiders and in the hopes of discovering interesting and entirely new discourses.

The selection of insiders was made by first seeking out Spanish insiders; through them, we attempted to broaden the scope of nationalities, first to other Southern countries and then beyond – a typical 'snowball' strategy.

We prioritised ideological and institutional diversity first and then national diversity; consequently, most of the interviews (all but four) were conducted in Spanish.

The total number of interviews was 22: ten from the European Parliament, four from the European Commission and eight from the Council of the European Union. Although the data are quantitatively scarce, the Commission was the institution with the best access to senior insiders (an ex-president of the European Commission, a Commissioner and two chiefs of cabinet of European Commissioners). In the case of the EU Council, we obtained interviews with councillors Antici and Mertens, a member of the Council Secretariat, a member of the cabinet of the president of the European Council, a legal councillor and an ex-secretary of state for the European Union. Furthermore, in the European Parliament, we interviewed eight MEPs, a member of the General Secretariat and a coordinator of a national delegation. The interviews had an average duration of 35 minutes. We did not use voice recorders, as we were after real insider discourses, not political ones. We wanted the interviewees to be able to express themselves with total freedom on the issues we brought up, so we took notes on the computer but did not record the interviews themselves.

The discourses of Southern European representatives in the institutions of the EU

Taking into account some exceptions in the European Parliament and certain technical and conceptual details, the interviews reveal the existence of discourses on the divisions between North, South and East. The insiders recognised these divisions, in some cases explicitly and with definite knowledge of which countries made up which coalitions on which issues and why; in other (most) cases, this knowledge was a vague perception that they had not thought about or analysed, but they were still aware of the coalitions and could elaborate on them when asked. There is, more or less, a consensus about the motivations for the divisions. The main factor that came up again and again was economic in nature: debtors vs creditors, net contributors vs net receivers, advocates of a bigger budget vs advocates of a better spending of the budget, Common Agricultural Policy (CAP) defenders vs opponents. The economic factor was omnipresent in the interviews, affecting almost all the issues raised in some way. As one insider pointed out:

> in Brussels, you start from a very simple point: you are managing economic issues. If you pay, do you have the power? Yes(Interview #4)

Discourse 1: Coalitions of countries

As part of the analysis of divisions, some of the insiders suggested the existence of different groups of countries that, on the basis of historical or geographical closeness, tend to coordinate or to form coalitions – in some special cases, explicit ones. For many of the insiders, the French-German friendship is essential for an understanding of the EU:

> The French-German friendship has a series of established practices to express that friendship. They have built a body of procedures to structure their bilateral relations with Europe.
>
> (Interview #2)

These French and German practices include many informal mechanisms, some of them surprising:

> Before each European Council, both the French and the German delegation stay in the Hotel Amigo. Supposedly, they meet in the morning of the second day to compare notes.
>
> (Interview #2)

However, most insiders expressed the opinion that nowadays this collaboration is weakened by the 'diminished France' (Interviev #16) – a France unable to serve as a counterweight for a resurgent Germany. This weakening of the French–German collaboration was mentioned in almost all the interviews; it is as though a kind of equilibrium has been lost.

Some insiders pointed to a coalition between the Nordic countries (Denmark, Sweden, Finland), which employ 'a structured coordination between them to coordinate their positions' (Interview #8), others to the Mediterranean countries (Italy, Portugal, Greece, Spain), the Baltic countries (Estonia, Latvia, Lithuania) or the Visegrad countries (the Czech Republic, Hungary, Poland, Slovakia). With regard to the Baltic countries, one interviewer said that 'they are very small countries, without resources. For some time, they had a common ambassador' (Interview #2).

To some interviewees, the Eastern countries tend to group together due to their common history, their experiences under Soviet rule, their market preferences and anti-regulation sentiments and also their vision of Europe as a passive bloc (in contrast to the more active US policies in relation to Russia). These experiences make them inclined to reject the attempts of the EU to promote common policies and to prefer a EU closer to the model defended by the UK a union exclusively as a common market. To many of those interviewed, the Eastern European enlargement seemed excessively hasty; they felt that the Eastern countries approach the EU with a very different vision than the older member states:

> I have the feeling that they do not see this club as we see it. They think that we didn't help them very much in the Soviet era, and that their true support came from the United States. In some ways, they are the Trojan horse of the United States and the UK in the EU.
>
> (Interview #10)

Another interviewer argued:

> The Eastern countries, the newcomers, joined the EU without an Europeanist culture. They seek to distance themselves from Russia. They want to keep their sovereignty and to be in the North Atlantic Treaty Organisation (NATO). But they don't have a European culture.
>
> (Interview #5)

To some of the insiders, the divisions or coalitions of countries are there in plain sight, but are not always easily perceived. As one interviewer explained:

> Only with years of experience can you perceive the patterns, but these patterns are not [explicitly] written out. They are more like habits that translate the fundamental conceptions of what the European Union truly is.
>
> (Interview #2)

However, the nature of negotiations is determined by the specific issue; thus, to some insiders, there are no coalitions because 'everything depends on the issue' (Interview #6). But some of the more senior insiders affirm that these dynamics are clear and that the countries' positions are stable and ultimately predictable: 'Germany says something and you know that Austria is going to say the same thing. Sometimes you don't even pay attention because you know what they are going to say' (Interview #8). Or, in the words of an insider with more than twenty years of experience: 'I could tell you what one minister or another is going to say. And that is because I know this game' (Interview #22).

For many of the interviewees, the economic crisis is exacerbating divisions based on cultural stereotypes and populist prejudices in both directions. Against the South, for example:

> During the European championship, I was with the chief of the cabinet of (Javier) Solana. The match: Germany vs Portugal. If you are watching the match and you are a German, you see that all the good players are playing for Real Madrid.
>
> (Interview #6)

To some insiders, all of this seems very dangerous:

> These stereotypes existed before. That northerners are stingy and take a Calvinist-type approach, and that the others, the southerners, are easy-going, a bit on the lazy side. That's the perception, which is very dangerous. They (Germany) are playing that card, and it is very dangerous.
>
> (Interview #13)

To others, the explanation is simpler: due to the crisis and the macroeconomic debate about the EU's policies, we see in the press that which is most obvious or most controversial, due to the crisis, the macroeconomic debate about the policies on the EU. For these interviewees, the emergence of the North–South division was nothing more than a perception stemming from public policy debates about the euro; on other issues, the division was not strong enough to carry real weight. This would explain why the Eastern countries are not part of the debate, as they are not members of the Eurozone or directly involved in the euro crisis.

Discourse 2: Culture and economic power in North–South perceptions

Many of the insiders connected these possible divisions or coalitions with economic factors: 'Net receivers vs net contributors is a real cleavage' (Interview #9). There were at least two insiders who identified the division as exclusively an economic issue, related to debt, and defined it as a 'centre–periphery' cleavage. One of them affirmed that the North vs South cleavage 'does not exist. What does exist is a tendency for periphery countries to understand one another' (Interview #7). One of the issues that frequently recurred in relation to the divisions was the CAP and structural funds. The Southern countries are, of course, net receivers from both sources: 'There are two different and strong interests: Mediterranean and Continental agriculture' (Interview #12).

Other insiders connected the divisions with cultural issues. For example, one of the insiders explained with clear conviction that the differences between countries and policies intended to solve the euro crisis were linked to the use of either negative incentives (punishments, austerity, North) or positive tools (cooperation, structural funds, South):

> You see a division between countries that are more concerned about risk, moral hazards and so on, always insisting on rules, sanctions and mechanisms to address moral hazards and things like that. And other groups tend to like positive incentives more; they want to foster more integration through more positive incentives.
>
> (Interview #13)

Another cultural factor is language, which can favour agreements between the Northern countries or the Southern countries. As one of the interviewees stated, 'Another element that fosters alliances is language: in the North, it is English. It is rare to see people from the North using French. In the South, it is French'

(Interview #2).

One of the insiders, the chief of cabinet of a Commissioner, explained:

> I have a list of everyone who speaks working-level Spanish in various places on the Commission. Because if I have to negotiate with them on behalf of Spain, people who speak your language are always going to be more open to the issue, because they like your country or maybe their spouse is a Spaniard …
>
> (Interview #22)

The cultural issue, although always subservient to economic issues, seems to impact in many of the answers. As one of the most senior insiders claimed, 'In the European Union, the 'non-dits', the unspoken issues, are not discussed' (Interview #4). Here, he is referring to a set of taboos or unwritten cultural norms for each country, things that cannot be questioned and are simply taken for granted. Others interpret 'non-dits' as policy issues that are sensitive, almost like the 'property' of each state. For some insiders, there are issues that are 'assigned' to certain states, and everybody understands that those states possess legitimacy on these issues or at the least enjoy greater influence over the decision-making process: 'It is very difficult for something about fishing, for example, to be approved against the will of Spain and Portugal' (Interview #14). For all those interviewed, the main issues for Germany are monetary union and the macroeconomy. Its demographic weight and GDP, along with the euro and Eurozone of predominantly German design and the European Central Bank (ECB) modelled along the principles of the German Bundesbank, all contributed to the leading role of the country during the Eurocrisis.

Particularly interesting was an interview with one of the Council civil servants, who revealed through negation the very existence of the coalitions he denied. When asked whether there are divisions or coalitions between countries in the Council, he clearly stated that such coalitions do not exist, as the Secretariat of the Council works hard to prevent countries from forming historical or geographical alliances. He explained that, for example, there is a meticulous seating order that attempts to avoid seating 'close' countries together an order specifically designed to prevent coalition-building:

> In the Parliament, you sit with your friends. In the Council, the order is based on the order of presidencies; it is designed so that you don't sit with your friends, so that there are no permanent coalitions. We seek consensus to avoid alliances.
>
> (Interview #20)

Discourse 3: The Eurocrisis and the salience of intergovernmentalism

With regard to intergovernmental drift, most of the insiders recognised that such mechanisms have developed outside of the institutional mechanisms of the EU, but the intensity and severity of the drift are in dispute: 'Perhaps it is not growing as much as it seems, but at the least it is not being reduced as it should' (Interview #19). As another insider reports:

> They [the Germans] have usurped the inter-institutional mechanisms and they are drifting towards a intergovernmental decision-making process. Merkel has betrayed the European mechanisms: they take decisions at dinners, in summits, in non-regulated institutions.
>
> (Interview #3)

To others, this intergovernmental drift, though not strictly justifiable, is due to haste or to the need to take quick decisions:

> Yes, there is that drift as a consequence of the crisis. The crisis has quickened the decision-making process. [Decisions] have been taken much more urgently, more in European Council meetings, and in the Council, Germany has the last word.
>
> (Interview #5)

This hastened decision-making process and related mechanisms are seen as bad for the EU:

> All that is decided in the European Council is what the big states decide – Germany, France. We are moving towards a European Union in which these states have more power.
>
> (Interview #8)

However, some insiders minimise this problem:

> any additional mechanism that helps to hasten decision-making is welcome', 'although the haste should be accompanied by legitimacy
>
> (Interview #11)

To others, the problem is not the need for haste but rather the need to create additional institutional mechanisms:

> We had to create mechanisms that don't exist. And to create them outside of the treaties, we had to do it in an intergovernmental way
>
> (Interview #15)

Less critical positions with regard to intergovernmentalism acknowledge the irregularity of these mechanisms but accept them because they are known to be temporary:

> Yes, there is a drift towards more intergovernmentalism. For the time being.
>
> (Interview #18)

> The institutions of the European Union have a strong attraction, a strong gravity. Whatever is created to deal with a problem, ultimately gets adapted to the institutions, one way or another.
>
> (Interview #21)

Discourse 4: Hegemonic Germany

With respect to Germany's leadership, there is virtual unanimity in the recognition of the country's role, but not so much in the evaluation of it as positive or negative, although the balance favours the latter opinion. To many, it is 'totally clear that Germany is imposing its view'; other countries perceive a hegemonic

Germany for which the counterweight of Spain, Italy and France is not effective (Interview #9). One of the insiders went even further: 'Germany is definitely imposing what it wants. We don't even know half of the things it imposes' (Interview #3) For other insiders in the European Parliament, Germany's actions are more attempts than *fait accompli*: 'Yes, I see that Germany is trying to impose its rhythm. Trying' (Interview #11) Similarly, a high-ranking civil servant claimed, 'The real issue is not that Germany is imposing [its views]; the real issue is that there is nobody there to tell Germany not to do so' (Interview #18).

To one Greek civil servant, the German position is highly rational in light of its interests:

> If I were German, I would prefer Merkel as my leader. She does what her citizens want. Merkel is horrid, but for the Germans, she is a wonderful chancellor and she would win by a landslide.
>
> (Interview #18)

Of particular interest is the discourse of a high-ranking civil servant about Germany: 'For better or for worse, Germany has become an overwhelming power. Very little can be decided if Germany is not on board' Notably, he recognises the 'doubtful hegemon' role that Germany is playing. To this insider, Germany is not prepared to lead Europe, as it is a 'provincial-thinking country' (Interview #13) but neither does it want to be led. This provincial mindset of Germany is a relatively simplistic view of the world with a short-term vision of the future; its main objective is to directly promote the German model. In addition, the German view of Europe is that of a collection of countries; if all behave well, things will go smoothly:

> They see the monetary union in particular not as one entity, but rather as a collection of member states. If all these countries were to do the right things and follow the rules, there would be no crisis.
>
> (Interview #13)

Germany also sees itself as very pro-European, and this is true; however, every time integration advances, the Germans stop it because they do not want to share the resulting risks. In the end, Germany is the leader by the absence of any other: 'They are becoming an overwhelming power because the others are becoming less and less influential' (Interview #13) – here, the interviewee is making a direct reference to France. In this evolution towards German hegemony, the Central and Eastern European enlargement has been critical: 'The voice we hear is the voice of Germany, supported by its backyard, the new member states' (Interview #7)

For most of the insiders, Germany's power (beyond the formal power granted to it in the treaties) can be explained through economics, mixed with its strong degree of influence among Eastern and Northern countries: 'The economy, Ignacio, the economy' (Interview #18). To most of the insiders, the German economy, its privileged relationship with Eastern countries, its economic contribution to the European Union, its 'capture' of some of the economic institutions of the EU and the perception that Germany is the country ultimately liable for economic and monetary policies – all of this together is what allows Germany to have its way in macroeconomic and monetary issues.

One of the most interesting discourses about Germany came from one of the most senior insiders interviewed. In his opinion, Germany does not have that kind of power, but the:

> level of pressure it can deploy is obviously not small, [and so it wields] the pressure of the biggest country of the EU; it is located at the centre of the EU together with France, at the very origins of European integration; [it is] an economic powerhouse – and, because of all that, its opinions are much more influential than the opinions of a small country [...].
>
> Lately, Germany has had very clear ideas; it has priorities, positions, red lines. And it has a lot of determination and energy when it has a position: it presents the position, explains it, reacts to other positions clearly, not with velvet gloves. There are other countries that, I'm not sure why, don't have that clarity, that determination, that capacity to develop convincing strategies in the debates. On each issue, Germany has a position. And it expresses that position coherently, from the *Länder*, trade unions, businesses, Parliament, Council … . It is not easy to negotiate with people with such clear, united and persistent positions. When these positions allow the EU to advance, it is fantastic, but when the position is more German than European, it is problematic.
>
> (Interview #21)

Another very interesting discourse came from a Council civil servant:

> Germany has a slow internal decision-making process. They can't be asked for a position early, because they have to make up their mind. They have a slow but highly structured decision-making process, but in the end, they take a position, and when they take it, they usually tip the scale because they act as a whole. This creates the impression that Germany is the country that decides, and so people assume that Germany decides and that carries a lot of weight.
>
> (Interview #10)

The actors in negotiations slowly come to assume that all decisions must take into account Germany's position, and this becomes a self-fulfilling prophecy. During the informal parts of the negotiations between the Commission and the Council or Parliament, it is always considered necessary to check the German opinion; because of this, Germany tends to informally determine many of the decisions taken in the Council.

Discourse 5: The role of informality in EU decision-making

To complete the analysis, there is near unanimity on the vision of the 'informal' EU. For the insiders, the formal rules are not the key to understanding the decision-making process:

> In theory, even the smallest country can veto a decision, but in practice a small country cannot isolate itself like that. The veto works for the big countries.
>
> (Interview #5)

Another example refers to crossed negotiations and the 'reserve of favors'. As one interviewee commented, 'The Italian told us that he was going to support us, but he didn't do it. We have taken note of that' (Interview number #10).

Civil servants' personalities, personal relationships, medium- and long-term agreements, informal mechanisms between countries, language, coincidences, common hobbies and a long list of minor issues can all play important roles in negotiations. Moreover, regular informal meetings may strengthen a common voting pattern, as one interviewee noted: 'There are periodic meetings, mostly of Northern countries. I think they meet to coordinate their positions' (Interview number #10). And, above all, there is a 'consensual culture' in the EU that is especially strong in the Council, as clearly expressed by Council civil servants:

> You want to get what's yours, but there are some general lines: you are a Europeanist country, one that doesn't start big fights, that doesn't hinder the process, [that takes a] constructive approach … . Those are your red lines. Why would you veto? You don't like to veto. You are 'nice'.
>
> (Interview #10)

Conclusions

This research has allowed us to verify the existence of the proposed discourses among EU insiders, albeit with varying levels of support. Some of the discourses are very different from the ones we can see in the media, but we were able to confirm that the insiders use discourses about the North and the South, and about the East as well. They recognise these divisions and talk about taking such divisions into account (and act accordingly, primarily in the Council). We can also say that, for the insiders, these divisions are mostly economic ones; in addition, there are cultural factors, such as language. On the issue of inter-governmentalism, there is also a clear discourse recognising the existence of this drift that wavers between being critical and cautious in its regard with that drift. With respect to Germany, again, there is almost a consensus: many insiders (all of those from the Council, most of those from the Commission and some of the EP insiders) expressed diverse discourses about the power of Germany, employing different theories or expressions, but basically all of them acknowledged the enormous power of Germany on macroeconomic and monetary issues. Finally, there are clear discourses about the importance of the informal mechanisms in the EU. For the insiders, it seems that there is no other way to understand negotiations than by taking into account such mechanisms.

However, if we could choose the most important finding of this research, it would be the recognition of the simplification of the terms of the debate as formulated in public opinion and the media. The discourses of the insiders are much more varied and precise and sometimes differ widely from what we are accustomed to reading in the press.

It is possible that the differences between media discourses and insider discourses is due to the fact that the media focuses on only one specific issue: macroeconomic and monetary policy, an issue featuring a great variety of interpretations and solutions in the North and in the South. This could explain the absolute absence of any discussion of Eastern countries in comparison to the omnipresent Greece. It might also explain why the debate is stereotyped between Northern and Southern public opinions.

But although the insiders' discourses are much less stereotypical than the media's, this does not mean that they do not view Germany as a hegemonic or semi-hegemonic power in the EU. How do they explain this view? Some insiders point to the 2004 enlargement of the EU as a decisive factor in Germany's growing power; it seems that Germany has a special relationship with its 'backyard'. As Naurin (2008) points out, Germany is located at the centre of two branches of countries (the North and the East), while France is at the centre of only one (the South).

A more conclusive, data-driven confirmation of these hypotheses would require research that exceeds the limitations of this qualitative study. However, at the least, we have confirmed and explored the discourses on the cleavages perceived by Southern insiders, as well as the discourses on intergovernmentalism, the weight and power of Germany and the importance of informal mechanisms in the European Union's decision-making processes.

Note

1 Part of this work was supported by the European Science Foundation COST Action IS1004 'WEBDATANET' (webdatanet.eu).

Bibliography

Arregui, J. (2007) 'Modelos de negociación en el proceso legislativo de la Unión Europea,' *Revista Española de Ciencia Política*, 17 October: 83–111.

Arregui, J. and R. Thomson (2009) 'States' bargaining success in the European Union,' *Journal of European Public Policy* 16(5): 655–676.

Arregui, J. and R. Thomson (2014) 'Domestic adjustment costs, interdependence and dissent in the Council of the European Union,' *European Journal of Political Research* 53(4): 692–708.

Bilal, S. and M. O. Hosli (1999) 'Connected Coalition Formation and Voting Power in the Council of the European Union: An Endogenous Policy Approach,' European Institute of Public Administration (EIPA) Working Paper, no. 99.

Dizard, J. (2008) 'Betting on the possibility of breaking up the eurozone,' *Financial Times*, 1 July. Online. Available at: www.ft.com/intl/cms/s/0/68e62338-4707-11dd-876a-0000779fd2ac.html#axzz3VVa7sJWw (accessed 26 March 2015].

Elgström, O., B. Bjurulf, J. Johansson and A. Sannerstedt (2001) 'Coalitions in European Union negotiations,' *Scandinavian Political Studies* 24(2): 111–128.

Esping-Andersen, G. (1990) *The Three Worlds of Welfare Capitalism.* Cambridge: Polity Press.

Financial Times, (2008) 'Pigs in muck,' *Financial Times*, 1 September. Online. Available at: http://web.archive.org/web/20080905133210/http://www.ft.com/cms/s/1/388a3e90-77bd-11dd-be24-0000779fd18c.html (accessed 26 March 2014).

Hardacre, A. (2011) *How the EU institutions Work and How to Work with the EU Institutions.* London: John Harper Publishing.

Heidar, K. (2003) 'Parties and Cleavages in the European Political Space,' ARENA Working Paper 03/7, ARENA seminar. Oslo, 18 February.

Heisenberg, D. (2008) 'How should we best study the Council of Ministers?' in D. Naurin and H. Wallace (eds) *Unveiling the Council of the European Union.* Basingstoke: Palgrave Macmillan, pp. 261–276.

Helbling, M., D. Hoeglinger and B. Wüest (2010) 'How political parties frame European integration'. *European Journal of Political Research* 49(4): 495–521.

Hix, S. (1999) 'Dimensions and alignments in European Union politics: Cognitive constraints and partisan responses,' *European Journal of Political Research* 35(1): 69–106.

Hix, S. (2008) *What's wrong with the European Union and How to Fix it.* Cambridge and Malden, MA: Polity Press.

Hix, S. and B. K. R. Høyland (2011) *The Political System of the European Union.* Basingstoke: Palgrave Macmillan.

Hooghe, L. and G. Marks (1997) 'Making of a Polity: The Struggle over European Integration,' European Community Studies Association Meeting, Seattle.

Hooghe, L., G. Marks and C. J. Wilson (2002) 'Does Left/Right structure party positions on European integration?,' *Comparative Political Studies* 35(8): 965–989.

Hosli, M. O. (2008) 'Coalition-Formation, Cleavages and Voting Behavior in the Council of the European Union,' paper presented at the CONNEX Final Conference, Mannheim, 6–8 March. Available at: www.mzes.uni-mannheim.de/projekte/typo3/site/fileadmin/Final_Conference/papers/Hosli%20Paper.pdfhttps://0-scholar.google.com.libra.naz.edu/citations?hl=ro&user=qEWKAFYAAAAJ&view_op=list_works&sortby=title (accessed 3 November 2015).

Hosli, M. O., M. Mattila and M. Uriot (2011) 'Voting behavior in the Council of the European Union after the 2004 Enlargement, *Journal of Common Market Studies* 49(6): 1249–1270.

Kaeding, M. and T. J. Selck (2005) 'Mapping out political Europe: Coalition patterns in EU decision-making,' *International Political Science Review/Revue internationale de science politique* 26(3): 271–290.

Lipset, S. and S. Rokkan (1967) 'Cleavage Structures, Party Systems, and Voter Alignments: An Introduction,' in *Party Systems and Voter Alignments.* New York: Free Press, pp. 1–64.

Mair, P. (2000) 'The limited impact of Europe on national party systems,' *West European Politics* 23(4): 27–51.

Naurin, D. and R. Lindahl (2008) 'East-North-South: Coalition-Building in the Council before and after Enlargement,' in D. Naurin and H. Wallace (eds) *Unveiling the Council of the European Union.* Basingstoke: Palgrave Macmillan, pp. 64–78.

Naurin, D. and H. Wallace (2008) *Unveiling the Council of the European Union: Games Governments Play in Brussels.* Basingstoke and New York: Palgrave Macmillan.

Parízek, M. (2012) 'After the Enlargement: Trends and threats in the European Union decision-making,' *Perspectives: Central European Review of International Affairs* 20: 33–58.

Plechanovová, B. (2011a) 'The EU Council enlarged: North–South–East or core–periphery?,' *European Union Politics* 12(1): 87–106.

Plechanovová, B. (2011b) 'Coalitions in the EU Council: Pitfalls of multidimensional analysis', *AUCO Czech Economic Review* 5(3): 249–266.

Riker, W. H. (1962) *The Theory of Political Coalition.* New Haven, CT: Yale University Press.

Rokkan, S., P. Flora, S. Kuhnle and D. W. Urwin (1999) *State Formation, Nation-building, and Mass Politics in Europe: The Theory of Stein Rokkan, Based on his Collected Works.* Oxford and New York: Oxford University Press.

The Economist (2008) A decade in the sun, *The Economist*, 5 June. Online. Available at: www.economist.com/node/11487440 (accessed 26 March 2014).

The Economist (2010) 'The PIIGS that won't fly,' *The Economist*, 18 May. Online. Available at: www.economist.com/node/15838029.

The Economist (2011) 'Grounded PIIGS,' *The Economist*, 4 June. Online. Available at: www.economist.com/blogs/dailychart/2011/01/gdp_forecasts.

Thomson, R. (2009) 'Actor alignments in the European Union before and after enlargement,' *European Journal of Political Research* 48(6): 756–781.

Thomson, R. (2011) *Resolving Controversy in the European Union: Legislative Decision-making Before and After Enlargement.* Cambridge and New York: Cambridge University Press.

Thomson, R., J. Arregui, D. Leuffen, R. Costello, J. Cross, R. Hertz and T. Jensen (2012) 'A new dataset on decision-making in the European Union before and after the 2004 and 2007 enlargements (DEUII),' *Journal of European Public Policy* 19(4): 604–622.

Thomson, R. and M. O. Hosli (2006) 'Who has power in the EU? The Commision, Council and Parliament in legislative decision-making,' *JCMS: Journal of Common Market Studies* 44(2): 391–417.

Tsebelis, G. and G. Garrett (2000) 'Legislative politics in the European Union,' *European Union Politics* 1(1): 9–36.

Weber, M. (2001) *The Protestant Ethic and the Spirit of Capitalism.* London and New York: Routledge.

Zimmer, C., G. Schneider and M. Dobbins (2005) 'The contested Council: Conflict dimensions of an intergovernmental EU institution,' *Political Studies* 53(2): 403–422.

List of interviews

#1. Member of European Parliament, Congress of Deputies. Madrid, 17 December 2012
#2. Member of COREPER, Council of the EU. Madrid, 26 December 2012
#3. Member of European Parliament, Madrid. 18 January 2013
#4. Ex-President of the European Commision. Madrid, 6 March 2013
#5. Ex-Secretary of State for the European Union, Congress of Deputies. Madrid, 6 March 2013
#6. Member of the European Parliament. Madrid, 15 March 2013
#7. Chief of Cabinet, European Parliament Berlaymont Building. Brussels, 16 May 2013
#8. Member of COREPER, Council of the European Union. Brussels, 22 May 2013
#9. Member of COREPER, Council of the European Union. Brussels, 6 June 2013
#10. Member of the COREPER, Council of the European Union. 6 June 2013
#11. Member of the European Parliament. Brussels, 6 June 2013
#12. Member of the European Parliament. Strasbourg, 12 June 2013

#13. Head of Directorate General, Council of the European Union. Brussels, 18 June 2013
#14. Member of General Secretariat, Council of the European Union. Brussels, 18 June 2013
#15. Member of the European Parliament. Brussels, 19 June 2013
#16. Member of the European Parliament. Brussels, 19 June 2013
#17. National Delegation Coordinator at European Parliament. Brussels, 20 June 2013
#18. High-ranking official of the General Secretariat of the Council of the EU. Brussels, 24 June 2013
#19. Member of European Parliament, Brussels. 26 June 2013
#20. Legal adviser of the Council of the European Union. Brussels, 1 July 2013
#21. European Commissioner. Brussels, 15 July 2013
#22. Chief of Cabinet, European Commission. Brussels, 25 July 2013

8 The increasing core–periphery divide and new member states

Diverging from the European Union's mainstream developments

Attila Ágh

Introduction: the increasing core–periphery divide and the current transformation crisis

There have recently been three markedly different periods of crisis in the EU: the 'immobility crisis' in the 2000s, the global crisis beginning in the late 2000s, and the 'transformation crisis' of the mid-2010s. *First*, the immobility crisis in the decade of disorder at the start of the new millennium arose from the asymmetrical nature of EU developments: the EU was advancing in some fields but was not ready to move further in other, closely interrelated fields. The establishment of the Eurozone is a case in point. *Second*, in the period of global crisis, there was a painful priority placed on direct crisis management. This crisis marginalised all other important EU problems, concentrating efforts on the saving the euro and maintaining the competitiveness of the EU core in a turbulent world. The selected method of crisis management meant that the EU had to pay a high price for the 'systemic misfit' in the Union resulting from the increasing core–periphery divide. *Third*, in the present transformation crisis, the EU must attempt to 'harmonise' its changing institutions and policies. This creative crisis has been facilitated by the substantial five-year change in EU institutions. The inauguration of the Juncker European Commission administration offers the possibility for a new start in attempts to reform the European architecture.[1]

The types of differentiated integration (DI) observable in these three periods have also been crucially different. Already in the first period, the lack of coherence between institutions and policies led to excessive fragmentation in the 2000s. This was further deepened in the second period of crisis management through 'economic nationalisms' and the increasing core–periphery divide within the Eurozone. The new member states (NMS) also had their own historical trajectory in DI, as the particular DI developments in NMS resulted in both domestic resistance against EU innovations and in the negative externalities or negative spill-overs within the EU. Overall, the core–periphery divide increased tremendously in the second period; in this paper, this will be discussed from the perspective of NMS divergence from mainstream EU developments. Now, in the third period, this increasing divide must be halted by the Juncker administration through institutional reforms elaborating both common EU regulations and the particular

DI spaces for individual member states in order to cope with divergence under the pressures of ongoing globalisation and promote flexible integration.[2]

There has been a sizable literature on DI, after the pioneering work of Dyson and Sepos (2010), the recent comprehensive works have both completely covered the history of the topic (see Tekin, 2012) and provided an overview of its horizontal and vertical integration structures (see Leuffen et al., 2013). The current research has analysed all three DI dimensions: first, 'differentiation of areas of political action (policy dimension)'; second, 'differentiation processes and decision-making within the EU (politics dimension)'; and, third, 'differentiation of the institutional and constitutional architecture of the EU (polity dimension)' (Diedrichs et al., 2011: 13). Moreover, with regard to the current situation, Nicolai Ondarza (2013) has issued serious warnings about the 'pitfalls' of DI potentially 'splitting' Europe even more drastically into centre and periphery. These works offer a good point of departure for the DI research; however, as this chapter tries to point out, the field has developed a Western bias and the research is based on a flawed concept of DI as politically 'neutral'. Consequently, a conceptual innovation is needed to provide a proper analysis of the special case of DI in the NMS.

Western bias as a conceptual trap in discussing DI in NMS

The sizable and impressive international DI literature has dealt almost exclusively with the problems of old member states (OMS). Paradoxically, although there have been many references in the mainstream literature to the drastic changes in DI following the 'Big Bang'-type Eastern enlargement, the particular character of DI in the NMS still remains under-researched. This DI literature has mostly discussed the impact of the enlargement on the OMS rather than the special DI developments in the NMS. The main conceptual issue is that from the very beginning, DI has been considered only as a vehicle for dealing with the neutral heterogeneity in the EU in the 'policy' dimension of socio-economic processes. Its 'political' dimension (the transnational decision-making process) in relation to the NMS has been rarely discussed. Finally, its 'polity' dimension – the democratic system of institutions in the member states as the embodiment of European values – has been completely neglected. Thus, DI has been reduced to the process of facilitating socio-economic development (the 'catching-up process') by other policy means. Consequently, the whole DI debate has been restricted to 'technical' aspects, side-lining the politics and polity dimensions. Overall, of the three dimensions of DI, the policy dimension has been comprehensively analysed, and the politics dimension (transnational decision-making) has been studied to some extent, but the polity dimension (the basic values of EU democracy) has been largely neglected, even though this aspect was crucial in both the South and the East. Generally speaking, it has been assumed that DI would not hurt European values as the structure of the democratic European polity.[3]

The EU has always been an organisation characterised by 'unity in diversity', but the differentiation across its membership has become more marked with expansion. With regard to polity DI, the Rome Treaty actually stipulates that only *democratic* European states can be members of the EU. Naturally, within European democracy, there can be various national models; this variety can be considered *positive* divergence. Before the Eastern enlargement, the EU stipulated in the Copenhagen criteria that a democratic polity was a precondition for accession. However, it was also evident that the NMS countries would become democratic and would stay democratic after their accession. The issue of *negative* divergence from the democratic polity has been raised very belatedly, although both the eastern and – much earlier – some southern states deserved closer examination. The EU has acted in a very restricted fashion when tackling polity, over-respecting the sovereignty of member states. In fact, all member states have supported this low-profile approach, since all of them prefer to avoid making precedents of interfering in the internal affairs of other member states. Nevertheless, negative divergence occurred long before the global crisis, and there was no EU reaction. Moreover, due to the global crisis, democracy backsliding has become a widespread phenomenon in some member states, resulting in an increasing democracy gap within the EU. Finally, the European Parliament (EP) as the guardian of democracy has announced that the regular violation of democratic European values is dangerous for the EU; the EP has realised that the EU will pay a high price for neglecting the negative divergence in NMS by over-respecting the principle of non-interference. In some cases, the EP has begun to act against the negative divergence related to democratic backsliding, although only with limited success thus far.[4]

The Copenhagen criteria stipulate not only the democratic polity but also the 'competitive policy', prescribing the capacity of member states to withstand the competitive pressure within the EU. However, the policy of DI has still been necessary in terms of socio-economic development because of the (growing) heterogeneity of the EU. In this policy aspect, however, there is a choice between *progressive* divergence, the creative capacity of DI for alternative developments, and *regressive* divergence, a lack of accommodation to changing external conditions.

The clear case for progressive divergence is the deepening of social dimension of the European integration in the Nordic states (enhanced interest representation and consultation, increasing investment in human and social capital and growing transparency of public affairs) and for regressive divergence its opposite trend in the NMS. Even progressive divergence, as a policy instrument intended to facilitate catching up with the mainstream in an optimal way, has generated many problems and complications in the cooperation of the EU member states.

Nonetheless, in the final analysis, progressive divergence can also be helpful for the EU's common future, since through its transitory stages and forms, it may lead to a more convergent EU. In contrast, regressive divergence entails refusing or avoiding the necessary policy adaptation to the EU and/or to changing external conditions. Such non-compliance with policy-orientated membership rules can result in socio-economic backsliding, with an increasing competitiveness gap.

At the same time, regressive divergence is a serious violation of the EU's competitive model as the mainstream policy, and thus it is also harmful for the effective polity and politics of DI. Obviously, the three types of DI divergence are closely interrelated. Their closest meeting point is at the elaboration, execution and monitoring of the *strategic direction* of socio-economic and political developments in the member states. It is easy to demonstrate that negative polity divergence produces regressive policy divergence, and vice versa. In fact, they are different sides of the same coin. The 'non-democratic' and 'non-competitive' member states are not just lagging behind quantitatively but also backsliding qualitatively to a 'low-performing' development trajectory. Thus, in the spirit of the Copenhagen criteria, the high-performing strong democracies and the low-performing weak democracies can be contrasted. In many cases, the Commission as the *Guardian of Treaties* has acted against regressive divergence where direct rules exist, but it cannot go beyond this narrow understanding of *acquis* because the strategic direction of socio-economic development has mostly remained in the competences of the member states.

Finally, negative and regressive DI has produced a weakened 'political' voice on the part of the NMS countries in EU transnational decision-making bodies, resulting in marginalised participation in political DI. The EU28 is much more than a 'multi-speed' Europe; it is already a 'multi-floor' Europe, since the different member states' positions have been institutionalised (i.e. rather strictly arranged and regulated in legal terms). Within the EU's operating system, there are in fact 'four floors' or institutionalised membership positions with different decision-making potentials in EU transnational bodies. Therefore, it is not sufficient to merely refer to the deep divide between the core and periphery in general; rather, it is necessary to specify these positions as Core-1, Core-2, Periphery-1 and Periphery-2. Above all, the core has two meanings. First, the developed and dynamic part of the EU (Core-1: 'West-Continental') features the *fully effective membership* of Eurozone members with deep integration and full decision-making capacity. There is a DI-related meaning of the core, referring to the second group of countries that have followed (almost) all common EU policies except for Eurozone membership (Core-2: 'Nordic EU'). This has resulted in *partly effective membership*, given the shallow integration of these countries in 'political' DI: they do not take part in the vital decision-making process in the Eurozone. This situation can be expressed as 'the political status of Euro opt-outs', because nowadays such participation has become even more important due to the further institutionalisation of the Eurozone.

However, in the political DI it is also important to distinguish between the southern and the eastern periphery. In the present situation, the 'South' can be defined as the Periphery-1, with *partly marginal membership*; these countries are Eurozone members at the legal level but have limited weight in actual EU decision-making processes. The 'East' (Periphery-2) group of new member states has *fully marginal membership*: even though some of them are Eurozone members, none of them – despite the growing influence of Poland – number among the real decision-makers (see Vida, 2010). As a result of the global crisis, there has been increasing differentiation between both Core-1 and Core-2 and between Periphery-1 (South) and Periphery-2 (East). In fact, the South has dropped out of Core-1; its formal inclusion was mostly a pseudo-convergence that has evolved from an asset into a liability for the Core-1 due to the serious burden of the huge sovereign debts of these nations. The NMS region of the Periphery-2 (East) has also declined in many ways, but its further socio-economic peripherialisation remains a forgotten crisis, a problem that has long gone relatively unnoticed in the EU. The decline of the Periphery-1 is much more dangerous for the Core-1, given that the South has been much more involved in the asymmetrical Eurozone integration; thus, for the Core-1, much more is at stake in the South than in the East.

In my understanding, this triple approach to DI explains the present situation in the EU28 better than the conventional DI analysis. This common divergence in NMS generates a vicious circle of backsliding democracies within the EU that could first be observed in the South and later in the East. Although this DI in NMS existed even before the global crisis, it has been very much intensified by the event. The triple approach makes it clear that basic divergence even in one country would hurt the EU as a whole. Thus, this approach is important in the evaluation of the case of NMS, in which pseudo-convergence has in fact generated a profound divergence from mainstream EU developments that can be described through its common features in the NMS.[5]

National resistance and negative externalities: the double evil in the NMS

In fact, in the DI analyses, both the negative externalities of the EU in general and the national resistance to the EU rules on the part of the weaker member states in particular have been largely neglected. The conventional wisdom was that Eurozone integration would force the less productive member states to undertake the structural reforms necessary to modernise their economies. Contrary to these previous assumptions, the new finding is that these modernising effects have appeared not in the South but in the North (see, e.g., Fernández-Villaverde et al., 2013). As to the negative externalities, the usual analyses in the core countries have not targeted the real issues in the case of the East, either. The East has become a special periphery of the Core-1, since it has been closely integrated into the core countries by means of its production structures. This situation, despite its strong modernising effects, has also unleashed dependent development with negative processes, as these NMS countries have become internally deeply divided between their modernised and declining sides. As Rupnik and Zielonka have noted (2013: 7), 'There are two Polands as there are two Hungaries.' Thus, domestic social cohesion has become the crucial issue in NMS: the problem is not only to become united with the EU, but also for the given country to become united as a whole. It comes as no surprise that these negative externalities have also resulted in national resistance and widespread disappointment in NMS, although the main reasons for this resistance have been domestic – 'Eastern-type' path dependence combined with the new reform fatigue.

Thus, the main problem of 'neutral heterogeneity' mentioned above returns with a vengeance in the case of NMS: from the very beginning of their membership, DI has been considered by the EU only as the legal-technical instrument for dealing with policy heterogeneity in the EU, not seriously taking into account European values ('polity' as democracy dimension). The EU mistakenly believed that in the case of NMS, their DI would not hurt European values in the democratic European polity. Originally, the Road Map of NMS was conceived only in terms of catching up with the average GDP in the EU. Even official EU progress reports were conceptualised and documented in terms of this GDP-based catching-up process; in the late 2000s, 'Going beyond GDP' ranked very high on the agenda in the EU. This type of 'quantitative' catching-up process was also a basic precondition of Cohesive Europe as an elementary aspect of the 'Convergence Machine'; however, without 'qualitative' catching-up based on sustainable social progress, it proved to be vastly insufficient, even before the onset of the global crisis. At present, all indicators have shown that the divergence in NMS appeared first in the new qualitative EU2020 terms; this has been the main reason for their competitive backsliding under the pressure of the global crisis (WEF, 2012, 2014). The divergence of the NMS region from mainstream EU developments has resulted in a decline in all aspects of democracy, governance and sustainability as a complex deficit, ultimately leading to a blind alley in global competitiveness. The main lesson from these painful NMS developments is that 'history does not move in straight lines' and that cycles of progress may be succeeded by cycles of decline. Obviously, due to the global crisis, the reverse wave in democratisation has become the new global trend, with setbacks evident in many countries (Demos, 2013; EIU, 2014). However, the East has exhibited a more serious decline in democracy than the South, with its backsliding process culminating in the mid-2010s. These democracy, governance and sustainability deficits have generated a deeper core-periphery divide between the Core-1 and the Periphery-2 than ever before.

The growing divergence of NMS provoked by the global crisis has in some ways reproduced the pre-accession situation for the NMS at a higher level. They are already members in the EU formally/legally; however, with regard to real, competitive-effective membership, their membership is still just 'partial'. Eurozone and Schengen memberships are mandatory for all NMS, but only after certain internal conditionalities have been met. This implies that the Eastern enlargement was not a full accession, but rather only a partial one that must be completed later through certain policy memberships. In fact, nowadays, all NMS have to 'enter' the EU again in terms of the triple membership – polity, politics and policy – under more difficult conditionalities than was originally the case. At present, a substantial revision of this construct is ongoing under the name of 'Copenhagen Revisited'. In the usual EU adjustment process, the NMS countries had to embrace at least minimal EU *compatibility* to qualify for formal-legal membership. The alternatives for them are either to remain at this minimal level of *formal membership* with low performance and weak competitiveness or to strive for the maximal level of *effective membership* with high performance and strong competitiveness within the EU. However, after a decade of membership, it is clear that the NMS countries are not yet competitive in the EU, as they have been either unable or unwilling to complete the Europeanization project by following and implementing all EU-level regulations for full membership. Instead, they have produced reduced, formal-legal, low-performing democracies with poor governance and non-sustainable social progress. Overall, after ten years, they still exhibit a 'thin', low-profile Europeanisation and democratisation in triple DI terms. In general, the declining NMS democracies feature weak party systems, fragile governments and increasing oligarchisation and corruption in polity terms. They have not yet achieved high-performing democracies in policy terms or effective EU membership in politics terms – in other words, they have not achieved genuine Europeanisation.

EU documents have been largely based on evolutionary ideas about (quicker or slower, but basically positive) converging development in NMS. The negative diverging process in NMS has not been dealt with seriously thus far by the EU leadership or by the experts, and therefore it has not been properly addressed. Nevertheless, apart from any delay in the proper adjustment process, in the real world there have been clear signs of distorted Europeanisation – divergences that may be termed de-Europeanisation and de-democratisation as the 'state capture' (Innes, 2014) in the backsliding, 'captured' or guided democracies (Sedelmeier, 2014). By neglecting or at least marginalising the negative-regressive divergences in NMS, and by concentrating exclusively on the short-term tasks of the Core-1 (or at most those of the Periphery-1), the long-term perspectives of the EU28 may become lost or distorted. Consequently, a strict distinction must be made between narrow, legally enforced EU adjustments and broad, social progress-based Europeanisation. These 'thin' and 'thick' types of Europeanisation can also be called 'facade Europeanisation' and 'substantial Europeanisation'. This distinction appears at the EU level between the formally/legally united Fragmented Europe and the substantially/socially united Cohesive Europe. Altogether, the further developments in NMS – with its alternative positive or negative reinforcing processes, its virtuous or vicious circles – could lead either to processes of catching-up or to peripherialisation. Only extended integrative balancing meeting the requirements of the triple approach (polity, politics and policy) can provide a remedy to the backsliding of democracy and competitiveness in NMS.

Conclusion and discussion: the need for a new start for NMS within the EU

The recent transformation crisis demands a progressive redefinition of the EU in response to the global pressure in all three DI dimensions: first, polity-wise, by reforming the European architecture on the basis of the 'quality of democracy'; second, politics-wise, by facilitating all member states' effective participation in EU transnational decision-making processes; and third, policy-wise, by dynamically extending the EU policy universe based on a long-term EU2020-type development strategy. The present decade will be a tough stress test for the EU with regard to intellectual learning and social innovation. In brief, the global crisis raised the choice between More Europe (integration) and Less Europe (fragmentation) – either re-establishing integrative balancing within the EU by moving forward to create harmonisation at a higher level or dismantling the latest achievements to restore balance at a much lower level. The true believers in Less Europe argue for simple coordination rather than integration and/or for the renationalisation of policies instead of their communitarisation. However, due to the neglect of the growing gap between the centre and the periphery, nowadays even the More Europe tendency still faces the dilemma of the divergence between the more competitive Core Europe with its thriving 'North–West' and the less competitive Cohesive Europe with its declining 'South–East'. Certainly, the core–periphery divide will grow further if the two evils of negative externalities and national resistance – a fatal deviation from EU mainstream developments – are not remedied in the near future in the East and South. Although DI must be maintained, it should be re-regulated in all three dimensions, and the proper control mechanisms must be set into motion to prevent serious divergences.[6]

In its present situation, the EU faces an alternative between More Europe and Less Europe in the form of the Cohesive-Integrated Europe and Fragmented-Disintegrated Europe scenarios. This alternative appears in all three DI dimensions as a division between more and less democratic polities, effective or limited participation and high or low competitive performance of member states as these gaps close or widen in the EU. In the final analysis, the EU28 has proven to be a Multi-Floor Europe in which the 'common denominator' must be redefined in the polity, politics and policy dimensions. If it is reduced to a minimum, then the EU28 will be fragmented and may ultimately fail: the current dangerous fragmentation processes will be accelerated and will produce new kinds of deep division in the EU28 due to deeply diverging sectorial and/or regional integrations of member states structured along the core-periphery divide. In the present unresolved situation, there is still a risk that the EU may produce strict regulations for some well-defined policy fields (first and foremost in the Single Market) but leave their wider policy linkages and basic social indicators unregulated or unbalanced, not only policy-wise but also in terms of both polity and politics.

The recent discussions about the priorities of the incoming Juncker presidency by the leading policy institutes – among them, the European Policy Centre (EPC, 2014a, b) and the Centre for European Policy Studies (CEPS, 2014a, b) – have emphasised that DI has been important but it must be limited to ensure the convergence of the EU28 and to guarantee that some kind of Competitive-Cohesive Europe emerges. The New Pact project organised by the EPC clearly states that 'An increasingly multi-speed approach seems likely, but a permanent 'multi-tier Europe' must be avoided' (EPC, 2014a: xi). In the same spirit, in discussing 'increasing differentiation', the CEPS team has stressed that 'The proliferation of 'opt-outs' from the treaties, enhanced cooperation and agreements between some members outside the EU legal framework are raising questions on where the boundaries of differentiated integration lie in an organization based on a unique legal order with common institutions and common principles' (CEPS, 2014a: 16).

The present DI model of 'diversity management' has proven to be a failure in NMS due to its neglect of their violations of the rules for democratic polities and competitive policies. It has been unable to facilitate convergence or to mitigate the core–periphery divide in the EU. In the final analysis, the NMS countries have been unable to achieve sustainable social progress; quite to the contrary, their historical trajectory in the EU has proven to be unsustainable and the global crisis has drastically aggravated their position. Although significant progress has been made in NMS in many policy fields, the setbacks have still dominated – not only with regard to volatile 'quantitative' development in GDP terms but above all in 'qualitative' development in terms of the quality of democracy and effective membership. In fact, this widening qualitative gap has also been the main reason behind their volatile quantitative catching-up process since these qualitative factors have been both the substantial institutional frameworks and the main drivers for the new type of economic growth (see IMF, 2014).

Generally speaking, it turns out that the NMS have been lagging behind in the new, more sophisticated terms of human investment, good governance and social progress – that is, in the complex indicators of social capital and well-being. This ever-increasing gap appeared first between their 'old-fashioned' socio-economic development and the 'new-fangled' demands for development in terms of well-being involving modern human and social services (see both the *Sixth Cohesion Report* (EC 2014b) and the *Member States' Competitiveness Report* (EC 2014c)). Their divergence can also be described as a return to the past, reviving anti-democratic traditions, sluggish socio-economic performance and marginal positions in the European arena. Thus far, the NMS have been unable to generate the proper extended reproduction of their society with its various functions to achieve the level of sustainability in social progress. On the contrary, they have downgraded themselves in a vicious circle to the reduced reproduction of society through serious cuts in education, health care and R&D – in fact, by divesting in human and social capital and undercutting the future. They must therefore launch a new Europeanisation programme, opening themselves to this new type of European development in order to ensure 'More Europe at Home'. They cannot continue even the simplest catching-up process without overcoming the democracy, good governance and sustainability deficits on their own; this would represent their proper 're-entry' into the EU.

In the second half of the 2000s, the first reports on NMS were positive and optimistic, but by the mid-2010s they turned more negative and pessimistic. The two special issues on 'ten years of membership' represent the turning point in the NMS literature from the convergence model towards the divergence model. Both volumes have described the polity, politics and policy dimensions, but they have emphasised this negative historical turning point first and foremost in polity terms as the 'de-democratisation' of NMS: 'Today the focus of political and academic debates is no longer on democratic transition or consolidation but on the quality of democracy' (Rupnik and Zielonka, 2013: 11). Due to the declining democracy in NMS, the East–West gap in the EU has not disappeared but has instead been reinforced after ten years of membership:

> Notable achievements of EU enlargements notwithstanding, the volume points to the continuing important differences between east and west and highlights the issue areas in which the EU transcends but also reinforces the centuries-old partition.
>
> (Epstein and Jacoby, 2014: 1)

Academics have thus 'refuted the kind of optimistic determinism, suggesting that the collapse of communism and the victory of Western liberalism would make a swift convergence between the east and west of Europe the most natural development' (Rupnik and Zielonka, 2013: 19).

Consequently, the optimistic and evolutionary approach of democratization and Europeanisation as an evolutionary catching-up model cannot be applied to the recent developments in NMS. In addition, the short and formalistic Copenhagen criteria for accession cannot be considered sufficient for the evaluation of the quarter-century developments in NMS, since the states have not fulfilled their developmental role during this period. As Rupnik and Zielonka have noted (2013: 16), in NMS '[t]he state becomes weak, unfair and volatile when partisan interests prevail over common good.'

This conclusion leads also to the identification of a task for the EU: to push the NMS countries more energetically towards convergence with mainstream European developments. In the extreme case, as it has often been stated in the current literature, 'if major institutions of liberal democracy in one member state radically deviate from the EU's member states' constitutional traditions, and undermine the rule of law, this is an issue that the EU needs to address directly' (Bugaric, 2014: 25). The competitiveness of the core can only be a pyrrhic victory for the EU, since the primary slogan of the Juncker administration – 'to set the EU into motion' – also seeks to unite the EU28 into a cohesive and convergent Europe.

Notes

1 This paper relies on the recent mainstream DI literature, but I focus here on the centre-periphery divide from the side of the NMS. The paper can only elaborate the conceptual framework of the NMS divergence, since there is no space for the detailed analysis I have presented in my previous papers (Ágh, 2012, 2013a, b and 2014, 2015). First, I elaborate this conceptual framework in contrast to the Western-centric views; I then attempt to present an overview of the common problems of the NMS. I have described the complex data of the international ranking institutions at length in my Progress Report (Ágh, 2013a) to show the governance, democracy and sustainability deficits in NMS.

2 The financial-economic crisis has developed into a deep political and social crisis in NMS, with all countries exhibiting similar negative trends (see the two edited volumes on the ten years of NMS – Epstein and Jacoby, 2014, and Rupnik and Zielonka, 2013 – or the data of the ranking institutions, especially WEF, 2012, 2014). At the start of the Juncker administration, there have also been many interesting discussions on DI, including those issued by the important policy institutes (EPC and CEPS), which will be addressed in this paper.

3 In this paper, to save space, I concentrate on the polity (negative) DI and policy (regressive) DI, but I also discuss the politics (marginalising) DI in Multi-Level Europe.

4 For instance, the EP has dealt with NMS divergence in the Tavares Report (July 2013) and the Commission in the Rule of Law Initiative (March 2014). It remains to be seen how energetically the Juncker administration will continue along these lines.
5 Obviously, the NMS countries differ widely in terms of their EU integration strategies, and their integration efforts can also change over time. Nowadays, the more pro-integration countries like Poland and Slovakia have been somewhat more 'convergent' with the EU, consolidating their position in the organisation, while certain others like Hungary and the Czech Republic have joined the 'Europe of nations' group. Hungary can be seen as the worst-case scenario, but there is no space here to discuss individual country cases.
6 The June 2014 Conclusions of the European Council (2014: 11) have confirmed the necessity of DI: 'the European Council noted that the concept of ever closer union allows for different paths of integration for different countries, allowing those that want to deepen integration to move ahead, while respecting the wish of those who do not want to deepen any further.' But, as Piris (2014: 5) notes, 'there is a tension between differentiation, unity and coherence. This is why there must be limits to differentiation'.

References

Ágh, Attila (2012) 'The Hungarian Rhapsodies: The Conflict of Adventurism and Professionalism in the European Union Presidency,' *Journal of Common Market Studies*, The JCMS Annual Review of the European Union 2011, 50(S2): 68–75.
Ágh, Attila (2013a) *Progress Report on the New Member States: Twenty Years of Social and Political Developments*. Budapest: Together for Europe Research Centre,
Ágh, Attila (2013b) 'The Triple Crisis in Hungary: The "Backsliding" of Hungarian Democracy after Twenty Years,' *Romanian Journal of Political Science* 13(1): 25–51.
Ágh, Attila (2014) 'Decline of Democracy in East-Central Europe: The Last Decade as the Lost Decade in Democratization,' *Journal of Comparative Politics* 7(2): 4–33.
Ágh, Attila (2015) 'The Fall of the Berlin Wall and European Politics: Perspectives of New Europe in the Early Twenty-first Century,' in José Magone (ed.) *Routledge Handbook of European Politics*. London: Routledge, pp. 116–131.
Bugaric, Bojan (2014) 'Protecting Democracy and the Rule of Law in the European Union: The Hungarian Challenge,' London School of Economics (LSE) 'Europe in Question' Paper Series, no. 79, July. Available at: www.lse.ac.uk/europeanInstitute/LEQS/LEQSPaper79.pdf.
Centre for European Policy Studies (CEPS) (2014a) Shifting EU Institutional Reform into High Gear: Report of the CEPS High Level Group, CEPS, Brussels. Available at: http://ceps.eu/book/shifting-eu-institutional-reform-high-gear-report-ceps-high-level-group (accessed 6 January 2016).
Centre for European Policy Studies (CEPS) (1014b) Priorities for the Juncker Commission, CEPS Special Report no. 92, October. Available at: www.ceps.eu/book/priorities-juncker-commission-policy-recommendations-and-advice (accessed 6 January 2016).
Demos (2013) 'Backsliders: Measuring Democracy in the EU'. Available at: www.demos.co.uk/publications/backsliders (accessed 6 January 2016).
Diedrichs, Udo, Anne Faber, Funda Tekin and Gaby Umbach (2011) 'Europe Reloaded: Differentiation or Fusion?,' in Udo Diedrichs, Anne Faber, Funda Tekin and Gaby Umbach (eds) (2011) *Europe Reloaded: Differentiation or Fusion?* Baden-Baden: Nomos, pp. 11–19.
Diedrichs, Udo, Anne Faber, Funda Tekin and Gaby Umbach (eds) (2011) *Europe Reloaded: Differentiation or Fusion?*. Baden-Baden: Nomos.

Dyson, Kenneth and Angelos Sepos (eds) (2010) *Which Europe? The Politics of Differentiated Integration*. London: Palgrave Macmillan.

Economist Intelligence Unit (EUI) (2014) 'What's Gone Wrong with Democracy and How to Revive it,' 1 March. Available at: www.economist.com/news/essays/21596796-democracy-was-most-successful-political-idea-20th-century-why-has-it-run-trouble-and-what-can-be-do (accessed 6 January 2016).

Emmanouilidis, Janis (2014a) 'The Beginning of a New Political Cycle: The Results and Consequences of a Nomination Summit,' Post-Summit Analysis, European Policy Centre (EPC), 30 June. Available at: www.epc.eu/documents/uploads/pub_4594_psa_-_30_june_2014.pdf (accessed 6 January 2016).

Emmanouilidis, Janis (2014b) 'Low Key But Not Low Impact: The Results of the EU's "Transition" Summit', Post-Summit Analysis, European Policy Centre (EPC), 27 October. Available at: www.epc.eu/documents/uploads/pub_4935_post-summit_analysis_-_27_october_2014.pdf (accessed 6 January 2016).

Epstein, Rachel and Wade Jacoby (2014) 'Eastern Enlargement Ten Years On: Transcending the East-West Divide?,' Special Issue, *Journal of Common Market Studies* 52(1): 1–16.

European Commission (EC) (2014a) 'A New EU Framework to Strengthen the Rule of Law,' Brussels, 11.3.2014, COM(2014) 158 final. Available at: http://register.consilium.europa.eu/doc/srv?l=EN&f=ST%207632%202014%20INIT (accessed 6 January 2016).

European Commission (EC) (2014b) 'Sixth Report on Economic, Social and Territorial Cohesion, Investment for Jobs and Growth,' 23 July, http://ec.europa.eu/regional_policy/sources/docoffic/official/reports/cohesion6/6cr_en.pdf (accessed 6 January 2016).

European Commission (EC) (2014c) 'Reindustrialising Europe, Member States' Competitiveness Report 2014,' SWD (2014) 278, 17.10.2014. Available at: http://ec.europa.eu/transparency/regdoc/rep/10102/2014/EN/10102-2014-278-EN-F1-6.Pdf (accessed 6 January 2016).

European Council (2014) 'Conclusions,' 26/27 June, EUCO 79/14. Available at: www.statewatch.org/news/2014/jun/eu-council-conclusions-jha.pdf (accessed 6 January 2016).

European Policy Centre (EPC) (2014a) 'New Pact for Europe,' April. Available via www.newpactforeurope.eu/ (accessed 6 January 2016).

European Policy Centre (EPC) (2014b) 'Challenge Europe,' September. Available at: www.epc.eu/documents/uploads/pub_4855_challenge_europe_issue_22.pdf (accessed 6 January 2016).

Fernández-Villaverde, Jesús, Luis Graziano and Tano Santos (2013) 'Did the Euro Kill Governance in the Periphery?,' *Vox*, 20 April. Available at: www.voxeu.org/article/did-euro-kill-governance-periphery (accessed 6 January 2016).

Innes, Abby (2014) 'The Political Economy of State Capture in Central Europe,' in Rachel A. Epstein and Wade Jacoby (eds) Eastern Enlargement Ten Years On: Transcending the East-West Divide?, *Journal of Common Market Studies* 52(1): 88–102.

International Monetary Fund (IMF) (2014) '25 Years of Transition, Post-Communist Europe and the IMF,' Regional Economic Issues, Special Report, October. Available at: www.imf.org/external/pubs/ft/reo/2014/eur/eng/pdf/erei_sr_102414.pdf (accessed 6 January 2016).

Leuffen, Dirk, Berthold Rittberger and Frank Schimmelfennig (2013) *Differentiated Integration in the European Union: Explaining Variation in the European Union*. London: Palgrave Macmillan.

Ondarza, Nicolai von (2013) 'Strengthening the Core or Splitting Europe? Prospects and Pitfalls of a Strategy of Differentiated Integration,' SWP Research Paper no. 2, Stiftung Wissenschaft und Politik, Berlin, March. Available at: www.swp-berlin.org/fileadmin/contents/products/research_papers/2013_RP02_orz.pdf (accessed 6 January 2016).

Piris, Jean-Claude (2014) 'The Acceleration of Differentiated Integration and Enhanced Cooperation,' Fondation Robert Schuman, no. 328, 13 October. Available at: www.robert-schuman.eu/en/european-issues/0328-the-acceleration-of-differentiated-integration-and-enhanced-cooperation (accessed 6 January 2016).

Rupnik, Jacques and Jan Zielonka (2013) 'The State of Democracy 20 Years on: Domestic and External Factors,' in Jacques Rupnik and Jan Zielonka (eds) Democracy in Central and Eastern Europe: The State of the Art, *East European Politics and Societies and Cultures* 27(1): 1–25.

Sedelmeier, Ulrich (2014) 'Anchoring Democracy from Above? The European Union and Democratic Backsliding in Hungary and Romania after Accession,' in Rachel A. Epstein and Wade Jacoby (eds) Eastern Enlargement Ten Years On: Transcending the East-West Divide?, *Journal of Common Market Studies* 52(1): 105–121.

Stubb, Alexander (2014) 'Differentiated Europe Needs Strong Institutions,' in European Policy Centre (EPC), Challenges and New Beginnings: Priorities for the EU's new leadership, *Challenge Europe* 22, September: 84–88. Available at: www.epc.eu/documents/uploads/pub_4855_challenge_europe_issue_22.pdf (accessed 6 January 2016).

Tavares, Rui (2013) 'Draft Report on the Situation of Human Rights: Standards and Practices in Hungary,' European Parliament, Committee on Civil Liberties, Justice and Home Affairs, 2012/2130(INI), 2.5.2013. Available at: www.europarl.europa.eu/sides/getDoc.do?pubRef=-//EP//NONSGML+COMPARL+PE-508.211+02+DOC+PDF+V0//EN&language=ENaccessed (accessed 6 January 2016).

Tekin, Funda (2012) *Differentiated Integration at Work*. Baden-Baden: Nomos.

Vida, Krisztina (ed.) (2010) 'The Impact of the 10 New Member States on EU Decision-Making,' Foundation for European Progressive Studies, Brussels and Institute for World Economy, Budapest, June. Available at: www.feps-europe.eu/fileadmin/downloads/framingeurope/1008_FEPS_IWE_NewEUMS.pdf (accessed 6 January 2016).

World Economic Forum (WEF) (2012) 'The Europe 2020 Competitiveness Report: Building a More Competitive Europe.' Available at: www3.weforum.org/docs/CSI/2012/Europe2020_Competitiveness_Report_2012.pdf (accessed 6 January 2016).

World Economic Forum (WEF) (2014) 'Global Competitiveness Report 2014–2015.' Available at: www3.weforum.org/docs/WEF_GlobalCompetitivenessReport_2014-15.pdf (accessed 6 January 2016).

9 The southern and eastern peripheries of Europe

Is convergence a lost cause?

Béla Galgóczi

Introduction

In this chapter we examine the prospects for growth and development of the European 'periphery', an area that encompasses the previously 'converging' countries of Eastern and Southern Europe that have been particularly harshly affected by the financial crisis that began in 2008 and its ongoing consequences. This involves not only the varying economic *growth rates* among member states but also the different economic *models* that have been affected by the crisis in divergent ways. The adjustments that came in the wake of this crisis (including austerity policies and competitiveness-enhancing measures based predominantly on wage cuts) have also had differing implications for individual economic models, such that what we currently observe is a 'patchwork Europe' with fault lines zigzagging across a variable combination of country groups. The practices imposed in the context of these adjustments are asymmetrically affecting the so-called 'deficit countries', those countries suffering a loss of national sovereignty as a result of interference from European institutions; a 'side effect' of this development is thus a democratic deficit.

This article focuses on key features of two peripheries, the East and the South of Europe, in order to demonstrate that the primary difference between them lies in their economic structures and (more importantly) in the different roles these peripheries play in the division of labour within the European economy. Section One is devoted to economic convergence with regard to the South and the East, with special attention to the period of the crisis. Section Two explores the main characteristics of the economic structures of these countries. Section Three, the core of this article, focuses on foreign direct investment (FDI), its characteristics and its impact. Section Four examines wages, emphasising that they are not the critical factor for competitiveness and were not a decisive element of the pre-crisis divergence within the eurozone.

The conclusions we can draw are important for understanding the challenges these peripheries are facing, but they also provide lessons regarding the overall process and practices of European crisis management.

From convergence to divergence

There is a fundamental clash between Europe's social ambitions and the way in which post-crisis adjustments are being made. The conditionality of all bailouts or support from the European Stability Mechanism (or, in the case of non-Economic and Monetary Union [EMU] member states from Central Eastern Europe [CEE], from International Monetary Fund-European Union [IMF-EU] bailout deals) is clearly geared in one direction: austerity, cost-cutting and the undermining of social standards – in other words, 'rebalancing' downward. Thus far, Greece has lost 25 per cent of its GDP during this process.

The idea of the European Social Model has always taken a back seat in the process of European integration. A number of contributions to the political science literature (Streeck, 2000; Scharpf, 2002; Martin, Ross, 2004) have argued that while the single market project has always been at the core of integration – backed by hard law and its flagship project the EMU, albeit on the basis of an incomplete architecture, as we bitterly learned during the crisis – the social dimension has always been based on declarations, wish lists and soft targets like those set out in the EU 2020 Strategy. Although the EMU clearly represented a new stage of integration, and much of the underlying regulatory framework was based on fiscal rules (highly unsatisfactory rules, as we again learned during the recent crisis), it is hard to imagine seriously a common fiscal platform among member states that have public expenditure ratios that range between 34 per cent and 57 per cent of GDP. Indeed, some elements of social spending came under scrutiny during the rebalancing act: in particular, pension systems and social spending have been placed under enormous pressure, again in the downwards direction.

Besides debt consolidation and fiscal austerity, the other main dimension of crisis management has focused on remedying the divergence between the competitive positions of EMU members.

In the context of the current Eurozone crisis it has been argued that the discrepancy in nominal unit labour costs (NULCs) between Germany and countries like Greece and Portugal has widened to unsustainable levels, thereby contributing to the crisis. Figure 9.1 shows these developments for CEE Eurozone member counties (Estonia, Slovakia and Slovenia) and Poland on the one hand and Germany and two Eurozone crisis countries (Greece and Portugal) on the other. NULCs increased by about 25 per cent in Greece and Portugal in comparison to Germany, but in Slovakia and Estonia the divergence was over 90 per cent. One might conclude from these figures that if Greece and Portugal are experiencing major competitiveness problems, then the competitiveness of the CEE countries exhibiting a much greater increase in unit labour costs must have completely tanked. Later in this chapter we will show that the European Commission believes this theory to some extent and has been exerting pressure in support of wage cuts in many CEE economies. However, we will demonstrate that this idea of competitiveness is misguided. The case of these CEE counties indicates that the nature of the supposed competitiveness problem is not predominantly cost-based.

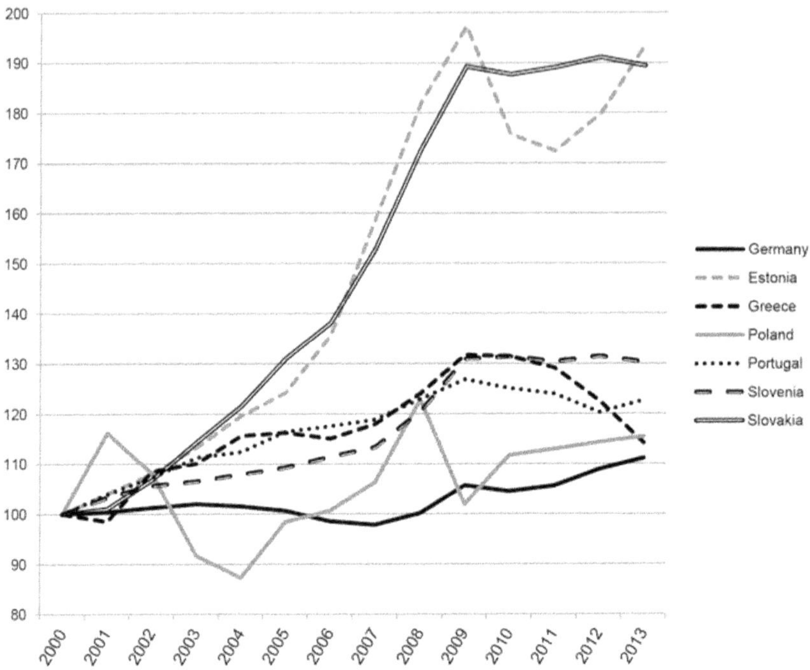

Figure 9.1 Development of total nominal unit labour costs in South and East Europe with Germany as reference, 2000–2013
Source: European Commission AMECO database, 2014.

Although CEE countries share some specific features, we also show that unit labour costs are not the only general measure of competitiveness (Felipe and Kumar, 2011).

Here, again, the institutional remedy is biased in one direction: downwards. Adjustment policies are asymmetrical, with the entire burden of correction placed on deficit countries, while surplus countries have not been seriously involved. In addition, the correction of the competitiveness gap (the gap in unit labour costs) has been elicited through the price channel (predominantly through cuts in labour costs, i.e., wages); the non-price aspects of competitiveness (position in the international division of labour, export structure, productivity, quality) have been ignored. This again results in a downward bias. As we will show in the second half of this paper, the majority of the competitiveness challenge in Southern Europe is due to results from the structure of the economy.

The applied strategy of asymmetric and downward adjustment in which mostly peripheral, lower-income countries are affected results in a persistently growing gap between surplus and deficit countries that manifests itself in a diverging Europe.

The historical founding principle of the EU concentrated on peace, but it was the prospect of convergence that embodied the European dream for millions of people. This ambition seemed to function for several decades. However, now that Europe's flagship project, the single currency, is having difficulty responding to the external shock imposed by the financial crisis and with adjustment therapy forcing some member states into a diverging downwards spiral, this essential and fundamental mission seems to be at risk.

The promise of income convergence – between poorer and richer member states and among the poorer and richer regions within states – has been an underlying feature of European integration from the outset. In this respect, a look back over fifty years of EU history up until the crisis provides confirmation of the project's unprecedented success. As a World Bank (2012) report states, 'The European convergence in consumption levels in the last four decades is unmatched. Except for East Asia, the rest of the world has seen little or no convergence.' Indeed, by the early 1990s, the incomes of more than one hundred million people in the poor southern regions of Europe (Greece, southern Italy, Portugal and Spain) had increased, moving closer to those of the more prosperous areas of Europe. Similarly, between the late 1990s and the mid-2000s, the income levels of one hundred million people in Central and Eastern Europe were dynamically converging towards levels in the richer parts of the continent. The year 2008, with the onset of the crisis, marked a halt in these processes of convergence and catching up on the part of the less prosperous countries and regions, raising questions about the sustainability of the progress achieved in earlier phases of European integration. Figure 9.2 offers a overview of the economic divide in Europe, showing that Central and Eastern European countries still have substantially lower per capita GDP levels (at PPS) than the EU27 average. The data

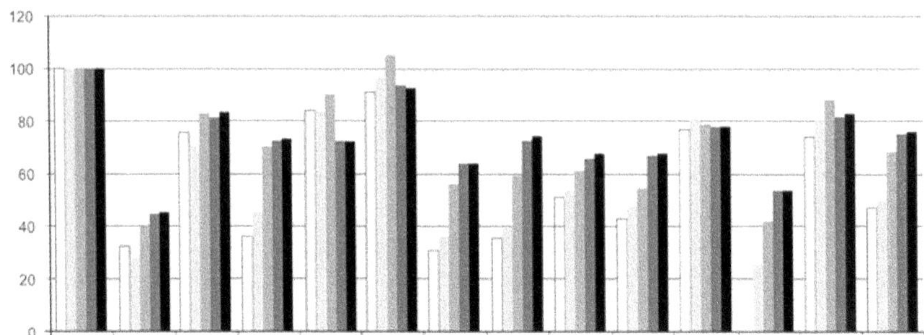

	European Union (27 countries)	Bulgaria	Czech Republic	Estonia	Greece	Spain	Latvia	Lithuania	Hungary	Poland	Portugal	Romania	Slovenia	Slovakia
1995	100	32	76	36	84	91	31	35	51	43	77	0	74	47
2000	100	28	71	45	84	97	36	40	54	48	81	26	80	50
2007	100	40	83	70	90	105	56	59	61	54	79	41	88	68
2013	100	45	82	73	73	94	64	73	66	67	78	54	82	75
2014	100	45	84	73	72	93	64	74	68	68	78	54	83	76

Figure 9.2 Income gaps and convergence: GDP/capita as a percentage of the EU27 total for selected years and countries (based on market prices at PPS)

Source: Eurostat (2014a).

also indicate milestones over the last fifteen years, illustrating the varying convergence dynamics of individual countries in different periods.

Most of the convergence took place between 2000 and 2007, after which momentum was lost or even reversed direction. It is also apparent from the graph that Greece and Portugal are outliers, displaying no convergence whatsoever over the entire 18-year period.

Although 2008 was a common point of fracture for Eastern and Southern Europe, the experiences of these two regions differed significantly. While convergence ground to a definite standstill in Southern Europe and even reversed, in the CEE countries the much stronger impetus towards convergence came to a more abrupt halt; however, in some cases, this proved to be only temporary. Indeed, in most CEE countries – particularly those with the lowest per capita GDP levels – a rapid process of catching up had been observable in the years before the crisis. In Southern Europe, however, the picture had been more mixed, even during the boom period: Spain achieved significant convergence, while Greece and Portugal tended towards stagnation. Latvia and Lithuania, the two countries that suffered the most dramatic falls in output in 2009 (17.7 per cent and 14.8 per cent, respectively), nonetheless still showed impressive overall convergence for the 1995–2013 period as a whole, with per capita GDP levels relative to the EU27 rising from 31 per cent to 64 per cent for Latvia and from 35 per cent to 73 per cent for Lithuania.

The picture for Southern Europe is much bleaker: between 1995 and 2013, Greece and Portugal showed no convergence, while Spain exhibited only limited convergence relative to EU27 levels. Thus, while Spain achieved some measure of catching up over these 18 years (increasing from 91 per cent to 94 per cent), Portugal saw almost no change (77 per cent in 1995, 78 per cent in 2013), and Greece actually suffered a decrease in convergence (from 80 per cent in 1995 to 73 per cent in 2013). All three countries suffered significant setbacks during the crisis, particularly Greece, with a 17 per centage-point drop in its relative income level between 2007 and 2013. The relative positions of lower-income member states also shifted dramatically; for example, Greece regressed in terms of its per capita GDP level relative to the EU27 average, falling behind not only Slovenia and the Czech Republic, but also Slovakia. Its current level matches those of Estonia and Lithuania. On the other hand, some of the CEE countries managed to catch up considerably despite the period of recession, as the examples of Poland, Lithuania and Slovakia show. What factors can these different developmental paths be attributed to? The key issue is certainly not wage dynamics, the main focus of adjustment policies. We will show that certain characteristics of the economic structures of these lower-income countries are highly influential, in particular foreign direct investment.

The role of the structure of the economy

Competitiveness is influenced by economic structure, not just by labour costs. The divergent patterns observed in Eastern and Southern Europe in the catching-up process result from a number of underlying structural differences among European countries that have affected their respective paths in economic integration. We examine four important drivers of economic integration that have played a key role in convergence: exports, the balance-of-payments situation and its structure, foreign direct investment (FDI) and the role of credit flows.

Currently, the most pronounced division in Europe is between 'surplus' and 'deficit' countries, as determined by their balance-of-payments position within the eurozone; the core 'surplus' countries are clustered around Germany, while the 'deficit' nations border the Mediterranean. A similar distinction applies beyond the eurozone: a number of CEE countries belong to the 'surplus' core (e.g. the Czech Republic and Poland), but the more peripheral and crisis-ridden CEE countries (e.g. the Baltic states) fall into the 'deficit' group. This differentiation between surplus and deficit countries thus cuts across the historical divisions between the continent's East and West.

The balance of payments encompasses all of a given country's financial flows with the outside world, including trade in goods and services, various forms of capital, asset and income flows and credit. We address here one of the most important components, a factor that played a crucial role for deficit countries both before and during the crisis – namely, the balance of trade in goods and services. The balance in the trade of goods (in both 2007 and 2011) reveals substantial differences between individual member states. A negative trade balance means that a country imports more than it exports; this difference must be financed. Persistent deficits not financed from other transactions within the balance of payments create debt, as happened in the cases of Latvia, Bulgaria and Greece (see Figure 9.3).

The data also allow an assessment of the degree to which countries were able to adjust to the crisis of 2008. The Czech Republic, Hungary and Slovakia had broadly balanced trade even before the crisis, whereas Latvia, Bulgaria, Greece, Romania and Portugal had to contend with persistent double-digit trade deficits.

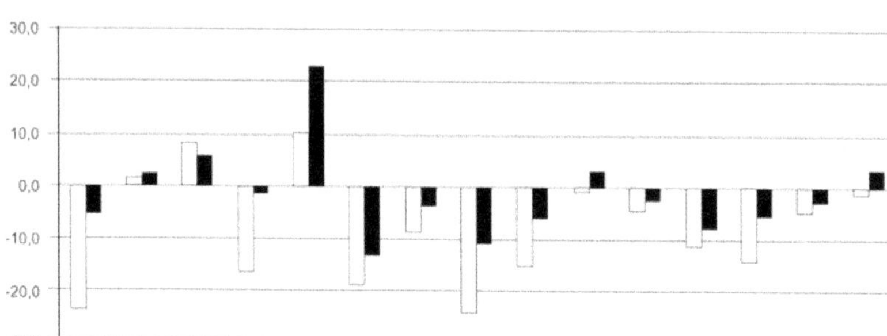

	Bulgaria	Czech Republic	Germany	Estonia	Ireland	Greece	Spain	Latvia	Lithuania	Hungary	Poland	Portugal	Romania	Slovenia	Slovakia
□ Goods 2007	-23,5	1,3	8,2	-16,4	10,5	-18,6	-8,7	-24,0	-14,9	-0,7	-4,4	-11,3	-14,3	-4,8	-1,2
■ Goods 2011	-5,6	2,4	6,0	-1,4	23,0	-13,1	-3,7	-10,8	-5,9	3,3	-2,7	-7,8	-5,5	-2,9	3,5

Figure 9.3 Balance of payments component: trade in goods (per cent of GDP)
Source: Eurostat (2013).

During the crisis, most CEE countries adjusted by substantially cutting their deficits or by achieving a positive trade balance. In most cases this was managed through a decrease in imports, a consequence of slowing growth or even recession. A balance thus achieved by means of 'deep-freezing' certain types of activity (such as consumption, investments and imports) can produce signs of rapid adjustment, but this cannot be regarded as a long-term solution. Moreover, it is still an open question to what extent adjustments in CEE deficit countries (for example, the Baltic states) might have a longer-term structural impact. In any case, even after having absorbed drastic measures intended to induce such a 'deep-freeze', Greece and Portugal still continued to exhibit high trade deficits in 2011, thereby revealing a much more limited ability to adjust in any of the abovementioned ways.

When we examine the key features of deficit and surplus countries in the periphery in more detail, we find further important structural differences in their economies. While surplus countries in the East have enjoyed large-scale foreign direct investment (FDI) in their productive sectors, this has not been the case for Southern European crisis states. In 2012, according to the World Investment Report released by United Nations Conference on Trade and Development (UNCTAD), Slovakia, the Czech Republic, Hungary and Estonia had FDI stocks in their economies ranging between 60 per cent and 80 per cent of GDP; for Greece, this stock amounted to just 9 per cent (UNCTAD, 2013).

Central and Eastern European countries also tend to have a high export share in their GDPs; again, this is not the case for the deficit countries in the South. To illustrate this discrepancy, Figure 9.4 shows the export shares for this group of countries.

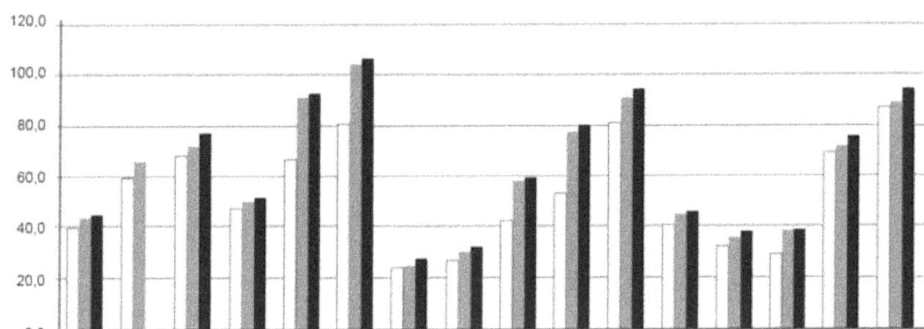

	European Union (27 countries)	Bulgaria	Czech Republic	Germany (including former GDR from 1991)	Estonia	Ireland	Greece	Spain	Latvia	Lithuania	Hungary	Poland	Portugal	Romania	Slovenia	Slovakia
2007	40,1	59,5	68,2	47,2	67,1	80,7	23,8	26,9	42,5	53,8	81,3	40,8	32,2	29,3	69,5	86,9
2011	43,7	66,5	72,2	50,2	91,1	104,9	25,1	30,3	58,8	77,6	91,3	45,2	35,5	38,3	72,5	89,7
2012	44,9	0	77,5	51,6	92,6	106,6	27,8	32,0	59,8	80,4	94,8	46,0	38,6	39,2	75,6	95,0

Figure 9.4 Exports of goods and services (per cent GDP)
Source: Eurostat (2012).

In 2012, Slovakia, Hungary and Estonia had export shares of around 90 per cent of their respective GDPs, whereas in the case of Greece, this share amounted to 27 per cent.

There are also substantial qualitative differences in the export profiles of individual countries. One important feature is the share of 'complex sectors' within the total exports of individual member states. The classification of export structures by means of Standard International Trade Classification (SITC) categories roughly corresponds to the level of technological sophistication of the products being exported. Accordingly, the 'complex sectors' include machinery and transport equipment, pharmaceuticals and scientific instruments. This classification is merely indicative, insofar as it does not take into account the role of the country in the division of labour within the sector or its R&D or innovation content. In terms of sectoral composition, Hungary and the Czech Republic thus had a higher rate of export complexity in both 2007 and 2011 than Germany, with a share of complex sectors of around 60 per cent of their total exports; in combination with the high export shares of these countries, this corresponds to nearly 50 per cent of their GDPs. Greece had the lowest share of complex sectors in its exports (13.8 per cent in 2011), and Bulgaria, the Baltic states and Portugal also had relatively low shares (between 20 and 30 per cent in 2011). During the four years of the crisis, a further downgrading of what were already relatively low export profiles in terms of complexity took place in Greece, Lithuania, Portugal and Spain. By contrast, Romania, Estonia, Bulgaria and Latvia were able to upgrade their export profiles during this period. Export complexity thus supplies a further indication of the roles of countries in the division of labour in Europe, demonstrating how certain small peripheral countries with limited domestic capital – like most of the CEE countries – were able to achieve high export complexity through foreign direct investment.

In addition to the size and composition of trade and foreign direct investment, the geographical orientation of exports also has a substantial impact. As Germany currently represents the economic core of Europe, the share it occupies in the exports of individual countries is a decisive factor.

Based on Eurostat data (Eurostat 2013), a quarter to a third of the exports of Hungary, Poland and the Czech Republic are bound for Germany, with a slightly decreasing trend over the years. Greece and the Baltic states, in contrast, send less than 10 per cent of their exports to Germany. Three further CEE member states (Slovakia, Slovenia and Romania) have German export shares of around 20 per cent, while the rest of the countries examined (including Portugal and Spain) have values closer to 10 per cent.

Summarising the above, with regard to foreign trade characteristics, the following trends emerge from the data: Central and Eastern European exporters tend to have balanced trade or even trade surpluses; a high share of their GDPs are generated by exports; and, in the case of the Czech Republic, Slovakia and Hungary, a substantial proportion of their exports consists of complex products, with a high proportion destined for Germany. These countries also exhibit high FDI penetration in their tradable sectors, with much of their manufacturing FDI originating from Germany (automobile, components and electronic sectors). On the other hand, the Baltic states and the Southern European states examined here show lower export shares, varying levels of trade deficits, low levels of export complexity and limited trade relations with Germany. All of this supports the view that, among the various fault lines in crisis-ridden Europe, one decisive dividing line lies between surplus and deficit countries, with the core CEE countries (in this context, the Czech Republic, Slovakia and Hungary) as part of the Germany-centred side in terms of trade and investment patterns within the European division of labour.

Within this framework, Western (mostly German) multinationals have benefited from cheap sourcing from Central and Eastern European locations and have used this to strengthen their market positions and competitiveness on a global level. However, the longer-term sustainability of this model poses serious questions. It can be maintained only if CEE subcontracting activities become higher-value-added in terms of both R&D and local value-added content. Although signs of such a trend were evident in the mid-2000s (see Broadman, 2005), the process was interrupted by the crisis; nowadays, the mainstream adjustment strategy as reflected in the European Semester (European Commission, 2011) is focused on low-wage competition. This is far from promising for the future.

Foreign direct investment as a key driver of convergence

In the CEE countries, FDI has been one main drivers of economic and wage convergence. Figure 9.5 shows that FDI has constituted a high share of GDP in the 10 CEEs as a group; recently, this figure increased from nearly 58 per cent in 2008 to over 66 per cent in 2011, a proportion considerably higher than the EU27 averages (41.1 per cent in 2008 and 42.0 per cent in 2011). Bulgaria had the most FDI stock in its GDP (130 per cent in 2008, 124 per cent in 2011), followed by Estonia (99 per cent and 103 per cent, respectively). With FDI stocks of 85 per cent and 81 per cent of their 2011 GDPs, Hungary and the Czech Republic also exhibited a considerable influx of FDI.

Poland, in contrast, with its 53 per cent FDI share in 2011, was closer to the EU27 average. The size of the Polish economy and the country's relatively large domestic market probably explain this divergence. This does not imply, however, that Poland is less integrated into European value chains than the Czech Republic or Hungary. With regard to FDI stocks, Romania, which features the second largest population among the CEE countries, was in the same league as Poland.

FDI, and especially investment targeting the exporting manufacturing sector, has clearly played a key role in modernising the industrial base of CEE countries. These investments have introduced new technology and work organisation, while also driving the need for qualified labour. Figure 9.6 shows the per centage share of manufacturing within green-field foreign direct investment projects in terms of their number, capital invested and jobs created during the period 2008–2012. The CEE countries and in particular the central European Visegrad 4 group (the

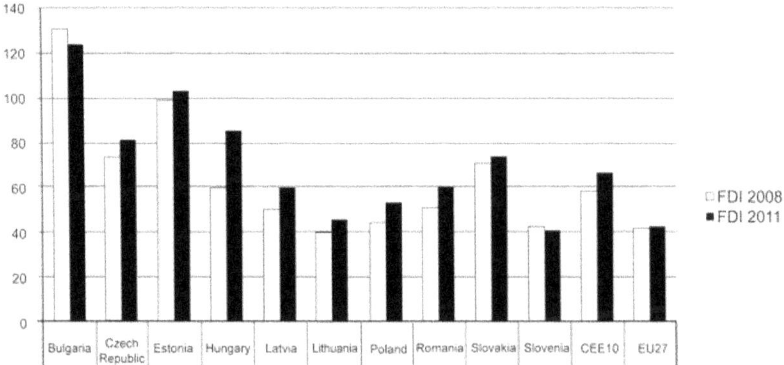

	Bulgaria	Czech Republic	Estonia	Hungary	Latvia	Lithuania	Poland	Romania	Slovakia	Slovenia	CEE10	EU27
FDI 2008	131	73	99	60	50	40	44	51	71	42	58	41
FDI 2011	124	81	103	85	60	45	53	60	74	41	66	42

Figure 9.5 Inward FDI stock as a percentage of GDP in EU27 and CEE countries, 2008 and 2011

Sources: UNCTAD 2013 (FDI stock); Eurostat (GDP).

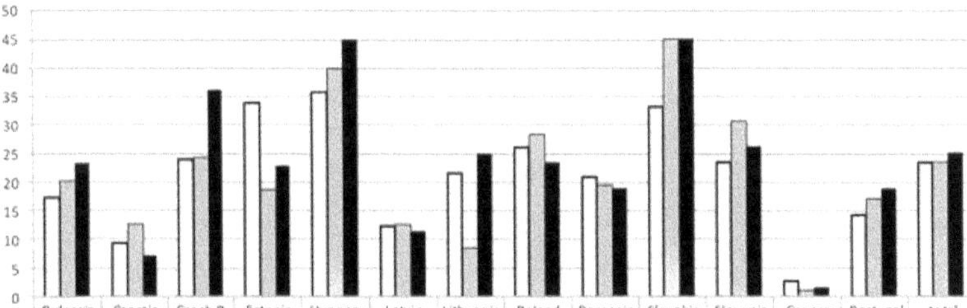

	Bulgaria	Croatia	Czech R.	Estonia	Hungary	Latvia	Lithuania	Poland	Romania	Slovakia	Slovenia	Greece	Portugal	total
FDI projects	17,2	9,3	23,9	33,8	35,7	12,3	21,5	26,1	21	33,3	23,5	2,7	14,2	23,6
FDI capex	20,4	12,8	24,4	18,7	40,1	12,7	8,8	28,4	19,6	45,2	30,9	1,2	17,4	23,8
FDI jobs	23,3	7,3	36,2	22,9	45	11,4	25	23,6	19	45,3	26,3	1,6	19	25,3

Figure 9.6 Share of manufacturing in green-field FDI projects between 2008 and 2012 by country (per cent)

Source: adapted by author from Hunya Schwarzhappel 2014.

Czech Republic, Hungary, Poland and Slovakia) exhibit the highest levels, whereas Greece is a negative outlier.

Geared by high productivity and the advantages of large-scale operations , exporting foreign-controlled or foreign investment enterprises (FIEs) paid substantially higher wages than domestic firms (Van Klaveren et al. 2013); due to the limited availability of qualified labour, the wages of skilled workers rose rapidly. These wage increases cannot be seen as threatening competitiveness, even when nominal unit labour costs for the economy as a whole rises. In the manufacturing sector and in the broader tradable sector of economy, productivity – to a great extent due to FDI – also increased, as Figure 9.9 illustrates. Figure 9.7 below displays the share of FIEs in total private employment in the CEE countries. For nine of the ten countries, these shares correlate highly with the FDI stocks in

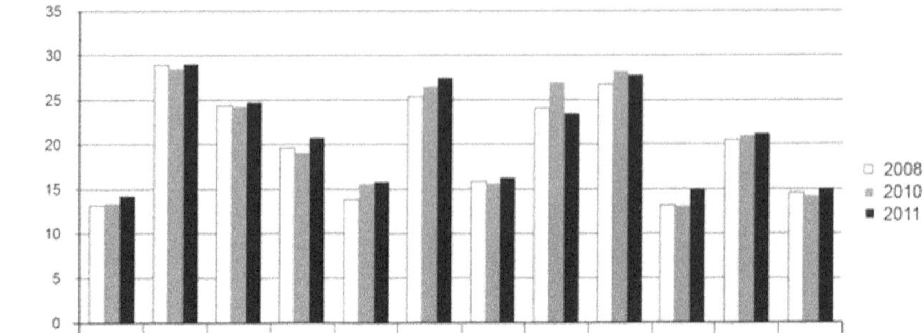

	Bulgaria	Czech Republic	Estonia	Lativa	Lithuania	Hungary	Poland	Romania	Slovakia	Slovenia	CEE10	EU27
□ 2008	13.1	29	24.3	19.7	13.8	25.4	15.7	24.1	26.9	13	20.5	14.6
▪ 2010	13.5	28.5	24.3	19.1	15.7	26.4	15.8	27	28.3	13.2	21.1	14.4
■ 2011	14.3	29.1	24.8	20.8	15.9	27.5	16.4	23.5	27.9	15	21.2	15.1

Figure 9.7 Employment in Foreign Investment Enterprises (FIEs) as a percentage of total private employment (excl. finance) in EU27 and CEE countries, 2008 and 2011

Sources: Eurostat 2014b (Annual enterprise and FATS statistics).

GDP shown in Figure 9.6. In the 10 countries in question, the already rather high total employment share of FIEs grew from 20.3 per cent in 2008 to 23.2 per cent in 2011, or 9 per centage points over the EU27 average (14.1 per cent in 2011). Thus, in the EU at large, about one in seven privately employed workers was employed by foreign-controlled firms, whereas in CEE, this was the case for nearly one in four workers. With such a large share in private employment, FIEs exerted a pull effect on general wage levels in the CEE countries. Later developments in employment indicate a continuing dependence on FDI. Between 2008 and 2011, the share of FIEs in employment in important industries showed overall growth, with only a few exceptions. Calculated over the ten countries, foreign direct investment was dominant in metal and electronics manufacturing, with the share of FIEs growing from 46.4 per cent in 2008 to 49.2 per cent in 2011; in the retail industry, the FIE share rose from 15.4 per cent to 18.2 per cent between 2008 and 2011, and in transport and telecom, from 11.4 per cent to 13.5 per cent (Van Klaveren et al. 2013; additional calculations by Maarten van Klaveren, based on Eurostat Annual enterprise and FATS statistics).

During the 2008/9 crisis, the high share of FDI in Central and Eastern Europe appeared to represent a risk factor, raising doubts about the sustainability of the export-based and FDI-driven growth model of these countries. At the time, the narrative was dominated by terms such as 'FDI dependence' and 'export dependence'. Notably, with regard to exports, the times are changing. Beginning in 2010, the exports of nearly all CEE countries began to surge, in particular because the German economy (with which the CEE countries are closely interlinked, especially through subcontracting chains via German manufacturing FDI) started to exert a strong pull effect. In 2011/12, except for Hungary, Slovenia and Croatia, the value of the exports of individual CEE countries grew by over 4 per cent; in all cases, this was more than imports increased, thus improving all trade balances (Eurostat, International trade statistics). Figure 9.8 also shows a correlation between changes in FDI stock and changes in GDP during the crisis. On the one hand, Poland experienced soaring FDI and good growth performance; Lithuania, Slovakia, Estonia and Bulgaria also witnessed FDI expansion and growth during the four years of the crisis (see also Hunya 2014). In the case of a number of countries, including Portugal, Hungary, Croatia and Slovenia, growth in FDI was not sufficient to prevent a contraction of the economy, and thus GDP decreased even as FDI rose. Greece, on the other hand, experienced an enormous drop in FDI and a significant decrease in GDP.

At the same time, a number of the economic problems of the Southern European countries during the intensifying eurozone crisis proved to be linked to low levels of export potential and productive FDI penetration. In the case of the CEE countries, although high FDI shares and reliance on exports can be seen as risk factors during turbulent times, for small countries that lack capital and natural resources (and were cut off from the European and global economies for four decades), there seems to be no better alternative. The primary lesson from the crisis, however, has been that what matters most with FDI (and in broader terms, with the external financing of the economy) are the potential economic repercussions. Productive FDI in the manufacturing industry that creates an export potential can clearly be considered an advantage and a driving economic force, although the spillover effects strengthening the role of domestic firms remain rather weak in most CEE countries. In contrast, FDI that targets the exploitation of the domestic market (finance, retail chains, real estate) is more controversial and may well be regarded as an actual risk factor.

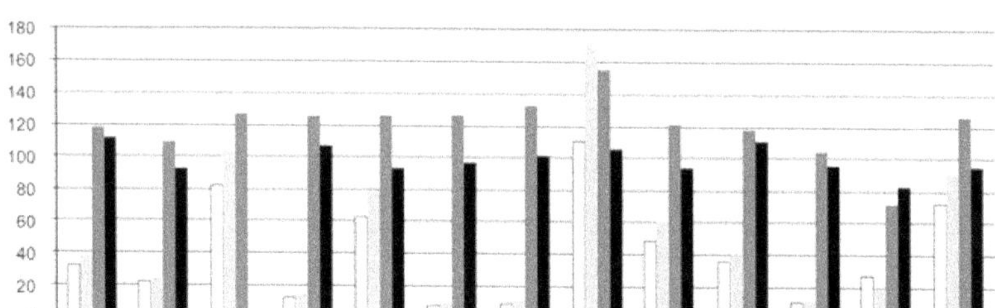

	Bulgaria	Croatia	Czech Republic	Estonia	Hungary	Latvia	Lithuania	Poland	Romania	Slovakia	Slovenia	Greece	Portugal
□ FDI 2008	31,65	22,19	81,3	11,77	62,45	8,12	9,19	110,42	48,79	36,22	11,32	27,39	71,83
FDI 2012	37,32	24,06	103,46	14,66	78,48	10,25	12,1	170,59	59,12	42,3	11,72	19,77	90,78
■ FDI index	118	108	127	125	126	126	132	155	121	117	104	72	126
■ GDP index	112	92		107	92	97	102	105	94	110	95	83	96

Figure 9.8 Changes in FDI stock and GDP, 2012/2008 in per cent (nominal EUR-based)
Source: adapted by author from Hunya, Schwarzhappel 2014.

Wages are just one factor of competitiveness

The data also indicate that even though developments in wages and unit labour costs showed a high degree of divergence in the decade leading up to the crisis (when the competitive positions of periphery countries in both the East and the South deteriorated substantially in comparison to Germany), there is no fundamental cost-competitiveness problem if we examine the levels of productivity and wage costs in tradable (manufacturing) sectors. Table 9.1 shows that based on the manufacturing sector, the peripheral countries did not have a cost-competitiveness problem with Germany. The problem some countries have experienced is more of a structural nature: specifically, their shares of manufacturing and exports in general are very low.

The case of the two peripheries in Europe demonstrates that the competitiveness problem of some Mediterranean countries results more from deeply rooted structural issues than from price and cost levels. Because the remedies have focused almost exclusively on cost and wage cuts, neglecting structural problems, not only have previous achievements in convergence been wiped out, but their future prospects have also been put at risk.

Although tackling these structural problems through cost adjustments (wage and spending cuts) can deliver temporary results in cost competitiveness at the price of dramatic increases in poverty and unemployment, the inevitable 'side effects' can ultimately jeopardise the success of the adjustment process. Cost adjustment is simply not an adequate way of addressing the longer-term structural problems (such as the share of manufacturing in the overall economy, export shares, the qualitative composition of exports, the country's position in the international division of labour, etc.).

To put it bluntly, the problem was not that consumers in the surplus countries were buying less olive oil and port wine due to rising unit labour costs in Greece or Portugal. In other words, the cure chosen by the EU tackles the symptoms but not the root causes of the problem.

Table 9.1 Wage-adjusted productivity in manufacturing in selected countries, 2009

Country	*Apparent labour productivity (EUR 1000 per employed)*	*Average personal costs (EUR 1000 per employed)*	*Wage-adjusted productivity (%)*
EU27	46	34.5	132.1
Czech Republic	22	14.0	154.6
Hungary	23	11.7	199.6
Greece	42	28.0	150.6
Germany	57	47.2	120.7
Portugal	23	15.8	146.7
Slovakia	17	12.3	134.7
Spain	48	35.1	137.2

Source: Eurostat 2012.

Some of the convergence achieved before the crisis might be regarded as unsustainable, but this also points to a policy failure. In a series of reports and communications issued up until 2007, European institutions proudly publicised rising employment levels and income convergence in many of the peripheral countries. This progress was also seen as a partial achievement of the Lisbon targets. If much of this progress is seen now as a result of a credit-fuelled bubble that was not based on real performance, it also represents a strong criticism of EU policies. European leaders cannot merely shrug their shoulders and say, 'We're sorry – what we welcomed as an achievement turned out to be an illusion.' The unsustainable expansion was due to an enormous capital allocation problem resulting in part from irresponsible financial and lending practices, predominantly through banks in surplus countries. Ordinary working people are now paying the price, and those who created the bubble are safeguarded from any future comeuppance.

Conclusions

The eurozone crisis has highlighted the diversity of economic models in the European 'peripheries' and their sustainability during hard times and external shocks. The convergence of income levels in the poorer regions of the South and the East towards the EU average has been one of the major European objectives, and the process seemed to be functioning for several decades. This strongly contributed to the legitimacy of and public support for the European Union. Although it was largely driven by economic processes, convergence was also a fundamental factor in maintaining the European Social Model despite diversity at member-state level.

The economic catching-up processes came to a sudden halt in 2008. While this proved to be a temporary setback or slowdown in the East, for the South the positive trend seems to have completely reversed. The credit crunch of 2008 highlighted the division between countries with current-account surpluses (the European 'core' based around Germany, including the largest Central and Eastern European exporters) and the 'deficit' countries, including Mediterranean countries and a number of smaller countries in Central and Eastern Europe (the Baltic states and Hungary). Given the lack of effective adjustment mechanisms in the eurozone, the surplus–deficit divide quickly evolved into a trickier creditor–debtor relationship. The 'debtor' countries then experienced a prolonged agony of negotiated and imposed adjustments in the context of crisis-driven Euro-Area institution-building. Fiscal retrenchment and wage cuts were the imposed remedies, even though the lack of competitiveness of some Southern European countries is largely due to accumulated problems in the structures of the national economies. We have shown that in comparison to most CEE countries, the shares of exports, foreign direct investment and especially green-field manufacturing FDI are significantly lower in the southern periphery. It is not wage levels and dynamics but rather these structural features that are key for competitiveness. Despite this, many of the adjustment measures focused on wage cuts and cost adjustments; the distortions in terms of economic structure were not addressed.

What should also be emphasised is that if convergence is exclusively driven by economic processes, the result will not be enduring and balanced. More political and institutional integration is needed, as the Single Market alone will not do the job. The paradoxical and most worrying point is that political integration in the form of the economic governance that has evolved through the current crisis management practices of the EU is doing precisely the opposite: it has further increased diversity, up to a point that may tear the Eurozone and the EU apart.

References

Broadman, H. (2005) *From Disintegration to Reintegration: Eastern Europe and the Former Soviet Union in International Trade.* Washington, DC: World Bank.

European Commission (2011) 'Annual Growth Survey 2011.' Available at: http://ec.europa.eu/economy_finance/articles/eu_economic_situation/pdf/2011/com2011_11_annex1_en.pdf (accessed 6 January 2016).

European Council (2012) 'The Treaty on Stability.' Available at: http://european-council.europa.eu/eurozone-governance/treaty-on-stability (accessed 6 January 2016).

European Commission (2014) 'DG ECFIN Annual Macro-Economic Database (AMECO).' Available at: http://ec.europa.eu/economy_finance/db_indicators/ameco/index_en.htm (accessed 15 May 2014).

Eurostat (2012) 'Manufacturing Statistics.' Available at: http://epp.eurostat.ec.europa.eu/statistics_explained/index.php/Manufacturing_statistics_-_NACE_Rev._2 (accessed 14 January 2015).

Eurostat (2013) 'International Trade in Goods: Intra EU Trade Data.' Available at: http://epp.eurostat.ec.europa.eu/statistics_explained/index.php/International_trade_in_goods#Intra-EU_trade (accessed 6 January 2016).

Eurostat (2014a) 'Structural Business Statistics.' Available at: http://epp.eurostat.ec.europa.eu/portal/page/portal/european_business/data/database; including 'Annual detailed enterprise statistics' and 'FATS statistics' (accessed 7 May 2014).

Eurostat (2014b) 'Annual Enterprise and FATS Statistics.' Available at: http://appsso.eurostat.ec.europa.eu/nui/show.do?dataset=nama_gdp_c&lang=en (accessed 6 January 2016).

Felipe, J. and U. Kumar (2011) 'Do Some Countries in the Eurozone Need an Internal Devaluation? A Reassessment of What Unit Labour Costs Really Mean,' *Vox EU.* Available at: www.voxeu.org/article/internal-devaluations-eurozone-mismeasured-and-misguided-argument (accessed 3 April 2015).

Hunya, G. (2014) 'Regional Policy and FDI Location,' wiiw Research Report no. 393, Vienna Institute for International Economic Studies. Available at: http://wiiw.ac.at/regional-policy-and-fdi-location–an-overview-of-the-larger-new-eu-member-states-dip-3310.pdf (accessed 14 January 2015).

Hunya, G. and M. Schwarzhappel (2014) 'Hit by Deleveraging,' wiiw FDI Report no. 2014-06, Vienna Institute for International Economic Studies. Available at: http://wiiw.ac.at/wiiw-fdi-reports-ps-11.html (accessed 6 January 2016).

Martin, Andrew and George Ross (2004) 'Introduction: EMU and the European Social Model,' in Andrew Martin and George Ross (eds) *Euros and Europeans. Monetary Integration and the European Social Model.* Cambridge: Cambridge University Press, pp. 1–19.

Scharpf, Fritz (2002) 'The European Social Model: Coping with the Challenges of Diversity,' *Journal of Common Market Studies* 40(4):645–670.

Streeck, Wolfgang (2000) 'Competitive Solidarity: Rethinking the "European Social Model",' in Karl Hinrichs, Claus Offe, Herbert Kitschelt and Helmut Wiesenthal (eds) *Kontingenz und Krise*. Frankfurt and New York: Campus, pp. 245–262.

United Nations Conference on Trade and Development (UNCTAD) (2013) 'World Investment Report, Global Value Chains for Investment and Trade Development,' New York and Geneva, 205. Available at: http://unctad.org/en/publicationslibrary/wir2013_en.pdf (accessed 14 January 2015).

Van Klaveren, M., K. Tijdens and D. Gregory (2013) *Multinational Companies and Domestic Firms in Europe: Comparing Wages, Working Conditions and Industrial Relations*. Basingstoke: Palgrave Macmillan.

World Bank (2012) *EU11 Regular Economic Report: Coping with External Headwinds*. Zagreb: World Bank Office.

Part III

Country studies on the political management of the Troika Adjustment Programmes and the sovereign debt crisis

10 Greece and the Troika in the context of the Eurozone crisis

Anna Visvizi

Introduction

The sovereign debt crisis made Greece the focal point of the Eurozone in 2010. The possibility of a Grexit ('Greek exit') sent shockwaves across Europe in 2012. However, it was the January 2015 victory of the Coalition of the Radical Left (Synaspismos tis Rizospastikis Aristeras – SYRIZA) in the early parliamentary elections that ignited a vicious and perplexing sequence of developments that culminated in an emergency EU summit stretching over the night of July 12/13, 2015. The truly dramatic negotiations of that night, in which Donald Tusk and François Holland may have played the roles of their lives, seem to have averted not only a Grexit but also a dissolution of the Eurozone and the EU. On early Monday morning July 13, Alexis Tsipras, Greece's prime minister, travelled back to Athens to have four laws passed by the Greek parliament until July 15; laws that SYRIZA and others had been resisting for the past five years. With New Democracy (Nea Dimokratia – ND) and other centrist groupings extending their support to Tsipras, the unthinkable happened: rather than continuing infighting, politicking and political blackmail, the Greeks united at last, hence raising hopes that a third bailout would be possible and Greece would remain in the Eurozone.

That being said, the unprecedented nature of the assistance programmes extended to Greece in 2010 and in 2012, the variability of the programmes' implementation and the prospect of the 2015 bailout render Greece one of the most interesting case studies in the debate on the nature of bailout programmes in the Eurozone. Therefore, the objective of this paper is to examine the developments in Greece under bailout conditions during the period 2010 through July 2015. The argument is structured as follows. In the first section, the bailout programme and the Troika's[1] engagement in Greece are placed in a historical perspective. In the next, the structural problems of the Greek economy are discussed, along with the principal factors leading to Greece's insolvency in 2010. In the following section, the negotiations over the 2010 and 2012 bailout programmes are examined and the content of the programmes described. In the next, the variability of the programmes' implementation and their outcomes are elaborated. In the final section the dramatic developments ignited by SYRIZA's win in

January 2015 elections and culminated in the emergency EURO Summit on 12 July 2015 are discussed. Conclusions follow.

Placing the crisis, the bailout and the Troika's engagement with Greece in perspective

Three interconnected issues should be mentioned by way of placing the discussion of Greece's bailout programme in a perspective conducive to its being properly understood. These are: the historically contingent state-building process in Greece and, effectively, the country's incomplete modernisation; the resultant dysfunctional state–society relationship that was consolidated in the 1980s and is the primary source of Greece's current political and ideological paralysis; and, finally, Greece's contentious position in the EEC/EU forum, which is largely due to domestic political developments in Greece.

With regard to the historical contingencies besetting Greece, as Pryce (2015: 1) notes: 'it is a nation that has existed in its modern form only since the First World War, a country that was still under Ottoman rule less than 200 years ago'. Admittedly, during the country's 400 years under Ottoman rule after the fall of the Byzantine Empire, Greece lost touch with many of the historical processes that have proven to be fundamental for modernisation and modern Western state-building processes. These processes included: the construction of a Western-style monarchy and its gradual dissolution, the resultant emergence of a dynamic spectrum of social classes and its evolution (with the Ionian Islands being the exception from the rule), full-scale industrial revolution and the ensuing urban/spatial re-organisation of the country, etc. If modern Greece is being torn apart by political and ideological paralysis, whereby its political establishment is unable to effectively address the economic and financial crisis, the roots of this drama are embedded in the unfinished process of state-building and modernisation.

Another issue that should be noted is that when Greece joined the European Economic Community (EEC) in 1981, its membership in the group was almost immediately referred to in the academic literature in terms of a 'return to democracy'. Over the years, this argument has been repeated and reinforced (Verney, 1987; Valinakis, 2012) obscuring the fact that the rationale behind Greece's EEC membership bid launched in the 1970s by Kostas Karamanlis, leader of the ND, was to restore Greece's position in the West, as opposed to the unspoken but real possibility of the country falling under the influence of the Soviet Union. In any case, Greece signed its Association Agreement with the EC in 1961 with the intention of joining the organisation by 1984 at the latest. That agreement was partially frozen for the period between 1967 and 1974, but it was immediately reinstated once the ND government was established in Athens in 1974 (Tsinisizelis, 2008: 14). From this perspective, the EEC bid was intended to create new geopolitical (rather than economic) prospects for the country. Therefore an alleged 'return to democracy' was in no way involved. Interestingly, neither was the notion of economic performance, as throughout the 1970s Greece recorded positive growth rates, and its fiscal position was outstanding. Even in

1981, the gross government debt-to-GDP ratio was only 25 per cent, although this figure increased dramatically in the 1980s as a result of extensive social spending.

Turning to the sources of Greece's historically contentious position in the EEC/EU forum, it should be noted that the ND – the party that promoted and successfully negotiated the country's entry into the EC – lost the national elections in 1981. The winner was the Panhellenic Socialist Movement (Panellinio Sosialistiko Kinima – PASOK), a political movement that 'had made its anti-communitarian rhetoric a central element of its political platform' (Mitsos, 2000: 53). Indeed, an attempt was soon made by the new government to renegotiate Greece's EEC Accession Treaty. As a result, in the first years of its membership in the EEC, Greece remained an introverted country, a receiver of European policies, beating the drum of Greek exceptionalism and yet incapable (due to a nearly exclusive focus on the intergovernmental and bilateral fora of decision-making) either of promoting its national interests or adjusting to the broader logic of cooperation within the EEC (Mitsos, 2000: 61).

The daunting observation at this point is that despite the tendency in the literature to cast Greece's membership in the EEC in terms of a 'return to democracy', the political system that emerged in Greece in the 1980s proved extremely susceptible to the maladies of nepotism, cronyism, the abuse of executive authority and the emergence of powerful interest groups. It may be argued that in some respects Greece's political system turned into a parody of democracy following Greece's accession to the EEC. The weaknesses of the Greek domestic political system hampered the expected positive impact of EEC/EU membership on the Greek polity, policies and politics, repeatedly prompting questions about the virtues of the Europeanisation of Greece. This influenced the role that Greece assumed in the EU forum. Moreover, it defined Greece's position vis-à-vis its creditors following the launch of bailout programmes as well as their implementation over the period 2010–2015. From a different perspective, the contingent nature of the state-building process in Greece, which gave rise to the argument of Greece as a failed state (Featherstone, 2011), made Greek voters extremely vulnerable to political manipulation; the financial and economic crisis intensified this vulnerability. The victory of SYRIZA in the early elections on 25 January 2015 serves as a good case in point, as does the referendum of 5 July 2015.

The key components of the Greek rescue programme

As a means of addressing the sovereign debt crisis in Greece and its implications, two financial assistance and reform programmes – the so-called Economic Adjustment Programmes (EAPs) – have been launched since 2010. The first EAP, with a value of €110 billion, was approved by the Eurogroup and the International Monetary Fund (IMF) board in May 2010. This loan was unprecedented in terms of its magnitude, the addressee (i.e. a Eurozone country) and the method of supervision (i.e. a 'Troika' of creditors consisting of the European Commission, the European Central Bank (ECB) and the IMF). The package consisted of €80 billion in bilateral loans from the euro-area member states centrally pooled by the European Commission (the so-called Greek Loan Facility (GLF)) and a €30 billion Stand-By Arrangement (SBA) approved by the IMF. In March 2012, the second EAP for Greece was approved. This consisted of the undisbursed amounts of the first EAP, specifically the undisbursed amounts of GLF, and an additional €130 billion for the years 2012–2014. Unlike in the case of the first EAP from 2010, the financial assistance offered to Greece under the provisions of the second EAP consisted of a contribution of the Eurozone member states, via the EFSF (€144.7 billion) and of the IMF (€19.8 billion, as part of a four-year €28 billion arrangement under the Extended Fund Facility for Greece approved in March 2012). As for the EFSF assistance for Greece, out of the initial €144 billion, €48.2 billion was intended to cover the costs of bank resolution and recapitalisation; during the course of the process, €10.9 billion in EFSF notes was found to be unnecessary and returned to the EFSF. Originally, the ESFF-funded programme was scheduled to end on 31 December 2014, but it was extended twice upon request of the Greek government (EFSF, 2015), i.e. until the end of February 2015 and then until the end of June 2015.

The first four tranches of the EAP 2010 were disbursed on time, suggesting that the corresponding programme outcomes for each tranche had been met. The fifth tranche was not disbursed until early July 2011, fuelling speculations as to the performance of the Greek economy and the Greek government. In order to remedy this uncertainty, amidst the havoc and further downgrading of Greek bonds (Standard & Poor's rating was lowered to CCC, i.e. substantial risk/extremely speculative), in June 2011 the Greek parliament approved a Medium-Term Fiscal Strategy (MTFS) for 2012–2015. In line with the provisions of this MTFS, additional fiscal consolidation measures valued at €28 billion were scheduled, based on a reduction in expenditures of €14.8 billion (6.3 per cent of GDP) and an increase in public revenue of €13.4 billion (5.7 per cent of GDP). A modest reshuffling of the government took place, essentially as a means of creating the image of a committed government aware of its failings. The fifth tranche of the loan was duly disbursed and discussions began on a new loan from the euro-area member states to replace the initial €110 billion rescue package under the first EAP. The new financial package for Greece was agreed upon on 21 July 2011; however, it was not until December 2011 that the new programme was approved by the European Council. The programme's implementation started in late February 2012.

With regard to the interest rates and maturity for the loans extended to Greece, a crucial decision signifying a de facto restructuring of the Greek debt was taken on 11 March 2011. The maturity of the euro-area loans to Greece was extended from three years to 7.5 years, in line with the IMF part of the package, and the interest rates were adjusted from 5.2 per cent to 4.2 per cent (European Council, 2011: 4). The interest rate paid by Greece for the IMF loan remained at 3.3 per cent. At the beginning of 2015, Greece numbered among the EU programme countries paying the lowest interest rates.

In line with agreements reached during the European Council meeting in December 2011, the launch of the second EAP in 2012 was conditional upon so-called private sector involvement (PSI) in the Greek programme, i.e. restructuring of the Greece's privately owned debt. Although the question of the sustainability of the Greek debt was debated by many, it was the confidential report (leaked to the press) released by the Troika on 21 October 2011 and depicting the Greek public debt as unsustainable that created the momentum for the PSI. The PSI, brokered by the Institute of International Finance (IIF), foresaw a 53 per cent restructuring of the privately held portion of the Greek debt. The programme turned out to be a success, in that out of the total of €205.6 billion in bonds eligible for the exchange offer, approximately €197 billion, or 95.7 per cent, have been exchanged, thereby contributing to the sustainability of the Greek debt.

The objectives of the EAPs included the restoration of Greece's fiscal balance, the attainment of solvency, the modernisation of the economy and economic growth. In this way, the first EAP in particular represented a standard set of solutions to the common problem of overspending, whereby fiscal consolidation and fiscal discipline coupled with structural reforms were expected to yield positive outcomes in the form of growth and increased revenue. Significantly, in the first version of the first EAP, the notion of privatisation was essentially neglected. On the contrary, provisions devoted to revenue-enhancing measures were meticulously designed. Drawing on the negative experiences with the implementation of the first EAP, the second EAP stressed very specific expenditure-reducing measures, especially the reform of the public health-care system and further reductions in pension levels. Moreover, an explicit emphasis was placed on both the privatisation process (conceived both as a revenue-enhancing measure and a tool of liberalisation of the economy) and the liberalisation of services and product markets. The most important policies in this respect concerned the functioning of the labour market, including a reduction in the minimum salary level and some deregulation measures. However, due to problems in transposition and implementation, these measures did not result in either the opening of or increased flexibility in the labour market. On the contrary, malfunctions that were particularly detrimental to young people entering the labour market emerged as a side effect.

In July 2011, a Task Force for Greece was established by the Commission. The rationale behind the establishment of this body (led by Horst Reichenbach) was to improve the perceived low quality and limited efficiency of implementation of the first EAP. Essentially, the Task Force played the role of a liaison between the Greek authorities and other EU member states and was meant to provide technical assistance in the form of recommendations on legislative, regulatory and administrative (re)programming measures related to the disbursement of EU funds.

In mid-2014, the Greek authorities opened a discussion on the possible end of the EAP and a so-called 'clean exit', but the Eurogroup did not approve. Instead, a decision was taken to offer Greece a precautionary credit line in the form of an existing ESM tool called ECCL (Enhanced Conditions Credit Line). The ECCL would draw on the undisbursed €11 billion granted to Greece for the recapitalisation of Greek banks. The Eurogroup and the Commission both made the case for involving the IMF as well. Implicit in the possibility of extending the ECCL to Greece was a new agreement between Greece and its creditors. Given the political instability in Greece and the prospect of snap elections, the decision was postponed to after the election scheduled for 25 January 2015.

Structural problems of the Greek economy and the insolvency issue

Prior to the Troika's engagement with Greece, the major structural weaknesses of Greece included *unsustainable fiscal policies* and *excessive public expenditures* that led to persistent deficits and high debt-to-GDP ratios. An overgrown, inefficient and costly public sector, including a large number of deficit-carrying and subsidised state-owned enterprises (SOEs), and neglected reforms (liberalisation and privatisation) constituted the major problems of the Greek economy. Greece's fiscal weaknesses, hidden in part by high revenues in the period preceding the global financial crisis, were revealed by the rising cost of financing its deficits and government debt after 2007. In turn, *rigid labour and product markets* precluded the private sector's ability to swiftly adjust to the changing dynamics of the domestic and international economy following the global financial crisis of 2008. This situation was aggravated by a *progressive loss in competitiveness* related to labour productivity, prices and a hostile domestic and international business environment following the global crisis. However, it would be an overstatement to suggest a direct link between these issues and Greece's insolvency in early 2010. The dramatic deterioration of Greece's fiscal position and the rating agencies' pessimistic outlook on the country's solvency should instead be associated with the implications of domestic politicking by the PASOK government throughout 2009 and 2010 and its unintended consequences; the salient hypothesis here being that the country's sovereign debt crisis was avoidable.

Following unsuccessful attempts by the Karamanlis administration to push a reformist agenda over the period 2004–2009, early elections were enforced in October 2009 by PASOK on the occasion of the election for the President of the Republic. The electoral campaign reflected the populism and demagogy of the time, peaking with the argument employed by Papandreou that 'the money is there [to be spent]'. This was essentially aimed at convincing the electorate that the ND had ignored the needs of society and the hardships being endured by the population. Georgios Papandreou, heir to the political legacy and charisma of Andreas Papandreou, was entrusted with victory by his father's supporters, winning 44 per cent of the vote. Shortly after the ballot, the newly elected PASOK government established a Solidarity Fund to disburse allowances to large segments of the population, thus putting a serious strain on the public budget. Moreover, in a move designed to discredit the previous administration and set a convenient benchmark for assessing the political efficiency of the new government, an official revision of the projected general government deficit was announced (from 8 to 12.7 per cent). At the same time, in the European Commission, Papandreou pressed charges against the Karamanlis government based on its alleged falsification of fiscal data (Papathanasiou, 2010: 9–15).

As argued elsewhere (Visvizi, 2012a: 21–22), what was initially viewed as a domestic strategy of discrediting the ND brought about uncontrolled hysterical responses on the part of a number of international third-party actors (markets, investors, rating agencies, governments) that began to question Greece's creditworthiness. The markets in particular were taken by surprise, which led to a dramatic deterioration of Greece's terms of lending in late October 2009, with yields for Greek treasury bills rising sharply. The new administration's response to this emergency was delayed. Rather than tackling the roots of the problem, Papandreou initiated a double-pronged communication strategy. One aim was to convince the political establishment in the EU and the US that Greece had fallen prey to massive speculative attacks, and thus that financial regulations should be strengthened to prevent market manipulation in the future. In addition, by means of an essentially anti-Greek discourse that Papandreou employed in the foreign media (Visvizi, 2014: 338–339), the strategy sought to separate the developments in Greece from Papandreou's actions (and eventually his policies). This allowed Papandreou to recast himself as a responsible modern politician, the saviour of the Eurozone and the euro, and a cosmopolitan. The enduring market hysteria was fuelled by statements in which Greece was likened to the sinking Titanic (Papakonstantinou, 2010) whereas the Greeks were portrayed as notorious tax-dodgers sipping cocktails and iced coffee next to their swimming pools. Eventually, economic reform measures were announced in January 2010 in the form of an Updated Hellenic Stability and Growth Programme (SP2010). However, this did not have any real impact on the market perceptions of the solvency of the Greek state, and thus the creditworthiness of Greece as assessed by Fitch, Standard & Poor's and Moody's continued to deteriorate.

In March and April 2010, with prices for Greek government bonds becoming increasingly prohibitive, discussions on how to address Greece's insolvency problem were held; these were especially important because the EU did not have any relevant mechanisms at its disposal. Of the two proposals suggested – one exclusively involving EU member states' bilateral loans to Greece and the other based on the IMF's participation – the second alternative was selected. At the time it seemed that the IMF's engagement, backed by the organisation's know-how, experience and policy of conditionality, would guarantee the efficient implementation of the Greek EAP. During the crisis, there had been some speculation as to why Papandreou and his minister of finance had waited so long to request the IMF's assistance, especially since – as reports suggest – the option had long been on the table.

Negotiations over the bailout programme and description of the final bailout programme

In the debate on the Troika's involvement in Ireland, Portugal and Greece, the following question has been frequently raised: to what extent the negotiations between a programme-country government and the Troika represented what the government actually wanted, as well as to what extent the outcome of the negotiation process was predetermined by the representatives of the Troika. The Greek case offers interesting insights in this regard.

The 2010 EAP contained provisions from the Updated Hellenic Stability and Growth Programme (SP2010) that the PASOK government had submitted to the European Commission earlier that year. In this sense, the first EAP was exactly what the PASOK government wanted. This suggests that in the initial stages of the EAP's implementation, the PASOK government was trusted and given considerable leeway; hence, it would be absurd to argue that anything was imposed on the government. On the contrary, shortly before submitting the official request for external financing to avoid insolvency, as a means of avoiding the necessity of consulting with Greece's creditors, the PASOK government passed an extremely strict tax law (Law 3842/2010) that effectively undermined business activity in the country and directly contributed to the subsequent recession. The law in question introduced multiple increases in the taxation of income, revenue, luxury goods and real estate, set special levies and established presumptive taxation. Several other punitive measures were included, one of which transformed the inability of natural persons to deliver on their fiscal obligations into a criminal offense. The law was published in the Official Government Gazette on 23 April 2010 (to enter into force as of 1 January 2010). The same day, Greece extended an official request to the EU, the ECB and the IMF for financial assistance. At the time, experts in the IMF circle considered that particular policy move by the PASOK government to be inappropriate, in terms of both political *savoir vivre* and economic policy choices. Nevertheless, the European Commission and specific EU member states (most notably, Germany) seemed to have uncritically embraced Papandreou's administration. For instance, in Summer 2010, Olli Rehn praised the Greek government for the progress it had achieved and predicted a quick end to the programme. That same year, Papandreou was honoured with the prestigious German Quadriga Award for 'the power of veracity' and was later named one of *Foreign Policy* magazine's Top 100 Global Thinkers for 'making the best of Greece's worst year'.

With respect to the negotiation process itself, the PASOK government very skilfully employed arguments regarding the alleged impunity of the (rich) tax-dodgers and succeeded in convincing the Troika that tax evasion was the culprit behind Greece's fiscal imbalance. Given that the sovereign debt crisis in Greece was the result of deep-seated structural problems and political paralysis, the fact that Troika actually considered the absurd arguments of tax evasion based on images of swimming pools and expensive cars suggests that in the initial stages of the negotiation process the Troika was open to dialogue and ready to listen rather than to impose policy choices on the Greek authorities. However, as time passed and the Troika found it increasingly difficult to write positive progress-assessment reports, its initial trust was replaced with suspicion towards the Greek establishment. The shift in the Troika's stance coincided with the elections of June 2012 and the formation of the coalition government of Antonis Samaras. As a result,

Samaras and his government had to deal with a triple challenge: an economic recession, the need to secure sources of funding by meeting the programme's objectives, and the negotiations with a suspicious and increasingly reluctant Troika that – mindful of its earlier experiences – was determined to be as efficient as possible this time.

Over the period 2010–2012, the PASOK government succeeded in channelling the burden of fiscal adjustment primarily to the private sector (via revenue-enhancing measures), thus shoring up its electoral base (i.e. the public sector). The fundamentally ill-advised policy mix thereby implemented was subject to Samaras' critique throughout the period 2010–2012. Nevertheless, once in power, Samaras' pleas to renegotiate the programme's provisions in hopes of reviving private-sector activities were rejected by the Troika. In political terms, Samaras found himself at an impasse, forced to negotiate the non-negotiable with an unrelenting Troika. In an uncharacteristic act of goodwill, in 2013 the Troika agreed to introduce a temporary reduction (from 23 to 13 per cent) in the VAT rate for hotels and restaurants, making the consolidation of this move conditional on increased revenues in the state budget. However, by the time this particular tax reduction was introduced, it was too late to expect significant results, and Samaras was forced to reinstate the 23 per cent VAT rate as of 2014. Most importantly, the negotiation process was hampered by the issue of tax evasion. Having grown to mythical proportions, the tax evasion issue undermined Samaras' arguments on liberalisation, reductions in taxes and potential growth. It is worth noting at this point that the Greek case highlights another very curious process. It shows that the instrumental use of certain arguments (here, tax evasion as the principal culprit of the crisis in Greece) in a path-dependent way contributed to the construction of an inaccurate depiction of the reality of the Greek crisis. This distorted depiction of reality in turn served as the basis for the negotiation process. This may explain why the Troika was unwilling to redesign some of the fundamentally misguided provisions of the policy mix implemented in Greece.

Another important set of factors that proved critical for the negotiation process, on the part of both the Troika and the Greek government, is related to the negotiating teams. The IMF is renowned for its professionalism, experience and excellence in negotiations, including negotiation techniques, preparation for talks and actual performance during negotiation sessions. With regard to their Greek counterparts, from 2010 to 2014, the Greek government employed the same chief negotiator and roughly the same team members. Insiders' observations suggest that on many occasions the Greek team was unable to win any points in the negotiations, largely due to insufficient preparation. Indeed, media reports on specific visits of the Troika to Athens produce an image of the Troika–Greek government relationship as full of misunderstandings and confusion. This was translated by the media into a rhetoric of conflict between the Troika and the government.

The really interesting (and troubling) observation here is that no changes were made in the design of the negotiating team, including the chief negotiator, even though substantial ideological differences as to the logic underlying the structural adjustment process could be observed between the PASOK and the ND governments. Although the major dividing line was drawn by the method of channelling the burden of fiscal adjustment (private vs public sector), Samaras kept the negotiating team that *en gros* represented a left-leaning political stance. In this context it is difficult to imagine that the team would effectively represent and defend centrist/right-leaning policy goals and a policy mix. By retaining the same chief negotiator, Samaras may have essentially shot himself in the foot; unless of course he had no choice in the matter, given that his government was a coalition government.

In discussing the negotiation process between the Greek authorities and the Troika, it is necessary to point out that the Troika is a complex and unprecedented institution of international cooperation with no strictly defined rules of conduct. The Troika represents three institutions, i.e. the European Commission, the ECB and the IMF. Apart from offering financial assistance, the Troika has also offered technical assistance on several less and more specific issues regarding the reform and fiscal adjustment process. For instance, in the context of the recapitalisation of the Greek banks in 2012 and 2013, the representatives of the European Commissions' DG Competition were praised for their professionalism, their zeal in blocking Greek proposals that represented breaches of EC law on competition and their generally supportive attitude towards the top managers of Greek private banks. Given its unprecedented nature and complex ad hoc design, the functioning of the Troika has been effectively an outcome of practices that were either reproduced from the IMF or the EU or established instantly for the purpose of delivering results in a given programme-country. In this respect, the impact of personalities on the functioning of the Troika needs to be taken into consideration as it weighs on the analysis. For instance, in the case of Greece the role played by Paul Thomsen was crucial.

Although divisions and conflicting opinions among its representatives in Greece would become more apparent over time, the Troika did a very good job overall in presenting the image of a coherent and unified actor to the media. In this way, assumptions that arguments and differences of opinions existed within the Troika remained in the sphere of unfounded speculations. This had a positive impact on the Troika's bargaining power. It was only in 2014 that some of the tension festering in the Troika forum leaked to the public in the form of a war of words between the Commission and the IMF (Fox, 2013). The IMF's uneasy status in the Troika forum and other contingencies related to the IMF's engagement with programme-countries were signalled in a report published by the IMF's watchdog in November 2014. Notably, the report suggested, 'Looking forward, to protect the institution's independence and to ensure uniform treatment of the entire membership, the IMF should develop guidelines for structuring such collaboration arrangements that clarify the parties' roles and accountabilities' (IEO, 2014: v).

The politics of the implementation of the programme provisions

The case of Greece highlights the importance of broad political consensus for effective EAP implementation. It also suggests that programme ownership, a feature frequently emphasised in the literature on structural adjustment programmes (Drazen, 2002), cannot be limited to the ruling party itself but needs to stretch across the political spectrum. Specifically, throughout 2010–2012, focused on domestic politicking and concerned with minimising the political cost of the EAP, the PASOK government essentially implemented a cherry-picking strategy with regard to the programme's implementation. It sought to implement the most politically neutral components of the programme, i.e. those that did not have any direct impact on the party's electoral base. As a result, the bulk of the fiscal adjustment was channelled through the private sector, leaving the overgrown, inefficient, corrupt and unaffordable public sector virtually intact. The few expenditure-reducing measures that the PASOK government introduced included dramatic reductions in pension levels. This strategy of cherry picking was legitimised by the discourse on tax evasion as the culprit behind Greece's predicament. Initiated by Papandreou and his minister of finance, over time this discourse on tax evasion grew to mythical proportions, misguidedly creating the image of Greece as a nation of tax-dodgers. The media then uncritically reproduced the revelations of the annual Corruption Perceptions Index (CPI), turning the instrumentally employed argument into an intersubjective reality. The problem is that by directing the Troika's focus towards the exaggerated tax-avoidance problem, the PASOK government neglected the most important programme components (such as liberalisation, privatisation, modernisation and growth) in the politics of the programme implementation. Over the period June 2012-December 2014, the coalition government led by Samaras attempted to implement several of the reforms scheduled, yet given the fragility of the coalition bold structural reforms bore the risk of the government's collapse. This explains why several of them have been postponed. Over the period January–June 2015, the SYRIZA government succeeded in reverting and/or stopping several reforms introduced earlier, e.g. privatisation and downsizing of the public sector. Overall, party-specific considerations as well as personal calculations would block the implementation of the EAPs' provisions over the period 2010–2015, rendering the prospects of growth and fiscal stability in Greece captive of politicking and personal ambitions.

The implementation process for both EAPs for Greece was accompanied by the increasing destabilisation and polarisation of Greece's political scene, the decline of the Greek economy and rising poverty and deprivation among Greek society. A mismatch between the fiscal performance and growth objectives set out in the programme and the actual performance of the economy was apparent. Tables 10.1 and 10.2 offer insights into the macroeconomic and fiscal targets laid out in the EAP of May 2010 and the most recent forecasts (at the time of writing) by the European Commission. Of the indicators presented in both tables, the most striking is the debt-to-GDP ratio: 115 per cent of GDP in 2009, forecast to stabilise at 175.5 per cent of GDP in 2015.

Table 10.1 The macroeconomic and fiscal targets set out in the Economic Adjustment Programme 2010

	2009	*2010*	*2011*	*2012*	*2013*	*2014*	*2015*
GDP growth (%, year on year)	−2	−4	−2.6	1.1	2.1	2.1	2.7
Public budget balance (% of GDP)	−13.6/ −15.4	−8.1	−7.6	−6.5	−4.8	−2.6	−2
Gross public debt (% of GDP)	115	133	145	149	149	146	140

Source: Adapted from MoF (2010).

Over the period of the EAPs' implementation, the Greek economy contracted more than 20 per cent and the investment level decreased by 86 per cent in comparison to 2008 (IMF, 2013). The unemployment level, a modest 9 per cent in 2009, will soar to 26.8 per cent in 2015 according to the Commission's forecast. At the end of 2014, the unemployment rate in several areas had reached 45 per cent. Decreased public spending and prohibitive prices for heating oil led to extreme (for a developed country) situations, where whole families would find it difficult to deal with low winter temperatures in several parts of Greece. Indeed, the at-risk-of-poverty rate increased from just above 20 per cent in 2008 to over 44 per cent in 2013 (ILO, 2014). At the beginning of 2015, empty shop fronts only added to the atmosphere of depression and hopelessness that even hung over districts once considered posh. Well-known top-flight brands have either left Greece or have significantly reduced their overall exposure. In return, Athens has been flooded with countless bakeries and confectioners serving as evidence of faltering income levels and the corresponding hierarchy of spending needs.

Even if by the end of 2013 and in the first quarter of 2014 there had been some positive signs regarding the Greek economy, such as the primary fiscal surplus of 0.8 per cent (European Commission, 2014a), these have been lost in the first quarters of 2015 when SYRIZA's government pushed Greece into a political limbo and nearly out of the Eurozone. The considerable achievements by Samaras' coalition government, which succeeded in getting the EAP back on track, were wasted and it remains to be seen if the major structural problems of the Greek economy (such as the overgrown and highly unionised public sector encompassing the state administration and state-owned enterprises, over-regulation, insufficient liberalisation, and – due to the measures introduced during the crisis – excessive taxation) will be eventually addressed following the breakthrough negotiations between Tsipras and the creditors leading to a third EAP for Greece.

As a result of increasing poverty and unemployment rates, the electorate has become extremely susceptible to populism, demagogy and manipulation. At the same time, the political scene is too small, too densely populated and too conflicted to contain the variety of divisive internal and external political pressures. Indeed, over the period 2010–2015, Greece has had five prime ministers, several

Table 10.2 Macroeconomic indicators for Greece: Forecast (2013–2016)

Forecasts for Greece	*2013*	*2014*	*2015*	*2016*
GDP growth (%, year on year)	−3.3	0.6	2.9	3.7
Inflation (%, year on year)	−0.9	−1	0.3	1.1
Unemployment (%)	27.5	26.8	25	22
Public budget balance (% of GDP)	−12.2	−1.6	−0.1	1.3
Gross public debt (% of GDP)	174.9	175.5	168.8	157.8
Current account balance (% of GDP)	−2.7	−2.8	−2.5	−2.2

Source: European Commission (2014b).

constellations of the cabinet, and three rounds of early general elections. In particular, the second half of 2011 was marked by the political demise of Papandreou, who unsuccessfully sought to rescue his position by proposing a national referendum on the second EAP (Visvizi, 2012b). Although Papandreou never said 'I step down', an agreement was brokered that led to the formation of an interim government under Lucas Papademos, the former vice president of the ECB. This government, dominated by PASOK, was inaugurated in Athens in mid-November 2011. Due to its provisional nature and lack of democratic legitimacy, it was endowed with a limited mandate. Its purpose was threefold: to ensure that the sixth tranche of the EU/IMF rescue package would be disbursed, to negotiate the 50 per cent voluntary bond exchange programme with private creditors, along with provisions for the Greek bank recapitalisation scheme, and to pave the way for parliamentary elections tentatively scheduled for 19 February 2012. These elections ultimately took place on 6 May 2012. However, as the political scene had been left fragmented, the victorious ND was unable to form a government; neither was SYRIZA, the runner-up. As a result, a second interim government was formed under the leadership of Panagiotis Pikramenos with the goal of preparing for the next round of elections. These national elections, held on 17 June 2012, led to a narrow victory for the ND[2] and the establishment of a coalition government under the leadership of Samaras.

At the end of 2014, two and a half years into the coalition government's attempts to implement the EAP's provisions, Greece recorded a slim primary fiscal surplus (2.7 per cent of GDP in 2014), raising hopes that, like Portugal and Ireland, it would be granted a 'clean exit' option from the EAP and the Troika's supervision. As Greece's European partners did not share Samaras' optimism (Visvizi, 2014), a negative decision concerning this exit was taken during the Eurogroup meeting on 9 December 2014 (Dijssenbloem, 2014), thus prompting speculation on the state of the Greek economy and placing additional ammunition in the hands of the Greek opposition (i.e. SYRIZA). Indeed, in what represents a political déjà vu reminiscent of the political blackmail employed by PASOK back in 2009, SYRIZA set in action a chain of events that forced Samaras to risk the possibility of early elections. Similarly as in 2009, the trigger for the 2015 ballot was the election for the post of president of the Republic, a largely symbolic position .The term of then-president Karolos Papoulias was due to expire in 2015, so it was necessary for candidates to be nominated in 2014. In a conflicted parliament with a growing number of independent MEPs leaning towards the possible future winning camp, it was impossible for Samaras to obtain the necessary majority. Several speculations floated as to why Samaras decided to speed up the elections. The most viable explanation is that given the pre-existing path-dependent constraints faced by Samaras (i.e. Troika and the EAPs), in combination with the extraordinary pressure exerted by SYRIZA, the governing process had become intractable. In good faith, foreign commentators would ask at that time whether cooperation between Samaras and SYRIZA would be an option as a means of avoiding the election and the likely destabilisation of the political scene. However, SYRIZA had no desire for any such cooperation. Tsipras' goal was the post of prime minister. Samaras, in contrast, for reasons of personal integrity could not cooperate with SYRIZA, i.e. a party that deliberately exploited cheap (detached from actual reality) anti-EAP rhetoric to leverage its popularity and political success and that employed the Troika's hesitation over the 'clean exit' to undermine the efforts and achievements of Samaras' government and Greek society as a whole.

In the months that followed SYRIZA's ascent to power in January 2015, the crisis in Greece once more became the centre of media attention, fuelled by frequently imprudent statements by certain cabinet members. With the advent of the Tsipras government and privatisation were halted, civil servants and administrative personnel at the universities rehired, perpetual students reinstated, new positions in the public sector were filled. In February 2015 the government negotiated a four-month extension of the bailout programme for Greece. Following several rounds of unsuccessful talks, the negotiations were eventually broken off by the Greek government, unwilling to succumb to the creditors' demands for a more prudent fiscal policy. In late June 2015, in a yet another déjà vu move (reminiscent of Papandreou and the infamous developments in Cannes in November 2011) and to the dismay of all observers, Tsipras called for a national referendum to be held on 5 July 2015. Capital controls were introduced on 28 June 2015, with ATMs dispensing up to €60 per day per citizen; Greece failed on its payment to the IMF on June 30. Regardless of the alleged dubious legality of the referendum (the constitution forbids referenda on fiscal policy matters), the Greeks were asked if they were against (or in favour) of the by that time defunct Eurogroup proposal concerning fiscal adjustment measures of the value of €8 billion. Following a very strong 'no' campaign by the SYRIZA government, 61.31 per cent of participants voted 'no' in the referendum, which had a high turnout (62.5 per cent) (MoI, 2015). In the week that followed, though, opinion polls would suggest that only 12 per cent of respondents were in favour of the return of the drachma. To the bewilderment of the voters, in a series of events suggesting a process of enforced, speedy political maturing of the Greek politicians, with Grexit and its consequences looming on the horizon, the Greek parliament passed a bill proposing a structural adjustment programme of the value of €13 billion. This proposal formed the basis for the negotiations with the

Eurogroup held during the emergency Euro Summit where the prospects of a bridge financing and a third bailout for Greece of the value of *c.* €89 billion were discussed.

Conclusion

The EAPs for Greece, like those for Ireland and Portugal, definitely 'stand out compared to typical IMF programmes because of their exceptionally long durations and the exceptionally large size of the financial assistance packages' (Pisani-Ferry et al., 2013: 4). The discussion of the developments in Greece under bailout conditions highlights the importance of domestic policy factors in the successful implementation of the EAP, as well as the crucial role of transparent and effective communication processes between creditors and the programme-country. A case could be made that several episodes of the Greek tragedy might have been avoided if the communication process had been better. The Greek case highlights as well that the nature of EAP ownership remains fundamental to the success of EAP implementation, that ownership needing to rest on a consensus stretching across the political spectrum. The Greek case suggests too that personalities matter and that the notion of personal responsibility for a nation's fate may sometimes weigh more than politicking and ideology. The apparent U-turn that Tsipras has made attests to that. It remains to be seen what happens next.

Note

1 Following SYRIZA's ascent to power in January 2015 and due to a Greek government's request the Troika has been referred to as 'institutions', while a representative of the European Parliament joined the "institutions".
2 Nea Democratia (ND) won 29.66 per cent of the vote and 129 seats (out of 300) in the Greek parliament. The Coalition of the Radical Left, SYRIZA, won 26.89 per cent of the overall vote and 71 seats. The socialist PASOK won 12.28 per cent of the vote and 33 seats, followed by the Independent Greeks (7.51 per cent and 20 seats), the Golden Dawn (6.92 per cent and 18 seats), the Democratic Left (6.26 per cent and 17 seats) and the Communist Party of Greece (4.50 per cent and 12 seats).

References

Dijsselbloem, J. (2014) 'Remarks by Jeroen Dijsselbloem at the press conference following the Eurogroup meeting of 6 November 2014,' Eurogroup, Remarks, Brussels, 6 November.
Drazen, A. (2002) 'Conditionality and ownership in IMF lending: A political economy approach,' *IMF Staff Papers* 49, Special Issue, International Monetary Fund.
European Commission (2014a) 'The Second Economic Adjustment Programme for Greece Fourth Review,' European Economy, Occasional Papers 192, Brussels. Available at http://ec.europa.eu/economy_finance/publications/occasional_paper/2014/pdf/ocp192_en.pdf (accessed 21 January 2014).
European Commission (2014b) 'European Economic Forecast: Autumn 2014,' European Economy 7/2014, 4 November.

European Council (2011) 'Conclusions of the Heads of State or Government of the Euro Area of 11 March 2011,' Brussels.
European Financial Stability Facility (EFSF) (2015) 'EFSF programme for Greece expires today,' EFSF Press Release, June 30. Available at: www.esm.europa.eu/press/releases/efsf-programme-for-greece-expires-today.htm (accessed 2 July 2015).
Featherstone, K. (2011) 'The Greek sovereign debt crisis and EMU: A failing state in a skewed regime,' *Journal of Common Market Studies* 49(2): 193–217.
Fox, B. (2013) 'Rehn in war of words with IMF,' *euobserver*, 7 June. Available at: http://euobserver.com/economic/120419 (accessed 5 November 2015).
Independent Evaluation Office (IEO) of the International Monetary Fund (2014) 'IMF Response to the Financial and Economic Crisis: An IEO Assessment,' 8 October, Washington, DC.
International Labour Organisation (ILO) (2014) 'Greece: Productive jobs for Greece/ International Labour Office,' Research Paper, ILO Research Department, Geneva.
International Monetary Fund (IMF) (2013) 'IMF Executive Board Concludes 2013 Article IV Consultation,' Public Information Notice (PIN) no. 13/64, 5 June.
International Monetary Fund (IMF) (2014) 'Adjustment in Euro Area Deficit Countries: Progress, Challenges, and Policies,' IMF Staff Note, European Department and Research Department, IMF, Washington, DC, July.
Minister of Finance of Greece (MoF) (2010) 'Hellenic Stability and Growth Programme Newsletter,' Hellenic Ministry of Economy and Finance, Athens, 17 May.
Ministry of Interior (MoI) 'Referendum July 2015, Results'. Available at: www.referendum 2015gov.gr/en/ (accessed 6 January 2016).
Mitsos, A. (2000) 'Maximising Contribution to the European Integration Process as a Prerequisite for the Maximisation of Gains,' in A. Mitsos and E. Mossialos (eds) *Contemporary Greece and Europe*. Aldershot: Ashgate, pp. 53–92.
Papakonstantinou, G. (2010) quoted in Bodoni, S. and E. Ross-Thomas (2010) 'Europe Economy Chief Calls for More Steps by Greece (Update5),' *Bloomberg*, 15 February. Available at: www.bloomberg.com/apps/news?pid=newsarchive&sid=aKPXdMFfM9Ok (accessed 5 November 2015).
Papathanasiou, G. (2010) Με τη γλώσσα των αριθμών: Η αλήθεια για την Οικονομία [Talking numbers: the truth about the economy], Athens, November.
Pisani-Ferry, J., A. Sapir and G. Wolff (2013) 'EU-IMF Assistance to Euro-area Countries: An Early Assessment,' Bruegel Blueprint Series no. 19, Brussels.
Pryce, V. (2015) 'The EU bears some responsibility for Greece's liquidity crisis,' *The World Today* 71(2): 44–45.
Tsinisizelis, M. (2008) 'Greece in the European Union: A Political/Institutional Balance Sheet,' in Ministry of the Press and Mass Media, *About Greece*, Hellenic Republic, Athens, 145–158. Available at: http://video.minpress.gr/wwwminpress/aboutgreece/aboutgreece_greece_eu.pdf (accessed 5 November 2015).
Valinakis, Y. (2012) 'Greece's European Policy Making,' GreeSE Paper no. 63, Hellenic Observatory papers on Greece and Southeast Europe, LSE, London, October.
Verney, S. (1987) 'Greece and the European Community,' in K. Featherstone and D. K. Katsoudas (eds) *Political Change in Greece: Before and After the Colonels*. London: Croom Helm.
Visvizi, A. (2012a) 'The crisis in Greece and the EU-IMF rescue package: determinants and pitfalls,' *Acta Oeconomica* 62(1): 15–39.

Visvizi, A. (2012b) 'The crisis in Greece, democracy, and the EU,' *Carnegie Council for Ethics in International Affairs*, 10 December. Available at: www.carnegiecouncil.org/publications/ethics_online/0076.html (accessed 5 November 2015).

Visvizi, A. (2013) 'Democracy or Demagogy? The Greek Political Actors on the Sovereign Debt Crisis,' in L. Rye (ed.) *Distant Voices: Ideas on Democracy and the Eurozone Crisis*, Rostra Books, Trondheim Studies in History. Trondheim, Norway: Akademika Publishing, pp. 23–50.

Visvizi, A. (2014) 'From Grexit to Grecovery: The paradox of the Troika's engagement with Greece,' *Perspectives on European Politics and Society* 15(3): 335–345.

11 Confronting interrelated crises in the EU's Western periphery

Steering Ireland–EU relations back to the centre

Bernadette Connaughton

Introduction

Ireland has been regarded as the most successful peripheral country required to implement austerity policies since the onset of the financial crisis in 2008. This is illustrated by Ireland's ability to exit the International Monetary Fund (IMF)/ European Union (EU) bailout programme in December 2013, which is regarded as a European success story as well as an Irish one. This chapter explores the features that have impacted on the sovereign debt crisis in Ireland and how this in turn has affected EU–Ireland relations. The Irish case is symptomatic of several interrelated crises – property market, banking, fiscal, financial, economic, social and reputational (NESC, 2009; Donovan and Murphy, 2013; O'Riain, 2014). The crisis was initiated by the collapse of the property market, which precipitated a banking crisis and a fiscal crisis. A fateful decision in September 2008 to guarantee all the private liabilities of the banking sector led to Irish taxpayers assuming a significant burden for the activities of domestic and foreign banks. In parallel government revenue collapsed and the budget moved promptly from surplus to a massive deficit. This culminated in the financial crisis leading to the bailout application to the EU/IMF in November 2010. Under the EU/IMF Programme, Ireland adhered to a series of targeted measures advocating banking stabilisation, fiscal consolidation and structural reform. The discussion will explore how Ireland confronted these challenges and subsequently implemented the Troika's programme while endeavouring to enhance its credibility and commitment to EU membership.

The interrelated crises: global, European or home-grown?

Ireland slid into recession in September 2008 and since then it has felt the reverberations from a series of shocks arising from the global credit crunch and a property bubble collapse which prompted and exposed an interrelated set of crises in banking, fiscal and financial pillars. On the home front an over-reliance on the construction industry and the sources of revenue associated with it narrowed the tax base in an era that was also characterised by increases in public expenditure, wage inflation and a loss of economic competitiveness. A Fianna Fáil

(Soldiers of Ireland)-led coalition government was elected in 2007 on the basis of an election manifesto espousing growth. This over-optimism led to a series of policy errors that left Ireland poorly placed for coping with an economic downturn and extremely vulnerable to international shock (Fitzgerald, 2012; Whelan, 2010). A complete failure was the negligence in banking regulation and lack of action to ensure that the domestic financial system operated in a prudent manner (Regling and Watson, 2010). The financing of the huge investment in construction was certainly problematic but its origins were not entirely home-grown. With EMU membership, the ready flow of cheap credit within the Eurozone, coupled with low interest rates, incentivised borrowing. The removal of exchange rate risk enabled the banks to access funding, thus ensuring the flow of credit could persist. Despite the sanctions built into the Stability and Growth Pact, weak EU coordinating capacity meant that there was little external vigilance on national decision-making and this extended to the design of European decision-making and the management of monetary union. In Ireland, given the straitjacket of monetary policy, changes in the role of fiscal policy needed to be introduced in order to cool down inflationary pressures and this was not recognised by either the government or regulators (Fitzgerald, 2012: 2). Hence, while European and global factors adversely impacted on Ireland, its exposure to risks and its capacity to cope with them was undoubtedly shaped by its own national policy frameworks, institutions and processes which did not adequately protect the economy and society (NESC, 2009).

Confronting the crisis: 'no bank can be allowed to fail'

During 2007/8 several events unfolded internationally and exposed the vulnerability of Irish banks. The authorities were initially convinced that the difficulties were a symptom of a short-term liquidity problem rather than one of solvency and a threat to the stability of financial institutions. The belief that 'no bank can be allowed to fail' was accepted as an overarching principle of government policy by those involved, including the Department of Finance, the Central Bank, and the Financial Regulator (Honohan, 2010; Nyberg, 2011). The mantra around saving the banks was in part due to a belief in their systemic importance and the necessity to avoid the contagion effects across the euro area. Irish actors were also of the viewpoint that 'no bank can fail' reflected the stance of the European Central Bank (ECB) (Donovan and Murphy, 2013).

It is evident that the Irish authorities and both the Central Bank and the Office of the Financial Regulator were ill prepared to deal with the crisis as the fractures in the Irish banking system became exposed. It was not due to complacency but rather that the authorities underestimated the impact and totally misdiagnosed the types of problems that the Irish banks were facing (Donovan and Murphy, 2013: 194). Looking back on this period it is worth noting that there was surprisingly little discussion on banking prior to September 2008, whether in parliament or at cabinet level (Boyle, 2012: 101). The official reports by Honohan (2010) and Nyberg (2011) on the causes of the Irish banking and financial crisis have also emphasised the significant shortage of written documentation relating to developments as the crisis unfolded.

Perhaps the most controversial, contested and impactful action by the Irish government during the crisis was the decision to provide a comprehensive government guarantee to almost all of the financial liabilities of the domestic banking system (Donovan and Murphy, 2013) – including Anglo Irish Bank, which was not part of the bank clearing system. On 30 September 2008, in the face of the imminent collapse of those institutions, the six domestic banks received a broad government guarantee on all deposits and specific debt instruments until September 2010. The guarantee was to run for two years, meaning any default on bank liabilities that occurred during that period would be covered by the Irish government (Whelan, 2013). This was subsequently extended until 28 March 2013.

Initially the bank guarantee was presented as a solution to the immediate crisis and heralded by the Minister for Finance, Brian Lenihan, as 'the cheapest bail out in the world so far' (Carswell, 2008). In time this fateful decision unwound and came to 'represent for many, the source of much of the enormous financial difficulties the State has faced' (Donovan and Murphy, 2013: 196). In essence, the decision to guarantee the vast bulk of the banks' liabilities, without knowing what those liabilities were, proved catastrophic. As Boyle (2012: 115) notes, 'There was no doubt subsequently that the banks lied about their situation that evening in government buildings, and that particularly the situation of Anglo Irish Bank was being grossly misrepresented.' The government appear to have believed that the guarantee would not have consequences for the state finances and that the banks were suffering from a short-term liquidity problem. The politicians are accountable for the decision and it has been argued that senior civil servants and financial advisers did warn against the dangers of a blanket guarantee (Whelan, 2013). The initial European Central Bank (ECB) reaction to the guarantee is not publicly known but the government asserted that the ECB would have opposed any attempt to burn senior bondholders. The lack of contact about the decision with other European capitals was deemed problematic, however, and it provoked anger in UK government circles given the fear of capital flight. Ironically, what this broad guarantee did was leave 'the Irish state on the hook for the vast majority of the costs of the banking crisis' (O'Riain, 2014: 246).

Enduring the crisis: from the guarantee to the bailout

Following the guarantee funds began to reflow in the Irish banking system. Although the guarantee was technically never actioned, the fact that bank liabilities were guaranteed by government played a role in limiting the options to restructure insolvent banks so that private creditors shared the losses (Whelan, 2013). The enormity of the potential liability of the Irish state sobered officials in the Department of Finance and attention was directed towards obtaining a clear picture of the financial implications of the banking collapse and the requirements for direct recapitalisation. By January 2009 Anglo Irish Bank was nationalised and its senior management was replaced as information of gross malpractice emerged. Four banking reviews were undertaken up to March 2011 and following each one the bills for bank recapitalisation mounted. These costs played a crucial role in presenting the Irish debt burden as unsustainable to financial markets and consequently triggering an EU/IMF bailout (Whelan, 2013).

A further issue was a systemic solution to address handling the non-performing property investment loans within Irish banking. In April 2009 the National Asset Management Agency (NAMA) was set up to issue government backed bonds to the banks to purchase the loans at a 'haircut'. What became apparent was that approximately two thirds of the toxic assets transferred to NAMA came from Anglo Irish Bank. Over 2010 the combination of the guarantee, the direct injection of funds and the acquisition of distressed loans within the banking system illustrated the attempts to build a firewall around the problems of the Irish financial sector. Although the ECB provided support for the financial system in terms of liquidity, the absence of a Eurozone bank resolution instrument led to this massive private sector loss being assumed by the Irish taxpayer. Ireland's experience is extreme and it has been debated as to how much of these losses the Irish state needed to take responsibility for. An eventual total of approximately €64 billion makes it one of the most expensive bailouts in history (Woods and O'Connell, 2012).

As 2009 progressed the banking crisis became more inextricably linked with the developing economic and fiscal crises. One area of political relief for the government was Ireland's approval of the second Lisbon referendum in October 2009 when a turnout of 59 per cent voted decisively to approve the treaty by 67.13 per cent. By budget 2010 the deficit was brought to 11 per cent GDP and while the state had made an adjustment of almost €15 billion the public finances remained precarious. The measures to wrest control over the deficit also have to be considered against the backdrop of the Commission's requirement to reduce the deficit to less than 3 per cent of GDP as provided under the Stability and Growth Pact. As the Irish government's difficulties became more starkly apparent, the timeframe for reaching such a target was repeatedly modified. In April, anxiety intensified in European sovereign debt markets following the Greek bailout. As Ireland's creditworthiness began to be eroded the guarantee ceased to be of much use. In September 2010 it was announced that the zombie bank – Anglo Irish – would cost the state about €30 billion. Its recapitalisation was by providing it with bonds called 'promissory notes' which would consist of cash payments over several years. Under EU rules the promissory notes were put against Ireland's general government deficit and this caused the deficit to rocket to record levels of 30.9 per cent of GDP. At the end of September the government announced its intention to withdraw from the market, which was 'portrayed as a tactical move' since officials indicated that the budget was already fully funded to mid-2011 (Donovan and Murphy, 2013: 232).

Although the Irish authorities were able to draw on ECB-Central Bank funding it was evident that the Irish banks faced very serious solvency problems. The combination of high estimates for the cost of bank recapitalisation, an unfavourable ratings assessment for Ireland by Standard & Poor's, and the Deauville announcement by German chancellor Angela Merkel and French president Nicolás Sarkozy all served to intensify pressures and bond yields leapt further. Throughout this period the Irish government's position was to rebut negative commentary, even though much of it was entirely correct. The international market's loss in confidence meant that Ireland could not possibly meet its massive debts and this finally pushed Ireland to seek the rescue package from the IMF in liaison with the ECB and European Commission announced on 28 November 2010.

As with the guarantee decision, the behind-the-scenes events leading up to the bailout have been the subject of much speculation. The refusal to acknowledge the magnitude of the crises went to the heart of Irish government. The Taoiseach, Brian Cowen, and minister for finance, Brian Lenihan, forcefully denied an application was imminent and communications both within government circles and in announcements to the public were inadequate. A group of EU officials also visited Dublin for discussions on a draft four-year plan to address fiscal consolidation. An important factor perceived to direct events towards the inevitable application was the alleged intervention from the ECB. A series of letters between ECB president Jean-Claude Trichet and minister Lenihan published on 7 November 2014 provide details of a warning from Trichet on 15 October 2010 that the large provision of emergency liquidity assistance (ELA) could not be relied on indefinitely. The text of the letters from the ECB president appears to reflect a frustration that the Irish government would not face up to the gravity of the situation and submit a formal aid application. In his reply on 4 November Lenihan argued, 'It is the case that many market commentators attribute these comments [political figures in large member states] as being the primary driver of the increased spreads of peripheral countries, including Ireland, in recent days' (Beesley, 2014).

The wall of denial was shattered on 18 November 2010 when the governor of the Central Bank, Patrick Honohan, broke the news of Ireland's receipt of a 'large loan' in an early morning radio interview. The Irish nation was shocked when he confirmed that an EU/IMF delegation was arriving in Ireland that day to work out the details. A letter from the ECB on 19 November explicitly states that its governing council would authorise further provision of ELA to Irish financial institutions only if they received a commitment in writing that Ireland was going to send a request for financial support to the Eurogroup. On 21 November Lenihan informed Trichet that the government had subsequently taken the decision to seek access to external support.

Introducing the Troika programme

Unlike the anticipation preceding the formal bailout announcement the actual discussions with the 'Troika' proceeded smoothly. The 'negotiations' with the Troika were run by the Department of Finance but in reality the bulk of the work on the programme had already been completed. The ensuing Memorandum of Understanding (MOU) was predominantly consistent with the measures included in the four-year National Recovery Plan 2011–2014 which included cuts in public spending of €10 billion and €5 billion in tax rises. The Troika was broadly happy with the fiscal reform underway and the real question of the bailout was about how much and at what interest rate (interview senior official, December 2014).

A total of €67.5 billion was approved in financial aid for over a period of seven-and-a-half years. In return for the funding the Irish government was committed to a timeline of measures that included restructuring the banks, implementing further fiscal adjustment and introducing various structural reforms. A further €17.5 billion from the national pension reserve fund was included to assist with bank recapitalisation. The terms of the package were controversial and came with a high level of conditionality, including the achievement of the government's austerity programme and a higher than expected interest rate of 5.85 per cent. Partly due to pressure from the US the MOU could not be finalised without commitment from the Irish government not to pursue the controversial issue of burning senior bondholders (Donovan and Murphy, 2013: 250). The assistance kept public services running but the unwillingness of the European institutions to share in the burdens of adjustment was highly criticised. A more moderate assessment of its impact is reflected in the view that 'the bailout supplied a means through which Ireland could make a gradual rather than a sudden, adjustment to living within its means' (Leahy, 2013).

At this point in 2010 national per capita income was already 20 per cent lower than it was in 2007 (Dellepiane and Hardiman, 2012) and a total of €6 billion was taken out of the economy in budget 2011 along with further tax increases. Much of the competitiveness lost during the boom had been won back at this stage and the strategy pursued was to meet the targets through front loading the fiscal adjustment and reducing the deficit to below 3 per cent GDP by 2014. In reality economic conditions further stagnated and this led to more fiscal contraction. The anger and dismay felt by the Irish people was represented at European level by various public representatives including the Socialist Party MEP for Dublin, Jim Higgins, who asserted that the EU/IMF financial aid was a mechanism to turn Irish taxpayers into 'vassals' for European banks. This was rebuffed by José Manuel Barroso who claimed that 'the problems of Ireland were created by the irresponsible financial behaviour of some Irish institutions and by the lack of supervision in the Irish market' (Beesley, 2011).

The domestic political fall-out from the loss of sovereignty was enormous. The incumbent Fianna Fáil-Green coalition was hugely unpopular and the public was intensely angry, not only because of the bailout circumstances but because of the way in which the entire debacle had been handled. Support in the polls plummeted and the government crumbled from within as the Green Party withdrew from government on 23 January 2011. The election in February 2011 was a landslide victory for the opposition parties of Fine Gael (Irish race) and Labour. Despite its traditional position as the dominant player in the Irish party system, Fianna Fáil lost 24 per cent of its vote and the Green Party lost all its seats. They were replaced by a Fine Gael and Labour coalition that commanded a large majority and were branded a Government of National Recovery.

Implementing the EU/IMF programme: institutional arrangements

Between December 2010 and Ireland's formal exit from the bailout, the Troika became an important focus of governance arrangements. Troika representatives paid periodic visits to Dublin to assess Ireland's programme performance and core Troika personnel were resident in central government departments. The IMF positioned a permanent representative in the Central Bank and officials were required to provide detailed data on all budgetary and banking transactions. The MOU included precise timetables for individual policy actions and all budget decisions had to be cleared with the Troika. During visits the teams from the EU and IMF swarmed over accounts and held the government to task for its financial activities. The reduction in sovereign control was repugnant to Irish people since the economic viability of the Irish state had largely ceased to be an issue following changes in policy direction and modernisation from the late 1950s. The loss of control over Irish budgetary policy was highlighted in November 2011 when details of Ireland's budget for 2012 were discussed by the Bundestag's budget committee in advance of being discussed in the Irish parliament (Dukes, 2013). The Irish budget 2012 blueprint had been given to the German finance ministry as part of the agreed quarterly reviews of Ireland's Troika programme.

The Troika visits were managed by officials in the Department of Finance and this period coincides with efforts to establish structures and processes to address regulatory governance challenges and build oversight and capacity at the centre of government. In particular, shortcomings in coordination, official capacity for policy evaluation, and risk assessment had been identified in the Department of Finance (Wright, 2010; Regling and Watson, 2010). Formal organisational structures include the External Programme Compliance Unit (EPCU) established within the Department of Finance to manage Ireland's official interaction with the EU/IMF and to ensure that all programme conditions met targets. The quarterly missions were normally two weeks in duration, concluded with a press conference and revised programme documents were circulated to the EU, IMF and ECB. Programme monitoring reviews were published in tandem with the disbursement of funding. To assist with internal monitoring and promote a reform agenda, a new government department, Public Expenditure and Reform, undertook a comprehensive expenditure appraisal and sought to introduce reforms of 'doing more with less' into the public service.

'Fixing the country': reputational, banking and fiscal adjustment

Building capacity and restoring Ireland's reputation in Europe

Avoiding paralysis in decision-making processes both at home and abroad, and nurturing coalition relations were integral to securing the success of the assistance programme. When the Fine Gael-Labour government took office in March 2011 the Taoiseach, Enda Kenny, and Tánaiste's, Eamon Gilmore, staff reconfigured structures at the centre of government which included a far more formalised and active system of cabinet committees for overseeing implementation. At the apex of this system is the Economic Management Council (EMC) on which senior political advisers sit together with the two finance ministers, the Taoiseach, the Tánaiste and their secretaries General. The EMC acts as a clearing-house arrangement for major budgetary matters and overseeing decisions within the Troika framework. It is a controversial structure but government has defended its work, insisting it has the status of a cabinet sub-committee and does not usurp cabinet decision-making. It also plays an important role in coalition dynamics and Labour's senior aides pushed for a structure that balanced the powerful role of the Department of Finance and ensured that it did not retreat into a silo as it had in the chaos leading up to the bailout (interview senior official, December 2014).

Further arrangements were promoted by the Fine Gael-Labour coalition's pledge to prioritise Ireland's engagement with Europe. The Taoiseach held a three-line whip on efforts to engage with the EU and restore Ireland's reputation. In the words of one official, 'restoration of reputation was part of the strategy, right there at the top with restoration of public finances and economic growth – inextricably linked' (interview senior official, December 2014). In Autumn 2011 a group of officials moved to the Department of Taoiseach from the Department of Foreign Affairs to embed the EU Division there. A second secretary general in the Department of Taoiseach was created to play a lead role in EU coordination and support the work of the EMC. Officials actively worked on building rapport with their counterparts in EU capitals and the role of embassies was deployed more effectively. For example, on Tuesdays at 3 p.m. a video conference was held with each of the embassies in the Eurozone to brief them on economic issues. In May 2012 Ireland passed a referendum on signing the Fiscal Treaty with 60.3 per cent of the vote. The government's ability to persuade the electorate to vote for a European treaty at a time of crisis underlines the conviction that Ireland is better off anchored in the EU, although this preoccupation has largely been about domestic challenges rather than fully engaging with how Europe might integrate further in the future.

Banking

In order to 'fix the country', restoring Ireland's banking system was considered to be a major priority. Ironically, the announcement that the government was injecting an additional €17.5 billion into bank recapitalisation did not immediately improve market sentiment. The announcement of the EU/IMF programme intensified the problem and reliance on the central bank increased further (Whelan, 2013). The Department of Finance and the Central Bank worked hard to assess the banks' capital needs and meet those needs with the lowest costs to the budget by attracting private investment and bailing in subordinated debt. The system began to stabilise in spring 2011 and new legislation enabled the minister for finance to enforce coercive write-downs of subordinated bonds in banks requiring assistance. Progress remained slow in dealing with non-performing loans, especially mortgages in arrears. Although the Fine Gael-Labour government had some modest success in renegotiating the terms of refinancing the zombie Anglo Irish Bank, they did not manage to persuade the ECB and European Commission to countenance some burden sharing for the direct refinancing of the banks. This had been an election campaign issue, along with the resolution to press for a reduction in the onerous interest rate. The latter was achieved in July 2011, along with an agreement to extend the maturity on the EU loans that helped to improve the country's debt sustainability.

Addressing the debt incurred by Ireland to recapitalise the banking system was investigated at the EU Summit in Brussels on 29 June 2012. The Euro Area statement announced that a single banking supervisory mechanism would be established and concluded that, 'We affirm that it is imperative to break the vicious cycle between banks and sovereigns.' The agreement to provide the ESM with the possibility of injecting funds into banks directly was regarded as a breakthrough by the government. It was hoped that it might be able to purchase the government's equity position in banks (other than the toxic banks) without the Irish government incurring any financial obligation to the ESM. The statement also noted that, 'The Eurogroup will examine the situation of the Irish financial sector with the view of further improving the sustainability of the well-performing adjustment programme' (European Council, 2012). Confidence in this happening waned as it became evident that Germany, the Netherlands and Finland would not support this mechanism for dealing with legacy debt. In general it is believed that the IMF was more sympathetic to the Irish authorities' request for burden sharing than the EU elements of the Troika (Donovan and Murphy, 2013).

A second priority was to improve the terms of the promissory notes. Again the Irish government stressed the degree to which the country's debt has been increased due to the assimilation of the banking debt and that the bank guarantee had assisted in avoiding not just a collapse of the Irish banking system but contagion across the Eurozone. The argument was that allowances should be made for these efforts plus the fact that Ireland had rigorously adhered to the terms of the rescue programme and was optimistic about a successful return to the market – therefore avoiding a second bailout. Following sustained negotiations an agreement was reached in February 2013 on a restructuring of the promissory notes through their conversion into long-term government bonds following the liquidation of the Irish Bank Resolution Corporation (vehicle for the liquidation of Anglo Irish Bank). The deal left the total nominal amount of the debt unchanged but with a significantly extended bond repayment schedule that assists Ireland's overall economic and budgetary position. The terms on which the bank recapitalisation is funded continues to be a contested issue in Ireland's relationship with Europe.

Fiscal adjustment

In terms of fiscal measures Ireland made steady progress in reducing the fiscal deficit and its 'capacity to implement a very severe adjustment programme has been in many ways remarkable' (Donovan and Murphy 2013: 255). Despite their protestations during the 2011 election campaign, the Fine Gael-Labour coalition continued with the implementation of the budget announced in December 2010. Further fiscal adjustments of €3.5 billion were introduced in budgets 2012 and 2013. The retention of Ireland's 12.5 per cent corporation tax rate remained staunchly defended by the Irish government and keeping income taxes constant was prioritised. The distributive impact of fiscal adjustment shifted to pressure on social welfare payments and a significant impact on the public sector through more pay cuts and reduced services. Expenditure on health and social welfare areas tended to overrun but despite these 'implementation risks' the quarterly and annual fiscal targets for deficit reduction were met consistently because adjustments were made elsewhere. It is perhaps unlikely that this level of spending discipline could have been maintained outside a formal programme (Whelan, 2013). Ireland earned the nickname of 'poster boy for austerity' for adhering to the Programme of Support from the Troika so conscientiously. The quarterly review reports positively highlighted Ireland's efforts and upheld that maintaining steady fiscal consolidation was central to Ireland's future (European Commission, 2012). A gain from these results was the return of investor confidence as evidenced by the decline in yields on long- and short-term government bonds. In July 2012, Ireland began to re-enter the bond markets for the first time since the bailout programme began in 2010. By October the Taoiseach, Enda Kenny, was lauded on the cover of *Time* magazine for enacting a 'Celtic comeback'.

Despite these successes and a marginal return to growth, Ireland remained vulnerable given the uncertainty of the economic outlook and questions over domestic demand dependent on the strength of Ireland's main export partners. Unemployment statistics began to demonstrate improvement in 2013 and structural reforms focused on maintaining flexibility in the labour market and enhancing competitiveness. Structural reforms in areas like health, education and legal services were more difficult to advance and incurred the veto of influential interest groups. For example, the legal profession sought to protect its self-regulation and the twelfth report of the Troika review noted that there was no genuine progress towards enacting the Legal Services Regulation Bill since the previous review. Although this was a less prominent part of Ireland's programme, the Troika prompts were important for addressing reforms to encourage durable savings. Fiscal policy was the clearest example of comprehensive implementation and in 2013 Christine Lagarde of the IMF lauded Ireland's progress as 'setting standards' (Telford, 2013). Although the trade unions and opposition parties loudly voiced that austerity was not working, Irish people accepted budget cuts peaceably and without the violent protests witnessed on the streets in Spain and Greece. Two large demonstrations took place when the Troika arrived in November 2010 and opposition mobilised against specific measures like the household charge (precursor to property tax). Although Sinn Féin and the United Left Alliance made political gains in 2011 along with 13 per cent of the vote going to Independents, there was no major swing towards radical politics in Ireland at this time. Arguably, social inequality did not worsen but lower- and middle-income sectors of the population carried the main burden of debt and austerity significantly depressed living standards, even for those at work.

Exiting the bailout

As Ireland took over the presidency of the EU in January 2013 the government announced its intention to exit the bailout programme within the year. By mid-2013 Ireland's sovereign debt rate returned to pre-crisis levels and the country issued a number of well-priced long-term bonds. On 14 November 2013, the decision to conclude the EU/IMF programme on 15 December without a pre-arranged precautionary credit line was publicised. Although the wisdom of this decision was debated internally, it served as a clear signal to the international markets, credit rating agencies and European counterparts that Ireland had regained sovereignty, put the public finances back on a sustainable path and restructured the banking system. A cash balance of €20 billion had been accumulated through bond auctions in 2012/13 to act as a backstop, interest rates on Irish bonds had declined significantly and GDP was forecast to grow by 2 per cent in 2014. Ireland was also 95 per cent of the way towards meeting the deficit target of less than 3 per cent in 2015. The ability to exit the bailout and 'get the job done' generated favourable headlines all over Europe and considerably enhanced Ireland's reputation within the EU. A sobering reality is that the economic situation remains challenging and while Ireland is recording higher rates of growth relative to other member states, public debt levels are inordinately high. It has been very difficult for the government to make any breakthrough on burden sharing at EU level and this in turn places an additional political burden on the Irish government to ensure public tolerance of this obligation. Social solidarity has been stretched and the Irish people have reached their limit with austerity policies, as evidenced by the bungled introduction of legitimate water charges that led to massive protests in October 2014.

Conclusions

The Troika may have 'gone home' but the legacy of the interrelated crisis remains as Ireland suffered one of the most severe economic contractions in Europe. Although the crisis bore the imprint of global and European influences it was conditioned by multiple 'home-grown' governance and policy failures (Regling and Watson, 2010; Dellepiane Avellanedania and Hardiman, 2010). Moving forward will depend on Ireland's prospects for growth, domestic institutional reform, sustained social solidarity, and whether Ireland's public debt can be resolved successfully. The Troika retains an oversight function which takes the form of bi-annual missions for post-programme surveillance. It has indicated that real GDP growth of approximately 4 per cent is projected for 2014/15 but the downside risks to Ireland's short-term outlook are linked to a weakening in economic momentum in the euro area and the sustainability of high export growth. They reiterate that the Irish government must stand ready to adopt additional measures to address 'potential future risks' (European Commission, 2014). Of significance is how Ireland's relationship with Europe continues to evolve in the context of architectural reforms of the Eurozone. A strengthened European economic governance framework will assist in preventing the kind of imbalances that led to Ireland's sovereign debt crisis. At the end of 2014 the country is coming to terms with a new normality in which tighter policy coordination is anticipated as part of the European semester framework.

References

Beesley, A. (2014) 'Letters between Brian Lenihan and Trichet pivotal in Irish history,' *The Irish Times*, 7 November.

Beesley, A. (2011) 'Angry Barroso Points Finger of Blame at Irish Institutions,' *The Irish Times*, 20 January.

Boyle, D. (2012) *Without Power or Glory: The Greens in Government*. Dublin: New Island.

Carswell, S. (2008) 'Cheapest Bailout in the World,' *The Irish Times*, 24 October.

Dellepiane, S. and N. Hardiman (2012) 'The New Politics of Austerity: Fiscal Responses to the Economic Crisis in Ireland and Spain,' UCD Geary Institute Discussion Papers, February.

Dellepiane Avellanedania, S. and N. Hardiman (2010) 'The European context of Ireland's economic crisis,' *Economic and Social Review* 41(4): 473–500.

Donovan, D. and A. E. Murphy (2013) *The Fall of the Celtic Tiger: Ireland and the Euro Debt Crisis*. Oxford: Oxford University Press.

Dukes, A. (2013) *Legitimacy and Democratic Accountability: The European Semester and the Irish Budget*, Economic Governance Paper no. 5. Dublin: Institute of International and European Affairs.

European Union/International Monetary Fund (EU/IMF), 'Programme of Financial Support for Ireland,' 16 December. Available at: www.finance.gov.ie/sites/default/files/euimfrevised.pdf (accessed 4 November 2014).

European Commission (2012) 'Economic Adjustment Programme for Ireland: Autumn 2012 Review'. Available at: http://ec.europa.eu/economy_finance/publications/occasional_paper/2013/op127_en.htm (accessed 4 November 2014).

European Council (2012) 'Euro Area Summit Statement,' Brussels, 29 June. Available at www.european-council.europa.eu/home-page/highlights/euro-area-summit-statement (accessed 13 January 2015).

European Commission (2013) 'Economic Adjustment Programme for Ireland: Autumn 2013 Review'. Available at: http://ec.europa.eu/economy_finance/publications/occasional_paper/2013/op167_en.htm (4 November 2014).

European Commission (2014) 'Statement by the European Commission and the European Central Bank following the conclusion of the second post-programme surveillance mission to Ireland,' Press Release, Brussels. 21 November.

Fitzgerald, J. (2012) 'Restoring credibility in policy making in Ireland,' *Public Money and Management* 2(1): 27–34.

Honohan, P. (2010) *The Irish Banking Crisis: Regulatory and Financial Stability Policy 2003–2008: A Report to the Minister for Finance by the Governor of the Central Bank*. Dublin: Government Publications.

Leahy, P. (2013) 'Independence Day?,' *Sunday Business Post*, 15 December.

National Economic and Social Council (NESC) (2009) *Ireland's Five-Part Crisis: An Integrated National Response*, NESC Report no. 118. Dublin: NESC.
Nyberg, P. (2011) *Misjudging Risks: Causes of the Systemic Banking Crisis in Ireland: Report of the Commission of Investigation into the Banking Sector in Ireland.* Dublin: Government Publications.
O'Riain, S. (2014) *The Rise and Fall of Ireland's Celtic Tiger: Liberalism, Boom and Bust.* Cambridge: Cambridge University Press.
Regling, K. and M. Watson (2010) *A Preliminary Report on the Sources of Ireland's Banking Crisis.* Dublin: Government Publications.
Telford, L. (2013) 'Irish women have it better in some aspects of life than others in Europe: Christine Lagarde,' *Irish Independent*, 8 March.
Thorhallsson, B. and P. Kirby (2012) 'Financial crisis in Iceland and Ireland: Does European union and Euro membership matter?,' *Journal of Common Market Studies* 50(5): 801–818.
Whelan, K. (2013) 'Ireland's economic crisis: The good, the bad and the ugly,' *Journal of Macroeconomics* 39 (part B): 424–440.
Whelan, K. (2010) 'Policy lessons from Ireland's latest depression,' *Economic and Social Review* 41(2): 225–254.
Woods, M. and S. O'Connell (2012) 'Ireland's Financial Crisis: A Comparative Context,' *Central Bank Quarterly Bulletin* 4: 97–118.
Wright, R. (2010) *Strengthening the Capacity of the Department of Finance*: Report of the Independent Review Panel, Department of Finance. Dublin: Government Publications.

12 Portugal as the 'good pupil of the European Union'

Living under the regime of the Troika

José M. Magone

Introduction: the tale of the 'good pupil of the European Union'

Although the Portuguese economy is still weak and characterised by permanent imbalances in its current trade balance deficit, the country's political elites are highly committed to EMU. This approach with regard to the European Union is best symbolised by the depiction of Portugal as 'a good pupil of the European Union' (Pureza, 2011). This basically means that successive Portuguese governments have uncritically accepted reform packages from the European Union in the hope that this compliance will be well regarded by their counterparts in the supranational institutions. The 'good pupil' image is orientated towards the outside world, the technocratic establishment in Brussels and relevant core member states such as Germany, while neglecting the suffering of the population. This persistent desire on the part of Portuguese political elites to be praised by the technocratic elites and German politicians reached a peak when the Portuguese government emphasised during the crisis that 'Portugal is not Greece' (*Portugal não é a Grécia*, see Magone, 2014b).

In 2002, Portugal was the first country to receive a letter on an excessive budget deficit from the European Commission. Even before the financial, Euro- and sovereign debt crises began in 2008, successive governments in Portugal had to implement austerity measures to keep the nation's deficit below 3 per cent. However, this was only achieved at considerable social cost and with a decrease in GDP growth to below zero. In 2008, Portugal had a budget deficit of 3.1 per cent and a public debt ratio of 71.7 per cent (Eurostat, 2014b, c)

Efforts aimed at convergence of the deficit were abandoned in 2009 when the government was forced to deal with an economic recession and the bailout of several banks that had been affected by either toxic assets following the collapse of Lehman Brothers or the subsequent credit crunch. Critical in this regard was the Portuguese Business Bank (Banco Português de Negócios – BPN), which was mostly affected by the US financial crisis; it had to be bailed out by the government and was subsequently nationalised. This bailout was estimated to cost at least € 3.4 billion, and the deficit soared to 10.2 and 9.8 per cent in 2009 and 2010, respectively. The BPN bailout was heavily politicised, in part because several politicians from one of the main parties, the Social Democratic Party (Partido

Social Democrata – PSD), held top positions in the bank. Afterwards, the bank was sold for just €40 million to the Angolan Bank BIC by the PSD and Democratic Social Centre-People's Party (Centro Democratico e Social-Partido Popular – CDS-PP) coalition government led by Prime Minister Pedro Passos Coelho. Parallel to this, public debt increased from 53.1 per cent of GDP in 2001 to 94 per cent at the end of 2010 (Eurostat, 2014b, c; for an excellent discussion of the problems of reform, see Torres, 2009). As one influential Portuguese political scientist has claimed, Portugal has a huge imbalance between its productive and distributive sectors. The country's stagnant economy has only reinforced this, leading ultimately to what he calls the 'end of illusions' with regard to the main problem of the Portuguese political economy (Aguiar, 2005: 58).

This chapter delineates the process that led to the intervention of the Troika in Portugal. In the next section, the relationship between the Portuguese government and the Troika is discussed, followed by an early assessment of the outcomes of the implemented programme of reforms. The subsequent section deals with the impact on democracy and society at large. Finally, some conclusions will be drawn.

The emergence of the Troika in Portugal

The Euro- and sovereign debt crises reached its peak during the second Socialist (Partido Socialista – PS) minority government of José Socrates (2009–11). As it had been under prime ministers from various parties before him, the image of the 'good pupil' was central to Socrates' European policy. In 2010 and 2011, he tried desperately to keep the Troika out of the country; however, he was constrained by several factors, of which two stand out prominently.

On the one hand, Socrates could not command an absolute majority in the Assembly of the Republic. He therefore had to negotiate the austerity packages that were recommended by the European Commission with the other parties, in particular with the Social Democratic Party (Partido Social Democrata – PSD). In 2010, there were three such packages, which discredited the government considerably. The main leader of the PSD passively supported the government by abstaining in the Assembly. The minority Socialist government of José Socrates had great difficulties getting its budgets for 2010 and 2011 approved. The 2010 budget was only approved in March 2010 after an intervention by the president of the Republic, Anibal Cavaco Silva, and because the PSD abstained in the vote. The same thing happened in 2011, and again, the role of President Cavaco Silva cannot be underestimated (Magone, 2011). Unfortunately, the campaign for Cavaco Silva's second term took place in December 2010 and January 2011. This complicated the relationship between the president (supported by the PSD and the conservative CDS-PP) and the PS minority government. Prime Minister Socrates allegedly tried to undermine Cavaco Silva's presidential campaign by disclosing the president's business interests. Despite this negative campaigning, Cavaco Silva won the elections in the first round on 23 January 2011 with 50.1 per cent of the vote (Magone, 2012: 257–62).

Afterwards, the relationship between Prime Minister Socrates and President Cavaco Silva was virtually non-existent. Thus, in a period of extraordinary international pressure and threatened national sovereignty, there was almost no communication between the prime minister and the president. At the same time, the cooperation between the two main parties collapsed. On 23 March 2011, the PSD joined the Communists (Partido Comunista Português – PCP) and the Block of the Left (Bloco da Esquerda – BE) in voting against the fourth revised Stability and Growth Pact (Pacto de Estabilidade e Crescimento – PEC IV), which included further, more drastic measures of austerity based on the recommendations of the European Commission. As previously announced, Prime Minister Socrates resigned on the same day. Problematic for the 'good pupil' image here is the fact that Portuguese politicians from the different mainstream parties – in particular, the PSD and the Socialists – did not work together properly, instead preferring to blame the other for the country's economic situation. Mistrust and partisan politics were more important than creating a grand coalition to confront the uncertainty of the markets (Luís, 2014: 59).

Indeed, the Portuguese government was under considerable pressure from the markets and the European institutions alike due to the danger of contagion from the sovereign debt crisis in Greece. In early January 2011, Prime Minister José Socrates became aware of the rising interest rates for Portuguese sovereign bonds. This was already a dangerous situation, as interest rates for sovereign bonds had reached 6.9 per cent; the cut-off point was 7 per cent. Moreover, it had become difficult for Portugal to place sovereign bonds in the markets at reasonable interest rates. This was further complicated by the downgrading of Portugal by the US rating agencies Fitch and Moody's in December 2010 (Dinis, Coelho, 2013: 19). In 2010 and early 2011, the Socrates government undertook a frantic and ultimately unsuccessful search for investors who would buy Portuguese sovereign debt bonds at reasonable interest rates. Despite two bailouts to Greece and one to Ireland totalling €96 billion by the end of 2010, the danger of contagion remained on the agenda. After the resignation of Prime Minister Socrates, a request for bailout funds for Portugal became inevitable. The resignation of Socrates also led to a collapse in the ratings for Portuguese sovereign debt bonds by the three main agencies (Moody's, Fitch and Standard & Poor's) between 24 March and 5 April 2011 (Santos, 2011: 95). Although Prime Minister Socrates had sought to avoid it, his finance minister Fernando Teixeira Santos was supportive of a bailout and went public with his contrary views (Dinis, Coelho, 2013: 190–3). These views reflected the opinions of the Portuguese banking sector, which had refused to buy the sovereign debt bonds issued by the government.

Due to the resignation of Prime Minister Socrates and the call for early elections issued by President Cavaco Silva on 5 June 2011, an interim government led by Socrates was in charge of negotiating the Memorandum of Understanding with the Troika. However, the European institutions also wanted a commitment to the Memorandum of Understanding from all the other political parties after the early elections. The three mainstream parties (PS, PSD and CDS-PP) supported the bailout and the implementation of the associated programme. Only the

Communist Party and the Block of the Left were against the Troika's intervention in Portugal and refused even to meet with them.

The negotiations with the Troika started on 11 April and lasted until 3 May 2011. In total, the bailout would comprise €78 billion, divided equally between the three institutions. About 60 experts from the Troika institutions negotiated the contents of the Memorandum of Understanding. These experts were divided into four working groups:

a budget implementation and the final public accounts of 2010;
b structural dossiers(e.g.privatisation, public administration reform, health sector reform);
c preparation of the budget plan;
d banking supervision and financial stability.

(Dinis, Coelho, 2013: 204)

The mission was led by Jürgen Kröger (European Commission), Rasmus Rüffer (European Central Bank) and Poul Thomsen (International Monetary Fund). Ironically, the basis for the Memorandum of Understanding was the PEC-IV programme of austerity measures that had been rejected in the Assembly of the Republic on 23 March 2011. In fact, Kröger and Rüffer had been involved in the negotiations with the Portuguese government over the PEC-IV (Dinis, Coelho, 2013: 202).

There is no single document from the Troika's intervention, but rather two Memorandums of Understanding. The IMF Memorandum covers economic and finance adjustment policies, while the Memorandum issued by the European institutions is on the conditionalities of economic policy. The former is a conjunctural package, the latter a package of structural reforms (Governo de Portugal, 2014: 10). Moreover, there were substantial differences in approach between the European institutions and the IMF. For one thing, the economic and financial adjustment programme of the IMF featured lower interest rates. Furthermore, the IMF wanted the European part of the programme to last longer and the interest rates to be lowered; however, this was allegedly rejected by the creditor countries in northern Europe (Dinis, Coelho, 2013: 209).

On 3 May 2011, the agreement on the Memorandum of Understanding was announced by the Interim Prime Minister José Socrates and his Finance Minister Fernando Teixeira Santos. Socrates presented it as a 'good agreement', better than those concluded with Greece and Ireland.

The bailout originally consisted of 222 measures to be implemented in several policy areas; over the course of the process, these were expanded to 450 measures. One part consisted of short- and medium-term measures to control the budget deficit, improve budget management and create the necessary conditions to increase the sustainability of the public debt. The other part focused on the reform of the public administration, as well as the privatisation of public enterprises and the liberalisation of sectoral markets in compliance with European internal market regulations (Governo de Portugal, 2014: 10).

The implementation of the programme of austerity measures: process and first assessment

On 5 June 2011, the conservative parties PSD and CDS-PP were able to obtain an absolute majority in early elections and form a coalition government. The difficult fiscal and economic situation required the implementation of several aspects of the programme of austerity measures within months. Consequently, the new government led by Prime Minister Pedro Passos Coelho worked throughout the summer to report to the Troika.

As a member of the European Union, and particularly of the EMU, Portugal shares sovereignty with all other member states (Wallace, 2005: 491–4; Wallace, 1999). The more European integration progresses, the less Portugal is able to take its own sovereign decisions. One of the differences in governing under the Troika regime is that most government policies become subject to continuous scrutiny by the representatives of the three institutions. A country under a Troika regime loses even its shared sovereignty and becomes dependent on the regular positive assessment of the Troika to receive its next tranche of funding.

Despite its electoral legitimacy, the coalition government of Prime Minister Pedro Passos Coelho was an agent of the Troika rather than of the Portuguese people. According to the European Parliament, the programme of austerity measures was never submitted to the Portuguese parliament and therefore was never endorsed by it (European Parliament, 2014: 17). Between 2011 and 2014, Portuguese policy-making was shaped by the demands of the Troika. The enormous number of measures put the Portuguese public administration under considerable pressure and stretched the limits of its capacity. From the very beginning, Prime Minister Passos Coelho was keen to play a leading role in the process, and so the small coordinating unit, the Unit of Monitoring the Implementation of the Memorandums (*Missão de Acompanhamento dos Memorandos*-ESAME), was attached to his office. The acronym ESAME is reminiscent of the word *exame* ('exam') in Portuguese, which fits well in the overall image of the 'good pupil': Portugal as a self-proclaimed 'good pupil' had to pass the exams of the Troika. ESAME was headed by the junior minister Carlos Moedas, an experienced manager with an international curriculum. He was supported by a team of 10–15 people who were in continuous contact with the relevant ministries. This team consisted of specialists from different backgrounds who were necessarily quite flexible in dealing with all the issues that had to be discussed with the Troika. ESAME was a temporary unit scheduled to operate until 30 June 2014 (Governo de Portugal, 2014: 12).

The main duty of ESAME was to coordinate the implementation of the programme of austerity measures agreed upon with the Troika. It was the primary unit monitoring the reforms carried out in the individual ministries, as well as serving as the central liaison between the government (in particular, the prime minister and the finance minister) and the representatives of the Troika. The most important points in terms of coordination were the meetings with the Troika representatives (Governo de Portugal, 2014: 12–13). The monitoring visits of the Troika took place every three months, and there were 12 visits in total. Successful completion of these review visits allowed Portugal to receive the next tranche of the €78 billion.

Prime Minister Pedro Passos Coelho belongs to a new generation of politicians in Portugal, and he himself was also a manager. He was quite successful in attracting knowledgeable ministers to his cabinet, such as Finance Minister Vitor Gaspar and Economy Minister Alvaro Santos Pereira. In addition, his former university professor Maria Luis Albuquerque became a junior minister of the treasury in the Ministry of Finance. This was a crucial position, as it dealt with the country's sovereign debt. Albuquerque had excellent experience on this issue: she had previously been a junior minister and one of the top officials in the Portuguese Management Agency of the Treasury and Public Debt (Agência de Gestão da Tesouraria e da Divida Pública – IGCP) before joining the government (Dinis, Coelho, 2013: 42–3). After the resignation of Gaspar in July 2013, Prime Minister Coelho appointed Albuquerque to be his new finance minister, but without consulting Paulo Portas, leader of the junior partner in the coalition. This led to a crisis in the coalition government that could only be overcome when Prime Minister Coelho offered Portas the post of deputy prime minister, which would give him a hierarchical ranking above that of the finance minister. Albuquerque was a crucial part of the handpicked technocratic team of Prime Minister Coelho and was highly respected by the Troika (Magone, 2014b).

Originally, the Passos Coelho government wanted to use the extensive reform programme to change the country for good. The first six months were quite successful and led to positive first results: the budget deficit was reduced from 9.8 to 4.4 per cent of GDP in 2011. However, this was only achieved through a transfer of the surplus in the pension fund of the public banking sector to make up for the shortfall. Such an extraordinary measure was not possible in the following years. The budget deficit soared to 6.4 per cent in 2012 but dropped again to 4.9 per cent in 2013. This decrease was achieved by means of the introduction of very unpopular measures that reduced wages in the public sector, imposed new taxes and instituted reforms in the tax system. Moreover, a serious programme of reducing expenditures in the public sector was carried out. However, at the same time, the public debt almost doubled from 68.7 per cent in 2007 to 129 per cent in 2013. This shortcoming will increase the pressure on subsequent Portuguese governments to maintain strict austerity policies.

Several public enterprises were privatised or the share of state ownership in them further reduced. Two cases of successful privatisation are the main energy company Electricity of Portugal (Electricidades de Portugal – EdP) and Airports of Portugal (Aeroportos de Portugal – ANA); in the former case, privatisation led to investment by the Chinese Three Gorges Corporation, which acquired a 21.74 per cent share for €2.3 billion, while the latter case resulted in the sale of the company for €3 billion to the French Vinci Corporation. One less successful case is that of Portuguese Airlines (Transportes Aéreos de Portugal – TAP), which in early 2015 was still looking for a buyer.

One important area of reform was the labour market. Following negotiations with the social partners, major changes in terms of flexibilisation were undertaken in order to make the economy more competitive. A central part of this reform was the reduction in costs of dismissal: severance compensation for workers was cut by 40 per cent. However, this change may simply exacerbate the already precarious labour market situation, allowing employers to reduce staff even further. In the second quarter of 2015, unemployment was still 11.9 per cent. It is difficult to make a final assessment of the impact of the Troika on the Portuguese economy and how patterns of behaviour in the country have changed. Although some control over the budget deficit was achieved, it is not clear whether this is sustainable. Moreover, many of the reforms were undertaken too rapidly and without proper funding, such that there may have been missed opportunities. In particular, the reform of the judiciary was completed without proper funding. Such a significant and enormous project should have been carried out more calmly and with more rigour, as it is crucial for improvements in the justice system and for the quality of democracy in the country.

One positive sign is the fact that Portugal has been able to maintain its high levels of exportation. Exporting enterprises have made major efforts to identify emerging markets such as Serbia, Poland and Angola that will allow them to expand their businesses. Strategically, the government has been (at least symbolically) quite supportive of these efforts. These high export levels were accompanied by a reduction in imports; this allowed an improvement in the trade balance account, which has traditionally been negative and has represented a major structural problem for the Portuguese economy. Between 2002 and 2013, Portugal had the highest growth in exports in the Eurozone at 1.1 per cent, but its export ratio of 30.7 per cent is still one of the lowest in the EU (Lisbon Council and Berenberg Bank, 2014: 87). Moreover, emigration has led to a considerable increase in remittances by Portuguese citizens abroad, a figure that grew to over €2.5 billion between 2007 and 2012. In 2013, remittances surpassed the €3 billion mark (Pordata, 2014).

Despite this good news, Portugal still has a relatively weak economy with too many micro-enterprises unable to invest in research and technology. There are about 1,000 large enterprises, but very few in innovative sectors. One major exception is the energy company EdP, which is a leader in renewable energy. In addition to its poor human resources record (explaining in part the country's low productivity per hour), Portugal has the lowest proportion of people who have completed secondary education. Almost two-thirds of the country's population has only completed the compulsory schooling of nine years or less. The lack of people who have completed secondary education is particularly problematic due to the resulting lack of intermediate skilled workers. In 2010, just 31.9 per cent of the Portuguese population had completed upper secondary education, in comparison to the EU27 average of 72.7 per cent (Carmo et al., 2010). For decades, the drop-out rate of pupils in upper secondary education was between 40 and 50 per cent. The Lisbon and Europe 2020 strategy have contributed to a reduction of about 20 per cent in recent years. In 2013, the Portuguese drop-out rate had declined to 18.9 per cent, but only Iceland, Malta and Spain had higher rates, at 20.5, 20.8 and 23.6 per cent, respectively (Eurostat, 2014d). The result is a significant inequality in education attainment that perpetuates a division in society: the one-third who have completed upper secondary or tertiary education are well integrated into the economy and have more options (including emigration), while the other two-thirds are struggling to make ends meet.

In sum, a major report entitled 'Euro Monitor Plus' ranked Portugal in fifth place in terms of the adjustment reforms it has undertaken, behind only Greece, Ireland, Latvia and Spain in the Eurozone. However, in terms of the health of its economy, Portugal only ranks in eighteenth place, before Italy, Cyprus and Greece but behind France. Although one can identify certain improvements, it is in particular the labour market that remains the focus of the study. It seems that the Portuguese economy has major difficulties in creating new jobs. One positive aspect is that Portugal has become one of the countries where it is easiest to open new businesses; however, there are still many obstacles to actual competition in the specific markets. One serious problem in terms of sovereign debt is the fact that Portugal will have to repay a considerable amount of money in the coming years (Lisbon Council and Berenberg Bank, 2014: 87).

Democratic institutions and rudimentary welfare states under pressure

The most important veto player in the political system in relation to the austerity measures was the Constitutional Court, which declared many of the measures involving cuts and new taxes unconstitutional. At first, MPs sent complaints and requests for checks on the constitutionality of the austerity measures included in the budget for the year 2011. From that point on, there was pressure on President Anibal Cavaco Silva to be more critical of the austerity measures proposed by the government, as he had obviously failed to do so in 2011. The Constitutional Court declared many austerity measures directed towards civil service wages to be unconstitutional, and the government had to find alternative solutions to close the funding gap. In all, the Constitutional Court vetoed austerity measures presented by the government four times between July 2012 and December 2013. This was an important sign that the institutional framework of checks and balances was working (for more details, see Magone, 2014b: 354–6).

Before the crisis, Portugal was already one of the most unequal societies in the European Union. The difference between the 20 per cent with the highest incomes and the 20 per cent with the lowest incomes was more than 6.5 times in 2007, although this gap was trending downwards. In 2010 it had narrowed to 5.6 times, however, it later increased again, reaching six times in 2013. This may be a consequence of the crisis, which led to a decline in income for the middle classes with a continuing low level of income in the lower stratum of society. The Gini coefficient confirms this unequal distribution, reaching 34.2 per cent in 2013 (Estanque, 2010).

The sociologist Boaventura Sousa Santos characterises Portugal as having a welfare society (*sociedade providência*) instead of a welfare state (*estado providência*); this means that family networks take over many of the functions that the weak state cannot supply. Sometimes these networks are linked to international connections (Santos, 2011: 73).

One tragedy of the Portuguese economy is the fact that in the years of cheap money Portugal accumulated one of the highest private debt ratios in the European Union. Many Portuguese people bought homes but could not pay their mortgages and later had their homes repossessed. This high level of private debt remains a major problem. In 2013, private debt was still 202.8 per cent of GDP, although this figure also includes enterprises (Eurostat, 2014h). In addition, the negative economic situation led to substantial emigration by the younger, highly skilled labour force throughout the crisis period. It is estimated that since 2006 more than half a million people have emigrated to the Lusophone countries of Brazil, Angola and Mozambique, as well as to the United Kingdom, France, Switzerland and Germany.

Conclusions

In 2014, Portugal celebrated the fortieth anniversary of its democracy; simultaneously, the country managed to complete the programme of austerity measures agreed upon with the Troika and returned to the markets without significant problems.

However, the country is still immersed in a major social and political crisis. The sovereign debt crisis was merely a symptom of an economy and society that is blocked. The high numbers of people who have chosen to emigrate since 2006 show that there is a growing scepticism about the future of the country. This is clearly related to the ill-thought-out policies by successive governments since Portugal's transition to democracy.

References

Aguiar, J. (2005) *Fim Das Ilusões Ilusões do Fim 1985–2005.* Lisbon: Aletheia Editores.

Carmo, Renato Miguel de, Frederico Cantante and Margarida Carvalho (2010) 'Inequalities in Portugal: recent and structural trends'. Available at: http://observatorio-das-desigualdades.cies.iscte.pt/index.jsp?page=projects&lang=en&id=126 (accessed 30 December 2014).

Dinis, David and Hugo Felipe Coelho (2013) *Resgatados: Os Bastidores da Ajuda Financeira a Portugal.* Lisbon: Esfera dos Livros.

Estanque, Elísio (2010) *A Classe Média: Ascensão e Declínio.* Lisbon: Fundação Francisco Manuel dos Santos.

European Commission, European Central Bank and International Monetary Fund (2011) 'Memorandum of Understanding on Specific Economic Conditionality'. Available at: http://economico.sapo.pt/public/uploads/memorando_04–05–2011.pdf (accessed 11 September 2012).

European Commission (2014) 'Cohesion Policy and Portugal'. Available at: http://ec.europa.eu/eurostat/tgm/table.do?tab=table&init=1&language=en&pcode=tsdde410&plugin=1 (accessed 30 December 2014).

European Parliament (2014) 'Report on the Enquiry of the Role and Operations of the Troika (ECB, Commission, and IMF)'. Committee on Economic and Monetary Affairs (rapporteurs Othmar Karas and Liem Hoang Ngoc), A7–0149/2014, 28 February. Available at: www.europarl.europa.eu/sides/getDoc.do?pubRef=-//EP//NONSGML+REPORT+A7-2014-0149+0+DOC+PDF+V0//EN (accessed 30 December 2014).

Eurostat (2014a) 'Real GDP growth rate: volume'. Available at: http://ec.europa.eu/eurostat/tgm/table.do?tab=table&init=1&language=en&pcode=tec00115&plugin=1 (accessed 30 December 2014).

Eurostat (2014b) 'General government deficit(-) and (+)- annual data'. Available at: http://ec.europa.eu/eurostat/tgm/table.do?tab=table&plugin=1&language=en&code=teina200 (accessed 30 December 2014).

Eurostat (2014c) 'General government gross debt'. Available at: http://ec.europa.eu/eurostat/tgm/table.do?tab=table&init=1&language=en&pcode=tsdde410&plugin=1 (accessed 30 December 2014).

Eurostat (2014d) 'Early leavers from school and training'. Available at: http://ec.europa.eu/eurostat/tgm/table.do?tab=table&init=1&language=en&pcode=tsdsc410&plugin=1 (accessed 30 December 2014).

Eurostat (2014e) 'Gini coefficient of equivalised disposable income'. Available at: http://ec.europa.eu/eurostat/tgm/table.do?tab=table&language=en&pcode=tessi190 (accessed 30 December 2014).

Eurostat (2014f) 'Inequality of income distribution'. Available at: http://ec.europa.eu/eurostat/tgm/table.do?tab=table&plugin=1&language=en&pcode=tsdsc260 (accessed 30 December 2014).

Eurostat (2014g) 'Social expenditure per capita in power purchasing power'. Available at: http://appsso.eurostat.ec.europa.eu (accessed 30 December 2014).

Eurostat (2014h) 'Private sector debt consolidated'. Available at: www.ec.europa.eu/eurostat/tgm/table.do?tab=table&language=en&pcode=tipspd20 (accessed 30 December 2014).

Ferrera, Maurizio (1996) 'The "Southern model" of welfare in social Europe,' *Journal of European Social Policy* 6(1): 17–37.

Governo de Portugal (2014) *A Gestão do Programa de Ajustamento: 1000 Dias and 450 Medidas Cumpridas*. Lisbon: Governo de Portugal, Estrutura de Acompanhamento de Memorandums (ESAME).

Lisbon Council and Berenberg Bank (2014) 'Euro Monitor Plus 201: Leaders and Laggards'. Available at: file:///C:/Users/Jos%C3%A9/Downloads/The%202014%20Euro%20Plus%20Monitor.pdf (accessed 30 December 2014).

Luís, Filipe (2014) *Crónica de um Resgate Anunciado: A História e os Bastidores da Intervenção. Os Desafios de um País sem Troika*. Lisbon: Clube de Autor.

Magone, José M. (2011) 'Portugal,' in Tim Bale, Daniele Caramani, Kevin Deegan-Krause and Rainbow Murray (eds) *Political Data Yearbook 2010*. Special issue of *European Journal of Political Research* 50(1): 1102–1107.

Magone, José M. (2012) 'Portugal,' in Daniele Caramani, Kevin Deegan-Krause and Rainbow Murray (eds) *Political Data Yearbook 2011*. Special issue of *European Journal of Political Research* 51(1): 257–258.

Magone, José M. (2013) 'Portugal,' in Andreas Bågenholm, Kevin Deegan-Krause and Liam Weeks (eds) *Political Data Yearbook 2012*. Special issue of *European Journal of Political Research* 52(1): 189–195.

Magone, José M. (2014a) *The Politics in Contemporary Portugal: Evolving Democracy*. Boulder, CO: Lynne Rienner.

Magone, José M. (2014b) 'Portugal is not Greece: policy responses in the sovereign debt crisis and the consequences for the Portuguese political economy,' *Perspectives on European Politics and Society* 15(3): 346–360.

Magone, José M. (2014c) 'Portugal,' in Andreas Bågenholm, Kevin Deegan-Krause and Rainbow Murray (eds) *Political Data Yearbook 2013*. Special issue of *European Journal of Political Research* 39(1): 257–264.

Pordata (2014) 'Remessas de emigrantes total'. Available at: www.pordata.pt/Portugal/Remessas+de+emigrantes+total-135 (accessed 30 December 2014).

Pureza, José Manuel (2011) 'A rábula do bom aluno,' *Diário de Notícias*, 7 October. Available at: www.dn.pt/inicio/opiniao/interior.aspx?content_id=2039800&seccao=Jos%25E9+Manuel+Pureza&tag=Opini%25E3o+-+Em+Foco (accessed 30 December 2014).

Rhodes, Martin (1996) 'Southern European Welfare States: Identity, Problems and Prospects of Reform,' in Martin Rhodes (ed.) *Southern European Welfare States*. Special issue of *South European Society and Politics* 1(3): 1–22.

Santos, Boaventura de Sousa (2011) *Portugal: Ensaio Contra a Autoflagelação*. Lisbon: Edições Almedina.

Statista (2014) 'Youth unemployment rate in EU member states as of May 2014 (seasonally adjusted)'. Available at: www.statista.com/statistics/266228/youth-unemployment-rate-in-eu-countries/ (accessed 30 September 2014).

Tribunal de Contas (2013) 'Acompanhamento dos mecanismos de assistência financeira a Portugal,' Relatório de Auditoria, no. 28/2013–2 S. Processo 23/2012 – Audit. December. Lisbon: Tribunal de Contas. Available at: www.tcontas.pt/pt/actos/rel_auditoria/2013/2s/audit-dgtc-rel028-2013-2s.pdf (accessed 29 December 2014).

Torres, Francisco (2009) 'Policy responses to the financial crisis in the Eurozone: the case of Portugal,' *South European Society and Politics* 14(1): 55–70.

Wallace, William (1999) 'The sharing of sovereignty: the European paradox,' *Political Studies* 47(3): 503–521.

Wallace, William (2005) 'Post-Sovereign Governance: The EU as a Partial Polity,' in Helen Wallace, William Wallace and Mark A. Pollack (eds) *Policy-Making in the European Union*. Oxford: Oxford University Press, pp. 483–503.

13 Cyprus

The Troika's new approach to resolving a financial crisis in a Eurozone member state

Thorsten Kruse

Introduction

The difficult financial situation of the Republic of Cyprus is the latest problem thus far in the European debt crisis or so-called 'Eurozone crisis'. The Cyprus crisis, which started in 2012, led the island to the brink of ruin. While the 2008 global financial crisis and its consequences hit other European countries hard, the Cypriot economy was only slightly affected by these events. Although in the following years, small declines in some of the main economic indicators (e.g. in the fields of tourism and the property market) were recorded, there were no reliable data indicating that the government was facing the threat of bankruptcy. The causes of the Cypriot financial crisis are manifold, and the approach employed by the international donors to resolve this crisis differs from the measures implemented in the other affected European countries.

In the first section of this chapter, a short historical overview of relevant developments in the Republic of Cyprus is presented. This is followed by a closer examination of the political and economic changes on the island that triggered the domestic crisis. The next section explores the planned measures and the mode of implementation suggested by the Troika. Subsequently, the impact these measures had on the government and society over 2013/14 is analysed, followed by an outlook for 2015. The chapter closes with a short conclusion.

From British Crown colony to a problem case in the Eurozone

In 1878, the island of Cyprus became part of the British Empire, and in 1925 it received the status of a British Crown colony. The effects of trilateral talks between the United Kingdom, Greece and Turkey gave Cyprus its independence in August 1960. When the Republic of Cyprus was founded, its first president, Archbishop Makarios III, who was also the spiritual leader of the Church of Cyprus, deemed it best to adopt an impartial and neutral stance, not only in foreign policy but also in economic relations. Nevertheless, in 1963, the Republic of Cyprus submitted its application for full membership in the European Economic Community (EEC), primarily because the United Kingdom – the island's largest trading partner – had also applied for membership. When the British application was vetoed by France, Cyprus decided to withdraw its own application as well. At the beginning of the 1970s, the United Kingdom launched a second attempt to become a full member of the EEC, and Cyprus was – again for economic reasons – in favour of closer contact with the EEC. This time, the government of Cyprus opted for an association agreement with the EEC, which was signed in December 1972.

In the summer of 1974, the Junta in Athens planned and carried out a *coup d'état* against President Makarios. This unilateral intervention was a breach of the tripartite agreements. Consequently, the Turkish army invaded Cyprus and occupied an area in the north, roughly one-third of the island's area. Since then, the island has been divided (for a detailed presentation of the history of Cyprus, see Richter, 2010).

In July 1990, the Republic of Cyprus submitted its application for full membership in the European Community (EC). Brussels accepted the application, in hopes that the difficult situation on the island might be resolved through the negotiation process. During the Copenhagen summit in 2002, it was decided that Cyprus would be accepted as a member of the European Union (EU) in 2004.

Shortly before the accession, Turkish and Greek Cypriots went to the polls to vote for a possible solution to the Cyprus problem – the so-called 'Annan-Plan V' prepared by the United Nations (United Nations, 2004). The majority of Turkish Cypriots (65 per cent) voted in favour of the plan, while nearly 76 per cent of Greek Cypriots rejected it. Consequently, the referendum failed. In May 2004, the whole island *de jure* became a member of the EU. But *de facto*, the *acquis communautaire* is only implemented in areas controlled by the government of the Republic of Cyprus.

Four years later, on 1 January 2008, Cyprus and Malta both acceded to the Eurozone and adopted the euro as their currency. At this time, the economy of Cyprus was flourishing and the public debt as a per centage of GDP was 48.7 per cent (RoC, 2010: 27). Cyprus' fast track to adopting the euro was primarily motivated by political rather than economic reasons. The government of Cyprus believed that the country would thereby be well anchored to the most influential core states, since the country had become a member not only of the EU but also of the Eurozone (c.f. Orphanides, 2013).

The beginnings of the Cypriot crisis

In February 2008, presidential elections were held in Cyprus. At this point it is worth mentioning that Cyprus has a presidential system of government; the president is directly elected for a five-year term and has far-reaching powers. Furthermore, the president's constitutional powers are formally independent of the parliament's confidence and of majorities in the parliament.

Surprisingly, the seemingly strong candidate Tassos Papadopoulos was eliminated in the first round of the 2008 elections. In the second round, the nominee of the Progressive Party of Working People (Ανορθωτικό Κόμμα Εργαζόμενου Λαού, AKEL), Dimitris Christofias, won the election against his opponent Ioannis

Kasoulidis (Democratic Rally, DISY). This was the first time that a member of the communist party of Cyprus had been elected president.

At first glance, Cyprus seemed to be in good shape economically when Christofias took over the presidency at the end of February 2008; many believe this was the main reason why he won the support of the electorate. He had been elected for political, not economic reasons: voters thought that he would be capable of finding a way to mitigate the conflict with Turkey and the Turkish Cypriots, the most significant problem facing Cyprus. Nevertheless, signs of financial risks for Cyprus were already emerging – specifically, risks of a structural nature. During a public hearing of the Investigation Commission on the Economy of Cyprus on 15 May 2013, the former minister of finance, Michalis Sarris, claimed that he had warned Papadopoulos that if he won a second mandate, the government might have to ask the EU for assistance towards the end of that term (Zenios, 2014: 3). One reason for this prognosis was the fact that private households and non-financial corporations had accumulated excessive debts. For example, by December 2007, private households in Cyprus had accumulated a debt of 105 per cent of GDP, a figure that rose to 130 per cent by December 2012. For comparison, in Italy and Germany this rate was below 60 per cent in December 2012 (FAZ, 2012).

In addition, the massive inflow of foreign capital into the Cypriot banking system, attracted by the supposed safety of the common European market and the common currency, seemed to represent a risk for the economy. The country's economic advisers should thus have been well aware of the fragile economic situation on the island at the time.

While everyone was looking for political developments in Cyprus, the government started to spend huge amounts of money unproductively, e.g. increasing state pensions, giving annual bonuses to pensioners and disbursing grants to students without proper differentiation of their social circumstances.

The obviously ill-advised spending policies of the Christofias government prompted other EU countries, relevant EU bodies and (most importantly) rating agencies to examine the financial developments in Cyprus more closely. When the crisis in Greece was exposed in 2010, the Cypriot banking sector and its ties to the Greek banking sector came increasingly into focus.

This caused the island's economic situation to deteriorate even further and in late 2010 rating agencies announced a series of downgrades. In May 2011, Cyprus lost its access to long-term sovereign debt markets. In mid-2011, yields on the ten-year government bond exceeded 10 per cent (IMF, 2011: 8). This was a grave problem for the Cypriot government, but it was not the only one. Starting in 2008, the general governmental gross debt of Cyprus grew from 44.7 per cent of GDP to 71.6 per cent at the end of 2011 (Eurostat, 2014; RoC, 2011: 14). The negative financial developments in Greece at the beginning of 2011 and the exposure of the Cypriot banking sector to Greece represented a further problem. At this time, the government of Cyprus should have asked for assistance from the relevant EU bodies. Stark warnings to seek EU help were also issued by the president of the European Central Bank (ECB), Jean-Claude Trichet, and the

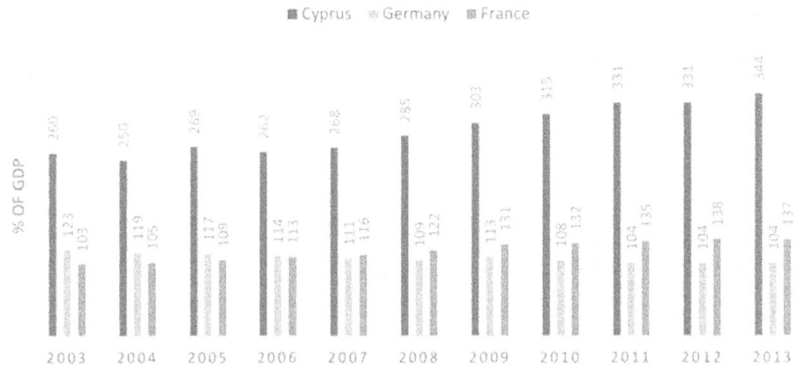

Figure 13.1 Cyprus: changes in private sector debt, 2003–2013
Source: Eurostat.

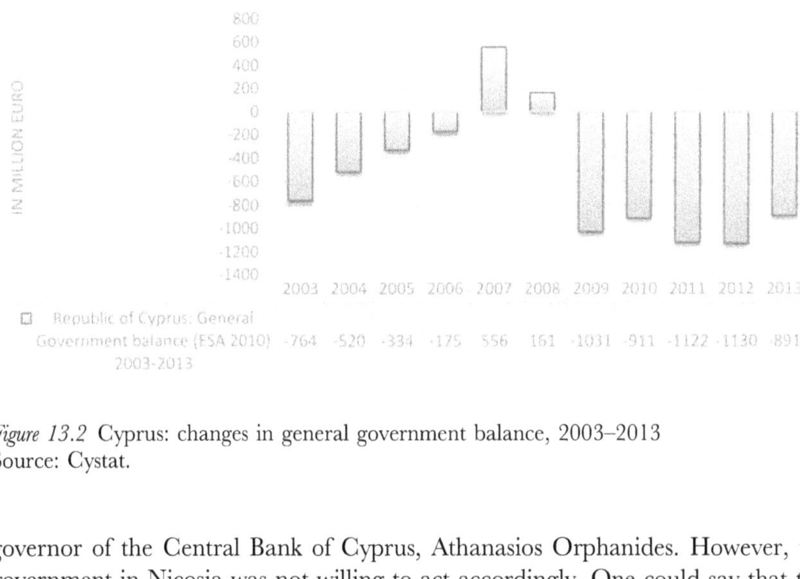

Figure 13.2 Cyprus: changes in general government balance, 2003–2013
Source: Cystat.

governor of the Central Bank of Cyprus, Athanasios Orphanides. However, the government in Nicosia was not willing to act accordingly. One could say that this was the start of the disastrous politics of procrastination employed by President Christofias in the financial crisis.

The Mari explosion

In the early hours of 11 July 2011, a catastrophic military accident took place at the Evangelos Florakis Naval Base near the village of Mari on the south coast of the island. Ninety-eight shipping containers filled with explosives self-detonated on the base, killing 13 people. The explosives had been discovered two and a half years previously when US naval forces intercepted a Cypriot-flagged ship in the

Red Sea on its way from Iran to Syria. After the ship was forced to dock at a port in Cyprus, the responsibility for the seized ammunition was handed over to the Cypriot navy. The shipping containers were stored in an open space at the Florakis base where they were exposed to the elements – in particular, to the sun, which ultimately led to the explosives' self-detonation in 2011 (for more details on the explosion and its background, see *Cyprus Mail*, 2011; BBC, 2011; *Telegraph*, 2011). The accident not only killed 13 people but also destroyed large parts of the adjacent Vasilikos power plant – the island's main power station, which provided more than half of the nation's electricity.

The political and economic consequences of this event were detrimental. Politically, the explosion triggered a veritable government crisis. Shortly after the accident, both the defence and foreign affairs ministers as well as the National Guard's commander-in-chief handed in their resignations. On 28 July 2011, due to political and public pressure, the entire cabinet tendered its resignation in order to give the president the opportunity to institute a political reshuffling, which he did a few days later. Even President Christofias came under increasing pressure, especially after the publication of an independent probe that attributed responsibility for the blast to him. The investigator, Polys Polyviou, reported during a press conference that the 'President of the Republic in this case failed to take elementary measures for the security of Cyprus's citizens' (Reuters, 2011). Despite further allegations of negligence issued by the investigator, Christofias denied any responsibility.

Economically, the explosion had an extremely high cost. Various sources have estimated that the total cost of the accident for the Cypriot economy ranged between €2.4 billion and €3 billion (14 to 17 per cent of GDP). The cost for repairs to and reconstruction of the Vasilikos power plant alone amounted to nearly €1.5 billion (Financial Mirror, 2013). With regard to effects on the nation's GDP, it is very difficult to separate the naval base explosion from the simultaneous impact of the financial crisis in Cyprus.

The 2011 Russian loan

In mid-2011, the situation in Cyprus deteriorated even further, and consequently the government sought out opportunities that might give them more leeway. The administration tried to find help from outside the EU in order to avoid the infamous austerity measures and structural adjustments implemented by the so-called 'Troika' in other Eurozone member countries when these countries asked for financial assistance. On 5 October, the Council of Ministers approved an agreement with Moscow for a €2.5 billion loan with an interest rate of 4.5 per cent. At a press conference, a government spokesman emphasised that 'the loan will enable Cyprus to cover its medium-term refinancing needs, avoiding liquidity strains on local commercial banks, as well as restore international investors' confidence and ease the rising tendencies on Cypriot bond spreads in the European secondary markets' (EurActiv, 2011). However, the governor of the Central Bank of Cyprus, Athanasios Orphanides, came to a different conclusion: he argued that at this stage in the process, the government should be applying for a small package from the Troika that would easily fix the island's financial problem. Instead, in turning to Russia, the administration was demonstrating that it did not want to carry out the necessary structural adjustments. Orphanides also stressed that in his opinion, the Russian loan was a mistake for Cyprus, as the considerable size of the loan (nearly 15 per cent of GDP) would enable the government to keep operating and to accumulate more deficits without being induced to take any corrective action (Orphanides, 2013: 2).

Just a few weeks after the loan agreement, rating agencies downgraded Cyprus' debt rating yet again, making it clear that the government's strategic and financial goals as originally pursued were unattainable in practice and that further action was urgently required.

The Greek haircut and its effects on Cyprus

When the financial crisis in Greece emerged in 2010, many European financial institutions decided to get rid of their Greek government bonds. Two major Cypriot players, namely the Bank of Cyprus and the Cyprus Popular Bank (better known as the Laiki Bank), which both played a systemic role in Cyprus' banking sector, took a different path for reasons that are still not clear. At the end of 2010, the two institutions held Greek bonds amounting to a value of €5.8 billion; this was €1 billion more than the amount held nine months previously. In 2011, both banks actually increased their purchase of Greek government bonds (*Spiegel Online*, 2013). However, to be fair, it should be noted that both the Bank of Cyprus and Laiki passed the EU-wide stress tests conducted by the European Banking Authority (EBA) in the years 2010 and 2011 without any reservations. This is surprising, but can be seen as a reflection of the EBA's position that as a strategic orientation, investing in Greek bonds was unproblematic.

At the end of October 2011, European leaders agreed on a second bailout package for Greece. This time, they decided to include private sector involvement (PSI) in the package as well. Here, the aim was to persuade private investors such as financial institutions, insurance companies and international funds to exchange Greek government bonds for new long-term Greek bonds and bonds provided by the European Stability Fund (EFSF) with a nominal discount of more than 50 per cent (Zenios, 2014: 2). The plan was finalised in February 2012, at which time private investors had to accept write-offs of between 53.5 per cent and 70 per cent of the value of the Greek bonds they held (SZ, 2012).

This decision also affected the Bank of Cyprus and Laiki, forcing them to write off much of the value of the Greek government bonds they had accumulated. Together, the two banks lost more than €4.1 billion in this 'Greek haircut', amounting to more than 23 per cent of the GDP of the Republic of Cyprus. A comparison of these figures with the losses of banks in the core countries (Germany: €3.6 billion or 0.14 per cent of GDP; France: €5.04 billion or 0.25 per cent of GDP) reveals the severity of the impact on Cyprus and on the island's economy (Zenios, 2014: 4). In December 2011, the EBA carried out another stress test. For the first time they included in their calculations potential losses arising from government loans in the deposits of the respective banks (i.e. market vs. book value of government bonds). Like 31 other banks in the Eurozone, the Bank of Cyprus and the Laiki Bank were found to require recapitalisation in order to meet the EBA's guidelines (Spiegel Online, 2013). In early 2012, the two largest banks in Cyprus urgently needed around €2 billion of recapitalisation to meet the so-called 'Core Tier 1' capital ratio of 9 per cent (Orphanides, 2013: 3).

Cyprus on the road to insolvency

With its impact on Cyprus' two major banks and the accumulation of public debt, the Greek haircut set into motion a negative feedback loop. Because the overall conditions were so threatening, concrete measures to reduce the public debt and to support the troubled banks should have been taken by the government of Cyprus, but again there were signs of tactical delays. Although the Ministry of Finance was well aware of the critical situation at the beginning of 2012 and the new minister of finance had tried to warn Christofias of the profound and severe repercussions should no action be taken, for months the president was unwilling to act, despite the significant impact this delay could have on the country's financial and social structures (for details, see Orphanides, 2014: 20). One example of Christofias' unsuitable political decisions can be seen at a press conference on 1 June 2012, when he was asked:

> Over the past several days there has been information that plans with fiscal measures have been advanced but these measures have not been announced as expected. Press reports today suggest that the Presidential Palace and AKEL have interfered with these plans. Is this correct?

The president answered:

> This President means what he says. And for this reason, I did not allow, and will not allow additional burdens imposed on the workers. […] We discuss plans with the ministers and, of course, if these plans are not agreeable to the President […] then this President can stop them. […] And I wish to reassure the public one more time, and the government workers, that neither their bonuses are at risk, nor their pensions are at risk and that no additional measures will be implemented that cut workers' benefits.
>
> (Orphanides, 2014: 22)

In mid-June 2012, the rating agency Moody's downgraded Cypriot ten-year bonds to the 'non-investment grade/speculative' level for the first time. This meant that it would be impossible for the government to acquire further loans from the markets. Cyprus was thus no longer able to recapitalise the two systemic banks of the island, nor could it reduce its budget deficit. Finally, on 25 June 2012, only a few days before assuming the presidency of the European Union, the

Cypriot government gave in and asked for financial support from the EU (for details, see BBC, 2012).

It is difficult to explain why President Christofias refused to take any concrete action for such a long time in light of the continuing deterioration of the country's economic and financial situation. Christofias may have had a number of reasons, among them political rationales. These might include the Republic of Cyprus' first-time EU Presidency beginning on 1 July 2012, the upcoming presidential elections in February 2013 and AKEL's goal of improving the standard of living for workers. Personal reasons may also have played a role: perhaps Christofias did not want to be the president who handed the island over to the control of the Troika with all the associated consequences. There is no clear evidence of Christofias' possible intentions; however, it is noteworthy that on 14 May 2012, the president announced that he would not seek re-election. He explained his decision by saying that he had been unable to unite the divided island and that he did not 'see any definitive progress in coming months' (Bloomberg, 2012a).

The Troika in Cyprus

At the beginning of July 2012, the Troika (composed of members of the European Commission, the ECB and the IMF) visited Cyprus for an initial fact-finding tour. The delegation returned on 23 July, this time to discuss for the first time the specific financial and restructuring needs of the island's economy. These talks included some of the political 'hot potatoes' – namely, the index-linked Cost of Living Allowance (CoLA), pensions and the corporate tax rate.

It very quickly became obvious that the government's invitation to the Troika had been only half-hearted. While some members of the government conducted talks with Troika representatives, others were trying to determine whether it would be possible to obtain credit from either Russia or China. The latter group's aim was to avoid the tough austerity measures that had been announced by the Troika before its first trip to Cyprus at the beginning of July and that were set out in concrete terms in a memorandum sent to the Cypriot government on 25 July. These conditions included an increase in the retirement age, strict balancing of the budget, the privatisation of semi-governmental organisations, pension reform, a 15-per cent cut in the state payroll, the loss of '13th-month' bonuses in the public sector, a wage freeze and other harsh and incisive measures (for details, see e.g. NZZ, 2012; FES 2012a: 4; FES 2012b: 6–8).

The memorandum's strict terms induced the president and the government to try their hand at blocking and evasive tactics; for example, the government delayed giving the Troika any answer to the abovementioned proposals for roughly three months. On 23 October, the European Commission confirmed that it had received Cyprus' counterproposals. From this response, it was clear that the government was again attempting to avoid making any deep cuts. Most of the proposals by the Troika were rejected or at least called into question (CNA, 2012; Bloomberg, 2012b). It seems plausible that the government's ambitions were reinforced by the highly negative public perception of the Troika and its work in other countries affected by the crisis. It was only on 4 December 2012 that President Christofias publicly conceded that there was no going back on the bailout deal with the Troika. A few days later, the parliament in Nicosia approved a provisional bailout agreement that included a tax hike, wage cuts in the public sector and a freeze in the cost of living allowance. However, the final agreement between the Troika and Cyprus would only be signed after the presidential elections at the end of February.

Between October 2012 and January 2013, it became evident that the bailout measures agreed upon for other countries (such as Ireland and Portugal) would not be introduced in the case of Cyprus. Germany in particular voiced disapproval of a bailout plan for Cyprus. The German allegations levelled against Cyprus were numerous; inter alia, it was claimed that the island was a tax haven and a site of Russian money laundering. The overriding German argument was that the usual bailout plan would simply consolidate the current state of affairs (for details, see e.g. *Spiegel Online*, 3 November 2012; *Handelsblatt*, 25 March 2013).

Presidential elections and the final agreement

In the second round of the 2013 presidential elections, Nicos Anastasiades (DISY) secured more than 57 per cent of the vote, defeating the independent candidate Stavros Malas, who was backed by AKEL. Just before the presidential elections, several newspapers had reported that a proposal had been made to 'bail-in' the investors and depositors of the affected banks in Cyprus. This was a completely new approach in the array of measures designed to help a Eurozone member in distress.

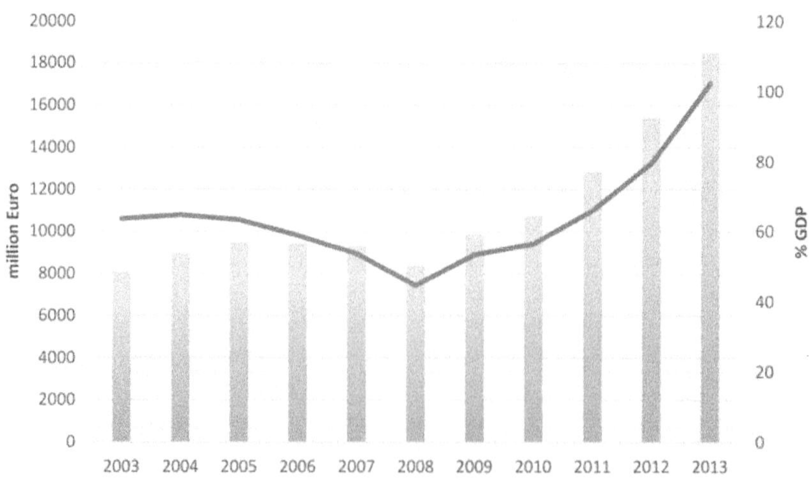

Figure 13.3 Cyprus: changes in general government debt, 2003–2013
Source: Roc 2013.

Following lengthy negotiations, the new president Anastasiades and the members of the Troika agreed to a €10 billion bailout deal covering the period from 2013 to 2016. Of the total sum, €9 billion was to be provided by the European Stability Mechanism and €1 billion would be contributed by the IMF. On 24 March 2013, the *Economic Adjustment Programme for Cyprus* passed the consultation process within the Eurogroup on the condition that the money would under no circumstances be used to recapitalise the troubled banks. Cyprus also had to agree to institute measures to identify and thwart money laundering – a key condition for some of the European core countries that suspected Cyprus of being a passive collaborator in such offenses. In addition to the measures laid out in the bailout plan, the government of Cyprus presented a bail-in plan that was intended to resolve the crisis of the two major banks and to obtain money through additional measures; this was agreed by the Eurogroup as well. This plan covered an additional €13 billion, a burden that was to be shouldered by the government of Cyprus alone. Thus, the final rescue package for Cyprus – approved at the Eurogroup meeting in April 2013 – had a total volume of €23 billion. On 30 April, the parliament in Nicosia approved the €10 billion bailout package with the marginal majority of 29 votes to 27.

It should be noted that it took nearly two years for the first indications of a severe crisis to be recognised and stern warnings to seek assistance to be voiced, and more than ten additional months before the first official request for help, representing a significant delay in the Cypriot government's acceptance of the need for intervention by its European and international partners.

The bail-in

The bail-in was designed as a new mechanism to (re-)capitalise the troubled banking sector, entailing a substantial contribution (or bail-in) on the part of share- and bondholders as well as depositors in the banks. In Cyprus, this approach led to the following scenario: only deposits under €100,000 at the two main banks would be fully protected (an initial plan to save the banking system sought to involve all depositors at the two banks, even those with miniscule savings). The Laiki Bank was liquidised and was thereby split into two units: the uninsured deposits (over €100,000) were kept in the Legacy Laiki, while the insured deposits as well as certain assets and liabilities were moved to the Bank of Cyprus. Of the uninsured deposits at the Bank of Cyprus, 47.5 per cent were used to recapitalise and restructure the bank (for details, see e.g. ESM, 2015; Reuters, 25 June 2013; *Financial Mirror*, 20 November 2014). In return, share- and bondholders received shares of the Bank of Cyprus and the Legacy Laiki, respectively, which at present have no significant value in comparison to the losses. Other banks in Cyprus such as the Hellenic Bank and the Cooperative Central Bank were not affected by these measures.

When the bail-in plan was publicised in mid-March, banks in Cyprus were closed and cash withdrawals from ATMs were limited to avert a bank run. However, bank branches abroad were not affected by these measures and there may thus have been a chance for foreign investors to adopt alternative security measures.

When the banks re-opened almost two weeks later, the Central Bank of Cyprus imposed capital controls and restrictions (e.g. a maximum of €1,000 in cash per person for trips abroad). Money transfers to accounts abroad were restricted to the sum of €5,000 per month; companies needed special permission for larger transfers, which were supervised in order to ensure that they were business-related (FES, 2013: 6). These capital controls were lifted gradually, with almost all revoked by January 2015.

The implementation of the bailout deal and its consequences

The main aims of the three-year Economic Adjustment Programme for Cyprus are threefold:

1 resolve the crisis in the banking sector and to restructure the systemic Bank of Cyprus;
2 correct the excessive general government deficit; and
3 implement structural reforms in order for the country to regain competitiveness and attain sustainable and balanced growth

(cf. EC, 2013).

The first point primarily relates to the bail-in process and part of the restructuring of the banking sector of Cyprus, whereas the other two were implemented through the austerity measures intended to effect changes and corrections in the design of the Cypriot spending policies and public welfare system.

Whereas President Christofias had tried to avoid any far-reaching changes to traditional structures, his successor Anastasiades began to carry out the demands of the Troika rather rapidly. This implementation led to massive impacts within the first few months, but it also promises long-term effects. Explaining all the measures would be beyond the scope of this discussion, but some of the features merit mention: the wages of public employees have been reduced even further; social transfers are being reformed, which will mean additional cuts in benefits; and pension schemes are to be revisited (e.g. an early retirement penalty will be introduced, the calculation of the final pension will take into account life-term service instead of end-career salary and there will be an increase in the retirement age). In addition, taxation measures have been introduced and others are planned (e.g. increases in excise duties, an increase in the VAT rate, etc.), and a reform of public healthcare provisions is underway.

All the measures carried out by the government of Cyprus are under quarterly review by members of the Troika; two reviews took place in 2013 and four in 2014. These reports show that Cyprus' programme is on track. On a positive note, the reports indicate that budgetary developments are good and that the government's primary deficit in 2014 is estimated at 1.7 per cent of GDP.

However, the final aim of the programme is a primary surplus of 4 per cent of GDP in the years after the programmes end in 2016. The members of the Troika also believe that the recession in Cyprus is bottoming out and that both reforms in the financial sector and structural reforms have progressed. It is worth noting that at the end of April 2014, Cyprus returned to the financial markets and sold a six-year bond for €100 million with a 6.5 per cent interest rate. The high unemployment figures are still problematic, as are the very high level of private sector debt and the high rate of non-performing loans, which will constrain the recovery (for details, see EC, 2013–14).

Challenging topics in 2015

By the end of 2014, it was obvious that the implementation process was not proceeding as smoothly as the government had planned. The parliament suspended the enforcement of the law on foreclosures, one of the key elements demanded by the international lenders. The opposition justified this step by arguing that the government's draft framework on insolvencies, which will give debtors a safety net, had been delayed. Because of this parliamentary decision, the lenders froze Cyprus' financing.

The final implementation of the foreclosure law represented a great challenge in 2015, as will to no lesser degree the law regarding the national health scheme and the already controversial privatisation of semi-governmental organisations (e.g. the Electricity Authority and the Cyprus Telecommunications Authority).

An additional challenge was the struggle to improve the conditions of significant parts of the population. The consequences of the bank crisis and the implementation of austerity measures have been the main causes of an extraordinary rise in the ranks of the unemployed (the per centage of unemployed

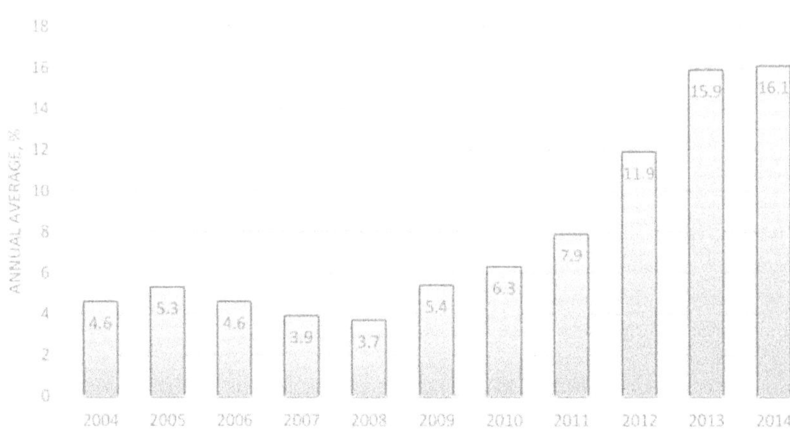

Figure 13.4 Cyprus: changes in the unemployment rate, 2004–2014
Source: Eurostat.

people increased from an average of 6.3 per cent in 2011 to an average of 16 per cent in 2014) and deep cuts in salaries and savings.

These developments have led to a vicious circle for many small and medium-sized enterprises as well as for many households. Much of the population can no longer spend money on consumer goods and services (e.g. on clothing, leisure activities, eating in restaurants, etc.) or even pay their rent or make loan payments. Consequently, many shops and companies have been forced to close and private debts are rising; the number of non-performing loans is growing as well. Due to this development and external risks (e.g. the crisis in Ukraine), it is unclear whether a turnaround in this sector during 2015 was possible or not.

Conclusions

It is expected that Cyprus will successfully finish the programme agreed upon with international lenders in 2016. Some economics experts have also estimated that Cyprus will not need the entire €10 billion that the Troika has offered. The ambitious approach taken by President Anastasiades and his government shows that they are willing to cooperate with the lenders and that they are trying to bring Cyprus closer to the core of Europe, even in these difficult times.

Although the government has emphasised the importance of creating closer links to Brussels, only one-third of the population believes that Cyprus' membership in the EU is 'good'. The latest Eurobarometer also reveals that 75 per cent of the Cypriot people believe that they have little or no say at all within the EU (Eurobarometer, no. 82). One reason for this negative attitude is the handling of the crisis by the big players, above all Germany. By publicly blaming Cyprus for its role in money laundering and harbouring Russian money and by accepting the bail-in mechanism instead of using previously proven methods of resolving financial crises in a Eurozone member countries, European policy-makers unnecessarily destroyed the credibility of the European institutions across large parts of Europe. As a result, large segments of the population in Cyprus believe that their country has been used as a guinea pig.

The coming years and the years following the completion of the programme in 2016 will be very challenging for Cyprus. The island's economy must be restructured and diversified, and its enormous mountain of debt must be reduced through a carefully monitored spending policy. The discovery of offshore natural gas near Cyprus' southern coast might represent a glimmer of hope for the reduction of the island's debt in the long run. But it will take some years to install the necessary infrastructure to utilise the natural resources, so no significant profits will be reaped before the end of the decade.

References

BBC (2011) 'Cyprus: Navy chief killed by base munitions blast,' 11 July. Available at: www.bbc.co.uk/news/world-europe-14115103 (accessed 10 February 2015).

BBC (2012) 'Cyprus to ask for bailout from eurozone partners,' 25 June. Available at: www.bbc.co.uk/news/business-18586532 (accessed 10 February 2015).

Bloomberg (2012a) 'Cypriot President Christofias says he won't seek re-election,' 14 May. Available at: www.bloomberg.com/news/articles/2012-05-14/cypriot-president-christofias-says-he-won-t-seek-re-election-1- (accessed 10 February 2015).

Bloomberg (2012b) 'Troika may laugh at Cypriot bailout proposal, lawmaker says,' 5 October. Available at: www.bloomberg.com/news/articles/2012-10-05/troika-may-laugh-at-cypriot-bailout-proposal-lawmaker-says (accessed 14 February 2015).

Cyprus News Agency (CNA) (2012) 'IMF receives Cyprus counter proposals, sources say, '23 October. Available at: www.cna.org.cy/webnewsEN.asp?a=d4d0c8c15d434ddeba34941558e3045e (accessed 10 February 2015).

Cyprus Mail (2011) 'A diplomatic vice with no room to wriggle,' 3 July. Available at: http://archives.cyprus-mail.com/2011/07/03/a-diplomatic-vice-with-no-room-to-wriggle/ (accessed 10 February 2015).

European Commission (EC) (2013) *The Economic Adjustment Programme for Cyprus*, Occasional Paper no. 149, May. Available at: http://ec.europa.eu/economy_finance/publications/ (accessed 16 February 2015).

European Commission (EC) (2013/14) *The Economic Adjustment Programme for Cyprus*, Occasional Papers on the Review of the Programme for Cyprus. Available at: http://ec.europa.eu/economy_finance/assistance_eu_ms/cyprus/index_en.htm (accessed 16 February 2015).

European Stability Mechanism (ESM) (2015) *ESM Financial Assistance for Cyprus* [with related documents]. Available at: www.esm.europa.eu/assistance/cyprus/index.htm (accessed 16 February 2015).

EurActiv (2011) 'Russia "bails out" cash-strapped Cyprus,' 7 October. Available at: www.euractiv.com/europes-east/russia-bails-cash-strapped-cypru-news-508182 (accessed 10 February 2015).

Eurostat (2014) 'General government gross debt.' Available at: http://ec.europa.eu/eurostat/tgm/table.do?tab=table&init=1&language=en&pcode=tsdde410&plugin=1 (accessed 10 February 2015).

Frankfurter Allgemeine Zeitung (FAZ) (2012) 'Zypern ertrinkt in Schulden' [Cyprus is drowning in debt]. Available at: www.faz.net/aktuell/finanzen/anleihen-zinsen/finanznot-zypern-ertrinkt-in-schulden-11977765.html (accessed 9 February 2015).

Friedrich Ebert Stiftung (FES) (2012a) *FES Cyprus Newsletter*, no. 3 (September).

Friedrich Ebert Stiftung (FES) (2012b) *FES Cyprus Newsletter*, no. 4 (October).

Friedrich Ebert Stiftung (FES) (2013) *FES Cyprus Newsletter*, no. 10 (April).

Financial Mirror (2013) 'How much did the Mari explosion cost?,' 9 July. Available at: www.financialmirror.com/blog-details.php?nid=1109 (accessed 10 February 2015).

Financial Mirror (2014) 'AGM: Ackermann takes charge at Bank of Cyprus,' 20 November). Available at: http://financialmirror.com/news-details.php?nid=33514 (accessed 10 February 2015).

Handelsblatt (2013) 'Russisches Schwarzgeld in Zypern gibt uns zu denken' [Russian black money gives us pause to reflect], 25 March. Available at: www.handelsblatt.com/politik/international/bnd-chef-schindler-russisches-schwarzgeld-in-zypern-gibt-uns-zu-denken/7981136.html (accessed 10 February 2015).

International Monetary Fund (IMF) (2011) *Cyprus: 2011 Article IV Consultation: Staff Report* (IMF Country Report no. 11/331), Washington, DC: IMF.

Neue Zürcher Zeitung (NZZ) (2012) 'Dritter Troika-Besuch im Inselstaat: Zyperns Regierung will das Sparpaket mildern' [Third visit auf the Troika on the island: the government of Cyprus tries to soften the austerity package]. Available at: www.nzz.ch/aktuell/wirt

schaft/wirtschaftsnachrichten/zypern-will-sparpaket-mildern-1.17634030 (accessed 10 February 2015).

Orphanides, Athanasios (2013) 'What happened in Cyprus', Policy Letter Series no. 6, Center of Excellence, SAFE – Sustainable Architecture for Finance in Europe.

Orphanides, Athanasios (2014) *What Happened in Cyprus: The Economic Consequences of the Last Communist Government in Europe*, LSE Financial Markets Group Special Paper Series, SP 232 (July).

Reuters (2011) 'Independent probe blames Cyprus leader for blast,' 3 October. Available at: www.reuters.com/article/2011/10/03/us-cyprus-blast-inquiry-idUSTRE7921L920111003 (accessed 10 February 2015).

Reuters (2012) 'And then there were five: Cyprus seeks EU aid,' 25 June. Available at: www.reuters.com/article/2012/06/25/us-eurozone-idUSBRE85O0CS20120625 (accessed 10 February 2015).

Richter, Heinz A. (2010) *A Concise History of Modern Cyprus 1878–2009*. Mainz: Rutzen.

Republic of Cyprus (RoC) (2010) *Public Debt Management Annual Report 2010*. Nicosia: Ministry of Finance.

Republic of Cyprus (RoC) (2011) *Public Debt Management Annual Report 2011*. Nicosia: Ministry of Finance.

Republic of Cyprus (RoC) (2013) *Public Debt Management Annual Report 2013*. Nicosia: Ministry of Finance.

Spiegel Online (2012) 'Russische Schwarzgeldkonten: BND warnt vor Rettungspaket für Zypern' [Russian clandestine accounts: German secret service warns against a bailout package for Cyprus], 3 November. Available at: www.spiegel.de/wirtschaft/soziales/russisches-schwarzgeld-bnd-warnt-vor-rettungspaket-fuer-zypern-a-865151.html (accessed 14 February 2015).

Spiegel Online (2013) '"Schuldenkrise" in Zypern' [Debt Crisis in Cyprus], 28 March. Available at: www.spiegel.de/wirtschaft/soziales/wie-sich-zyperns-banken-in-den-ruin-spekulierten-a-891456.html(accessed 10 February 2015).

Süddeutsche Zeitung (2012) 'Das Rettungspaket kommt, die Zweifel bleiben' [The rescue package comes, the doubts remain], 21 February. Available at: www.sueddeutsche.de/wirtschaft/geld-fuer-griechenland-freigegeben-das-rettungspaket-kommt-die-zweifel-bleiben-1.1289418 (accessed 10 February 2015).

The Telegraph (2011) 'Anger grows in Cyprus over "criminal errors" behind explosion,' 12 July. Available at: www.telegraph.co.uk/news/worldnews/europe/cyprus/8632718/Anger-grows-in-Cyprus-over-criminal-errors-behind-explosion.html (accessed 10 February 2015).

United Nations (2004) 'The Comprehensive Settlement of the Cyprus Problem (UN-Annan-Plan, V). Available at: www.bbc.co.uk/greek/Annan_plan_31_march.doc (accessed 2 February 2015).

Zenios, Stavros A. (2014) 'Fairness and reflexivity in the Cyprus bail-in', Working Paper no. 14-04, The Wharton Financial Institutions Center, University of Pennsylvania

14 The politics of Troika avoidance

The case of Spain

José M. Magone

Introduction

Although Spain was able to escape the strict monitoring of the Troika (the combined forces of the International Monetary Fund (IMF), the European Commission and the ECB), unlike Greece, Ireland, Portugal and Cyprus, Prime Minister Mariano Rajoy and his government had to pledge to introduce major reforms in the Spanish economic system in order to increase competitivity in the long run. As a trade-off, in June 2012, the Spanish government received confirmation of a loan of up to €100 billion from the European Stability Mechanism (ESM) to resolve the country's ailing post-crisis banking sector. Spain is therefore an interesting case study: as one of the larger member states in the European Union (thus entailing much stronger negative systemic repercussions on the EMU should it fail), it was able to prevent the intervention of the Troika in its domestic endeavours.

This chapter will focus on the relations between Spain and the European Union during the period of economic crisis that started in 2008 and is still ongoing. In order to explain the emergence of the economic crisis in Spain, the following section will describe the development and main features of the Spanish economy. A discussion of the most important aspects of the economic crisis is then presented. This is followed by two separate sections on how the crisis was managed by the Zapatero and Rajoy governments. Finally, the political and social impacts of the crisis are analysed, and some conclusions are drawn.

The development of the Spanish economy

After Spain joined the European Community in 1986, the community structural funds played a major role in improving infrastructure in the country. Spain was the largest recipient of structural funds in the 1980s and 1990s, a status achieved through a very successful alliance between Spain and the other southern European countries, Portugal and Greece. This so-called 'Club Med' group was instrumental in supporting the attempts of Jacques Delors' European Commission between 1985 and 1995 to substantially increase successive long-term budgets of the European Community. In 1988, the European Commission managed to double its budget, an increase that was primarily allocated to the (reformed) structural funds. Most of this funding was intended to be used to help the southern European economies overcome their peripheral status in order to allow them to compete in the upcoming Single European Market (SEM).

However, most of this funding was used to upgrade the country's infrastructure; little was allocated to strengthening and modernising enterprises. Moreover, due to the low capacity of both enterprises and civil society, regional governments dominated governance systems in the allocation of funding. This clearly had implications for the development of the country: the allocation of structural funds was dominated by a process of governmentalisation and politicisation instead of sound economic decisions (Magone, 2003: 243–58; Magone, 2009: 350–1; Centorrino, Perez-Urdiales, 2014).

The Spanish economy has considerable potential, both as a large economy in the Eurozone and because of its special access (through language and culture) to the many national markets in Latin America. The economy has undergone major transformations over the past four decades of democracy. However, despite these seemingly excellent conditions, the Spanish economy is still structurally weak and lags behind the core countries of the European Union. Most reforms have targeted the labour market, but in reality the crucial problem of the Spanish economy is the low level of investment in research and development in enterprises (see chapter 1, Figure 1.2).

Progress in this regard is hampered by the high level of fragmentation of enterprises. The lack of a sufficient number of large companies is a major problem for the future of the Spanish economy. Companies such as Telefonica, Repsol, Endesa, Iberdrol, Inditex (the parent of Zara, a blockbuster success) and Santander Bank are the exceptions rather than the rule in the Spanish business landscape. Instead, the landscape is dominated by an enormous number of small and medium-sized enterprises with low capital capacity. Consequently, most enterprises produce traditional products for the domestic market. If we compare Spain's economy to the highly successful economy of the Netherlands, a country with half the population, it becomes clear that Spain still has a great deal of work to do in terms of creating more competitive, larger companies. In the Spanish case, the majority of micro-companies are most likely survival enterprises. One statistic in particular highlights this difference: in 2009, Spain manufactured US$ 4,750 in goods for export per capita, whereas the Netherlands produced US$ 30,201 (Chislett, 2011: 32).

Although the globalisation and internationalisation of the Spanish economy began in the 1980s, the country's share in the global market for manufactured goods has remained at about 1.6 per cent since the 1990s. However, in the food industry, this figure has reached up to 3.17 per cent (Chislett, 2011: 31). Spain's main export markets are Latin America and Europe. Latin America was a critical market for the internationalisation of the Spanish economy until the sovereign debt crisis hit Argentina in 2001. In its first phase of expansion between 1993 and 2001, Spain was the second-largest provider of FDI in the region, just behind the United States; however, after 2001, the country's investments mainly shifted to

Europe. In 2010, Spain provided just 4 per cent of FDI in Latin America, in comparison to 17 per cent from the US, 13 per cent from the Netherlands and 9 per cent from China (Chislett, 2011: 3–4).

According to the 2013–2014 Competitiveness Index compiled by the World Economic Forum, Spain was ranked thirty-fifth out of 144 countries. This pales in comparison to the larger economies of the European Union: Germany was ranked fifth, the Netherlands eighth, the UK ninth and France twenty-third, although Italy was only ranked forty-ninth. Among the factors contributing to Spain's poor showing were the country's limited innovation capability, its ailing educational system, its (still) rigid labour market and the low level of university-industry collaboration. Political corruption and government inefficiency are additional factors that generally hamper competitiveness in Spain (World Economic Forum, 2015: 13, 24).

A further factor is the poor secondary education section, which has one of highest drop-out rates in the European Union: in 2014, the drop-out rate in Spain (and Portugal and Malta) was 22.4 per cent (Eurostat, 2015).

Another issue regularly flagged up is the fact that the labour market continues to be quite rigid. One notable characteristic of the Spanish labour market is its dualist nature. Large, capital-rich enterprises in the public and private sectors are able to provide their employees and workers with permanent contracts and the associated benefits, but a significant part of the economy consists of workers in precarious situations, particularly those employed in micro-, small and medium-sized enterprises. This links to a less -researched aspect of the Spanish economy is its large informal sector, which was estimated to represent 21 per cent of the nation's GDP in 2004 (Rodriguez Cabrero, 2010:7). Micro-, small and medium-sized enterprises may avoid paying taxes and employ people informally. The informal economy tends to increase in times of crisis, including the previously identified phenomenon of 'invisible factories' that produce goods outside of the formal economy (*New York Times*, 16 May 2012).

Managing the crisis I: the José Luis Zapatero administration (2008–2011)

Over the past four decades, Spain has had a relatively stable political system, despite the major difficulties experienced by its economy up through 1997. Major reforms undertaken in the 1990s led to the further liberalisation and flexibilisation of the labour market. In addition, Spain profited from a construction boom that radically increased consumer spending. Between 1997 and 2008, Spain grew about 3.5 per cent per year, and unemployment declined from 20.1 per cent to 8.3 per cent (Magone, 2009: 304, 309). Prime Minister Zapatero and his Socialist party came to power in 2004 after eight years of a Conservative government under José Maria Aznar. Between 2004 and 2008, Zapatero's government managed to preserve the economic stability and success of the Aznar administration. However, after the Socialists won re-election in 2008, Prime Minister Zapatero and his government ignored the signs of the financial crisis originating in the

United States and its potential impact on European markets for some time (for a review of the second Zapatero government, see Colino, Cotarelo, 2012). The catastrophic slump in the US financial market led to a credit crunch in most European countries and put an end to the speculative boom in Spain fuelled by the construction sector (Royo, 2009; Carballo-Cruz, 2011). In order to understand the management of the crisis by the Zapatero government, one must differentiate between the domestic and international dimensions. Until mid-2009, the domestic dimension was the focus of Spanish policy; after that point, the international dimension becomes an increasingly significant aspect of the country's economic policy-making. The systemic effects of the collapse of Lehman Brothers in 2008/9 and the subsequent Greek debt crisis beginning in 2009 were major factors constraining the policy options of the Spanish government. According to a seminal study conducted by Ignacio Molina, Zapatero's economic policy can be divided into three main phases, which he calls the phase of crisis denial (January 2008–July 2008), the phase of Keynesian response (August 2008–April 2010) and the phase of austerity and structural reforms (May 2010–December 2011).

As mentioned above, the phase of crisis denial was heavily influenced by the general elections of 14 March 2008. Electioneering was an important factor preserving the limited role of the government (Molina, 2012: 60–62). However, after the signs of a global crisis began to emerge, particularly the collapse of Lehman Brothers, Spanish policy-makers began to use neo-Keynesian instruments in order to stimulate the economy. This second phase led to increased public spending. Probably the most important measure in this phase was the 'E Plan', which involved expenditures of € 50 billion in order to stimulate employment at the local level and increase investment in infrastructure and enterprises. The Zapatero government also tried to revitalise the dialogue with social partners in order to achieve stability pacts. This phase was very much influenced by similar decisions taken at the global level in the G20, by the United States, and in the EU forums. Despite these measures, unemployment rose from 11.8 per cent in 2008 to 18 per cent in 2009 and to 20.1 per cent in 2010. In terms of GDP growth, there was a decrease from 0.9 per cent in 2008 to -3.7 per cent in 2009 and -0.1 per cent in 2010 (Molina, 2012: 62–5). The last phase was that of fiscal austerity and internal devaluation after the Greek sovereign debt crisis became a major problem for all peripheral economies. During this phase, Spain and Italy were targeted by speculating hedge funds. Particularly, insurance instruments, the so-called 'Credit Default Swaps' (CDS) could come into force should states default on their sovereign bonds obligations. Hedge funds speculated that in case of default of the big countries such as Spain, Italy and France their CDS in case of default could be activated. The contagion of the sovereign debt crisis made it difficult for the Spanish government to obtain funding from the markets due to the high interest rates demanded. In this last phase, Spain struggled to keep afloat, fighting against the efforts of the markets. Ultimately, a package of structural reforms was agreed upon with the European Commission in the hopes of restoring investor confidence. In this period, the Zapatero government worked closely with the social partners to further flexibilise the labour market. However, in the end, the administration acted unilaterally due to the pressure coming from the European Union. Among the measures introduced with the support of the People's Party was a debt-brake article inserted into the Spanish constitution. This set a limit for the structural deficit at a maximum of 0.4 per cent by 2020 (*The Economist*, 3 September 2011). Spain thereby largely followed the austerity policies advocated by the German government.

Unlike Portugal and Greece, which had major difficulties in dealing with the pressures of the markets, the external crisis management of the Spanish Socialist government up until November 2011 was, under the circumstances, quite successful. One important difference from the cases of Greece and Portugal is that Spain is a much larger economy with a larger population. The Spanish banking sector is also more robust and internationalised than those of Greece and Portugal. Moreover, the Zapatero government waged a battle against the rating agencies by providing transparent information that contrasted favourably to the speculative issuances of the agencies.

The result is that Spain gained control over its economic narrative, in contrast to Portugal and Greece. Spain refused to be a victim or to be victimised by the rating agencies and the markets. For the agencies and the markets, a default by Spain would be the ultimate proof of contagion, such that Spain was always linked to the contagion hypothesis. However, Prime Minister Zapatero was quite combative in relation to the rating agencies. At the time of the World Economic Forum in 2010, the Greek situation was already threatening to contaminate the Spanish economy. The resolute policies of the Spanish government throughout 2010 sought to negate this threat, including a tough package of austerity measures approved with only the support of the smaller regionalist parties in December 2010 (*The Economist*, 20 May 2010; *The Guardian*, 28 May 2010; *Der Spiegel*, 22 December 2010). However, the polarised relationship between the two main parties created major problems for the government in its attempts to present a united front against the markets and rating agencies. In order to counteract speculation from the rating agencies, the Spanish government continually issued updated data on all aspects of government and private debt.

A special website called 'The Spanish Economy.com' was set up to disprove the speculative claims of the ratings agencies. The weakest link in the Spanish economy was the regional savings banks within the banking sector, which were strongly affected by the financial crisis. A major restructuring of regional saving banks took place in order to reduce their burden. However, in March 2011 it became clear that there was still some way to go before the banking sector would be healthy again, as none of the major banks were able to pass the stress tests set by the European Central Bank. There was a shortfall of capital in many institutions, estimated at about €20 billion (*The Guardian*, 10 March 2011; *El Pais*, 23 March 2011; *The Telegraph*, 10 March 2011).

Despite the relatively positive external management of the crisis, the Spanish presidency of the Council of the European Union in the first half of 2010 was a rather unsuccessful enterprise for a variety of reasons. The Greek sovereign debt crisis came to the fore during the Spanish presidency, but it was sidelined by the

Franco-German directoire represented by German Chancellor Angela Merkel and French President Nicolas Sarkozy (also known as 'Merkozy' due to the strong coordination between the two leaders with regard to positions on issues). In addition, due to the country's deteriorating domestic economy and the attention drawn to it, the Spanish presidency became almost invisible in the management of the Eurocrisis (Molina, 2010: 69; Millet et al., 2011: 80–1).

Managing the crisis II: the Mariano Rajoy administration (2011–2015)

In the elections on 20 November 2011, Mariano Rajoy, the leader of the conservative People's Party, won with a comfortable absolute majority. The main reason for his high level of support was the fact that the population wanted a radical change from the policies of the Socialist government. Before the elections, Rajoy had been silent about his plans for dealing with the crisis. In fact, when he came to power, the new government really had no alternative programme to that of Zapatero. Rajoy had to learn the hard way about the continuing scepticism of the markets with regard to the willingness of the Spanish government to commit to the necessary structural reforms. Like Zapatero, Rajoy had to develop a positive communication strategy in order to prevent negative repercussions for Spanish sovereign bonds in the markets. President of ECB Mario Draghi's announcement that the ECB would do whatever it took to protect the euro was an important turning point for the situation in Spain.

Mariano Rajoy was very keen to restore confidence in the Spanish market. The high level of unemployment (and youth unemployment in particular) played a major role in the relatively severe package of austerity measures and structural reforms. One of the most difficult issues was the need to further flexibilise the labour market. Again, measures focused on reducing the costs of dismissal for permanent workers. Beginning in 2011, there have been three labour market reforms that have had the unintended side effects of increasing unemployment and decreasing wages; as a result, one-third of the population or more is now struggling to make ends meet. These reforms were part of the austerity package based on the internal devaluation of the country. The lack of funds also led to a major reform of the unemployment benefit system, restricting entitlement and reducing the amounts received and the time period of eligibility. Many enterprises seem to have used this flexibilisation of the labour market to reduce their workforce. Unemployment thus rose considerably despite the labour market reforms. In particular, young people and women have been strongly affected by the crisis. The unemployment rate among young people has been over 50 per cent throughout the crisis (*Financial Times*, 23 May 2014). Apart from the crisis, one major factor contributing to this high level of unemployment is the lack of adjustment to the needs of the markets on the part of new job seekers. Moreover, during the crisis, other governments such as Germany and Austria played a major role in helping their domestic enterprises to survive. For example, the government funded jobs by allowing enterprises to reduce the number of hours; the difference was paid for by the state. In addition, the well-established apprenticeship system in both countries allowed for a better match between the skills of young people and the needs of the labour markets. These programmes are underdeveloped or non-existent in Spain. Throughout the Spanish economy, industrial relations are still not completely internalised. According to Sergio González Begega and David Luque Balbona, neither the Zapatero nor the Rajoy government was able to achieve agreements with the social partners during the economic crisis. Consequently, the labour market reforms were imposed by the government without adequate dialogue with unions and employers' organisations. The scholars conclude that this may have destroyed any future prospects of a positive relationship between the government and the social partners (Gonzalez Begega, Luque Balbona, 2014). According to El Pais, in February 2015, the per centage of unemployed covered by unemployment benefit was 55.72 per cent. The average benefit was about 812 Euros. This clearly is an indication of the precariousness of large part of the population (*El Pais*, 6 April 2015).

Spain had to cope with massive capital flight during the first half of 2012, thereby becoming quite dependent on support to its banks from the European Central Bank. In order to preserve the liquidity of the banking sector, over €200 billion was poured into the banking sector each month in March, April and May of 2012 (*El Pais*, 14 June 2012). Finally, on 9 June, a soft bailout programme of up to €100 billion from the new permanent European Stability Mechanism (ESM) was agreed upon with the Eurogroup. One of the reasons for avoiding the Troika was that the Eurogroup based on reports of the European Commission were convinced of the efforts of successive Spanish governments to introduce major reforms. The continuity of reform between the Zapatero and Rajoy government were seen as proof of a strong commitment by Spain to make the necessary reforms. This restored calmness to the markets, from which the southern European peripheral economies were able to profit. After a review by the International Monetary Fund (IMF) and two independent commissions, the sum of €40 billion was requested in November 2012. These funds were used for the complete restructuring of the Spanish banking sector. However, one major victory for Rajoy was the fact that Spain would be able to avoid the Troika's control as long as the specified reforms were carried out. Although the much hated Troika was not involved in monitoring the bailout programme to the banks, Spain had to endure a soft Troika arrangement of European institutions consisting of the European Commission, European Central Bank and the newly founded European Banking Authority (EBA). They would monitor the progress made every three months. However, their remit was just restricted to the restructuring of the banking sector. Several banks needed capitalisation in order to remain in business. The largest and most complicated bank was Bankia, which was nationalised. One of the main reasons is that an insolvency of Bankia could have unleashed a similar systemic collapse of the finance system as Lehman brothers. Meanwhile, Bankia was able to make small profits in the €100 millions in 2013 and 2014. It had received €22.5 billion from the so-called Fund for the orderly Restructuring of the Banking Sector (Fondo de restruturación ordenada bancaria – FROB). In 2015, Bankia had still not paid back any of the borrowed funding. In January 2014, the Spanish government managed to exit the bailout programme without any precautionary backup funding. However, the restructuring of the local banking sector still remains to be completed (*The Telegraph*, 13 November 2015; EurActiv, 2013).

The lack of funding at the central level additionally resulted in conflicts with the decentralised 17 autonomous communities, which were also affected by the crisis.

This naturally led to discussions about the state of finances of these communities. In particular, the rich region of Catalonia felt disadvantaged, as it was transferring funds to the central government that were badly needed in the region itself. Some regions, including Catalonia and Valencia, were unable to pay their public bills. In particular, the public health sector had major problems dealing with the crisis. According to a study by the IMF, Spain had trouble limiting the deficits of the autonomous communities; these deficits increased from 6 per cent of GDP in 2007 to 18 per cent at the end of 2012, with more than half concentrated in the three most indebted regions: Catalonia, Andalucia and Valencia. This was clearly a major problem, in part because it made it difficult to estimate the exact budget deficit of the government. In 2012, the budget deficit had to be revised several times due to revisions in the regional budget deficits. The Rajoy government had to act fast in order to get this problem under control. Consequently, three main instruments were created in order to help the regions. First, in February 2012 the regions were provided with a €10 billion credit through the state-owned Institute of Official Credit (Instituto de Crédito Oficial – ICO bank). Second, in March 2012, the Fund for the Financing of Payments to Suppliers was established with up to €35 billion to help the regions pay their bills. Third, a Regional Liquidity Fund (Fondo de Liquidad Autonomo – FLA) was created and endowed with €18 billion in 2012 and €23 billion in 2013. All these short- to medium-term measures were linked to a long-term law on budget stability (*Ley de estabilidad presupuestaria*). In 2012, regional budget deficits were set at 1.8 per cent (Jenkner, Lu, 2014: 7–8; see also Dominguez Martinez and Lopez Jimenez, 2012). However, as of the end of 2014, most of the autonomous communities had not been able to meet the public debt targets that they had agreed upon with the central government. Only the Basque Country, Navarra and Madrid were able to meet their targets; all the other regions continue to have major problems controlling their public debt. In 2014, the regions with the highest public debt-to-GDP ratios were the Valencian Community (37.4 per cent), Castilla-La Mancha (33.5 per cent) and Catalonia (32.4 per cent). In contrast, Madrid (12.5 per cent) and the Canary Islands (14.5 per cent) have the lowest public debt ratios. One piece of good news is that the local authorities have thus far been the most disciplined tier of government in terms of public expenditures, resulting in an aggregate budget surplus in 2013 and 2014. Unfortunately, the crisis has increased the overall public debt of regional and central administrations from 36 per cent in 2007 to 97.7 per cent in 2014 (*El Pais*, 14 March 2015) and the public deficit from 1.9 per cent of GDP surplus to -6.8 per cent deficit at the end of 2013

In 2015, the government was offering loans at a 0 per cent interest rate, due to the fact that after peaking in 2011 and 2012, the interest rates of Spanish sovereign bonds have decreased to their lowest levels ever, about 1.52 per cent for ten-year bonds in March 2014 (*El Pais*, 26 February 2015).

Conclusions

Despite major reforms of the public administration, the economy and the labour market, the structural problems of the Spanish economy remain unresolved. Spain needs to tackle its ailing school system, which is reproducing the class system and inequality in the structure of opportunities, particularly for young people. Enterprises need to become larger and more capital-strong and must invest in research and development. Such structural changes can only be achieved over time.

References

Cárdenas, Amalia (2013) 'The Spanish Savings Bank Crisis: History, Causes and Responses'. Internet Interdisciplinary Institute Working Paper 13-003, Open University of Catalonia, Barcelona

Centorrino, Samuele and Maria Pérez-Urdiales (2014) *Convergence in the Spanish Regions: Too Little or too much European Structural Funds?* Madrid: Fundación Alternativas, Estudios de Progreso.

Chislett, William (2011) 'Spain's Multinationals: The Dynamic Part of an Ailing Economy'. Working Paper 17/2011, Instituto Real Elcano, Madrid

Closa, Carlos and Paul Heywood (2004) *Spain and the European Union*. Basingstoke: Palgrave.

Colino, César and Ramón Cotarelo (2012) 'Introducción: La Primera Legislatura de Rodriguez Zapatero,' in César Colino and Ramón Cotarelo (eds) *España en Crisis: Balance de la Segunda Legislatura de Rodriguez Zapatero*. Valencia: Tirant Humanidades, pp. 21–47.

Cruz, Francisco Carballo-Cruz (2011) 'Causes and consequences of the Spanish economic crisis: Why the recovery is taking so long,' *Panoeconomicus* 3: 309–328.

Dominguez Martinez, José M. and José M. López Jiménez (2012) 'La Reforma de la Politica de Estabilidad Presupuestaria en España: Análisis de la Ley Orgánica de Estabilidad Presupuestaria y Sostenibilidad Financiera.' Working Paper 9/12, Universidad de Alcalá-Instituto Universitario de Analisis Economico y Social, Madrid. Available at: www2.uah.es/iaes/publicaciones/DT_09_12.pdf (accessed 16 March 2015).

EurActiv (2013) 'Spain quits EU's aid programme for its banking sector,' 18 November. Available at: www.euractiv.com/euro-finance/spain-quits-eu-aid-program-banki-news-531718 (accessed 16 March 2015).

Eurostat (2014a) 'General government deficit(-) and (+)- annual data.' Available at: http://ec.europa.eu/eurostat/tgm/table.do?tab=table&plugin=1&language=en&code=teina200 (accessed 30 December 2014).

Eurostat (2014b) 'General government gross debt.' Available at: http://ec.europa.eu/eurostat/tgm/table.do?tab=table&init=1&language=en&pcode=tsdde410&plugin=1 (accessed 30 December 2014).

Eurostat (2015a) 'Private sector debt non-consolidated.' Available at: http://ec.europa.eu/eurostat/tgm/table.do?tab=table&language=en&pcode=tipspd10 (accessed 22 March 2015).

Eurostat (2015b) 'Early leavers from education and training by sex and labour status,' 24 February. Available at: http://appsso.eurostat.ec.europa.eu/nui/show.do?dataset=edat_lfse_14&lang=en (updated 24 February 2015) (accessed 15 March 2015).

Eurostat (2015c) 'Third quarter of 2014 compared with second quarter of 2014. Government debt fell to 92.1 per cent of GDP in euro area. Down to 86.6 per cent in EU28,' 22 January. Available at: http://ec.europa.eu/eurostat/documents/2995521/6483082/2-22012015-AP-EN.pdf/765eba70-6a88-4771-8af7-48f6665e3c67 (accessed 3 October 2015).

Garrido Medina, Luis (2010) 'Mercado de Trabajo, Ocupación y Clases Sociales,' in Juan Jesús González and Miguel Requena (eds) *Trés Décadas de Cambio Social en España*, Second edition. Madrid: Alianza Editorial, pp. 89–134.

Colino, César, Oriol Homs and Ignacio Molina (2013) 'Sustainable Governance Indicators: 2014 Spain Report,' Bertelsmann Foundation. Available at: www.sgi-network.org/docs/2014/country/SGI2014_Spain.pdf (accessed 17 March 2015).

González Begega, Sergio and David Luque Balbona (2014) 'Goodbye to competitive corporatism in Spain? Social pacting and conflict in the economic crisis,' *Revista Española de Investigaciones Sociologicas* 148: 78–102.

Jenkner, Eva and Zongjin Lu (2014) 'Subnational Credit Risk and Sovereign Bailouts: Who Pays the Premium?' Working Paper 14/20, International Monetary Fund, Washington, DC. Available at: www.imf.org/external/pubs/ft/wp/2014/wp1420.pdf (accessed 16 March 2015).

Jimenez, Fernando and Miguel Cainzos (2003) 'Political Corruption in Spain,' in Martin J. Bull and James L. Newell (eds) *Corruption in Contemporary Politics*. Basingstoke: Palgrave, pp. 9–23.

Magone, José (2009) *Contemporary Spanish Politics*. Second edition. London: Routledge.

Millet, Monserrat, Patricia Garcia-Durán and Elisa Casanova (2011) 'Gobernanza Económica: Cumpliendo con la Agenda en un Entorno Dificil para España,' in Esther Barbé Izuel (ed.) *Entre la irrelevancia internacional y el aprendizaje institucional:la presidencia española de la Unión Europea*. Barcelona: Institut Universitari d´Estudis Europeus, pp. 77–84.

Molina, Ignacio (2010) 'The 2010 Spanish Presidency: Trying to Innovate Europe in Troubled Times,' occasional Paper 2010/1. Swedish Institute of European Policy Studies, Stockholm

Molina, Ignacio (2012) 'Gobierno y Desgobierno de la Economia: Las Politicas de Respuesta a la Crisis,' in César Colino and Ramón Cotarelo (eds) *España en Crisis: Balance de la Segunda Legislatura de Rodriguez Zapatero*. Valencia: Tirant Humanidades, pp. 49–71.

Molina, Oscar (2014) 'Self-regulation and the state in industrial relations in Southern Europe: Back to the future?,' *European Journal of Industrial Relations* 20(1): 21–36.

Ortega, Eloisa and Juan Peñalosa (2012) '*The Spanish Economic Crisis: Key Factors and Growth Challenges in the Euro Area*,' occasional Paper no.1201, Banco de España, Madrid

Quaglia, Lucia and Sebastian Royo (2014) 'Banks and the Political Economy of the Sovereign Debt Crisis in Italy and Spain,'.CES Papers (Open Forum) 18, Minda de Gunzburg Centre for European Studies, Harvard University. Available at: https://ces.fas.harvard.edu/files/working_papers/CES_OFWP_18.pdf (accessed 16 July 2015).

Royo, Sebastian (2009) 'After the fiesta: The Spanish economy meets the global financial crisis,' *South European Society and Politics* 14(1): 19–34.

Royo, Sebastian (2013) *Lessons from the Economic Crisis in Spain*. Basingstoke: Palgrave.

Royo, Sebastian (2013) 'How did the Spanish financial system survive the first stage of the global crisis?,' *Governance* 26(4): 631–656.

Royo, Sebastian (2014) 'Austerity: Lessons from the Spanish Experience,' working paper 11/2014, Real Instituto Elcano, Madrid. Available at: www.realinstitutoelcano.org/wps/wcm/connect/8dc5a200456f1f1685d0e511646dbfa9/WP11-2014-Royo-After-austerity-lessons-from-the-Spanish-experience.pdf?MOD=AJPERES&CACHEID=8dc5a200456f1f1685d0e511646dbfa9 (accessed 16 July 2015).

Serrano, José Maria (2010) 'La Economia Española en el Siglo XXI: Perspectivas y Potencialidades,' in Salustiano del Campo and José Felix Tezanos (eds) *España: Una Sociedad en Cambio*. Madrid: Biblioteca Nueva, pp. 317–342.

World Economic Forum (WEF) (2014) *The Global Competitiveness Report 2014–2015*. Edited by Klaus Schwab. Geneva: World Economic Forum.

World Bank (2014) *Doing Business 2015: Going Beyond Efficiency*. Washington, DC: World Bank.

15 Italy between *transformismo* and transformation

Marco Brunazzo and Vincent Della Sala

Narratives of Italy and the EU have swung wildly during the course of the economic crisis: from the "sick man" of Europe in the dying days of the Berlusconi government in 2011 to the member state that was going to save the euro and Europe with the Monti government weeks later. It is presented as either the catalyst to bring about a major change in economic policy in the Eurozone, led by Matteo Renzi after the European Parliament elections in May 2014, or the proverbial straw that will precipitate a collapse of the single currency, again with the Renzi government. More than the search to find a narrative scheme for the economic crisis, we argue, these volatile gyrations reflect a deeper ambiguity about Italy's place in the European Union and the role of European integration in the regulation of social and economic life in the country. Italy is, by some measures, clearly part of the southern periphery, not only geographically but also with respect to its distance from meeting the objectives set by European policies and from the centres of power where those policies are made. Arguably, reticence by some northern EU member states to embark forms of burden and debt sharing derive from concern about taking on Italy's enormous public debt and, more generally, its deep regional disparities and public sector inefficiencies. On the other hand, Italy is very much at the centre of Europe. It is the second leading industrial economy in the EU, has very low levels of private debt and is an important transatlantic ally, not to mention a member of the G8. Moreover, Italy has provided ideational and political leadership for a federal Europe, with figures from Altiero Spinelli to Romano Prodi and Mario Monti leading the way. The very idea of a federal Europe has Italy at its centre. Both these views of Italy, as a peripheral member state that is more a subject of European integration than an object and as a central player that shapes it, have been present throughout the history of the EU in Italy. We will argue that the economic crisis has shown that it is difficult for this ambiguity to continue.

The aim of this chapter is twofold. First, it wants to illustrate that the traditional consensus that has existed amongst Italian political elites and in public opinion about the centrality of Europe for Italy's modernization has eroded over the last two decades. We will argue that the durability of this consensus was due, in part, to the ambiguity of Italy's position as both central and peripheral to the Union. The second aim is to demonstrate that it became increasingly hard to argue that Italy was central to the European project as the crisis evolved and that, consequently, it became easier for those political forces that did not want European commitments as the lynchpin of Italian policy to claim that Europe's approach to its periphery, which included Italy, condemned the country not only to the margins of the EU but to austerity for an indefinite period. Our discussion will be divided into two sections. The first will trace the evolution of Italy in the EU, highlighting its ambivalent position between centre and periphery. The second will focus on how the centre–periphery tension was at the heart of Italy's position throughout the recent economic crisis.

Italy and Europe: on the margins of both centre and periphery

There have been many different ways in which Italy's role and position within the European Union have been described. According to Antonio Varsori, Italy is Europe's "Cinderella", never quite accepted by her sisters and having to disguise herself to attend the ball and hoping that she will find her prince before she is noticed (Varsori 2010). Others have described Italy as neither a "giant" nor a "pygmy", pointing to its middling status and resources (Fabbrini and Piattoni 2004). While these metaphors are useful to trace Italy's role in different areas of policy-making, they are somewhat limited in understanding how they relate to the role European integration has played within Italian politics and society in the post-war period. We argue that it is much more useful to use the centre–periphery framework developed in this volume to illustrate Italy's ambivalent position within the Union, how its historical role and economic weight place it at the centre but its pressing need for structural policy reforms push it to the periphery. The centre–periphery scheme also helps to highlight a parallel ambiguity in Italy's relationship with Europe; that is, Europe has been seen both as "transformative", in that it was the catalyst for Italy's modernization, as well as something to be "transformed"—*trasformismo* is the Italian word used to describe the co-opting of political forces that threaten disruption—so as to provide a shield to protect Italian society and politics from broader global pressures.

In the aftermath of the Second World War, the Treaty of Rome and European integration had two important related and legitimizing roles for Italy. First, it gave Italy the means to re-enter the family of nations at the international level and to firmly place itself as a member of the Atlantic alliance (Varsori 2010). Moreover, European integration also provided an opportunity to shed its image of the "least of the great European powers" and to be one of the architects of a new post-war order. This was not a hard argument to make for both domestic and international audiences. Germany was hamstrung by its recent history, France was devastated by war and the United Kingdom chose to stay out of the fledgling union. Second, Europe meant liberal democracy and market capitalism, two essential features that were highly contested in the immediate aftermath of the war, thus entwining the idea of Europe with the new democratic Republic (Willis 1971). Even the presence of the largest communist party in western Europe did not prevent the emergence of an elite consensus on the role that

European integration would play in ensuring that Italy was at the centre of Europe; as well as looking to Europe as an anchor to bring about economic and political modernization. Italy's long-standing commitment to push for deeper integration is found as much in the belief that it would be one of the drivers of a major global actor as it was in the perceived need for a "*vincolo esterno*" to complete its social and economic modernization (Della Sala 2004, Dyson and Featherstone 1996).

These two pillars of Italy's relationship with Europe—that Italy was at the centre of the EU and that European integration would act as a catalyst to complete Italy's transformation as a modern European state and society—were central to both Italy's policy towards Europe and domestic politics for the first decades of the Republic and the EU. Whether Italy was really one of the four "great powers" and architects of the EU is open to debate. But it was an important argument that helped legitimize the political order established in the wake of the war and the Fascist experience. It also made it easier to claim that Italy was shaping and transforming European rules so that Italian approaches to governing could be preserved. But to be at the centre of Europe also meant becoming more "European"; that is, there was also the sense that despite its size and material resources, Italy still needed to prove that it deserved to be one of the drivers of integration. Italy needed to be "saved by Europe" as much as it was "condemned to success" by European integration (Ferrera and Gualmini 1999, Freddi et al. 2000). However, so long as there was the credible claim that Italy was shaping Europe as much as it was being shaped by it, popular support for Europe remained strong, as did the consensus amongst political elites. The consensus began to erode with the introduction of the single currency, which brought into relief the challenges Italy faced to become "more" European in its macroeconomic governance (Dastoli and Santaniello 2013).

While the reform of the many areas of public policy that needed to be addressed in the wake of entry into the single currency would garner attention (for example, labor market policy), none would capture the attention of policy-makers and European officials as the governing of the Italian economy, especially the state of public finances (Reviglio 1998, Spaventa and Chiorazzo 2000). The ink was not yet dry on the signatures of the Maastricht Treaty when Italy was forced to drop out of the Exchange Rate Mechanism (ERM) in the midst of a serious financial crisis in September 1992. The lira was devalued by as much as 25 per cent, leading to further strains on public finances. The devaluation would prove to be a swansong, which would raise more serious challenges once Italy entered the single currency; that is, it helped generate an export boom that allowed policy-makers to put off making difficult decisions about productivity and competitiveness. The exit from the ERM and the devaluation also sparked fears that Italy was reverting back to the old practices of avoiding difficult choices in the governing of its economy. Italy was once again the "sick man" of Europe (Graham 1996).

There are a number of reasons why the "health" of Italian public finances was the focal point for a broader discussion about the need to provide Italy with adequate policy responses in a rapidly changing world. The first, and most obvious, was the dimension of the problem. Italy's long road to enter the single currency is well documented but it is worth remembering here that its public deficit level in 1991 was in double digits and Italian budgets had to service a debt level that exceeded 110 per cent of GDP. It would have been hard for any kind of discussion about public policy in the 1990s to ignore these levels of public sector debt and deficit, even without the objective of bringing them within the parameters set by the convergence criteria. Any modernization of Italian public policy would have to begin with public finances; and given already high tax levels, this meant having to make decisions about spending.

Second, public finances put into relief many of the problems endemic in Italian decision-making. A consensual policy style combined with a political stalemate ensured that weak governments would loosen purse strings to hold together wobbly coalitions as well as maintain social peace. Necessary for reform was not only a first order change in the policy instruments but also in the decision-making mechanisms themselves (Hall 1993). It is not a coincidence that Italy's hyper-consensual polity ran into problems at the beginning of the 1990s, at precisely the same time that it was faced with difficult decisions about maintaining Exchange Rate Mechanism (ERM) commitments as well as beginning to take the steps necessary to meet the convergence criteria (Salvati 1997). This is not to argue that the "First Republic", as the political system of the first four decades of the post-war period has come to be known, collapsed because of public finances. It is simply to point out that Europe, by the 1990s, meant having to make difficult choices that constrained the ability of political parties to use public finances to mobilize support. Moreover, the narrative of Italy in Europe became one of the need for reforms to remain at the centre of the EU or risk being marginalized to the peripheries. Italian parties tried to avoid the day of reckoning as much as possible in the two decades since the start of the process to create and implement the single currency. By the time the financial crisis hit in 2011, it was that being part of the Eurozone meant it was harder to "transform" exogenous pressures rather than be transformed by them.

It is not surprising, then, that despite the enormity of the challenge at hand, Italian political leaders were undeterred in the quest to ensure that Italy did not miss entering the single currency in the first round. The overarching narrative of the 1990s was that Italy needed to enter the single currency in order to continue to present itself as one of the major powers in the EU. However, joining the euro area also had important domestic consequences, as it was the ultimate external pressure that would complete the modernization process. As one commentator argued, "The euro was the path of a solid currency, lower costs for energy and credit … . It was an alternative to the traditional policies, and certainly a healthier and more modern one" (Cafagna 2005). There was no debate as to whether Italy *should* strive to meet the convergence criteria; it was only a question of whether it could. Moreover, there clearly was little doubt that many felt that Italy had no choice but to try. The titles of books—for example, *Condemned to Succeed?* or *Saved by Europe?* (Freddi et al. 2000; Ferrera and Gualmini 1999)—were graphic summaries not only of the challenges ahead but also the implications of the convergence process. Europe would "condemn" Italy to reform, and the price for resisting might be to lose Europe and the modernization of Italy.

Italy's entry into the single currency, then, did not create political cleavages in the 1990s. The consensus that Italy *had* to adopt the euro was widespread and deeply rooted. However, Italy's "success" was not met with a great deal of enthusiasm and Italy had no sooner entered into the single currency when it became apparent that, rather than be an opportunity for solving Italy's policy dilemmas, the euro itself was now becoming a problem. In fact, there was even nostalgia for the lira. Ministers from the Northern League (LN) in the centre-right Berlusconi government made public declarations in favour of the return of the old currency. The LN's position was understandable. Its core constituency is in the industrial provincial cities of northern Italy, an area that benefited enormously from the export boom of the 1990s but which paid the cost once the cover of a devalued currency was lifted. However, they remained marginal voices in the political debate until the onset of the economic crisis.

The growing lack of consensus became more emphatic with the onset of the economic crisis, whose impact was seriously underestimated by the fourth Berlusconi government between 2008 and 2011. The official government position was that the economy was doing well. Berlusconi himself continued to claim that there was no "crisis" in Italy as late as November 2011, even as international financial markets were condemning his government and other European leaders were speaking openly about a rescue for its troubled public finances. This only highlighted that the lack of the needed structural reforms condemned the Italian economy to extremely low rates of growth if not recession. Confidence in Italy in international financial markets was undermined by the fact that these reforms were not carried out by the Berlusconi government despite having the largest majority in Italian parliamentary history. Berlusconi, his own credibility shaken by a string of personal scandals, presided over a fragile coalition that became more divided over the course of the legislature. Newspaper and media reports in the second half of 2011 were dominated by data of the "spread", that is to say the difference between Italian and German interest rates. This came to be considered an indicator of the capacity of Italy to cope with the economic crisis and to adopt the inevitable reforms. It also served to mark the distance that between Italy and the "centre" of Europe. Struggling to maintain the confidence of international markets was something that the member states on the periphery had to contend with, not a state that sought to be a central factor in determining European policy.

If the numerous pressures on the Italian government coming from the EU institutions requiring more incisive economic reforms did not succeed, this was also due to the fact that Europe was no longer seen singularly as the "answer" to Italian problems; becoming, instead, one of the sources of these Italian "problems" (Brunazzo and Della Sala 2011). For many politicians (mainly on the centre-right but also on the extremes wings of the political spectrum) and for a growing part of the public opinion, the EU (and, more specifically, the euro) was neither able to guarantee modernization nor protect Italian society from broader global pressures. Whereas in the first decades of the European project, this positive view of Europe's role in Italy's transformation would have been largely unchallenged, recent governments have had to deal with a very different landscape. Critical voices on the role of the EU in national economies and on the limit posed by the Euro to national sovereignty have become louder and louder (Bellucci and Conti 2012). The party manifestoes and the discourse of the political leaders are now much more diversified and politicized than in the past in defining the relation between Italy and the EU. A book like the one published in 2008 by Giulio Tremonti, the economy minister during the Berlusconi governments, entitled *La paura e la speranza* (Fear and Hope), criticized the role of Europe in managing the pressures generated by the globalization process in a way that would have been unthinkable in Italy only a few years earlier (Tremonti 2010). In his book, Tremonti tries to answer the following question: "Why is Europe no longer the master of history and risks exclusion from history, reduced to a geographical agglomeration?" His conclusion is that Europe has lost its identity and is no longer able to provide the right answers to the difficulties of national and international economies. Tremonti is an important figure not just for the central role that he played in governing the Italian economy for most of the period since the introduction of the Euro. He was the lynchpin of the different strands in the Berlusconi coalition, close to both the Northern League and Berlusconi. He was at the same time skeptical of many aspects of economic integration yet a proponent of Eurobonds. He saw in Europe not an engine of change but a bulwark against global pressures. In this way, he captured the position of the Italian government for most of the last decade. Moreover, by 2014, Tremonti's views would be considered too conciliatory towards Europe by most of his political allies.

The arrival of Mario Monti was supposed to represent a return to "salvation" through transformation. His government was met with an initial sigh of relief as the drama surrounding the figure of Silvio Berlusconi was replaced with a serious concern with restoring credibility in international markets and with European partners. However, relief quickly gave way to frustration amongst the electorate as the social and economic consequences of the crisis only worsened in 2012. More importantly, it was clear that not only was the esteem and credibility of the Monti government not an asset, in many ways it was a liability. It represented the transformative power of Europe but underestimated the extent to which Italian politics is still very much constrained by the dynamics of *trasformismo*. The success of the Movimento 5 Stelle (M5S) in the 2013 national election suggests that what the electorate was looking for was not political leadership that would gain favour in Europe but one that would ensure that a central place in Europe would guarantee that the impact of Europe on basic policies and politics would be limited. This was confirmed by the results of the 2014 European Parliament elections, as the parties that actively campaigned against European policies garnered clearly more than half the vote cast; while the governing party of Prime Minister Renzi emerged with 40 per cent of the vote on the basis of a campaign that it would be at the centre of Europe to change European policy for the periphery.

The 2013 and 2014 elections are striking in that the only political force that defended the importance of the transformative power of Europe, Mario Monti's Scelta Civica (Civic Choice), was soundly defeated. More importantly, not a single major political party, including the centre-left Democratic Party (Partito Democratico—PD), sent out unambiguous signals of support for the need to use Europe to modernize Italian society. The M5S has been dismissed as a protest and populist party that will in all likelihood fade away. However, it clearly campaigned on a platform that claimed the euro compromised sovereignty and was transforming Italian society and institutions. It touched a nerve with a part of the electorate that was feeling increasingly threatened by changes it saw as out of the control of its institutions and political leaders. It is not a coincidence that amongst the many targets of the M5S's leader, Beppe Grillo, are not only the European institutions but also international financial institutions, immigration and economic liberalization. Grillo has consistently said that he is not opposed to the EU but that he wants a Union that protects Italy from these elements of globalization. His success has not been lost on other parties. Indeed, the refrain that we want a different Europe was sung by the major parties of the centre-left and centre-right in the election campaign.

The centre does not hold

It would be hard not to find a period in the 150-year history of unified Italy when there was not a discussion of the need for major reforms to complete the process of modernization and meet the challenges of the contemporary period. However, arguably, the last twenty years may stand out as they have been characterized by, on the one hand, a great deal of political ferment and even convulsions and, on the other, yet another period when forces of resistance to change prevailed. Since the signing of the Maastricht treaty, Italy has had, amongst other important political developments, at least two major reforms of its electoral laws (subsequently rejected by the constitutional court), changes to the distribution of powers between the central and regional governments, the disappearance of all the major parties that dominated politics in the post-war period and then many of those that replaced them, two distinct phases in which the country was governed by technocrats and the emergence (and possible collapse) of a nascent bipolar party system. Yet, despite the volatility of the period, politics and policies have stayed remarkably consistent; and some basic social and economic structures have proven to be remarkably resilient.

It is this resilience that is at play in Italy's ambiguous relationship with the centre and periphery of the EU. One way to measure the limited impact that European pressure has had on Italy in the last two decades is to examine the letter sent by the then president of the European Central Bank, Jean-Claude Trichet, and his successor and governor of the Bank of Italy at the time, Mario Draghi, to Italian prime minister Silvio Berlusconi on 5 August 2011. The letter is remarkable both for what it represents and for its content. Written just as Italy entered into the sovereign debt storm in July 2011, it set out quite clearly what the Italian government had to do if it wanted to benefit from the ECB's intervention in the secondary debt markets. It was a form of conditionality that one would not expect to find applied to a member of the G8 and the third largest economy of the Eurozone. The August letter to the Berlusconi government set off an exchange of missives between the European institutions and the Italian government in October and November 2011. They were supplemented by reports from the IMF and the OECD, not to mention assessments by financial market operators (IMF 2011).

The missives from the EU institutions have two striking features. First, there was nothing new in the reforms that were being solicited. More than a list of conditions to be met in return for help on financial markets, they were an admonition of the inability of Italian governments of all political stripes in the period since the Maastricht treaty to carry out basic structural changes that should have been part of being in the single currency. This was a refrain that the Commission would continue with successive governments, culminating in heated exchanges between the Renzi government and the incoming Juncker Commission in 2014 (Pop 2014). The tension that Italian governments had to manage was between the very pressing need to transmit the urgency behind the demanded reforms and trying to convey them not as the result of being designated as part of the periphery. Second, it is hard not to read in the exchanges between EU institutions and Italian governments an underlying lack of faith that there is the political will to carry out reforms. The Berlusconi response, as well as the policy agenda of successive governments, was full of vague references and promises that were not so different from those presented by Italian governments for the last twenty years. Italy's oscillation between saying reforms are necessary to meet European commitments and that those commitments need to be changed are the embodiment of the centre–periphery tension in Italy's relationship with Europe.

The exchanges, then, provide an interesting lens through which to examine some of the structural problems that Italy continues to face and which seem resistant to attempts, mostly feeble, by governments to address. The Commission's and the ECB's concerns continued to fall into two categories in 2014: public finances and obstacles to economic growth. In many ways, the case of public finances has been the easier story for Italian governments to tell. Italy has emerged from Excessive Deficit Procedure (EDP), has remained below the 3 per cent threshold and has run an impressive primary surplus. However, the major problem with Italian public finances, apart from the rather obvious point that there is an exceptionally high level of public debt, is its structure. Public sector spending, as a per centage of GDP, has remained fairly constant over the last two decades, as has its distribution: from 50.2 per cent in 1997 to 50.5 per cent in 2010 after a slight drop in the intervening period (OECD 2011b). Yet Italy continues to spend a disproportionate amount on income maintenance for protected sectors such as pensioners while lagging in areas such as education and research. On the revenue side, tax revenue as a per centage of GDP has crept up from 40.1 per cent in 1995 to 43 per cent in 2010 (OECD 2011a: 19).

There may be a number of ways to explain this relative consistency in public finances but what emerges is a political system that has been unwilling and/or unable to address redistributive questions. Fragile governments, even with electoral majorities, have not mobilized the political capital to change the basic structures of taxation and government spending. Moreover, governments, from the Romano Prodi coalitions that brought Italy into the single currency to the recent Renzi government, have met public finance targets largely through tax increases rather than spending cuts. It, like its predecessors, has discovered that there is no major political force that can be mobilized to address some of the structural problems of Italian public finances nor to deal with productivity and competitiveness issues. The centre-left has proposed very little in terms of changes to public spending and has focused on revenue measures aimed at high-income earners and cracking down on tax evasion. The centre-right, on the other hand, is more fractured on the question and at the end of the day has supported tax measures rather than address spending questions especially those that affect local and sectoral electoral constituencies. The best example of this has been the Northern League, whose identity as an anti-politics movement is betrayed by its opposition to structural reforms such as eliminating provincial governments (equivalent to counties) which would have brought yearly savings of over €1 billion.

While there can be no doubt that European institutions and other member states have sought to put pressure on Italian governments to maintain fiscal discipline, they were more concerned with Italy's poor record on economic growth since the introduction of the Euro. For instance, only six of the 39 sets of issues raised by former European commissioner Rehn dealt with public finances while questions about structural reform to promote growth occupied 32. They essentially concurred with the assessment of the IMF, whose country report on Italy in July 2011 stated that fiscal consolidation was essential, "But only sustained growth will reduce the burden of public debt. Increasing potential growth should be the main policy goal. Comprehensive structural reforms in the areas of labor and product markets and public administration should be promptly implemented" (IMF 2011: 1). Structural changes to public finances were needed but these would be of limited use and politically difficult to sustain if they were not accompanied by measures to sustain economic growth.

A close reading of EU statements, as well as the IMF documents, presents a list of areas that represent the spectrum of social and political life. There are the usual references to the burden of an inefficient public administration and excessive regulation. But there are also queries about reform of the judicial system, universities, teacher training, evaluation of schools and transportation. The assessment of external actors, especially strident since 2011, seemed to imply that it was the Berlusconi government that had become the obstacle to these reforms seen as essential for growth. And while it is true that the centre-right was in power for most of the period since the introduction of the euro, there are deeper structural factors at play and successive technocratic and centre-left governments have had only marginal success. For instance, the poor capitalization of Italian firms (and banks) reflects a model of capitalism that has relied on close (often familial) networks deeply embedded in social and political life, from the local to the national level. Attempts to create new ownership structures that would subject firms to control based on return on equity rather than the more complex relationships in Italian capitalism have and will continue to run into fierce resistance even in light of stress tests conducted by the ECB. What emerges is a picture of Italian governments trying to convince their electorates that they are at the centre of the European debate and have the capacity to shape it or least ensure that the difficult reforming impulses are resisted; and those very same governments, including the Renzi government in 2014, struggling to have their European partners recognize that Italy is too important to the European project and could not be considered part of the periphery.

As the crisis evolved after the end of the Berlusconi government in 2011, Italy's position in Europe became increasing affected by the growing tide of anti-Euro sentiment in popular opinion and the electorate. Matteo Renzi became the leader of the centre-left PD and then prime minister largely on the back of the growing fear that this populist and anti-establishment wave would pick up enough momentum to bring back the close scrutiny by financial markets and European institutions of the country's commitment to fiscal discipline and European rules. However, the Renzi government sent out mixed signals in 2014. It set out an ambitious list of policy reforms that move in the direction consistent with demands from external pressures. Admittedly, these remained more stated intentions that concrete policy outputs. On the other hand, and relatedly, it argued that Italy was a sovereign state and a major European power that would set out its own course and would work to transform European rules. The government's success in Europe depended on its ability to convince domestic audience that Italy was sliding to the periphery, while its success domestically required it to be a central European actor that could transform European rules.

Conclusion

Italy has always occupied an ambiguous position in Europe and the role of European integration in domestic Italian politics has become increasingly ambivalent, swaying from support for an external constraint to ensure economic modernization and fiscal discipline to growing skepticism that Italy was at the centre of the European project or, at least, increasing concern that the reforms needed to be at the heart of Europe lacked sufficient popular support. While there is no serious political challenge to Italy's support for the EU and even for "more" Europe, there also is no political movement on the horizon able and willing to bring about the transformations that result from being part of the single currency. As the impact of being at the heart of Europe becomes more apparent to Italian society, the greater is the sense that integration is no longer the shield many sought. It is becoming increasingly difficult to hide between the ambiguity of Europe being both transformative and subject to *trasformismo*, as well as hide behind the ambivalence of being both at the centre and from the periphery. This is clearly evident in the actions of Italian governments after 2011. They argued that Italy needed to carry out major structural reforms of its basic institutions and policy areas if it was to have any leverage to change policies at the centre of Europe. Yet they also sought to change the terms of being at the centre of Europe so as to ease the burden of the difficult choices that needed to be made. However, the political consequences of having to choose and of the choices are only just beginning to become apparent. What is clear is that it is no longer possible to use the ambiguities of being centre and periphery as cover from both domestic and European pressures.

References

Bellucci, Paolo and Niccolo Conti (eds) (2012) *Gli Italiani e L'europa: Opinione Pubblica, Élite Politiche e Media*. Rome: Carrocci Editore.

Brunazzo, Marco and Vincent Della Sala (2011) 'From Salvation to Pragmatic Indifference?: Europe in Italian Political Discourse,' in R. Harmsen and J. Schild (eds) *Debating Europe: The 2009 European Parliament Elections and Beyond*. Baden-Baden: Nomos, pp. 69–84.

Cafagna, Luciano (2005) 'Europeismo realizzato', *Corriere della Sera*, Economia, 25 April, 1.

Dastoli, Pier Virgilio and Santaniello, Roberto (2013) *C'eravamo Tanti Amati: Italia, Europe E Poi?* Milano: Università Bocconi Editore.

Della Sala, Vincent (2004) 'From Maastricht to Modernization: Emu and the Italian Social State,' in A. Martin and G. Ross (eds) *Euros and Europeans: Monetary Integration and the European Model of Society*. Cambridge: Cambridge University Press, pp. 126–149.

Dyson, Kenneth and Kevin Featherstone (1996) 'Italy and Emu as a *vincolo esterno*: Empowering the technocrats, transforming the state,' *South European Politics and Society* 1(2): 279–299.

Fabbrini, Sergio and Simona Piattoni (2004) 'Introduction: Italy in the EU—Pigmy or Giant?,' *Modern Italy* 9(2): 149–157.

Ferrera, Maurizio and Elisabetta Gualmini (1999) *Salvati Dall'europa?* Bologna: Il Mulino.

Freddi, Giorgio, Giuseppe Di Palma and Sergio Fabbrini (eds) (2000) *Condannata Al Successo? L'italia Nell'europa Integrata*. Bologna: Il Mulino.

Graham, Robert (1996) 'Italy keen to leave sick man image behind: Rome paves way to be among the first group to join European Monetary Union,' *Financial Times*, 25 November, 2.

Hall, Peter (1993) 'Policy paradigms, social learning, and the state: The case of economic policymaking in Britain,' *Comparative Politics* 25(3): 275–296.

International Monetary Fund (IMF) (2011) 'Italy: Staff Report for the 2011 Article IV Consultation,' IMF Country Report no. 11/173. Washington, DC: IMF.

Organisation of Economic Cooperation and Development (OECD) (2011a) 'Revenue Statistics 2011.' Paris: OECD Publishing.

Organisation of Economic Cooperation and Development (OECD) (2011b) 'Statextracts.' Available at: http://stats.oecd.org/Index.aspx?DataSetCode=SNA_TABLE11 (accessed 18 January 2015).

Pop, Valentina (2014) 'Renzi continues row with new EU Commission chief,' *EUobserver*, 5 November. Available at: https://euobserver.com/political/126380 (accessed 18 January 2015).

Reviglio, Franco (1998) *Come Siamo Entrati in Europa*. Milano: UTET.

Salvati, Michele (1997) 'Moneta unica, rivoluzione Copernicana,' *Il Mulino* 46(1): 5–23.

Spaventa, Luigi and Vincenzo Chiorazzo (2000) *Astuzia O Virtù: Come Accadde Che L'italia Fu Ammessa All'unione Monetaria*. Roma: Donizelli.

Tremonti, Giulio (2010) *La Paura e La Speranza*. Milan: Edizioni Mondadori.
Varsori, Antonio (2010) *La Cenerentola D'europa? L'italia e L'integrazione Europea Dal 1947 a Oggi*. Soveria Mannelli: Rubbettino Editore.
Willis, Frank Roy (1971) *Italy Chooses Europe*. Oxford: Oxford University Press.

Part IV

Case studies on the impact of the crisis on non-Eurozone member states in the periphery

16 The Hungarian agony over Eurozone accession

Olivér Kovács

Introduction

> No idea, no opportunity that could be excluded. No distinct boundaries, no unalterable points, no rigid fundaments that could stabilise [...].
>
> Any kind of behaviour of individuals and governments is conceivable; we shall be prepared even for the most absurd and abnormal thing.
>
> Wilhelm Röpke (1950)

The advent of the Great Recession sets into motion a comprehensive refinement of the macroeconomic policy toolkit to include more pro-growth and pro-development features. This was especially the case because the European Union (EU) has proven not to be a facilitator of developmental integration (Csaba 2014). As the history of the Eurozone demonstrates, the mere fulfilment of the entry criteria in mathematical terms does not guarantee successful integration afterwards. Additionally, uncertainty regarding the future has begun to intensify (Kovács 2014), mainly due to the juggernaut effect of the recent financial and economic crisis as well as the subsequent lacklustre crisis management.

It would be pointless to behave with the naiveté of Tuzenbach[1] in this situation. The relevant homework must be completed by each member state, as the urgent need for uncertainty-reducing macroeconomic stability has not diminished. An examination of the evolution of economic development theory *per se* suggests that contemporary scholars should refocus on the role of the state and its institutional settings by going back to its origins. It has been argued that the public sector in general plays a critical role in socio-economic development (Evans et al. 1985); however, trust and confidence are of paramount importance in this regard (Akerlof and Shiller 2009). This contribution demonstrates that Hungary must also do its homework.

In the Western scientific world of politics, financial markets and the media, the current Hungarian governmental policy has been varyingly evaluated with respect to the country's economic situation and its EU-conformity. The variety of views is understandable, as there is no effective and efficient opposition to the ruling party, and thus the otherwise adequate system of checks and balances is suffering. In addition, at the moment, the administration enjoys a two-thirds majority in parliament, meaning that it has absolute legislative power, and the support of 38–40 per cent of the population. Formally, this scenario meets the requirements of democracy, but in practice a kind of authoritarian system has emerged due to the impaired mechanism of checks and balances. Although this form of governance has produced improvements in certain areas, certain costs must be reckoned with. This is one reason behind the partially conflicting perceptions about the Hungarian rule of law and the long-term effectiveness of the country's economic governance. The present chapter is intended to temper these views by calling attention to important nuances. It first addresses the issue of Hungarian macroeconomic instability from a comparative perspective – specifically, in a comparison of the Visegrád countries (the Czech Republic, Hungary, Poland and Slovakia – henceforth, V4). In so doing, it highlights the Hungarian 'lagging behind' phenomenon and calls for a more systemic approach to the Hungarian Eurozone accession. The chapter then focuses on the relationships between governance, institutional quality and innovation; the synergy among these factors drives the dynamism of the innovation ecosystem upon which the potential reduction of socio-economic cleavages (the foundation of healthy socio-economic development, including enhanced integration in the EU) greatly depends. Finally, the chapter unravels the major intertwined social and political factors behind agonising uncertainties and derives some general implications from the Hungarian *différance.*

The socio-economic development landscape in Hungary

Macroeconomic (in)stability

There is a broad consensus among economists that macroeconomic stability is a *conditio sine qua non* of international competitiveness. Rankings in this regard can offer a rudimentary overview of the consequences of the complex interplay between the institutions that influence innovation (and thereby also productivity and economic policies that seek to enhance competitiveness over the long term).

Figure 16.1 provides a snapshot of such international rankings, depicting the competitiveness of the V4 countries along with those of the EU periphery (Greece, Ireland, Italy, Portugal and Spain). As is evident, by 2014 Hungary and Slovakia had become the worst performers in terms of global competitiveness and global enabling trade.[2]

As a sign of macroeconomic shortcomings, deteriorating competitiveness reflects not only an ailing innovation performance[3] but also anomalies in the process of catching up to the EU average in terms of GDP per capita, a statistic that is often seen as an indicator of a country's preparedness for Eurozone entry. Figures 16.2 and 16.3 convey the message that the Hungarian path has diverged completely from the trends of the other V4 countries since 2006.

It should be emphasised that Hungary's seemingly dynamic growth trajectory in the period 2000–2006 was mainly driven by increasing indebtedness (Figure 16.4), especially foreign indebtedness (Figure 16.5). As a corollary, Hungarian fiscal governance was by and large pro-cyclical and lax, raising concerns over the sustainability of the country's public finances.

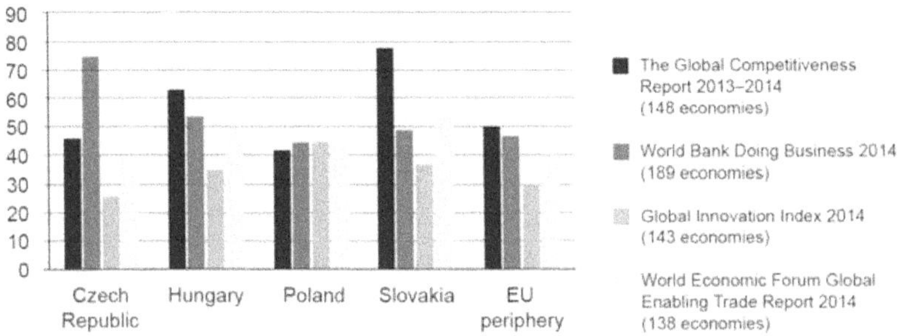

Figure 16.1 International competitiveness (rankings) in 2014
Note: The EU periphery comprises Greece, Ireland, Italy, Portugal and Spain.
Source: Author's compilation.

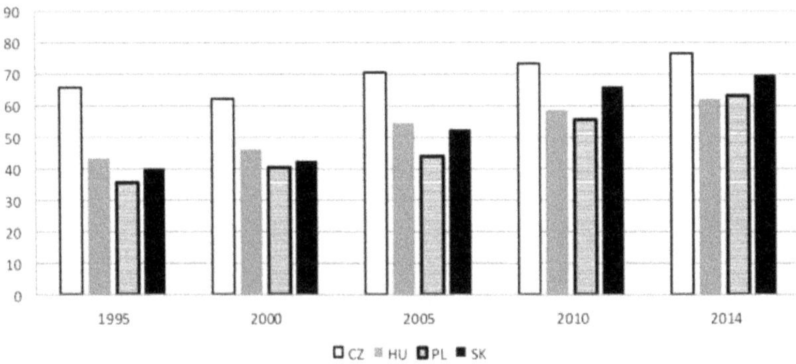

Figure 16.2 The catching-up process of the V4 (GDP per capita, PPP, EU15=100)
Source: Eurostat, National Accounts.

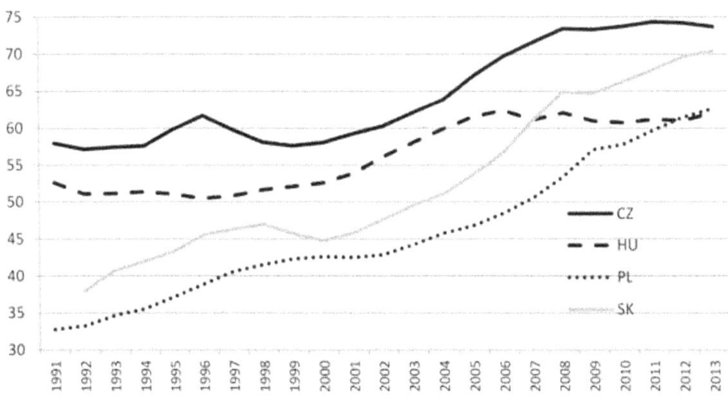

Figure 16.3 The 'getting stuck' phenomena in Hungary (GDP per capita, PPP, reference year 2005, EU15=100)
Source: Eurostat, National Accounts.

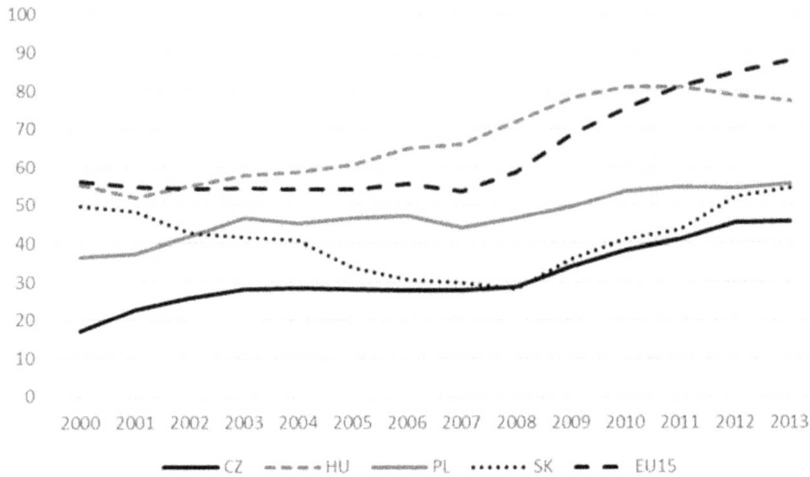

Figure 16.4 Changes in gross public debt (per cent of GDP)
Note: Estimations were used for 2013.
Source: Eurostat, National Accounts.

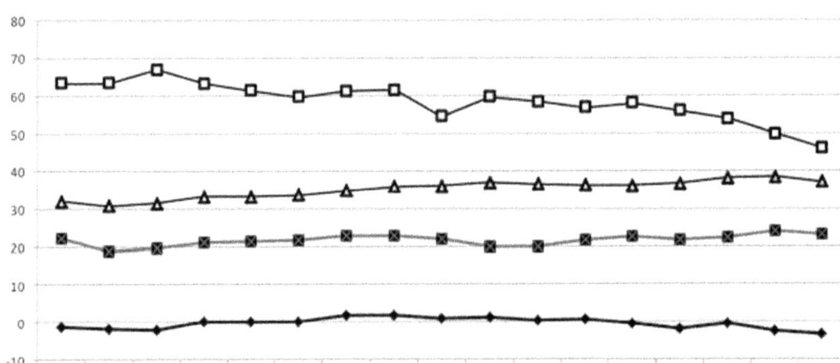

	2009Q4	2010Q1	2010Q2	2010Q3	2010Q4	2011Q1	2011Q2	2011Q3	2011Q4	2012Q1	2012Q2	2012Q3	2012Q4	2013Q1	2013Q2	2013Q3	2013Q4
CZ	-1,3	-1,9	-2,2	0,1	0,1	0	1,9	1,9	0,9	1,3	0,5	0,7	-0,4	-1,8	-0,6	-2,5	-3,4
HU	63,4	63,4	66,9	63,3	61,4	59,7	61,2	61,5	54,5	59,6	58,3	56,8	57,9	55,9	53,8	49,7	46
PL	32	30,7	31,4	33,2	33,1	33,6	34,7	35,9	36	36,9	36,5	36,1	36	36,6	38	38,3	37
SK	22,2	18,7	19,7	21,1	21,2	21,6	22,8	22,8	21,9	20	20	21,5	22,4	21,7	22,2	24	23,1

Figure 16.5 Changes in net foreign debt (per cent of GDP)
Note: Estimations were used for 2013.
Source: Eurostat, National Accounts, Oblath (2014).

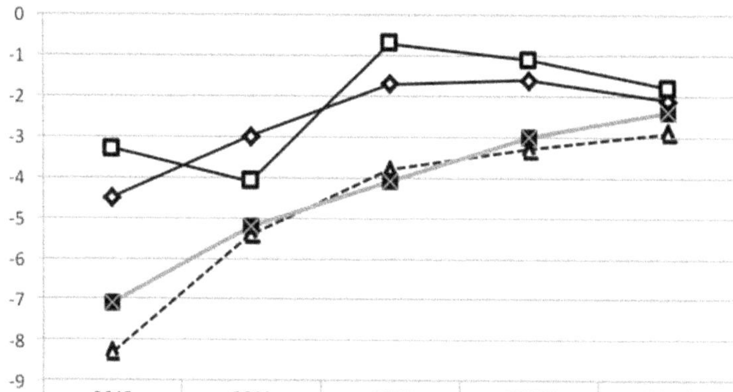

	2010	2011	2012	2013*	2014*
CZ	-4,5	-3	-1,7	-1,6	-2,1
HU	-3,3	-4,1	-0,7	-1,1	-1,8
PL	-8,3	-5,4	-3,8	-3,3	-2,9
SK	-7,1	-5,2	-4,1	-3	-2,4

Figure 16.6 Budgetary changes, Visegrad 4 (per cent of GDP)
Note: Estimations were used for 2013 and 2014.
Source: European Commission (2013), AMECO database.

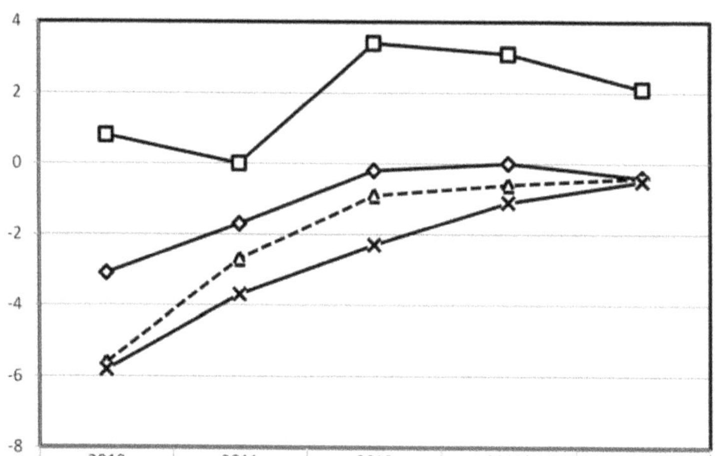

	2010	2011	2012	2013*	2014*
CZ	-3.1	-1.7	-0.2	0	-0.4
HU	0.8	0	3.4	3.1	2.1
PL	-5.6	-2.7	-0.9	-0.6	-0.4
SK	-5.8	-3.7	-2.3	-1.1	-0.5

Figure 16.7 Primary budgetary balance, Visegrad 4 (per cent of GDP)
Note: Estimations were used for 2013 and 2014.
Source: European Commission, AMECO database (http://ec.europa.eu/economy_finance/ameco/user/serie/SelectSerie.cfm).

To capture the government's intentions to mitigate indebtedness, the structural primary balance can be used. This figure shows that substantial surpluses were realised after 2011 due to fiscal adjustments (spending cuts and tax hikes; see Figure 16.6 and Figure 16.7.).

The fiscal sustainability-related economic literature suggests that pro-cyclical fiscal policy with the exclusive aim of stabilisation that focuses on mechanistically derived deficit targets via one-off measures[4] cannot be considered a panacea, as it paradoxically leads to destabilisation. This was reflected in Hungary's real GDP growth (Figure 16.7), which declined significantly after 2011. As a result, the country's debt-to-GDP ratio has not improved (the slight improvement in 2012 was only temporary; the ratio rose to 84.5 per cent by the end of the second quarter of 2014).

In the period 2009–2012, primarily expenditure-based fiscal consolidation (Figure 16.8) combined with unconventional economic policies led to growing uncertainties that paved the way for shrinking net investment (Figure 16.9) and depressed internal demand, as demonstrated by Hungary's current account balance surpluses (Figure 16.10). These overall developments are manifested in the country's disappointing near-zero potential economic growth.[5]

With regard to inflation, its low level seems to meet the target set out in the Maastricht Treaty; however, it is worth mentioning that exchange rate stability does not seem to be a priority of the Hungarian government, as can be deduced from the exchange rate's highly volatile nature (for example, based on the data of the European Central Bank, the EUR/HUF exchange rate of 270 in September 2009 skyrocketed to more than 320 in 2011). As Baker et al. (2013) have emphasised, volatility can be seen as a definite sign of uncertainty.

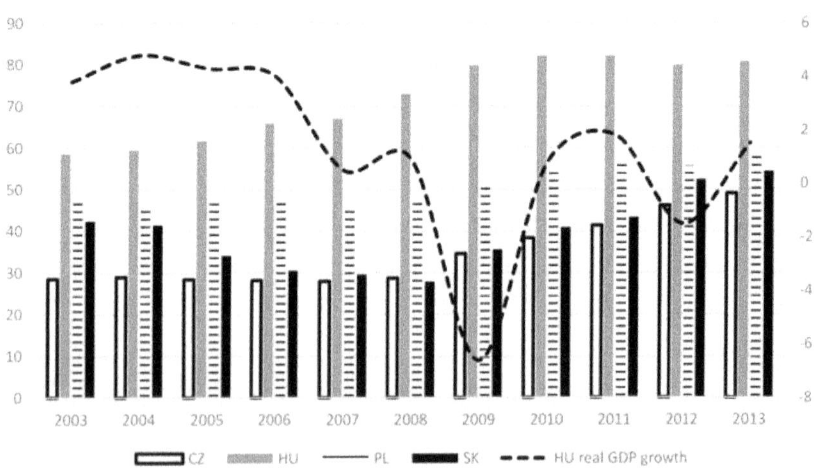

Figure 16.8 Gross debt and real GDP growth in Hungary (per cent of GDP)
Note: The left axis refers to gross debt, while the right axis refers to Hungarian real GDP growth.
Source: Eurostat, AMECO database.

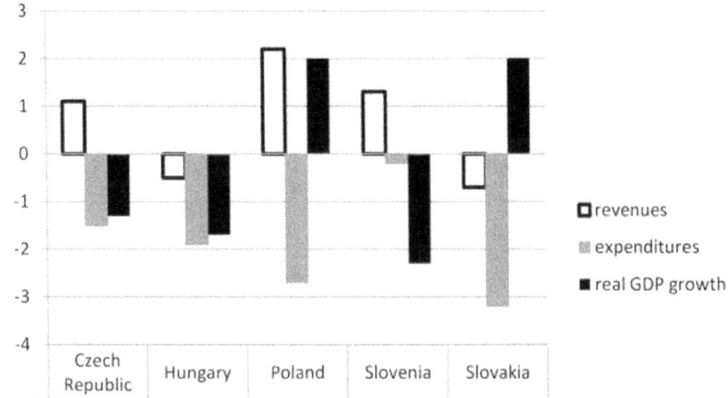

	Czech Republic	Hungary	Poland	Slovenia	Slovakia
revenues	1.1	-0.5	2.2	1.3	-0.7
expenditures	-1.5	-1.9	-2.7	-0.2	-3.2
real GDP growth	-1.3	-1.7	2	-2.3	2

Figure 16.9 Changes in cyclically adjusted revenues, expenditures and real GDP growth (in percentage points, 2009–2012)
Source: Eurostat.

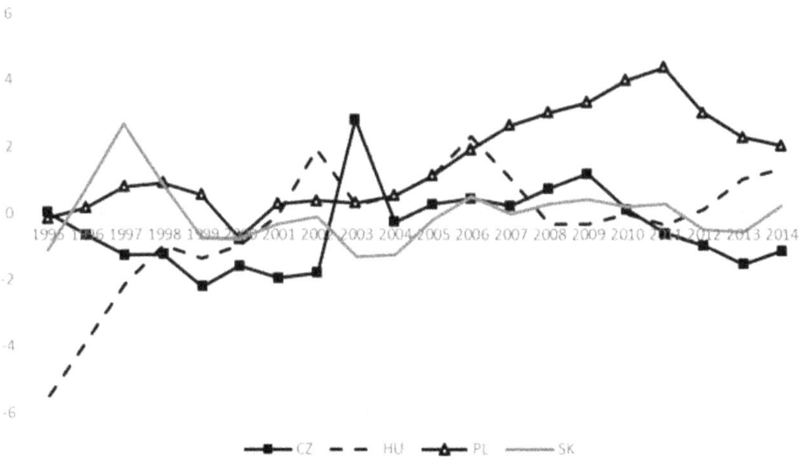

Figure 16.10 Net investment (per cent of GDP without amortisation): Public sector
Source: National Accounts, Oblath (2014).

Although Hungary appears to meet the inflation and deficit targets of the Maastricht Treaty in terms of pure numbers, this achievement is merely a Pyrrhic victory that does not truly represent a step forward in the process of adopting the euro. In addition, the Hungarian government has not thus far declared a target date for Eurozone accession, a fact that calls its commitment into question.

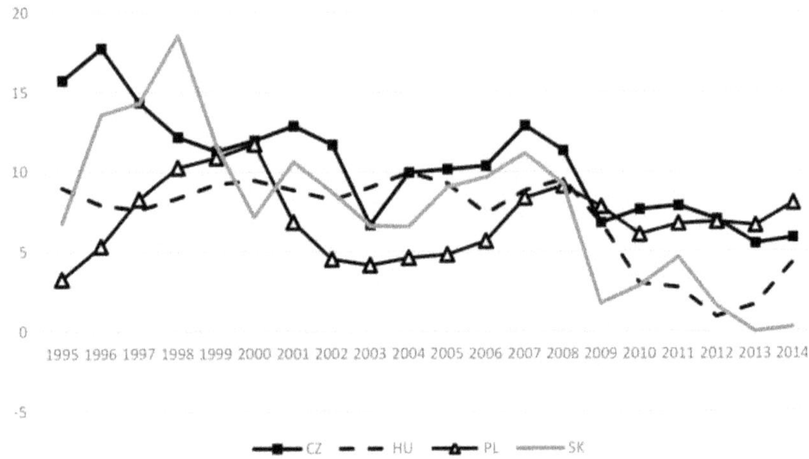

Figure 16.11 Net investment (per cent of GDP without amortisation): Private sector
Source: National Accounts, Oblath (2014).

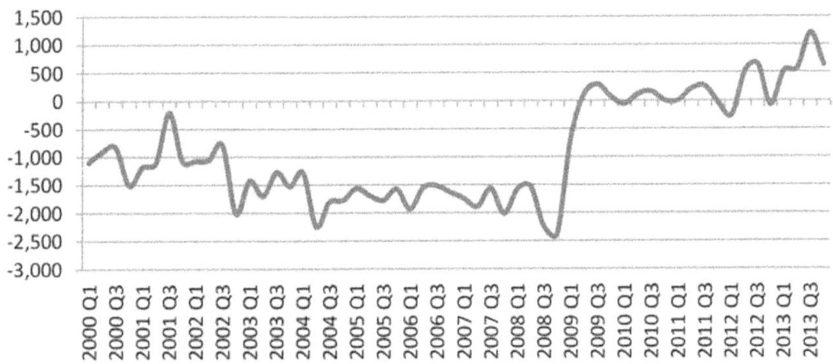

Figure 16.12 Current account balance (millions of EUR)
Source: Central Bank of Hungary.

Beyond the impulsive and uncertainty-generating nature of the Hungarian government's actions, certain policy measures have virtually eliminated any hope of reducing income inequality and poverty. The gap between rich and poor started to rise after 2009,[6] in part due to the harmful effects of the 2008 financial and economic crisis. However, the flat tax reform introduced between 2010 and 2013 was also a factor in the nation's growing income inequality, since the contribution to total tax revenue of the top tenth of the population sharply decreased – from 61 to 42 per cent![7] In addition, regional disparities (Pénzes et al. 2014), together with the poverty headcount ratio at the national poverty line, have also been on the rise since 2009.[8]

Table 16.1 Criteria for euro adoption

Criteria		*Reference rate*	*Hungary*
HICP inflation rate (12-month average of annual rates)		Max. 2.5%	August 2014: 0.2%
Public finance	Budget deficit (% of GDP)	Max. 3%	2013: 2.2% 2014: 2.5%
	Gross public debt-to-GDP ratio (% of GDP)	Max. 60%, or sufficiently approaching the reference rate	2014 Q2: 84.5% 2014: 76.2% 2015 Q2: 79.6%
Long-term interest rate (12-month average of 10-year bond yields)		Max. 4.81%	May 2014: 5.01%
ERM II member		Min. 2 years	No

Source: Hungarian Central Statistical Office, Central Bank of Hungary.

As a result, Hungary is situated on the periphery of the political and economic core of the EU. If the country is to truly and fully participate in European integration ultimately move beyond its *différance*, it cannot neglect its 'homework'.[9] With the term *différance*, we simultaneously refer to both differences and deferments, such as the Hungarian policy of sacrificing macroeconomic stability for mechanistically improved fiscal conditions. Because international competitiveness and innovation are heavily intertwined (Porter 1990) and sustained socio-economic development relies upon learning via innovations and smart adaptations, a more nuanced view is needed to understand the Hungarian agony. The country's economic policy should therefore be *more systemic* in targeting euro adoption in a way that cultivates good and more effective *national governance*.

Governance, institutional quality and innovation

An expedient way to create a more systemic description of the Hungarian agony is by examining the performance of the country's *innovation ecosystem*. This perspective is derived from complexity science theory, which states that many systems consist of a large number of entities that interact in a complex way and exhibit nonlinear behaviour (Aschwanden 2013). We thus recognise that innovations take place in the network of collaborating actors that are mutually interdependent and embedded within a wider institutional framework. By looking at *relationships* and *interactions*, we can obtain a more nuanced understanding of the Hungarian peripheral identity within the EU.

To this end, we devote special attention to the relationships between governance, institutional quality and innovation, as the synergy among these three factors drives the dynamism of the innovation ecosystem upon which the potential reduction of socio-economic cleavages – the foundation of healthy development, including better integration in the EU – greatly depends. We apply some of the

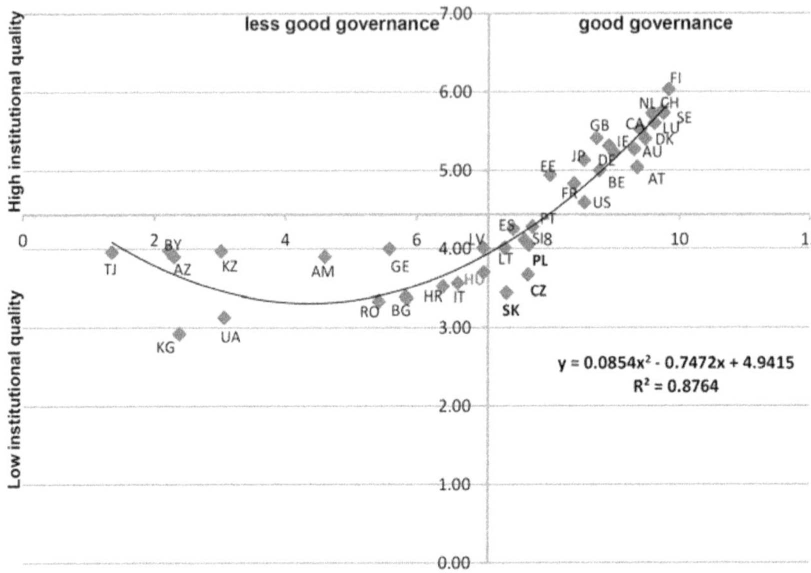

Figure 16.13 Quality of governance and institutional architecture in selected countries (2012)
Note: The vertical axis refers to the institutional competitiveness of countries as assessed by the World Economic Forum in its Global Competitiveness Report 2012, while the horizontal axis represents the aggregated Worldwide Governance Indicators prepared by the World Bank (see Kaufmann, Kraay and Mastruzzi 2008). The intersection reflects their averages.
Source: Author's compilation.

hard-won lessons of development economics and new political economics by recognising that the role of *institutions* is unquestionable in terms of framing and incentivising the behaviour of stakeholders, which are of paramount importance in coping with socio-economic cleavages and encouraging economic development. The rationale behind this approach is based on the fact that the Hungarian *différance* is partially attributable to inefficient governmental policies and the (maladaptive) functioning of formal and informal institutions.

Despite the limitations of measuring governance quality, Figure 16.13 suggests a strong correlation between good governance and competitive institutional settings. Generally speaking, in the context of core–periphery relations, *Hungary is found to have relatively worse governance and lower institutional quality*. As a corollary, *Hungary exhibits features characteristic of the EU periphery*.

Notably, the best-performing countries in terms of good governance and high institutional quality are either innovation leaders or followers, and also the most competitive nations in international rankings. *The quality of governance thus indigenously depends on the institutional framework in which innovation takes place*. As the pioneers of new political economics and public choice theory – Knut Wicksell (1896) and James Buchanan (1978) – argued, economists should look at the *structures* within which political decisions are made and behaviours are influenced.

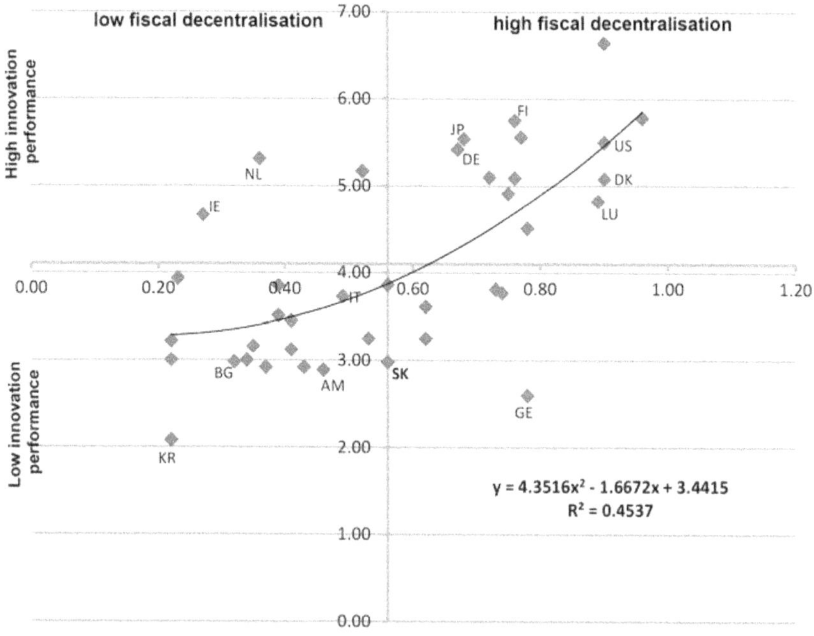

Figure 16.14 Fiscal decentralisation and innovation performance (2012)
Note: The vertical axis refers to the well-known fiscal decentralisation index developed by Ivanyna and Shah (2013), while the horizontal axis refers to the Innovation subindex of the Global Competitiveness Report 2012. The intersection reflects their averages.
Source: Author's compilation.

In this regard, a more decentralised system seems to offer more innovative freedom and thus greater competitiveness.[10] More freedom to innovate means (i) a greater role for decentralised initiation, and (ii) much more closeness among stakeholders, who are thus more likely to cooperate when innovating.

The role of decentralised initiation can be captured by examining the relationship between *fiscal decentralisation* (i.e. the higher the degree, the more fiscal autonomy enjoyed by the lower tiers of government) and *innovation performance* (Figure 16.14). This relationship is likely to be indirect: a higher degree of fiscal decentralisation will have *multiple positive spillover effects* on a country's overall innovation performance. This is primarily because highly decentralised countries typically perform better in terms of fiscal policy (i.e. more sustainable debt-to-GDP ratios, less risky sovereign credits[11]), which provides fiscal latitude in supporting innovation as well as more fertile ground for risky innovations (since urgent revenue-generating taxation is unnecessary). This structure offers more space for decentralised initiation than can be found in more centralised countries, which are generally associated with worse innovation performance (e.g. moderate innovators like Hungary).[12]

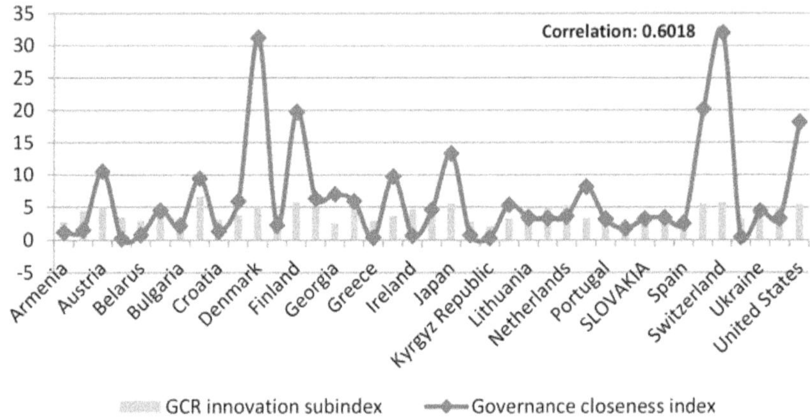

Figure 16.15 Governance closeness index and innovation performance
Notes: The governance closeness index comes from Ivanyna and Shah (2013); for innovation performance, the Innovation subindex of the Global Competitiveness Report 2012 was used.
Source: Author's compilation.

Although Hungary has a relatively high level of fiscal decentralisation (similar to that of Poland), its international competitiveness ranks below not only that of Poland but also the southern EU countries. This indicates that the expected multiple positive spillover effects in Hungary are being impeded by uncertainty-triggering political-economic factors.

Additionally, by virtue of the fact that the correlation between *governance closeness to society* [13] and *innovation performance* is relatively strong (Figure 16.15), increased closeness implies a greater chance for meaningful collaboration and a more fertile innovation milieu.[14] Although Hungary should have better performance in terms of innovation, there is a substantial gap between the innovation subindex and the governance closeness index. Economic governance therefore does not serve as a catalyst for the country's innovation activities.

The current decisions of innovation ecosystem stakeholders depend on their expected future, but their expected future itself depends in part on current decisions, in particular those determined by governance. In development economics and new political economy, what has become clear is that political institutions determine economic institutions and influence the psychic capital of society.[15] In this respect, a broader perspective should be applied in order to identify the hard and soft factors resulting in the 'getting stuck' phenomena.

Political-social factors behind agonising uncertainties

In the following section, building in part on research in the fields of political economy and psychology, some pivotal factors are identified that played an influential role in triggering and maintaining the uncertainties that reinforced the 'getting stuck' phenomena in Hungary. Uncertainties have a detrimental effect on economic performance (Baker et al. 2013) and thus on a country's capability to enter the Eurozone, as the case of Hungary illustrates. Together, these factors may perpetuate the EU-peripheral role of a country by contributing to the detrimental core–periphery divide in the EU.

First, in the case of Hungary, the inadequately addressed legacy of the pre-crisis period had long-lasting negative effects. The extensive external indebtedness of the Hungarian private sector up until 2006 indicates that households treated potential crises as rare events, underestimating their probability. This behaviour (the 'bias of experience') was sensitively described in the prospect theory developed by Kahneman and Tversky (1979). A lack of experience with crises thus led Hungarian households to behave in a risky manner.

In addition, *hedonic editing* also played an important role in the Hungarian fiscal dysfunction. This term refers to a situation in which people convince themselves that their earlier failure is inconsequential. Given the lack of penalties for rule-breaking (e.g. the non-sanctioned violations of France and Germany with respect to the Stability and Growth Pact in 2004), a government might easily get the misguided impression that non-compliance with external rules does not really matter and conclude that it can allow its fiscal deficit to skyrocket. Hedonic editing also served as a counter-incentive to commitment to stringent fiscal consolidation and structural reforms. However, the actual price for indebtedness was enormous, especially when the 2008 crisis hit and Hungary was forced to ask for IMF assistance. Ultimately, fiscal consolidation took place, resulting in improvements in the country's public finances by 2010.

Second, after 2010, the government confronted the zeitgeist by striving for a sort of economic liberation (the 'fight for economic freedom') from Brussels, the International Monetary Fund (IMF) and foreign companies.[16] Upon examining the changes and measures introduced,[17] one might find the emerging governance to be increasingly interspersed with characteristics of Weberian plebiscitary leadership democracy, but for the most part, the system resembles populistic leadership.[18] As Janos Kornai (2014) observes, with the government's actions, the cabinet made a perceptible shift from a post-communist democracy towards a post-communist autocracy. This seems to have been facilitated by the absence of a popularly supported and efficient opposition, which is currently the case in Hungary. As one of the central philosophies of democracy is that it is the temporary nature of the decisions which guarantees our freedom, if a government seeks to eliminate or at least drastically restrict some of the fundamental institutions of democracy in order to extend the scope of its decisions and power, psychic capital suffers and uncertainty grows. Such changes ushered in the development of extractive institutions and lingering concerns regarding the policies that kept Hungary's sovereign Credit Default Swap (CDS) spreads at an elevated level.[19] This put a spotlight on the country's socio-economic problems.

From 2010 onwards, the Hungarian populistic leadership system has had two primary guiding principles (which, of course, may change in the future): (i) the pursuit of nationalism and (ii) macroeconomic populism.

The pursuit of nationalism in the guise of the fight for economic freedom can easily lead to a situation of *certa amittimus, dum incerta petimus.* [20] It goes without saying that refusing to accept IMF credit and the stabilisation package simply because the effectiveness and efficiency of IMF stabilisation programmes have been long debated and criticised would be illogical. There is a good deal of uncertainty involved in such a freedom-targeting approach. For example, development economics suggests that ignoring the necessity of autochthonous integration into the highly globalised economy cannot be seen as a real alternative for sustained growth and development, but rather as a move that inevitably reinforces destabilisation (Röpke 1942; Szentes 2003). Because there is an asymmetrical interdependence between Hungary and the EU (i.e. 97 per cent of all public investment in Hungary is financed to a significant degree by the European Union), turning against Brussels would merely be an act of bravado (a pretence of bravery). By the same token, an economic fight would eliminate trust and stifle innovation dynamism. In the financially frail European setting, aspirations for the economic liberation of the export-orientated small and open Hungarian economy through burdens imposed on the banking sector would by no means be conducive to the development of domestic SMEs (since risky innovations often require greater front-load investment).[21]

Another aspect of the pursuit of nationalism offers us insight into theories on political budget cycles in the field of new political economics. Hungary has been struggling with its public debt, largely because the discussions over future EU governance have stressed that if a country faces severe financial problems, the EU authorities will have the right to intervene in its national economic policy.[22] The Hungarian government thus sought to bring its deficit down mechanistically via one-off measures in order to avoid such a situation (and in particular, any chance of the suspension of EU funds). By the 2014 election, the country's fiscal deficit was hovering around the Maastricht threshold. This was the first time after the regime change in 1990 that the political budget cycle was not at issue in an election campaign. To be sure, the government's pursuit of a populistic leadership system with greater independence – not society's ability to learn over the course of electoral cycles and to force fiscal prudency, as Brender and Drazen (2005) have suggested in the case of new democracies – was the main reason behind this development.

Furthermore, a populistic leadership system can give rise to *increasing sensitivity* (i.e. a decreasing level of tolerance to macroeconomic instability on the part of financial markets).[23] The Nobel-laureate Ilja Prigogine (1977) ascertained that in an open, adaptive and complex system such as the innovation ecosystem, the arrow of time plays a pivotal role, in that it makes it impossible to remove all of the effects of an event (e.g. economic measures, utterances of leaders) from the entire system. These effects become part of the memory of the socio-economic-political system in question, which in turn has an impact on psychological factors and behaviour. For instance, in times of economic hardship, political events (e.g. summits, elections) increase in importance because they tend to trigger news reports and speculation about changes, thereby creating uncertainty (Lubos and

Veronesi 2013), affecting the perceptions of financial investors (as reflected in the heightened volatility of risk premiums) and also conspicuously influencing real economic activity. It thus becomes clear why Hungarian financial vulnerability worsened further in reaction to the statements of leaders on the probability of state bankruptcy.[24] Moreover, as uncertainties reached critical levels, foreign companies began to close down some of their operations in Hungary or move them to other countries.[25]

As part of its new strategy of macroeconomic populism, in addition to the economic fight it proposed with great fanfare, the Hungarian government sought to signal only positive messages (e.g. the historically low level of inflation, employment development stated as a positive trend[26]) and to implement coaxing measures such as utility price cuts.[27] With these 'lightning rods', re-election became a real perspective, if for no other reason than because of the selectivity and short-sightedness of public memory, which ultimately makes decisions according to time-tested psychological findings (Kahneman 2013: 444). In this way, the one-track nature of the Hungarian mindset – specifically, the state paternalism demanded by the country's socialist heritage – resulted in a preference for short-term gains with longer-term pains as the electorate closed its eyes to the shift to a more populistic leadership system. Despite the agonising uncertainties in play, it seems that the Hungarian case offers a new verification on an old Hungarian saying: humanity is predisposed to think that certainty is everything (i.e. voters like to get short term gains with high certainty by neglecting the rationality and harmfulness of the same governmental measures). The populism implemented in the run-up to the parliamentary election appears to prove this.

Concluding remarks

It would be ridiculous to assume that an easy exit strategy from the *différance* presented in this chapter exists, but six main conclusions can be drawn based upon the Hungarian experience.

First, political interests are critical. According to Wilhelm Röpke, cited in the introduction, any kind of behaviour on the part of individuals and governments is conceivable. Even though its institutional architecture would seem to promise Hungary opportunities for a socially more egalitarian system (higher fiscal decentralisation), politicians' vested interests resulted in significant detours from 'optimal' policies by way of deteriorating institutional quality. In addition, policies geared towards building a populistic leadership system do not enhance good governance, nor do they spark the innovation ecosystem to eventually foster real socio-economic development. Broadening the research scope by incorporating the fields of new political economy, development economics, psychology, and complexity science would therefore be conducive to overcoming the one-sided approaches of purely political science or economics.

Second, Eurozone accession requires the full commitment of the Hungarian government, since the EU's external anchoring mechanisms by no means apply enough pressure on countries to adopt the euro (e.g. stipulating and announcing a target date).

Third, socio-economic development-supporting macroeconomic stability cannot and should not be created via mechanistic consolidation on the basis of numerical targets. Such an approach is doomed to destabilise rather than stabilise. Socio-economic development should therefore be grounded in not only quantifiable but also (scientifically sound) non-quantifiable aspects (e.g. trust, credibility, the quality of regulation, responsible public management, good governance, transparency, informal institutions). Such soft categories should also be better integrated into economic analyses.

Fourth, more holistic fiscal consolidation is required. The mechanistic pursuit of deficit and debt targets in the attempt to support fiscal sustainability and sustained growth would represent a fatal conceit in the Hayekian sense. There is a solid claim to be made for some kind of *aurea mediocritas* fiscal consolidation with a more systemic approach – for example, a strategy addressing aspects that are of paramount importance in the new techno-economic paradigm (Perez 2009) such as R&D, innovation and education through fiscal impulses designed to revitalise similar activities in the private sector in order to propel sustained growth. A mixture of pro- and anti-cyclical measures is therefore essential (i.e. cuts in unproductive fields like social transfers and public sector salaries and additional spending on R&D and innovation, aspects upon which growth currently depends the most) (Kovács 2013). Hungary has carried out a strategy of fiscal consolidation with a view to increasing spending on R&D and innovation; however, the one-off and thus unsustainable measures have triggered uncertainties that have impeded innovation in the private sector.

Fifth, socio-economic learning through Hayekian trial and error still remains a key driving force of real progress, a process that requires the integral functioning of politics and institutions. As we have illustrated, institutional architecture affects innovation performance. In addition, politics and policy have inevitable uncertainty-influencing features that are often related to psychological factors. If uncertainty grows, trust and confidence – prerequisites of socio-economic development – may be undermined. Consequently, sparking innovation in the public sector as a trust-builder is of paramount importance (i.e. achieving radical efficiency, cost savings, improved service quality and accessibility)[28] when painful measures are required. The Hungarian public sector should be *toujours à l'affût* for more innovation, not only in supporting its citizens' trust and confidence, but also to have on-the-ground-reality for euro adoption.

Sixth, structural reforms are a must, but the issue of sequencing initiatives is substantially more important in times of crisis. The old Roman wisdom of *festina lente* (move forward, but with adequate preparation) should guide policy-makers when it comes to reducing uncertainty. This implies that *limited discretionalism* is in order, with incremental changes organised around a clear and consistent strategy.

Notes

1 Baron Tuzenbach is an overly optimistic character in Anton Chekhov's *Three Sisters*.

2 Hungary and Slovakia have been exceeding the international competitiveness of the EU periphery for years. See the rankings in the issues of the Global Competitiveness Report. It is also worth noting that the Czech Republic performed the worst in terms of Doing Business in 2014, and the EU periphery average is improved by the Irish data. With regard to the latter, the Celtic Tiger's alleged recovery is very tentative, and pent-up domestic demand prevails; evaluating Ireland's international competitiveness is therefore not without ambiguities.

3 Hungary's innovation performance has been stagnating since 2009/10; its ranking of 25 in the Global Innovation Index 2011 fell to the 31 in the 2013 issue.

4 I.e. imposing substantial taxes on the banking system as well as crisis taxes on certain sectors such as the pharmaceutical industry, the nationalisation of private pension funds, etc.

5 Uncertainty is found to negatively correlate with economic performance. For instance, Ball (2014) estimated a loss in output of more than 30 per cent in Hungary during the Great Recession.

6 According to OECD statistics, the country's Gini index was 27.2 per cent in 2007, climbing to 29 per cent in 2012. Szívós and Tóth (2013) and Szikra (2014) demonstrate the increasing trend of income inequality in Hungary.

7 For more on the flat tax reform in Hungary, see Tóth and Virovácz (2013).

8 World Bank Development Indicators.

9 Here, the term *différance* is borrowed from the French post-modern philosopher Jacques Derrida. It is deliberately homophonous with the word *différence*. *Différance* plays on the fact that the French word *différer* means both 'to defer' and 'to differ'. See Derrida (1963).

10 There is a non-negligible proportion of federal states among the countries with good governance and high institutional quality. For more on the efficient nature of federalism, see Buchanan (1995) and Weingast (2013).

11 See Bloomberg, European CDS Spreads.

12 According to the Innovation Union Scoreboard 2014, moderate innovators are as follows: Croatia, the Czech Republic, Greece, Hungary, Italy, Lithuania, Malta, Poland, Portugal, Slovakia and Spain. See http://ec.europa.eu/enterprise/policies/innovation/files/ius/ius-2014_en.pdf (accessed 15.12.2014).

13 Higher decentralisation means greater financial and functional autonomy of lower tiers of governance which lead to a more visible public sector operation, and thus to greater pressure to do the right thing and to seek options how to do it better.

14 This intuitive insight was recently tested econometrically by Ivanyna and Shah (2013). More decentralised governance is likely to be associated with higher levels of human capital development, less corruption, and higher growth. Still, we emphasise that fiscal decentralisation could be high without any shift of actual decision-making power to the lower tiers (Rodden 2003).

15 The aggregated memory of actors is reminiscent of the concept of psychic capital, a term coined by Kenneth E. Boulding (1950: 140). Psychic capital encompasses memories of pleasure, success, achievement and recognition as well as memories of failures, disasters, atrocities or perceived injustices and indignities. It would be hard to overlook the fact that support for economic policy actions greatly depends on the current status of (positive or negative) psychic capital.

16 The term 'fight for economic freedom' was repeatedly used in governmental speeches (e.g. George Matolcsy used the term with respect to the IMF credit agreement in the Hungarian parliament on 21 November 2011 when he was minister for national economy).

17 The main actions were as follows: eradicating the original form of Hungary's Fiscal Council; amending the constitution and adapting the authority of the Constitutional Court to the planned laws and regulations in an *ad hoc* fashion; introducing special taxes on the energy, telecommunications, retail and banking industries that discriminate against foreign companies; rejecting any commitment to preserving and strengthening the sanctity of private property by nationalising private pension funds; introducing flat income taxes, which are more beneficial for high earners; reducing the autonomy of

higher education and cutting its budget by HUF 84 billion between 2010 and 2013; strict regulations on the media; and establishing and adopting Hungary's new Fundamental Law, which *inter alia* constrains the power of the Constitutional Court and limits the room for manoeuvre of future governments without a two-thirds majority. In addition, in 2014, the Hungarian prime minister explicitly expressed the government's ambition to create an 'illiberal democracy'.

18 Here, plebiscitary leadership democracy is a form of governance in which the ruling cabinet governs by referring to the people's will, but its intention is to subvert that will to its own purposes. In such a system, a strong charismatic leader represents the political elite, which shapes rather than follows the public will. See Urbinati (2014).

19 The Credit Default Swap (CDS) is a country's perceived risk for default.

20 'We lose things that are certain in pursuing things uncertain', as Plautus observed.

21 With the shrinking access to external financing due to the more risk-averse atmosphere triggered by the 2008 financial and economic crisis and the subsequent sovereign debt crisis, the critical mass of SMEs is likely to become ineffective in terms of innovativeness because of problems in accessing external financing (European Commission, 2014: 50).

22 See Trichet (2011).

23 Since the importance of an event can be even greater if it generates significant differences in the experience and perceptions of another event, uncertainties become a complex web of mutually reinforcing phenomena perceived dynamically over time. This was explicitly the case after the onset of the Greek crisis, when financial markets' confidence also crumbled with regard to Spain and Portugal because their sensitivity (tolerance level) to the degree of macroeconomic instability (linked to international competitiveness and the sustainability of public finances) had dropped substantially. This was also the case by 2007 in Hungary, and, to some extent, during the failed IMF negotiations in early 2012 when the Hungarian currency dropped to a record low.

24 In early June 2010, the Hungarian vice-chairman stated that Hungary's chances of avoiding the fate of Greece were rather slim.

25 The motivation for this exodus is reflected in the number of companies, including Elqoteq, Cora, Bricostore, Nord Sea, ElectroWorld and Saturn, that decided to leave the country in 2011. In April 2014, the Samsung plant in Göd was closed down. In all, 4,000 people were laid off at Nokia and Flextronics. Job cuts will also take place at the Michelin plant in Budapest by 2015. Another good proxy for uncertainty is the willingness of people to move abroad permanently to work and live. In 2010–2013, almost 400,000 Hungarians decided to go abroad. The negative impetus was manifested in the increasing number of people living in poverty or social exclusion. According to Eurostat, that figure grew by 100,000 between 2012 and 2013.

26 Welfare states can ostensibly better manage their employment situation by extending public employment. This was exemplified in Hungary, where the biggest increase in employment was registered in the fields of public administration and defence; and compulsory social security. Between 2008 and 2013, more than 78,000 people were absorbed by these fields. It is also telling that the government did not allocate money for poverty or socio-economic cleavage-related official research by the Central Statistical Office in 2014.

27 Importantly, cutting energy prices undermines one of the key demand-side incentives of behavioural changes in consumers to be more committed to increasing energy efficiency.

28 On radical efficiency, see Gillinson et al. (2010); for policy considerations of public sector innovation, see Kovács (2012).

References

Akerlof, G. A. and R. J. Shiller (2009) *Animal Spirits: How Human Psychology Drives the Economy, and Why it Matters for Global Capitalism.* Princeton, NJ: Princeton University Press.

Aschwanden, M. J. (ed.) (2013) *Self-Organized Criticality Systems.* Warsaw and Berlin: Open Academic Press.

Baker, S. R., N. Bloom and S. J. Davis (2013) 'Measuring Economic Policy Uncertainty,' Chicago Booth Research Paper no. 13-02.

Ball, L. (2014) 'Long-term Damage from the Great Recession in OECD Countries', *European Journal of Economics and Economic Policies: Intervention* 11(2): 149–160.

Boulding, K. E. (1950) *A Reconstruction of Economics.* New York: Wiley.

Brender, A. and A. Drazen (2005) 'Political Budget Cycles in New Versus Established Democracies,' *Journal of Monetary Economics* 52(7): 1271–1295.

Buchanan, J. M. (1978) *The Consequence of Mr Keynes.* London: Institute of Economic Affairs.

Buchanan, J. M. (1995) 'Federalism as an Ideal Political Order and an Objective for Constitutional Reform,' *Publius: The Journal of Federalism* 25(2): 19–28.

Csaba, L. (2014) 'A New Political Economy – For Development,' in G. W. Kołodko (ed.) *Management And Economic Policy For Development.* New York: Nova Science Publishers, pp. 239–250.

Derrida, J. (1963) 'Cogito et Histoire de la Folie,' *Revue de Métaphysique et de Morale* 68(4): 460–494.

European Commission (2014) 'Helping Firms Growth. European Competitiveness Report 2014,' DG Enterprise and Industry, Brussels. Available from: http://ec.europa.eu/DocsRoom/documents/6706/attachments/1/translations/en/renditions/native (accessed 1 April 2015).

Evans, P. B., D. Rueschemeyer and T. Skocpol (1985) *Bringing the State Back In.* Cambridge: Cambridge University Press.

Gillinson, S., M. Horne and P. Baeck (2010) 'Radical Efficiency: Different, Better, Lower-cost Public Services,' NESTA Research Paper no. 180610. Available at: www.networkfor europe.eu/files/files/radical-efficiency-nesta-180610.pdf (accessed 2 November 2015).

Ivanyna, M. and A. Shah (2013) 'How Close is Your Government to Its People? Worldwide Indicators on Localization and Decentralization,' World Bank Policy Research Working Paper no. 6138.

Kahneman, D. (2013) *Thinking, Fast and Slow.* New York: Farrar, Straus & Giroux.

Kahneman, D. and Tversky, A. (1979) 'Prospect Theory: An Analysis of Decision Under Risk,' *Econometrica* 47(2): 263–292.

Kaufmann, D., A. Kraay and M. Mastruzzi (2008) 'The Worldwide Governance Indicators: Methodology and Analytical Issues,' World Bank Policy Research Working Paper no. 5430.

Kornai, J. (2014) 'Threatening Dangers,' keynote lecture at the Transition in Perspective: 25 Years After the Fall of Communism conference (Peterson Institute for International Relations and School of Public Policy, Central European University), Budapest, 6–7 May.

Kovács, O. (2012) 'Policies Supporting Innovation In Public Service Provision,' Inno-Grips Policy Brief no. 5, European Commission, DG Enterprise and Industry. Available at: http://innogrips.empirica.biz/fileadmin/INNOGRIPS/documents/01_Policy%20Briefs/IG_PolicyBrief_5_Public-sector-innovation_final.pdf (accessed 1 April 2015).

Kovács, O. (2013) 'Black Swans or Creeping Normalcy? An Attempt to a Holistic Crisis Analysis,' *Eastern Journal of European Studies* 4(1): 127–143.

Kovács, O. (2014) 'Endogenously Increasing Uncertainties and Governance,' Tiger Working Paper no. 130.

Lubos, P. and Veronesi, P. (2013) 'Political Uncertainty and Risk Premia,' *Journal of Financial Economics* 110(3): 520–545.

Oblath, G. (2014) 'Makrogazdasági Instabilitás és Regionális Lemaradás: Magyarország Esete' [Marcoeconomic Instability and Regional Lag: The Case of Hungary],*Külgazdaság* 58(5/6): 5–42.

Perez, C. (2009) 'Technological Revolutions and Techno-Economic Paradigms,' TOC/TUT Working Paper no. 20, Working Papers in Technology Governance and Economic Dynamics, Other Canon Foundation (Norway) and Tallinn University of Technology (Tallinn).

Pénzes, J., Z. Bujdosó, L. Dávid, Z. Radics and G. Kozma (2014) 'Differing Development Paths of Spatial Income Inequalities after the Political Transition: By the Example of Hungary and Its Regions,' *Economy of Region* 33(1): 73–84.

Porter, M. E. (1990) *The Competitive Advantage of Nations*. London and New York: Macmillan.

Prigogine, I. (1977) 'Time, Structure and Fluctuations,' Nobel Lecture, 8 December. Available at: www.Nobelprize.Org/Nobel_Prizes/ Chemistry/Laureates/1977/Prigogine-Lecture.Pdf (accessed 1 April 2015).

Rodden, J. (2003) 'Reviving Leviathan: Fiscal Federalism and the Growth of Government,' *International Organization* 57(4): 695–729.

Röpke, W. (1942) *International Economic Disintegration*. London: William Hodge.

Röpke, W. (1950) *Mass und Mitte*. Erlenbach-Zürich: Eugen Rentsch.

Szentes, T. (2003) *World Economics 2: The Political Economy of Development Globalisation and System Transformation*. Budapest: Akadémiai Kiadó.

Szikra, D. (2014) 'Democracy and Welfare in Hard Times: The Social Policy of the Orbán Government in Hungary between 2010 and 2014,' *Journal Of European Social Policy* 24(5): 486–500.

Szívós, P. and I. G. Tóth (eds) (2013) 'Egyenlőtlenség és Polarizálódás a Magyar Társadalomban' [Equality and Polarisation in Hungarian Society], Tárki Monitor Jelentések 2012, Budapest: Tárki.

Tóth, C. G. and P. Virovácz (2013) 'Winners and Losers: An Assessment of the Hungarian Flat Tax Reform with Microsimulation,' *Public Finance Quarterly* 58(4): 369–385.

Trichet, J. C. (2011) 'Tomorrow and the Day after Tomorrow: A Vision for Europe,' speech delivered at Humboldt University, Berlin, 24 October.

Urbinati, N. (2014) *Democracy Disfigured: Opinion, Truth, and the People*. Cambridge, MA: Harvard University Press.

Weingast, B. R. (2013) 'Second Generation Fiscal Federalism: Political Aspects of Decentralization and Economic Development,' *World Development* 20. Available at: http://Dx.Doi.Org/10.1016/J.Worlddev.2013.01.003 (accessed 1 April 2015).

Wicksell, K. (1896) *Finanztheoretische Untersuchung*. Jena: Gustav Fischer.

17 Periphery, or perhaps already the centre?

The impact of ten years of membership in the European Union on the position and perceptions of Poland

Maciej Duszczyk

Introduction

This paper attempts to answer the question of to what extent the decade that has elapsed since the biggest European Union enlargement in history has helped Poland to shift from Community periphery to the centre. To this end, an analysis has been conducted regarding changes across selected economic and social indices and selected press articles about Poland published in 2013 and 2014; in addition, an assessment has been made of the political role of Poland in discussions on major issues addressed at the EU level. The analysis foregoes cultural and religious issues, in recognition of the fact that over the last decade they have not had a relevant impact on changes in the status of Poland within the European Union. Moreover, the chapter ignores the issue of the regional diversification of Poland; this subject has been well described by T. Zarycki, who identifies the eastern regions of Poland as a periphery area not only within Poland but also in the EU as a whole, thus treating them as so-called 'internal peripheries' (Zarycki 2011).[1] Consequently, this paper refers to entire states rather than examining particular regions.

The theoretical foundations of the analysis are based on the classic contribution by Immanuel Wallerstein that divided the world into four groups of states: core, semi-peripheries, peripheries and external areas (Wallerstein 1979). Poland has experienced a shift across the first three categories. Within the European Union, the status of external area is granted only to overseas regions of certain member states, such as the Canary Islands and French Polynesia.

To assess the changes in the political role of Poland over the past decade, I will apply the approach proposed by Stein Rokkan, who defines the centre as the place of growing political domination over the functioning of periphery territories (or states) (Lipset and Rokkan 1967: 9–13). In the case of the European Union, this influence should be understood as a significant impact on decisions made during meetings of the European Council and the Council of the European Union, as well as on the agenda of the activities of the European Commission. For periphery states, this may entail becoming dependent on the decisions of the states of the core; the concept also involves the perception of the core states on the part of periphery states as dominant polities that only sporadically take the interests of the less powerful group into account. In this context, when the European Union was enlarged in 2004 following accession negotiations that obliged aspiring member states to adopt the entire *acquis communautaire* without gaining scarcely any influence over it,[2] the European Union was divided into regions. According to this approach, the western European states constituted the core, the southern European and Scandinavian states were semi-peripheries, and the accession states from CEE regions became peripheries within the Community. Upon its accession to the EU, Poland thus became the largest periphery state. The rest of the chapter explores how much this situation has changed within the recent decade.

The economic and political situation of Poland before accession to the European Union

Along with seven other CEE countries, Poland completed its accession negotiations with the European Union on 13 December 2002 during the European Council summit in Copenhagen. The referendum carried out on 7 and 8 June 2003 was also successful, with 77 per cent of Poles voting in support of accession to the EU. Poland's accession to the Community came at a time when the EU was experiencing one of the most difficult moments in its history after 1989. In the period 2001/2, the EU's economic growth was only slightly above 1 per cent, while the unemployment rate (calculated according to Eurostat's methodology) approached the level of 19.1 per cent in 2003. Neither of these indices had reached similar levels since 1990. In early 2004, inflation exceeded 5 per cent, adversely affecting the economic situation of many households. The main reason underlying this difficult economic situation was the necessity to adjust to European Union requirements; this primarily generated costs for small and medium-sized enterprises (SMEs), a category upon which the Polish economy is largely based. In contrast to what happened in Spain and Portugal, in Poland the majority of harmonisation efforts were carried out before accession to the EU. As a result, rejection of membership by means of the referendum (which was not quite unlikely) would basically translate into incurring costs while refusing the benefits afforded by accession to the European Union. Poland would thereby have lost its chance to shift from Europe's periphery to its core.

The political situation prior to accession was not much better than the economic one. Beginning in June 2003, a minority government headed by Prime Minister Leszek Miller came to power in Poland. This government dissolved itself immediately after Poland's accession to the EU on 2 May 2004, replaced by a transitional government under Prime Minister Marek Belka. The situation was not conducive to political stabilisation in the country, and in practice it hampered Poland's ability to achieve any significant impact on EU functioning immediately after the country's accession.

In sum, Poland acceded to the European Union at a difficult economic and political time, which comprises an additional argument contributing to its peripheralisation in the initial period after accession.

Ten years of economic and social development: sufficient to change Poland's status within the EU?

On 28 June 2014, the magazine *The Economist* published an article on Poland that advanced a highly controversial thesis, namely that Poland had moved from the periphery to the core. However, at the same time, the author indicated that if measures seeking to avoid the middle-income trap were not continued, Poland's position among the core countries would not necessarily be guaranteed (The Economist 2014a).

When analysing Poland's economic results over the last decade, it is difficult to avoid the conclusion that the country has succeeded in doing things that no other EU nation has managed to achieve, in contradiction of the theories put forward by the editors of *The Economist.* But is one post-accession decade truly sufficient for the civilisational leap represented by a status change from the periphery to the core?

Economic growth

Poland has been the only country in the EU to have passed virtually painlessly through the two phases of the economic crisis that started in 2007. Generally speaking, this achievement was determined by four issues: the high flexibility of Polish SMEs, the reform package proposed and implemented by the Polish government, the German stimulation package (which, owing to economic ties, also had an impact on the Polish economy) and the country's exemplary use of structural funds from the EU budget (Duszczyk 2014). In this respect, Poland has fared very well compared to the other countries that acceded to the EU in 2004 and 2007. The data contained in Figure 17.1 suggest that in recent years, Poland – along with Slovakia – has recorded the highest economic growth of all states in the region, with both countries increasing their GDPs by almost 50 per cent. This result came during the crisis years when other countries in the region recorded much deeper and longer economic slowdowns or, as in the case of the Baltic states, experienced many months of recession.

Income level

The dynamic economic growth over the last decade has translated into a narrowing of the development gap between Poland and the EU member states with core status. According to Eurostat data, Poland's current GDP per capita amounts to approximately 70 per cent of the EU27 average. This translates into a growth of approximately 20 per centage points in comparison to 2003. However, it should be noted that after the accession of Romania and Bulgaria into the EU, the average per-capita GDP dropped, such that actual growth is less than straightforward comparisons would suggest. Of much greater relevance for conclusions related to Poland's shift from the periphery to the core, therefore, are the indices presenting median-equalised net income in PPS (Eurostat). These data suggest that in 2013, the median-equalised income of a Pole corresponded to

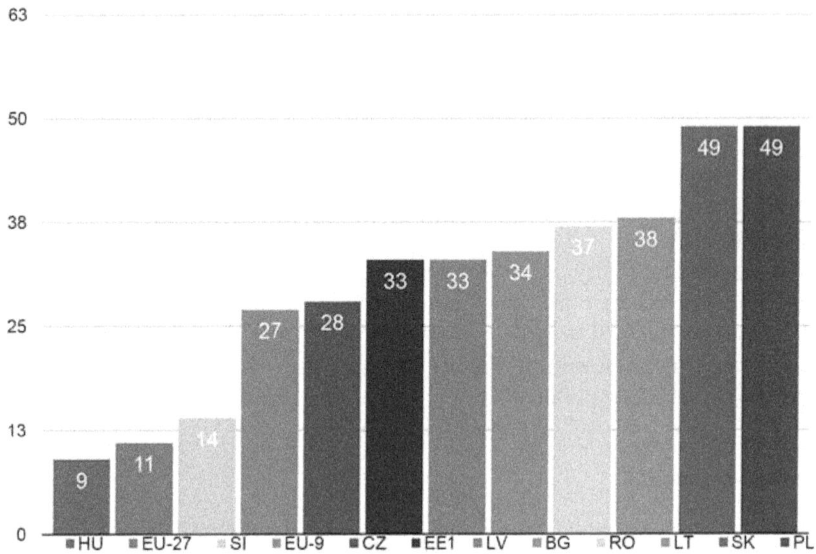

Figure 17.1 Accumulated GDP growth (per cent) in CEE countries in the period 2003–2013 (2003=100)
Source: Ministry of Foreign Affairs (2014): 61.

approximately 45 per cent of the income of a German, approximately 55 per cent of the income of a UK citizen and approximately 75 per cent of the income of a Spaniard. Immediately after accession, these differences were notably higher (approximately 35 per cent, 30 per cent and 45 per cent, respectively). This means that Poland has significantly narrowed the gap separating it from the development core of the EU. Nevertheless, considerable income differences remain.

The labour market situation

The unemployment level is another relevant indicator demonstrating the economic position of a given state that should be taken into account in any assessment of the state's status. It can be assumed that states with high unemployment rates, particularly among the young, have comparatively limited development potential owing to lower revenue from taxes and social insurance contributions and higher welfare payment obligations. As has already been noted, upon its accession to the EU, Poland had the highest unemployment rate of all EU25 states. The data displayed in Figure 17.2 indicate that since 2004, this unemployment rate has been steadily declining; even during the crisis, Poland has not recorded any significant increase in its unemployment rate.

The data related to unemployment suggest that for several years now, Poland's unemployment rate has been similar to the EU27 average. Of course, the EU average has been significantly inflated by states including Greece, Spain and

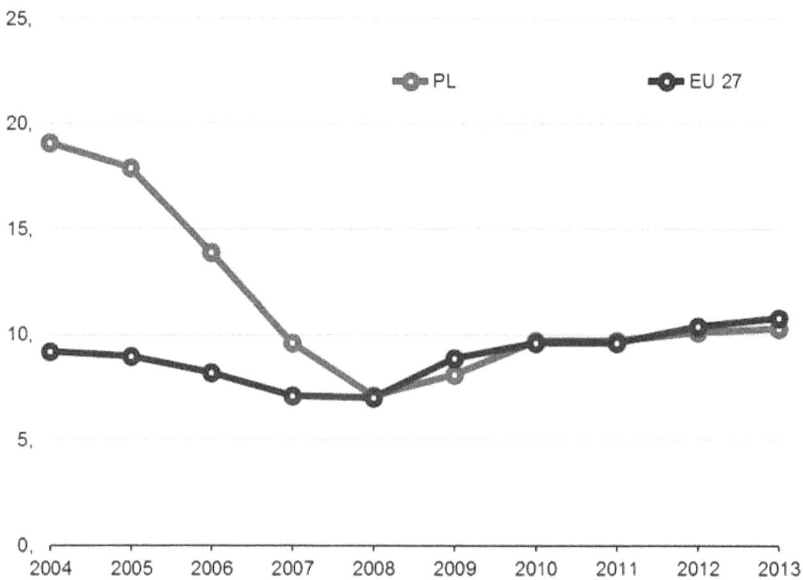

Figure 17.2 Changes in unemployment in Poland and the EU27 over the period 2004–2013
Source: Eurostat (2014).

Portugal, whose unemployment rates at the end of 2013 were 27.5 per cent, 26.1 per cent and 16.4 per cent, respectively. Notably, unemployment rates in the majority of the states of the core were much lower than in Poland. For example, in late 2013, Germany had an unemployment rate of 5.2 per cent, and the United Kingdom's rate was 7.6 per cent. The rate in France was similar to the level in Poland (Eurostat 2014). It should be pointed out that in the case of Poland, migration processes have resulted in a decline in the unemployment rate, while for Germany and the United Kingdom they have instead contributed to an increase through the immigration of third-country nationals (the issue of migration will be discussed later in this chapter). Thus, when analysing the changes in the situation of the Polish labour market over the period 2004–2013, significant improvements in the related indicators can be observed, as was the case with income. Poland has significantly shifted towards the EU average; however, when we compare the situation of Poland to that of the core states, there are still clear differences yet to be resolved.

Infrastructural connections between the peripheries and the centre

It is difficult to imagine a core state without sufficient transport connections to other states of the same status. These connections are key for investments, the living standards of citizens and economic competitiveness. In contrast, a majority of periphery states have only limited access to centres of development, a circumstance that adversely affects their development. Therefore, it comes as no surprise that in the initial period after accession to the EU, Poland adopted infrastructure improvement as one of its top priorities, taking advantage of funding under cohesion policy. The country's financial perspective for 2007–2013 envisaged almost EUR 30 billion for improvements in the quality of railway and road infrastructure (Ministry of Regional Development, 2007).

Upon its accession to the EU, Poland was definitely an infrastructural periphery. At the time, Poland had the lowest per centage of motorways and expressways in the entire European Union. Ten years later, the network of motorways in Poland has grown by over 1,100 km, and that of expressways by almost 1,000 km (Generalna Dyrekcja … 2013). At present, Warsaw, the capital of Poland, has two direct motorway connections to Germany (via Poznań and Wrocław) and additional connections to other European states. The connections along the eastern border of Poland are also being expanded. The travel time from Warsaw to Berlin has been reduced by approximately five hours, and from Warsaw to Dresden by approximately six hours.

The situation with regard to railway infrastructure is slightly less positive. Only in late 2014 did Poland manage to launch a backbone network of fast domestic railway connections. Travel by train from Warsaw to Berlin presently takes approximately five hours, while the travel time from Gdańsk to Warsaw, a distance of almost 400 km, is three hours.

The issue of the expansion of the country's airport network has aroused a great deal of controversy in Poland. At present, Poland has one large international airport (Warsaw), several regional airports (e.g. Wrocław, Poznań, Gdańsk, Rzeszów) and a network of local airports that has been expanded in recent years (e.g. Radom, Łódź, Lublin). At the local level, the decision to construct new airports reflects the desire to reduce travel time to Warsaw, and then to other European states and the United States. However, the financial returns of these airports remain unsatisfactory, raising the question of whether it makes sense to maintain them in the future (Onet 2014).

The investments in infrastructure made since Poland's accession to the European Union have definitely brought the country closer to development centres within the EU, particularly Germany. This has reduced the costs of pursuing international economic activity and has positively contributed to investments. There is still the problem of the lack of an airport from which one can travel to non-European regions of the world without connecting flights. This problem could be resolved through the opening of an airline hub in Berlin. If there are good railway and car connections, travelling through Berlin will only add a few hours to the trip from Warsaw. Thus, the lack of air connections need not adversely affect Poland's shift towards the states of the core.

Accession to the Eurozone as the completion of European integration

European integration is composed of three phases of membership: membership in the European Union, in the Schengen zone and in the Eurozone. To date,

Poland has completed the first two phases, but it is still not a Eurozone member, despite the fact that its Accession Treaty stipulates that Poland will accede to the Eurozone when it meets pre-defined conditions. In general, Poland still asserts its willingness to accede to the Eurozone, although it has not set any specific date for when this might happen. The main argument in support of such an approach is the belief that the adoption of the euro in Poland during a time of economic instability in the EU would be detrimental, both for Poland and for the states that already have the euro in place (Rostowski 2013). However, it is also clear that Poland directly links its accession not only to economic but also to political issues (Schweiger 2014: 182). It is difficult to imagine Poland's shift from the periphery to the core without the adoption of the euro. It should be noted that many key decisions related to the future of the European Union are made during meetings of the heads of the states of the monetary union. In this context, the voices of member states that have not yet adopted the euro are rarely heard. This viewpoint has been expressed for many years, among others by a former Polish prime minister and present head of the National Bank of Poland, Marek Belka (Belka 2014). Thus, if Poland wants to play the role of a core state within the European Union, it should reaffirm its willingness to accede to the Eurozone. However, it should be kept in mind that this may be extremely difficult for political rather than economic reasons, in part because it will be necessary to amend the Polish constitution, which stipulates that the 'Polish zloty' is the national currency. Consequently, in the coming or subsequent elections, the political parties supporting the adoption of the euro in Poland would have to achieve a majority that would enable constitutional amendments to pass. Given the political reality in Poland, this seems very unlikely. This inability to accede to the Eurozone owing to a 'constitutional stalemate' can be regarded as one of the major difficulties in Poland's assumption of a central role in the discussion about the future of the economic dimension of the European Union, a step that seems indispensable in achieving the status of a state of the core.

Migration from and to Poland

Employment migration is one of the key processes that must be considered in any assessment of the status of Poland. Following its accession to the European Union, Poland has experienced a significant outflow of nationals to other member states. Within a decade, the number of Poles residing and employed in other member states has increased by approximately 1.3 million (see Table 17.1).

The per centage of emigrants in the Polish population is approaching 5 per cent, with the United Kingdom being the main destination country for Poles going abroad (Table 17.2).

An analysis of migration data for the last decade allows the assertion that Poles have been leaving the periphery and moving to the core in far greater numbers than was previously assumed. In this case, the core (identified in terms of the labour market situation) consists mainly of the United Kingdom, and to a lesser extent Ireland, the Netherlands and Norway. Germany has ceased to be the

Table 17.1 The number of Poles residing in other member states of the European Union (as of 1 January of a given year)

	2004	*2006*	*2008*	*2010*	*2012*	*2013*
Poles resident in other EU member states	580,000	776,000	1,328,000	1,497,000	1,798,000	1,883,000

Source: Eurostat, 'Population by sex, age group and citizenship'.

Table 17.2 Emigration of Poles as of 1 January 2013

Emigration scale	*Population*	*Percentage of emigrants*	*Main receiving state*
1,883,000	38,533,000	4.9 %	United Kingdom

Source: Eurostat, 'Population by sex, age group and citizenship'.

primary destination for Poles; migration has increased only to a very limited extent despite the lifting of restrictions on the free movement of workers in 2011. However, Germany still remains an emigration country for Poles, as befits a country of the EU's core.

The data on migration within the European Union allow little room for doubt. In terms of its labour market, Poland is a periphery state with a negative migration balance. This status cannot be changed by the growing numbers of nationals of other member states (mainly Germany, the UK and Spain) residing and settling in Poland. Compared to emigration and return migrations of Poles, the scale of immigration is still very limited.

However, various conclusions can be drawn through an analysis of immigration to Poland from third countries. Poland is beginning to receive increasing numbers of non-EU immigrants, primarily from Ukraine. Table 17.3 indicates that the number of work permits issued to such immigrants has been regularly increasing over the last decade, reaching the level of approximately 40,000 annually in recent years.

Additional data related to the status of the Polish labour market are provided by figures on declarations of the intention to employ a foreigner.[3] The introduction of declarations, which liberalised the access of seasonal workers to the Polish labour market, followed from the need to remedy the emerging shortages, particularly in labour-intensive sectors in which there are not enough Polish nationals willing to undertake employment. The data contained in Table 17.4 suggest that the introduction of this instrument resulted in an exponential rise in the number of registered declarations and employees hired on this basis. The number of declarations registered in 2014 was the greatest since the introduction of this measure, reaching approximately 400,000. An analysis of the nationalities of the foreigners for whom these declarations are registered suggests that over 95 per cent of them come from Ukraine.

Table 17.3 The number of work permits issued in the period 2004–2014

Year	*Number of issue permits*		
	New	*Extended*	*Total*
2004	6,971	5,410	12,381
2005	5,905	4,399	10,304
2006	6,629	4,125	10,754
2007	7,667	4,486	12,153
2008	12,390	5,632	18,022
2009	20,806	8,534	29,340
2010	N/A*	N/A[c]	32,126
2011	32,519	8,289	40,808
2012	30,062	9,082	39,144
2013	29,609	9,469	39,078
2014	37,808	5,855	43,663

Source: Own work based on data from the Ministry of Labour and Social Policy.

Table 17.4 Employers' declared intentions to hire foreign workers (with breakdown into nationalities) from 2007 to 2014

Year	*Nationality*						
	Ukrainian	*Belarussian*	*Russian*	*Moldovan*	*Georgian*	*Armenian*	*Total*
2007	20,260	1,347	190	0	0	0	21,797
2008	142,960	12,606	1,147	0	0	0	156,713
2009	180,133	4,860	674	2,747	0	0	188,414
2010	169,490	3,623	595	5,912	453	0	180,073
2011	239,646	4,370	963	13,024	1,774	0	259,777
2012	223,671	7,636	1,624	9,421	1,384	0	243,736
2013	217,571	5,194	1,260	9,248	2,343	0	235,616
2014	372,946	4,017	1,227	6,331	2,103	774	387,398

Note: The system of employers' declarations of the intention to employ a foreigner entered into force in 2007.
Source: own work based on data from the Ministry of Labour and Social Policy.

To recapitulate the reflections related to emigration and immigration, over its ten years of membership in the European Union, Poland remains a periphery country for migration taking place under the free movement of workers. At the same time, it has become a country of the core for immigrants from third countries, particularly from Eastern Partnership states and especially Ukraine. At the same time it needs to be stressed that under the approach differentiating between centre and periphery states (within the European Union) adopted in this publication, Poland still remains a periphery state.

The political importance of Poland

One of the main objectives of Poland since its accession to the European Union has been to gain real influence over the development directions of the European integration. Poland is determined to enter the group of states that comprise the decision-making core within the EU. At the same time, the general view was adopted that owing to Poland's location and negative historical connotations, it would be beneficial to promote the idea that the more integration, the better for the country. Apart from rare exceptions,[4] this view still holds today.

An analysis of the evolution of Poland's part in the decision-making process at the EU level allows the conclusion that the country's role has increased greatly over the last decade. This thesis is corroborated by an analysis of the areas of responsibility of European Commission members coming from Poland (see Table 17.5). Thus far, there have been three such members: Danuta Hübner, Janusz Lewandowski and Elzbieta Bienkowska.[5] The data displayed in Table 17.5 indicate that the areas for which 'Polish' commissioners have been responsible correspond precisely to Poland's priorities during their respective terms in office.[6]

In the initial period of membership it was crucial for Poland to obtain real influence over changes in spending under cohesion policy. Danuta Hübner was responsible for this area. In the subsequent period, it was of the utmost importance for Poland that the financial budget for 2014–2020 not reduce the allocations to the states that acceded to the EU in 2004 and 2007. Janusz Lewandowski was the commissioner responsible for that area. At present, the defence of single-market

Table 17.5 'Polish' members of the European Commission in the period 2004–2014

First name	*Surname*	*Function*	*Term in office*	*Comments*
Danuta	Hübner	Commissioner for Regional Policy	November 2004–July 2009	As of July 2009, following her election to the European Parliament, she was replaced by Paweł Samecki
Janusz	Lewandowski	Commissioner for Financial Programming and Budget	February 2010–July 2014	As of July 2009, following his election to the European Parliament, he was replaced by Jacek Dominik.
Elżbieta	Bieńkowska	Commissioner for Internal Market, Industry, Entrepreneurship and SMEs	November 2014–	

Source: European Commission.

principles and improvements in the competitiveness of enterprises are top-priority issues for Poland. These areas were assigned to Elzbieta Bienkowska.

However, it is the appointment of Donald Tusk, one of the longest-serving prime ministers in the EU, to the position of president of the European Council that could prove critical for perceptions of Poland. Tusk is a definite enthusiast of European integration and may play a significant role during the first two and a half years of his term in office. However, it is clear that he will not be able to unequivocally promote the interests of Poland in the EU arena. However, it seems that recent years have proven that promotion of European integration is good for Poland, so any measures initiated by Donald Tusk in support of European integration and in defence of fundamental values will be beneficial for both the European Union and Poland. Given this context, his situation seems quite comfortable. In late 2014 *The Economist* published an article about Donald Tusk as the new president of the European Council. In the opinion of the author of this article, as a former Polish prime minister Donald Tusk can do things that seemed unlikely just a few years ago, namely secure to Poland the membership in the decision-making core of the European Union (*The Economist* 2014b).

In order to assess the political power of Poland, it is also necessary to analyse the effects of the country's actions initiated at the EU level. One good example of such an initiative is the Eastern Partnership, a project intended to establish closer relations between the European Union and East European states, although these states should not expect to join the EU anytime soon.[7] The effects of this initiative have been rather modest. The partnership was signed despite overt opposition from Russia, but many of the planned measures have remained just wishful thinking. It is difficult to argue against the advisability of the Eastern Partnership, but the enormous difficulties in its implementation must be acknowledged (Youngs and Pishchikova 2013). These difficulties have been aggravated even further by Russia's annexation of the Crimea and its attempts to destabilise the economic and political situation in Ukraine. Nevertheless, it must be unequivocally stressed that with regard to its purposes, the Eastern Partnership idea remains as pertinent as ever, as the Partnership creates a space for the tightening of cooperation between the European Union and East European states (Wojna and Gniazdowski 2009). Therefore, the initiative itself is very much necessary and – given the geopolitical circumstances of the time – it has been carried out as well as humanly possible. Nevertheless, the problems faced in the implementation of the Eastern Partnership demonstrate that Poland may encounter significant obstacles in its attempts to promote the tightening of EU-East relations in the future. It is difficult to expect EU member states to be willing to become involved in projects whose success is highly doubtful.

Another issue that may prove extremely significant in strengthening the political role of Poland in the European Union is related to the Weimar Triangle, an informal organisation uniting Poland, Germany and France. Thus far, the participants have not found a formula that would take the meetings of leaders of the three countries beyond the courtesy level, transforming them into a major forum where joint positions can be agreed upon and later presented at the European

Union level. In the source literature, some authors have asserted that the Weimar Triangle lost its chance to become a 'new driving force for Europe' after the 2004 EU enlargement (Lang and Schwarzer 2011: 2). A joint position supported by Poland, Germany and France would be of major, if not central, significance in discussions at the EU level, as it is difficult to imagine a situation in which positions developed by the Triangle would not be taken into account. Therefore, if Poland wants to stay on course towards becoming a core state within the European Union, the country must convince both of its partners to enhance their involvement in this cooperation. This task should be easier for Francois Hollande than it was when Nicolas Sarkozy was the president of France. Angela Merkel seems determined to maintain Germany's good relations with Poland. Poland should take advantage of this favourable situation.

Articles in the most popular European magazines also confirm the growing significance of Poland. Particularly visible is the change in the tone of articles in such periodicals as *The Economist* or *Financial Times*. The former one regularly publishes articles demonstrating the growing role of Poland both within the EU and on the global scale. As an example, in June 2014 a dedicated insert on Poland was published (*The Economist* 2014c). The articles contained in the insert presented Poland as a new leader, not only in the Central Eastern Europe (CEE) region but also in the entire European Union. By referencing history, the authors of the article claim that for the first time in centuries Poland succeeded in changing its role from 'order-taker' to 'playmaker'. According to the authors, this is attributable to the policy of opening to the European Union and building s strategic partnership with Germany while maintaining at least correct relationships with France and the United Kingdom. Perhaps less enthusiastic – but still very positive – opinions about Poland were also published in the *Financial Times*. As an example, in late August 2014 an article was published corroborating the hypotheses put forward by *The Economist* that Poland presently has a unique opportunity to enter the group of states deciding about the directions of a further European integration (*Financial Times* 2014a).

In its articles, the *Financial Times* also demonstrated the ability of Poland to initiate at the EU level coalitions enabling attainment of its political goals. As an example, during the European Council summit dedicated to combating global warming, which took place in October 2014, Poland managed to establish a coalition that blocked adoption of conclusions that might limit in the coming years the competitiveness of Polish plants, which would be unable to adjust to more stringent CO2 emission standards (*Financial Times* 2014b).

An analysis of articles published in the most popular European magazines may lead to a conclusion that already today, after appointment of Donald Tusk to the position of the president of the European Council, Poland has become a country of the centre of the European Union. At the same time this conclusion seems too far-reaching. One must be aware that the enthusiasm of the press vanishes as fast as it emerges. Press articles alone – although they certainly help build a positive image of a country and are conducive for transformation – do not suffice for a country to attain the formal status of a state of the centre.

Conclusions

This paper has analysed the decade of Poland's membership in the European Union in the context of the change in its status from the periphery to the centre. Despite the country's indisputable economic, social and political successes, it cannot be unequivocally asserted that Poland has managed to attain the status of a core member state with direct influence over both ad hoc decisions and the future of the European Union. The picture is much more complex than what can be inferred from articles about Poland published in the European press in the period 2013/14.

Needless to say, a decade of membership is too short a period for Poland to make up for 45 years of a centrally planned economy. Thus, we can only assert that Poland is a very powerful periphery state. However, the country plays a highly important role in this context as a bridge between countries in the core and those in the periphery – including non-EU states. Here, we can cite the example of the Eastern Partnership, especially Ukraine.

More convincing than the economic context is the situation in terms of the political role of Poland. Here, one can venture to say that Poland has entered the group of states that represent the immediate neighbours (backup) of the core. It has not yet attained a position akin to that of Germany or France, but it can probably be compared to Spain, despite not being a Eurozone member. Poland would not have been able to attain such a position if it were not for the country's success in coping with the effects of the economic crisis. The economic developments of the last decade have not yet allowed Poland to enter the group of core states of the European Union in terms of economic competitiveness, but they have been an indispensable factor in enhancing the political role of Poland. Nevertheless, in order to be able to participate directly in the decisions made in the Eurozone forum, it is crucial for Poland to access the zone. This would allow the country to complete the integration process and confirm its status as a core state and part of the process of political decision-making within the EU.

In summary, as of the end of 2014, Poland experienced one of the best periods in its history. One can safely assume that this period will continue unabated, as Poland has managed to negotiate a high level of support from cohesion policy for another seven years, among other successes. In addition, forecasts related to the country's endogenic development are very positive. However, the Russian aggression against Ukraine has raised some degree of doubt. As a country bordering on Russia and heavily involved in conflict resolution, it cannot be ruled out that the region around Poland will begin to be perceived as likely to decrease in stability, although this is related more to the issue of the security of economic investments rather than military acts. Fortunately, this scenario is still fairly unlikely. Much more likely is a scenario in which Poland will be able to use its economic and political potentials to its advantage in the coming decade and make a significant shift towards the European Union's centre.

Notes

1 He assigned a similar status to the eastern *Länder* of Germany.
2 The only exceptions were transitional periods, which provided accession states with longer adjustment times. These were applied mainly in the field of environmental protection.
3 An instrument of Polish immigration policy enabling nationals of Ukraine, Belarus, Russia, Georgia, Moldova and Armenia to accept seasonal employment in Poland without a permit (for the period of six months within a consecutive 12 months).
4 For example, Poland has not yet decided to recognise the EU Charter of Fundamental Rights. Failure to adopt the Charter resulted despite negotiations carried out by the government of Prime Minister Jarosław Kaczyński with the active participation of President Lech Kaczyński; this was a pre-condition for Poland's signing of the Lisbon Treaty.
5 They were temporarily replaced by other people, but this did not result in a change of the areas of their responsibility.
6 As a rule, members of the European Commission should not represent national interests. However, is a widespread practice for governments of certain states to strive for their candidates' assignment to areas of particular relevance for those states.
7 The Eastern Partnership states are: Armenia, Azerbaijan, Belarus, Georgia, Moldova and Ukraine.

References

Belka, M. (2014) 'Polska w strefie euro? Nie teraz. Jesteśmy tylko "małymi Chinami Europy"' [Poland in the euro zone? Not yet. We are just a 'small China of Europe'], *Polska*, 26 April. Available at: www.polskatimes.pl/artykul/3416147,prof-marek-belka-polska-w-strefie-euro-nie-teraz-jestesmy-tylko-malymi-chinami-europy,id,t.html (accessed 9 December 2014).

Duszczyk, M. (2014) 'Poland under economic crisis conditions,' *Perspectives on European Politics and Society* 15(3): 370–384.

The Economist (2014a) 'Poland's second golden age: Europe's unlikely star,' 28 June. Available at: www.economist.com/news/leaders/21605910-poland-just-had-best-25-years-half-millennium-its-transformation-remains (accessed 14 December 2014).

The Economist (2014b) 'Poland's progress: Donald Tusk's appointment caps Poland's journey to Europe's core,' 6 December. Available at: www.economist.com/news/europe/21635506-donald-tusks-appointment-caps-polands-journey-europes-core-polands-progress (accessed 16 December 2014).

The Economist (2014c) 'Special Report. Poland: a golden opportunity,' 28 June. Available at: www.economist.com/sites/default/files/20140628_poland.pdf (accessed 12 December 2014).

Eurostat (2014) 'Unemployment Rate by Sex'. Available at: http://ec.europa.eu/eurostat/tgm/table.do?tab=table&init=1&language=en&pcode=tsdec450&plugin=1 (accessed 15 December 2014).

Financial Times (2014a) 'Donald Tusk takes Poland to the "big table",' 30 August. Available at: www.ft.com/intl/cms/s/0/2b7fc0ce-2f9c-11e4-83e4-00144feabdc0.html (accessed 12 December 2014).

Financial Times (2014b) 'Eastern Europe attacks planned EU emissions curb,' 20 October. Available at: www.ft.com/intl/cms/s/0/eee0069a-5784-11e4-8493-00144feab7de.html#axzz3Tp0rmgTF (accessed 13 December 2014).

Generalna Dyrekcja Dróg Krajowych i Autostrad (2013) 'Budowa dróg w Polsce: Fakty i mity, doświadczenia i perspektywy' [Road construction in Poland: Facts and myths, experiences and prospects]. Warsaw.

Lang, K. O. and D. Schwarzer (2011) 'Consolidating the Weimar Triangle: European Policy Functions of German-Polish-French Co-operation,' Comments 2011C 30, Stiftung Wissenschaft und Politik, October.

Lipset, S. M. and S. Rokkan (1967) 'Cleavage Structures, Party Systems, and Voter Alignments: An Introduction,' in S. M. Lipset and S. Rokkan (eds) *Party Systems and Voter Alignments*. New York: Free Press, pp. 9–13.

Ministry of Regional Development (2007) *Narodowe Strategiczne Ramy Odniesienia* [National Strategic Terms of Reference]. Warsaw.

Ministry of Foreign Affairs (2014) *Polskie 10 lat w Unii: Raport* [Poland's decade in the EU: A Report]. Warsaw.

Onet (2014) 'Kto marzy o Ryanairze?' [Who is dreaming of Ryanair?], 31 October. Available at: http://wiadomosci.onet.pl/kto-marzy-o-ryanairze/nem2h (accessed 14 December 2014).

Rostowski, V. (2013) 'Nie będzie dramatu jak opóźnimy wejście do strefy euro' [Delaying our accession to the euro zone will be no tragedy], *Gazeta Wyborcza*, 24 April. Available at: http://wyborcza.biz/Waluty/1,111132,13799554,Rostowski__Nie_bedzie_dramatu__jesli_opoznimy_wejscie.html (accessed 2 November 2015)..

Schweiger, C. (2014) *The EU and the Global Financial Crisis: New Varieties of Capitalism*. Cheltenham: Edward Elgar Publishing.

Wallerstein, I. (1979) *The Capitalist World-Economy*. New York: Cambridge University Press.

Wojna, B. and M. Gniazdowski (eds) (2009) 'Eastern Partnership: The Opening Report,' Polish Institute of International Affairs, Warsaw.

Zarycki, T. (2011) 'Eastern Poland in a Center–Periphery Perspective,' in M. Stefański (ed.) *Strategic Issues of the Development of the Lublin Region*. Lublin: Innovatio Press Scientific, University of Economics and Innovation, 95–112.

Youngs, R. and K. Pishchikova (2013) 'Smart Geostrategy for the Eastern Partnership,' *Carnegie Europe*. Available at: http://carnegieeurope.eu/publications/?fa=53571 (accessed 4 November 2015).

Part V

Global dimension

18 From core to periphery?

The impact of the crisis on the EU's role in the world

Carolin Rüger

Introduction

When the Lisbon Treaty entered into force in December 2009, many observers in academia and politics assumed that the new institutional set-up would fundamentally strengthen the European Union (EU), not least regarding the Union's profile and standing on the global stage. Five years later, those who had hoped for a Lisbon upgrade for the EU's global role were dismayed to read sobering assessments of 'the world's biggest losers':

> As Europe's financial resources and political energy are sucked up by the euro black hole, the EU is losing its capacity to shape events in the neighbourhood. The chaos in Libya, the abject failures of western policy in Lebanon and Syria, the loss in Ukraine, Turkey's continuing drift away from a European orientation, the steady disappearance of the climate agenda in global governance: all these testify to the continuing decline in Europe's clout.
>
> (Mead, 2014)

When the financial and economic crisis hit the EU, the Lisbon moment seemed to fizzle out.

The objective of this chapter is to unfold the external dimension of the economic, financial and sovereign debt crisis and to explore the negative spillover of the crisis on the EU's political role in the world. The key question is not whether the crisis has had any consequences for the EU as a global player but how and to what degree the financial and economic turmoil has affected the formulation and implementation of EU foreign policy.

The first section briefly outlines the multidimensional mosaic of EU foreign policy post-Lisbon. Drawing on this conceptual background, the analysis examines the consequences the crisis has had for various dimensions of the EU's global role. The study focuses on the Common Foreign and Security Policy (CFSP) and the Common Security and Defence Policy (CSDP), but also considers other important external dimensions such as development cooperation, enlargement and the EU's policy on climate change. Moving beyond this policy-orientated approach, the chapter then turns to recent developments from a more strategic perspective: What strategic implications has the crisis had for both the inner-European power structure and for the EU's standing and image in the world? The concluding section studies the question of whether the crisis will only represent a blow to global Europe or whether there is evidence that it may also boost the EU's international role.

Understanding the multidimensional mosaic of the EU's role in the world

EU foreign policy is multifaceted and multidimensional. It cannot be reduced to CFSP, which was launched only with the Maastricht Treaty in 1993. Although the European Community (EC) was not a full-fledged institutionalised international actor, there is consensus among scholars of EU foreign policy that the EC gained a 'presence' on the international stage even before Maastricht (Ginsberg, 1989). Allen and Smith (1990: 20) stated that the EC 'is a variable and multidimensional presence, which plays an active role in some areas of international interaction and a less active one in others'. With the establishment of the CFSP, the literature on the EU's global role has increasingly focused on the question of whether the Union would be able to become an actor in international relations. 'Actorness' differs from 'presence' insofar as it implies intentional and strategic action: an entity can have *presence* by its mere existence, even though it does not *act* strategically (Bretherton and Vogler, 1999; Jupille and Caporaso, 1998; Jopp and Schlotter, 2007: 11).

Today, the EU's role and actorness in the world is shaped by a multitude of policies that can be best and most objectively systematised by reference to the treaties (Müller-Brandeck-Bocquet and Rüger, 2015). According to the Treaty of Lisbon, the mosaic of EU foreign policy consists of:

- the intergovernmental realm comprising CFSP and CSDP (Title V, Chapter 2 TEU);
- the external policies traditionally steered by the European Commission (Title V, Chapter 1 TEU and Part 5 TFEU);
- external aspects of other policies (expression based on Art. 21 (3) TEU) such as climate policy, external energy policy or migration and asylum policy as external aspects of the (internal) area of freedom, security and justice;
- enlargement policy (Art. 49 TEU) and the European Neighbourhood Policy (Art. 8 TEU).

This multidimensional conception of the EU's global role entails a broad understanding of EU foreign policy. It goes beyond the notion of EU external action (as laid down in Title 5 TEU) to also encompass aspects such as the enlargement policy, which is – according to the treaties – not an official part of EU external action. However, it has had significant effects, shaping the EU's environment; consequently, it can be regarded as a highly powerful tool and, in the words of the previous Commissioner for Enlargement and Neighbourhood Policy, 'the top external policy instrument of the Union' (Füle, 2014). This comprehensive conception of EU foreign policy also recognises the external implications of internal policies that are more often than not forgotten in discussions of the Union's global role. However, 'there is not one single internal policy that doesn't also have an external impact' (Mogherini, 2014). Therefore, the EU's role in the world is shaped not only by CFSP and CSDP and the supranationally governed external policies including the trade policy, development cooperation and humanitarian aid, but also (among others) by the Common Agricultural Policy and EU rules on competition, transportation, public health, consumer protection and the common European currency.

By resorting to these various dimensions of the foreign policy mosaic, the EU as an international actor can make use of both soft and hard power instruments (Nye, 2004). While the enlargement policy can be considered 'EU soft power at its best' (Ratiu, 2011), the Union can also use hard power instruments like EU military operations or – as could recently be witnessed in the case of Russia – restrictive measures, commonly known as sanctions.

Against this backdrop, the subsequent sections study how the crisis has affected various dimensions of the EU's global role in both material and ideational terms. The questions that frame and guide the analysis are: what implications did the crisis have for CFSP, CSDP and other external EU policies?[1] How did the crisis affect the hard and soft power instruments of the EU? And, more generally: what implications has the crisis had for the international actorness of the EU?

Consequences of the crisis for CFSP and CSDP

First of all, it must be stressed that not each and every deficit and failure of CFSP and CSDP can be blamed on the crisis. This specific intergovernmental dimension of EU foreign policy had definite shortfalls (mainly a lack of coherence and political will) even before the economic and financial tsunami hit the continent. The crisis aggravated and accelerated certain longer-term developments and structural shortcomings in CFSP and CSDP (see also Kempin and Overhaus, 2013; Kempin and Overhaus, 2014; Youngs, 2014). Three aspects are particularly relevant when analysing the consequences for CFSP and CSDP: the shift in agenda, the intensification of strategic disorientation and financial constraints.

In recent years, the management of the sovereign debt crisis has increasingly become the script for EU policies in general. With the intense focus on the euro, other issues had to take a backseat, especially EU foreign and security policy. CFSP and CSDP were intended for crises outside the EU; in recent years, however, crisis management has primarily happened *inside* the EU. This is particularly true for the period from 2008 to 2013. To be sure, this development is not due to a lack of crises beyond European borders but rather to a noticeable shift in the European agenda towards economic and financial issues. It seems telling that the number of CSDP missions sharply decreased between 2008 and 2013 in comparison to the significantly higher numbers during the golden age of CSDP beginning in 2003. However, these doldrum years of CSDP may also have been caused by a general mission fatigue and therefore cannot necessarily be regarded as a negative spillover of the crisis. The agendas of the European Council provide a more objective indicator of a thematic shift. The goal of the first permanent president of the European Council, Herman Van Rompuy, to devote one summit per year to EU foreign policy could not be realised. Since 2008, when the European Council under the French presidency held an intense and non-event-driven debate on security issues for the last time (European Council, 2008), there has been only one broader discussion on 'how to give new momentum to the Union's external relations, taking full advantage of the opportunities provided by the Lisbon Treaty', at the European Council meeting of September 2010 (European Council, 2010). In the past, foreign and security policy events had often hijacked the agendas of summits that were dedicated to economic issues, but now it was the other way around. The extraordinary meeting on Libya on 11 March 2011, for example, was flanked by a Eurozone summit.

Naturally, this shift in agendas does not imply that CFSP and CSDP issues were entirely absent from meetings. The conclusions of the European Council show that there were debates on foreign and security policy issues in meetings also during the heights of the crisis, which is not surprising considering (for example) the upheaval in the Arab world from 2010/11 onwards. However, the European Council addressed foreign and security policy more in reaction to international events (e.g. the extraordinary meeting on Libya on 11 March 2011) than in a proactive manner. Moreover, when the European Council conclusions referred to foreign and security issues, it was predominantly under the category of 'other issues'. Von Ondarza (2013) points out that most of these topics were already pre-discussed and settled at lower levels so that the heads of state or government could focus on the management of the euro crisis. Even the controversial European engagement in Mali in 2013 was only documented in the conclusions, not debated by the heads of state or government themselves at their meeting in February 2013 (Von Ondarza, 2013: 86).

CFSP and CSDP management from 2008 onwards was not only low profile and reactive but also characterised by a strategic vacuum that continued and reinforced a longer-term trend of strategic disorientation often deplored by many observers (see, for example, Howorth, 2009; Biscop and Coelmont, 2013). After the European Security Strategy (ESS; European Council, 2003) was introduced in December 2003, the European Council in December 2008 only endorsed a report on the implementation of the ESS, which was actually merely an update of the strategy rather than an upgrade to a veritable 'ESS 2.0'. An initiative (led by think tanks from Italy, Poland, Spain and Sweden) to formulate a new 'European Global Strategy' did not catch on, as it was more or less ignored by the 'Big Three' (Germany, France and the UK) and was not promoted by the then High Representative Catherine Ashton. Confronted with severe economic conditions domestically, time for and interest in talking about the big picture of CFSP, CSDP and the EU's global role has been scarce over the last five years (Helwig and Rüger, 2014: 13).

Serious financial constraints are an additional impact the crisis has had on CFSP and CSDP. As the following section will show, austerity measures had negative effects on all dimensions of EU foreign policy. In the area of defence, the cuts are clearly visible. Already between 2008 and 2010, during the early phase of the crisis, the EU-26[2] reduced their aggregate defence expenditure by 4 per cent. The degree of cutbacks varied across the EU: the deepest cuts in this period were made in Latvia, which almost halved its defence budget, but other crisis-ridden countries such as Greece, Ireland, France and Spain also made substantial cuts (Möckli, 2012: 76). In its 2014 report on military spending, the Stockholm International Peace Research Institute (SIPRI) recorded decreases in military expenditures since 2008 of over 10 per cent in real terms for Austria, Belgium, Greece, Ireland, Italy, the Netherlands, Spain and the UK, as well as for all countries in Central Europe with the significant exception of Poland (Perlo-Freeman and Solmirano, 2014: 3). This downsizing of defence expenditures in the EU was accelerated by the crisis, aggravating a longer-term trend that could be observed since the 1990s. The problem here is not only the decreasing level of expenditures but also the fact that member states have decided on cuts in an uncoordinated manner. Despite pooling and sharing initiatives (see the last section of this chapter), national perspectives still prevail in EU security and defence matters.

EU member states face the challenge of doing more with less. This is true not only for security and defence expenditures but also for CFSP. Cash-stripped budgets hit the EU just as the new Lisbon foreign policy set-up with the European External Action Service (EEAS) was scheduled to be established. At the EU level, the financial resources for CFSP could at least be maintained at previous levels, but national budgets were undergoing serious constraints. Spain, for example, had to reduce the budget for its foreign ministry by two-thirds (from €3.64 billion in 2009 to €1.34 billion in 2013; Kempin and Overhaus, 2013: 183) and, on the basis of economic considerations, tried to integrate some of its own embassies (for example, in Yemen) into the EEAS (Molina and Sorroza, 2013: 49).

The crisis-induced shift in agendas towards economic aspects, the intensified strategic disorientation among EU member states and serious financial constraints were aggravated by a general climate of rising nationalism, decreasing solidarity and centrifugal tendencies, all of which further complicated cooperation in CFSP and CSDP, two dimensions of EU foreign policy that have always been characterised by strong national reflexes.

2013/14 can be regarded as a tipping point with respect to the developments described above. 2013 saw the first summit on CSDP in five years. The heads of state or government emphasised that 'defence matters' and identified several priority actions for strengthening and deepening the CSDP. New CSDP missions were launched. In 2014, the spotlight focused even more on foreign and security issues, particularly following the bloody events in Ukraine and the advance of ISIS/Daesh. The changes in personnel at the helm of the EU also generated a new momentum, in particular the new High Representative/Vice President Federica Mogherini, who resuscitated the strategic debate after she was mandated by the European Council. This renewed drive with respect to CFSP and CSDP implies that some consequences of the crisis may only be of a short-term nature.

Consequences of the crisis for other EU external policies

The crisis also caused collateral damage in other dimensions of EU foreign policy. Here, the impacts of austerity measures are particularly evident. Development policy is a prime example of a casualty of the crisis: austerity-hit member states made substantial cuts in their development budgets. In 2012, for example, all but two EU-DAC countries[3] (Austria and Luxemburg being the exceptions) cut their official development aid (ODA). Spain, which nearly halved its budget, topped the list, followed by Italy (−34.7 per cent), Greece (−17.0 per cent) and Portugal (−13.1 per cent). ODA from the 15 EU countries that were DAC members in 2012 fell by 7.4 per cent in comparison to 2011 levels (OECD, 2013). The latest OECD figures for 2013 show a mixed picture: on the one hand, aid to developing countries rebounded in 2013, with the EU-DAC countries showing a rise in ODA of 5.2 per cent in real terms compared to 2012. The UK, for example, raised its expenditures by 27.8 per cent and for the first time achieved the long-standing UN target of an ODA/GNI ratio of 0.7 per cent. Italy also increased its ODA allocations by 13.4 per cent. On the other hand, some EU-DAC countries like France (-9.8 per cent) and Portugal (-20.4 per cent) further trimmed their development budgets (OECD, 2014). Despite these cuts, the EU (member states and institutions) is still the leading donor of development assistance, providing more than 50 per cent of global aid, but it is obvious that the crisis did not leave development policy unscathed.

The same holds true for the policy on climate change, where the EU likes to stress its role as the global model pupil. Economic considerations jeopardised the Union's self-proclaimed leadership in this dimension of EU foreign policy. Instead of discussing climate change as one of the most pressing international challenges, Europeans have increasingly been debating climate and energy policy in terms of economic disadvantages or a feared loss in competitiveness (Kempin and Overhaus, 2014: 186). It is particularly striking that even countries that survived the crisis rather well economically (such as Germany and Poland) seem to fear more ambitious climate targets. The European Council's 2014 agreement on EU energy and climate goals for 2030 was preceded by a heated debate. The conference in Paris in December 2015 (COP21) will demonstrate whether the EU, despite its internal economic turmoil, can live up to the expectation of globally leading by example.

Economic considerations also had consequences for one of the most successful and effective instruments of EU foreign policy: enlargement. Internally, European support for the idea of including additional countries into the Union decreased. In 2008, a majority of Europeans (47 per cent) had expressed their support for further enlargement, while 39 per cent were against the idea (European Commission, 2008). More recently, the numbers have flipped: 49 per cent of Europeans oppose further enlargement, and only 37 per cent speak out in favour (European Commission, 2014). Enlargement fatigue is not a new phenomenon, but it seems that the economic crisis has increased the general unwillingness to support new member states – especially since these nations are generally poorer and in worse condition than the current EU members. This holds particularly true for public opinion in the Eurozone, where an absolute majority of respondents (56 per cent) are against the idea of future enlargement, which differs significantly from non-Eurozone respondents, of which a majority of 47 per cent are in favour (European Commission, 2014). Moreover, the crisis and EU internal bickering have also diminished the attractiveness of joining the EU club for candidate countries. Although the Ukraine crisis showed that people are ready to fight and – in the worst case – die for Europe, the EU's force of attraction has decreased. A statement by Volkan Bozkir, Turkish ambassador to the EU from 2005 to 2009, is telling in this regard: 'The EU dream has come to an end for the world. There is a paradigm shift. The EU is no longer the same Union that provided comfort, prosperity and wealth to its citizens as in the past' (Rettmann, 2011; for the loss of the EU's soft power, see also the next section on strategic implications).

Strategic implications for the inner-European power structure and the EU's role in global power plays

If we examine the implications of the crisis not from a policy-oriented perspective but rather from a more strategic point of view, two levels must be considered: the inner-European constellation of power, and the EU's role in global power plays.

Internally, the crisis has had a multitude of strategic implications (see other chapters on the various perspectives of core–periphery relations, the North–South/North–South–East divide, centrifugal/centripetal tendencies, etc.). Some of them have also had an impact on EU foreign policy-making. One strategic consequence of the crisis is particularly notable in this respect: the power shift among the 'Big Three' – the UK, France and Germany – a constellation that is pivotal for EU foreign policy (see, for example, Brummer, 2006; Müller-Brandeck-Bocquet, 2006; Lehne, 2012). The position of the UK and France has weakened vis-à-vis Germany, which has emerged from the crisis as the 'reluctant hegemon' (Paterson, 2011; Schweiger, 2015). This economically induced shift in the power balance has also hindered cooperation among the 'trirectoire' (Brummer, 2006: 8) in EU foreign policy. Although some areas such as the EU–Iran negotiations led by the High Representative and the E3 (France, the UK and Germany) were not harmed (Helwig and Rüger, 2014), the power shift in this triumvirate implies that the essential trilateral leadership in EU foreign policy is 'more difficult to accomplish than ever' (Möckli, 2012: 64). The European Foreign Policy Scorecard, a thorough year-by-year analysis of 'leaders' and 'slackers' in EU foreign policy issued by the European Council on Foreign Relations (ECFR), reveals that there has been a 'drop in leadership by the big three' that was particularly notable in 2012 (ECFR, 2013: 16). The looming 'Brexit' does not make this *ménage à trois* any easier: although the question of British EU membership has been a hot topic for some time (Melcher, 2014; see Chapter 4 in this volume), the euro crisis and particularly David Cameron's refusal to sign the fiscal compact have further widened the gap between the 'awkward partner' and the continent. Overall, the crisis-induced shift has definitely put a strain on the E3, the indispensable engine of EU foreign policy.

Globally, the crisis has also had strategic consequences. The implications for the EU's role in the concert of world powers can be categorised as both material and ideational. Material effects can be observed with regard to the EU's global economic power, but also in terms of its military power. The downsizing of European defence budgets mentioned above has taken place in a challenging international context. The abundance of ongoing and emerging international crises in recent years cannot be elaborated on here, but the often-cited statement made by former US secretary of state Madeleine Albright in a CBS interview in July 2014 definitely gets to the point: 'To put it mildly: the world is a mess.' According to SIPRI data, in recent years, despite the highly volatile international context, military spending has fallen in the West (Western and Central Europe, North America, Oceania), while it has increased in all other regions. China, for example, has raised its military expenditures by more than 7 per cent, representing a long-term policy of increasing military spending in line with its economic growth. Russia has also augmented its expenditures by nearly 5 per cent and, for the first time in more than ten years, is spending a larger share of its GDP on the military than the US. The US is still the world's top military spender, but it cut its military expenditures by nearly 8 per cent in 2013 (Perlo-Freeman and Solmirano, 2014: 1). For years, US administrations have insisted on more burden-sharing in NATO; Robert Gates, when he left office as US secretary of defence in 2011, warned of a 'collective military irrelevance' unless member states (especially European states) reversed this trend of military downsizing (Gates, 2011). Austerity measures in European budgets, however, run counter to these demands. This is particularly worrisome considering the American 'pivot' towards Asia, which implies that Europe should get its act together in its own neighbourhood. The 'Arab Spring' and in particular the uprising in Libya once more exposed the transatlantic gap in military capabilities that has been exacerbated by recent austerity measures in European budgets. During the air strikes in 2011, according to a US Air Force planner, the US and European armies resembled 'Snow White and the 27 dwarfs, all standing up to her knees' (Kaplan, 2012). As Mölling (2011: 3–4) has shown in a long-term scenario analysis, the European 'defence budget crunch' may have serious strategic repercussions: 'If Europe further ignores the consequences of the defence-economic imperative, it will run the danger of losing its operational military capability'. According to his analysis, 'the defence-economic imperative' may, in the long run, not only entail '27 bonsai armies' but also a 'defence industrial exodus', the loss of technological leadership and 'a Europe that is incapable of defending its strategic interest outside its borders'.

Methodologically, it is much more difficult to gauge the non-material, ideational implications of the crisis than to quantify the hard power losses of the EU as a global actor. Recognition (Jupille and Caporaso, 1998) and external perceptions (Lucarelli and Fioramonti, 2009) form an essential part of the EU's international actorness. A deterioration of the EU's image – as described above with regard to the EU's neighbourhood in the context of enlargement policy – is also suggested by the findings of various scholars studying global perceptions of the EU (for the latest overview, see the contributions in Chaban and Holland, 2014). The image of the EU as an economic giant has always been prevalent in external perceptions. Its soft power is closely linked to its ability to provide welfare, prosperity and stability to its members. When this economic powerhouse was shaken in terms of its economic strength, its soft power and perceived influence also began to erode. Empirical evidence of this decline can be found in the yearly world public opinion polls published by the BBC (2012), which show a sizable drop in positive views of the EU worldwide. In 2012 in particular, (i.e. in the aftermath of the turbulence in 2011 related to Eurozone crisis management), the EU's global influence rating sharply declined. On average, 48 per cent of respondents in the 22 countries surveyed still had positive views of the Union, but positive perceptions dropped steeply (in comparison to 2011), for example, in Ghana (−26 per centage points), Indonesia (−20), Chile (−18), Australia and South Korea (−17), Japan and Russia (−13), Brazil and India (−12), Canada (−9) and the US and China (−5).

Chaban and Holland (2014: 249) also conclude that the crisis vaulted the EU into the headlines and increased its salience but that media coverage, public opinion and the views of influential stakeholders in various third countries have been detrimentally affected by the crisis. The crisis has left a substantial dent in the EU's external image: the circle of golden stars seems to have lost some of its shine worldwide and the Union's self-proclaimed image as a role model and a provider of solutions for global challenges has been jeopardised. This image reversal from an anchor of stability to a trouble-maker is also mirrored in the EU's strategic partnerships, which nowadays seem to be more about reassuring the EU about its own global role than about cooperation on global challenges. In this sense, the crisis has functioned as a 'game changer' for the EU's strategic partnerships. In particular, the EU's relations with emerging powers experienced a 'role reversal' in mutual perceptions, with the EU transforming from an aid provider into an aid recipient. The EU is no longer in a position to dictate good economic practices to the rest of the world (Grevi and Renard, 2012). All in all, the Union's global strategic decline (in terms of both hard power and perceived influence) was accelerated by the crisis.

The euro crisis: blow or boost for the EU as a global actor?

This analysis has painted a rather gloomy picture of the crisis-ridden EU's political and military role in the world. One must not forget, however, that many elements of EU foreign policy have kept on working despite the crisis (for example, advances in nuclear negotiations with Iran, mediation between Serbia and Kosovo, sanction policies against Syria and Russia, the launch of TTIP negotiations with the US and the general functioning of bilateral relationships[4]).

Moreover, the EU can be regarded as a master of resilience. European integration history has proven Jean Monnet's dictum true: 'L'Europe se fera dans les crises et elle sera la somme des solutions apportées à ces crises.'[5] Crises have thus often functioned as the grand unifiers for Europe. Is the 'crisis as a catalyst' pattern also true in this particular time and context? In other words, can this crisis ultimately represent not only a blow but also a boost for the EU's global political and military role? There seem to be certain indications in support of this assumption. One case in point relates to the pooling and sharing of military capabilities. For many years, the sensitive realm of defence was highly resistant to European cooperation, but the recent times of austerity have made member states more willing to cooperate. At the European Council meeting in December 2013, the heads of state or government agreed on 'increasing the effectiveness, visibility and impact of CSDP; enhancing the development of capabilities and strengthening Europe's defence industry" (European Council, 2013). Cash-stripped national budgets definitely triggered this willingness to cooperate. Defence was even framed in a new way, using economic arguments. In a speech at the European Defence Agency, Van Rompuy (2013) echoed this new framing by stating that 'European defence matters' – not only for security reasons but also 'because of the jobs, the cutting edge technologies, the potential for growth'. The strong and high-level advocacy of this 'CSDP as a job engine' argument is clearly linked to the crisis and the renewed interest of member states in cooperation could prevent the above-mentioned bleak scenario of a European decline in military capabilities (Mölling, 2011). However, thus far, the cost-saving initiatives such as pooling and sharing still await full implementation. They may provide an opportunity to halt European military decline, but member states must still 'walk the talk' or move 'from discussion to delivery', as Catherine Ashton (2013) succinctly asserted.

Conclusions

Politically speaking, in a final examination of core–periphery relations from a global perspective, the EU has never belonged to the core of global actors. Without a doubt, former Belgian foreign minister Mark Eyskens' comment that the EU is an economic giant, a political dwarf and a military worm still rings true. The crisis hit the Union at a moment when conditions were favourable for the economic giant to enhance its political clout. However, when the economic giant tumbled, it also lost its newly gained political ambitions. There is no question that the financial, economic and sovereign debt crisis not only affected core–periphery relations in the EU but also took its toll on the EU's global role. Intra-EU centrifugal forces additionally hindered external action. Some repercussions of the crisis seem to be more ephemeral (for example, the shifts in agenda), while others (such as financial constraints in all policy dimensions and the battered external image of the EU) will probably prove more persistent. By reinforcing internal fragmentation, the crisis aggravated the long-term structural problems of the EU's global actorness. Half a decade post-Lisbon, the perpetual dilemma of EU foreign policy still remains: all member states – both core and periphery – would like the

Union to wield the joint weight of the 28 states; however, the willingness of each member state to cooperate with the other 27 for this purpose is much more limited. Today, the European neighbourhood resembles more 'a ring of fire' (*The Economist*, 2014) than the 'ring of friends' Romano Prodi had aimed for at the launch of the European Neighbourhood Policy in 2004. It remains to be seen whether these international challenges will revitalise global Europe's ambitions and whether the EU will be able to revive the 'Lisbon moment' and finally make the leap from the periphery to the core of global political actors.

Notes

1 Geo-economic aspects will be excluded in this chapter. See the chapter by Edward Yencken in this volume.
2 Denmark has an opt-out in CSDP.
3 EU countries that are members of the OECD Development Assistance Committee (DAC). The DAC comprises the world's major donors.
4 On the latter, see the chapter by Edward Yencken in this volume.
5 Europe will be forged in crises and will be the sum of the solutions adopted for those crises.

References

Allen, D. and M. Smith (1990) 'Western Europe's presence in the contemporary international arena,' *Review of International Studies* 16(1): 19–37.

Ashton, C. (2013) 'Final Report by the High Representative/Head of the EDA on the CSDP,' 15 October. Available at: http://eeas.europa.eu/statements/docs/2013/131015_02_en.pdf (accessed 11 January 2015).

British Broadcasting Corporation (BBC) (2012) 'Views of Europe slide sharply in global poll, while views of China improve,' May. Available at: www.globescan.com/images/images/pressreleases/bbc2012_country_ratings/2012_bbc_country%20rating%20final%20080512.pdf (accessed 11 January 2015).

Biscop, S. and J. Coelmont (2013) *Europe, Strategy and Armed Forces: The Making of a Distinctive Power*. New York: Routledge.

Bretherton, C. and J. Vogler (1999) *The European Union as a Global Actor*. London: Routledge.

Brummer, K. (ed.) (2006) *The Big Three and ESDP: France, Germany, and the United Kingdom*. Gütersloh: Bertelsmann.

Chaban, N. and M. Holland (eds) (2014) *Communicating Europe in Times of Crisis: External Perceptions of the European Union*. Basingstoke: Palgrave Macmillan.

European Council of Foreign Relations (ECFR) (2013) 'European Foreign Policy Scorecard 2013,' January. Available at: www.ecfr.eu/page/-/ECFR73_SCORECARD_2013_AW.pdf (accessed 11 January 2015).

European Commission (2008) 'Standard Eurobarometer 69'. Available at: http://ec.europa.eu/public_opinion/archives/eb/eb69/eb69_en.htm (accessed 11 January 2015).

European Commission (2014) 'Standard Eurobarometer 81'. Available at: http://ec.europa.eu/public_opinion/archives/eb/eb81/eb81_en.htm (accessed 11 January 2015).

European Council (2003) 'A Secure Europe in a Better World: European Security Strategy,' 12 December. Available at: www.consilium.europa.eu/uedocs/cmsUpload/78367.pdf (accessed 11 January 2015).

European Council (2008a) 'Conclusions,' 11/12 December, 17271/1/08 REV 1. Available at: www.consilium.europa.eu/uedocs/cms_data/docs/pressdata/en/ec/104692.pdf (accessed 11 January 2015).

European Council (2008b) 'Report on the Implementation of the European Security Strategy,' 11 December. Available at: www.consilium.europa.eu/uedocs/cms_data/docs/pressdata/en/reports/104630.pdf (accessed 11 January 2015).

European Council (2010) 'Conclusions', 16 September, EUCO 21/1/10 REV 1. Available at: www.consilium.europa.eu/uedocs/cms_data/docs/pressdata/en/ec/116547.pdf (accessed 11 January 2015).

European Council (2013) 'Conclusions,' 19/20 December 2013, EUCO 217/13. Available at: www.consilium.europa.eu/uedocs/cms_data/docs/pressdata/en/ec/140245.pdf (accessed 11 January 2015).

Füle, S. (2014) Speech on the '2014 enlargement package', Committee of Foreign Affairs, European Parliament, 8 October. Available at: www.europa-nu.nl/id/vjnui9bnctzh/nieuws/speech_fule_on_the_2014_enlargement?ctx=vg09llio1gvn&tab=0 (accessed 11 January 2015).

Gates, R. (2011) 'The security and defense agenda (Future of NATO),' speech delivered in Brussels, 10 June. Available at: www.defense.gov/speeches/speech.aspx?speechid=1581 (accessed 11 January 2015).

Ginsberg, R. H. (1989) *Foreign Policy Actions of the European Community: The Politics of Scale.* Boulder, CO: Lynne Rienner.

Grevi, G. and T. Renard (eds) (2012) 'Partners in Crisis: EU Strategic Partnerships and the Global Economic Downturn,' *FRIDE*, Madrid. Available at: http://fride.org/download/RP1_Partners_in_crisis.pdf (accessed 11 January 2015).

Helwig, N. and C. Rüger (2014) 'In search of a role for the high representative: The legacy of Catherine Ashton,' *International Spectator* 49(4): 1–17.

Howorth, J. (2009) 'What Europe badly needs is a "Grand Strategy",' *Europe's World*, 1 October. Available at: http://europesworld.org/2009/10/01/what-europe-badly-needs-is-a-grand-strategy/#.VKg_kyx0zDc (accessed 11 January 2015).

Jopp, M. and P. Schlotter (2007) 'Die Europäische Union: ein kollektiver außenpolitischer Akteur? Theoretische Annäherung und Einführung,' in M. Jopp and P. Schlotter (eds) *Kollektive Außenpolitik: Die Europäische Union als internationaler Akteur.* Baden-Baden: Nomos, pp. 9–28.

Jupille, J. and J. A. Caporaso (1998) 'States, Agency, and Rules: The European Union in Global Environmental Politics,' in C. Rhodes (ed.) *The European Union in the World Community.* Boulder, CO: Lynne Rienner, pp. 213–229.

Kaplan, R. D. (2012) 'NATO's Ordinary Future,' *Stratfor*, 9 May. Available at: www.stratfor.com/weekly/natos-ordinary-future#axzz3O3cPI0wQ (accessed 11 January 2015).

Kempin, R. and M. Overhaus (eds) (2013) 'EU-Außenpolitik in Zeiten der Finanz- und Schuldenkrise,' SWP Study S9, April. Available at: www.swp-berlin.org/fileadmin/contents/products/studien/2013_S09_kmp_ovs.pdf (accessed 11 January 2015).

Kempin, R. and M. Overhaus (2014) 'EU foreign policy in times of the financial and debt crisis,' *European Foreign Affairs Review* 19(2): 179–194.

Lehne, S. (2012) *The Big Three in EU Foreign Policy.* Washington, DC: Carnegie Endowment for International Peace.

Lucarelli, S. and L. Fioramonti (eds) (2009) *External Perceptions of the European Union as a Global Actor.* London: Routledge.

Mead, W. R. (2014) '2013: The world's biggest losers,' *The American Interest*, 5 January. Available at: www.the-american-interest.com/2014/01/05/2013-the-worlds-biggest-losers (accessed 11 January 2015).

Melcher, M. (2014) *Awkwardness and Reliability: Die britische Europapolitik von 1997 bis 2013*. Marburg: Tectum.

Möckli, D. (2012) 'The Strategic Weakening of Debt-ridden Europe,' in D. Möckli (ed.) *Strategic Trends 2012: Key Developments in Global Affairs*. Zurich: Center for Security Studies, pp. 55–78.

Mogherini, F. (2014) Speech at the Berlin Forum for Foreign Policy, 11 November. Available at: www.koerber-stiftung.de/mediathek/player/rede-zur-eroeffnung-des-berliner-forums-aussenpolitik-2014-von-federica-mogherini.html (accessed 11 January 2015).

Molina, I. and A. Sorroza (2013) 'Spain and the European External Action Service,' in R. Balfour and K. Raik (eds) 'The European External Action Service and National Diplomacies,' EPC Issue Paper no. 73, March. Available at: www.fiia.fi/assets/news/The%20EEAS%20and%20National%20Diplomacies.pdf (accessed 11 January 2015).

Mölling, C. (2011) 'Europe without defence,' Stiftung Wissenschaft und Politik (SWP), Comments 38, November 2011. Available at: www.swp-berlin.org/fileadmin/contents/products/comments/2011C38_mlg_ks.pdf (accessed 11 January 2015).

Müller-Brandeck-Bocquet, G. (2006) 'The big Member States' Influence on the Shaping of the European Union's Foreign, Security and Defence Policy',' in G. Müller-Brandeck-Bocquet (ed.) *The Future of the European Foreign, Security and Defence Policy after Enlargement*. Baden-Baden: Nomos, pp. 25–53.

Müller-Brandeck-Bocquet, G. and C. Rüger (2015) *Die Außenpolitik der Europäischen Union*. München: Oldenburg (forthcoming).

Nye, J. S. (2004) *Soft Power: The Means to Success in World Politics*. New York: Public Affairs.

Organisation for Economic Cooperation and Development (OECD) (2013) 'Aid to poor countries slips further as governments tighten budget,' 3 April. Available at: www.oecd.org/newsroom/aidtopoorcountriesslipsfurtherasgovernmentstightenbudgets.htm (accessed 11 January 2015).

Organisation for Economic Cooperation and Development (OECD) (2014) 'Aid to developing countries rebounds in 2013 to reach an all-time high,' 8 April. Available at: www.oecd.org/newsroom/aid-to-developing-countries-rebounds-in-2013-to-reach-an-all-time-high.htm (accessed 11 January 2015).

Paterson, W. E. (2011) 'The reluctant hegemon? Germany moves centre stage in the European Union,' *Journal of Common Market Studies* (Annual Review of the European Union in 2010) 49(S): 57–75.

Perlo-Freeman, S. and C. Solmirano (2014) 'Trends in World Military Expenditure, 2013,' SIPRI Fact Sheet, April. Available at: http://books.sipri.org/files/FS/SIPRIFS1404.pdf (accessed 11 January 2015).

Ratiu, C. E. (2011) *EU Soft Power at its Best: Zur Leistungsfähigkeit der Europäischen Union als Demokratieförderer in Transformationsstaaten. Eine vergleichende Analyse der EU-Demokratieförderungspolitik in Slowenien, Kroatien und Serbien*. Hamburg: Dr. Kovac (VDK).

Rettmann, A. (2011) 'Former Turkish ambassador: "EU dream is dead",' *euobserver.com*, 18 November. Available at: https://euobserver.com/enlargement/114324 (accessed 11 January 2015).

Schweiger, C. (2015) 'The "Reluctant Hegemon": Germany in the EU's Post-Crisis Constellation,' in K. N. Demetriou (ed.) *The European Union in Crisis: Explorations in Representation and Democratic Legitimacy*. Cham, Heidelberg, New York, Dordrecht and London: Springer, pp. 16–32.

The Economist (2014) 'Europe's ring of fire: the European Union's neighbourhood is more troubled than ever,' 20 September.

Van Rompuy, H. (2013) *Defence in Europe: Pragmatically Forward.* Speech at the Annual Conference of the European Defence Agency, 21 March 2013, available at: www.consilium.europa.eu/uedocs/cms_data/docs/pressdata/en/ec/136394.pdf (accessed 11 January 2015).

Von Ondarza, N. (2013) 'Weniger Geld und politischer Stillstand: Interne Effekte der Finanz- und Schuldenkrise auf die GASP,' in R. Kempin and M. Overhaus (eds) *EU-Außenpolitik in Zeiten der Finanz- und Schuldenkrise*, SWP Study S9, April. Available at: www.swp-berlin.org/fileadmin/contents/products/studien/2013_S09_kmp_ovs.pdf (accessed 11 January 2015).

Youngs, R. (2014) *The Uncertain Legacy of Crisis: European Foreign Policy Faces the Future.* Washington, DC: Carnegie Endowment for International Peace.

19 The undermining of 'global Europe'?

The impact of the Eurozone crisis on third country perceptions of the European Union

Edward Yencken

Introduction

The Eurozone crisis as an issue has been predominately analysed in the context of its impact internally within the European Union (EU). This focus, while understandable, tends to ignore the impact of the Eurozone crisis on the EU's external relations with third countries. The intention of this chapter is to redress this situation by examining the impact, thus far, of the Eurozone crisis externally. Through the utilisation of the case study of EU–Australian relations and interviews with EU and Australian officials, this chapter will argue that while the Eurozone crisis has affected public perceptions of the EU, it has yet to impact on the EU's external relations in a discernable way.

This chapter will commence with an investigation of the economic implications of the Eurozone crisis and the subsequent extent to which constraints have been placed on EU foreign policy. As surmised by Spyros Economides (2013), 'a vulnerable single currency weakens the competitiveness of the single market; a less competitive single market weakens the foreign policy of a polity which is dependent – to a great extent – on its commercial prowess to be able to influence'. Consequently, the link between the Eurozone crisis and the potential undermining of the EU's ability to project itself as an international economic actor becomes apparent. As Björn Fägersten (2012) has suggested, the EU is likely to have 'less sway over issues of global economic governance', until such time as 'they put their own house in order'. Following economic implications, this chapter will then consider the broader foreign policy repercussions of the Eurozone crisis. Richard Youngs (2011) argues that 'the precariousness of the whole EU integration project means that external policies have little priority – on the grounds that if the euro fails, all bets on a common foreign policy are off'. A further problem, however, may be the extent to which economic problems and lack of a coherent foreign policy are limiting the EU's perceived importance as an international actor. As a result, the EU's ability to engage successfully with third countries may be 'impeded by structural issues, reduced economic resources, and clashing political agendas' that have come to be associated with the Eurozone crisis (Mirtchev, 2013).

The EU–Australia bilateral relationship, as the case study of this chapter, will be utilised to ascertain the extent to which an otherwise healthy bilateral relationship can be negatively influenced by the Eurozone crisis. Analysis will first focus on commonalities in values and interests that are at the core of the modern EU–Australia relationship. This will then provide the pretext for examining how the Eurozone crisis, as a newly emerged issue, can detract from the broader bilateral relationship. The often hostile tone of Australia and EU elites, suggests that, at the very least, the Eurozone crisis may serve to negatively influence the tone of bilateral relations at the public level. Despite the emergence of the Eurozone crisis as an irritant in bilateral relations, this chapter will argue that the EU–Australia relationship remains sufficiently durable to withstand such public disagreements. As an interviewed Australian Department of Foreign Affairs and Trade (DFAT) official noted, 'it does have an impact but I don't feel that it has an impact that really changes the overall relationship' (DFAT official 1, 2012).[1] This is particularly the case when viewed in the context of ongoing negotiations for a treaty-level Framework Agreement and the potential opening of negotiations for a Free Trade Agreement (FTA). Similarly, it will be suggested that the Eurozone crisis may by itself not be a significant enough issue to alter substantially the core dynamics of the EU's relationships with other third countries.

From internal to external: the emergence of the Eurozone crisis as a potential factor in EU external relations

The financial implications of the Eurozone crisis and its impact on EU foreign policy

The implications of the Eurozone crisis on the EU's foreign policy capabilities are in the first instance quite obvious when considering economic issues. This has been evident with regard to the current EU budget, with funds available for external relations under heading Number 4 'Europe as a global player' undoing significant reduction. While a 'negative trend in resource allocation' was a feature of the 2011 and 2012 budgets, the 2013 budget's share for external policies has been particularly affected. Ultimately, the allocation of €6.4 billion to EU external action represented 4.8 per cent of the total EU budget, as compared 'to the 6.4 per cent of the total budget that heading 4 counted for in 2012' (Nicoletti, 2013). Despite assurances from an interviewed Commission official that reduced funding has 'not come at the expense of external relations' (DG Trade official 1, 2012), the decline in the budget for external activities suggests that the EU will face at least some difficulties in promoting itself as an effective international actor. Moreover, the lack of resources available further underlines previous criticism of EU foreign policy capabilities, such as have been associated with the so-called 'capabilities expectation gap' (Hill, 1993). This 'gap' between the expectations placed on the EU compared to its actual capacity as an international actor could then be potentially exacerbated by financial constraints associated with the Eurozone crisis.

A relatively clear result of the Eurozone crisis has been the creation of a perception that the EU will have fewer resources available with which to manage external relations. In particular, this is associated with the single European market, the largest in the world, which has often been seen as a key factor in the EU's perceived importance as an international actor. As Martin Holland and Natalia Chaban (2013) note, in the context of Asian elite perceptions of the EU:

> the on-going sovereign euro debt crisis has led economic external profiles of the EU to once again become dominant, yet they are now depicted from a different vantage point. In the eyes of Asia, the EU turned from an 'economic giant and powerhouse' into a 'hobbled economic giant'.

Such a negative view from an economic standpoint thus has the potential to cloud more generally the way third countries perceive the EU. As surmised by Simon Duke (2012), the Eurozone crisis due to its duration 'is in danger of defining the EU's external image in the absence of any concerted efforts to otherwise define the Union's global role'.

Given the importance of the EU's status as a major economic actor, it is important to further investigate the extent to which this has been undermined by the Eurozone crisis. In particular, it is necessary to consider whether the Eurozone crisis has further enhanced perceptions of the EU as an ineffective actor. This has been evident in the Asia-Pacific region where the EU has traditionally been perceived as not being 'a significant player' (Mehta, 2013). The Eurozone crisis further enhances this perception, with Pratap Bhanu Mehta suggesting that the EU is facing greater pressure on its ability 'to speak with an independent (and coherent) voice in Asia'. Nevertheless, it is important to remain cognisant of the fact that such perspectives do have the tendency to ignore the continuing importance of the EU as an economic actor and, by inference, international actor. As the Commission (2013d) notes, 'although growth is projected to be slow, the EU remains the largest economy in the world with a GDP per head of €25,000 for its 500 million consumers'. Should the Eurozone crises continue in its duration for a number of years, however, such assertions regarding the economic importance of the EU may be brought into question.

The Eurozone crisis and the undermining of the credibility of the EU as an international actor

Aside from the financial constraints placed on the EU by the continuation of the Eurozone crisis, a secondary problem has emerged with respect to external relations. As Economides (2013) argues:

> the severity of the internal financial crisis, and its inescapable political and social consequences, has resulted in a heavy dose of 'Euro-introspection'. Europe is turning away from the world as it is consumed with its internal arrangements and future prospects for European integration.

The nature of such developments then poses obvious questions regarding the EU's ability to focus on relations with third countries while it is consumed with internal issues. Fraser Cameron (2013) has specifically noted that the 'first casualty' of the continuation of the Eurozone crisis has been 'the time available for foreign policy. EU leaders are devoting 90 per cent of their time to economic and financial matters with a consequent reduction in time available for foreign policy'. Criticisms such as Cameron's, regardless of their validity, reflect a widespread perception that the Eurozone crisis is so substantial that it is curtailing the EU's ability to focus on anything aside from internal issues. Such a perception has obvious repercussions for the EU regarding its ability to present itself as a credible international actor.

A key aspect of the damage to the EU as a result of the Eurozone crisis has been the extent to which it has undermined perceptions of the EU as an important international interlocutor. As Simon Duke (2012) has noted, 'the Euro crisis is already shaping third party perception of the EU due to the simple fact that much of the Union's presumed external attractiveness has been based upon the export of its internal values and principles'. The Eurozone crisis then serves as fundamental challenge to the EU's continuing ability to promote itself as a successful and coherent actor. Much of this problem stems from the reality that the Eurozone crisis has contributed fundamentally to 'the degradation of the reputation of the European Union as a whole on two accounts: as a model of competent economic policy management and as a model of enlightened regional integration' (Emerson, 2012). The notion of the EU as pioneering model of regional integration is particularly important to its image as an international actor. The duration of the Eurozone crisis then presents obvious challenges to the credibility of such suggestions.

Perhaps the most important aspect of the EU's approach to foreign policy has been its desire to emphasise its 'soft power' credentials. Former high representative for foreign affairs and security policy Catherine Ashton (2011) referred to the EU as having a 'soft power with a hard edge – more than the power to set a good example and promote our values. But less than the power to impose its will'. The Eurozone crisis, however, poses a specific threat to such aspirations given the extent to which it has undermined the EU's 'economic health', thereby causing 'damage to the EU's image as a well-governed entity, an important basis for the EU's attraction as a soft power' (Cameron, 2013). It is important to remember, however, that criticism of the EU effectiveness as an international actor predates the beginning of the Eurozone crisis. As Duke (2012) argues, the EU's ability to present a 'coherent, effective and visible face to the world' has been a longstanding problem for the EU. Consequently, the continuation of the Eurozone crisis would potentially cause 'further damage the Union's soft power and its global credibility'. This argument illustrates the fact that although the Eurozone crisis is not in itself the major source of the EU's perceived ineffectiveness as an international actor, it has nevertheless served to magnify pre-existing problems with regard to the EU's ability to successfully manage external relations.

EU–Australia relations and the Eurozone crisis: from stability to instability?

Common norms and values at the core of the EU–Australia relationship

Despite previous difficulties, surrounding predominantly the issue of the Common Agricultural Policy (CAP), the EU–Australia relationship has been fundamentally transformed over the past two decades. As an interviewed European External Action Service (EEAS) official remarked:

> Relations between the EU and Australia are on a remarkably improving trend. Previously we had considerable difference of opinion on agricultural policy. From what I see now we have managed to move substantially out of that mode of discourse and are on a much better path to develop a closer and effective bilateral relationship in a wide number of areas.
>
> (EEAS official 1, 2012)

At the core of the rapid improvement in the EU–Australia relationship, however, has been an emphasis on common norms and values. These common norms and values are outlined in the most recent agreement to be signed in 2008 between the EU and Australia, the Partnership Framework agreement. The Partnership Framework specifically noted the strength of cooperation between the EU and Australia both bilaterally on issues such as human rights and terrorism and multilaterally with regard to trade and climate change through their shared desire to strengthen the role of the United Nations (UN) and the World Trade Organisation (WTO), respectively (EU Delegation Australia, 2009).

An undeniably important aspect of the close nature of contemporary EU–Australia relations has been the extent to which both interlocutors have become increasingly cognisant of their shared values and interests in the Asia-Pacific region. These shared values and interests were noted by an interviewed member of the European Parliament (MEP) who suggested that 'Europe's interest in relations with Asia is similar to Australia' given the desire of both interlocutors to promote in the region 'values such as democracy, human rights and freedom of expression' (MEP 1, 2012). Similar sentiments were also expressed by former Commission president José Manuel Barroso (2011) who suggested that 'Australia and the European Union share the objectives of enjoying peace, security and trade with Asia'. The shared objectives of the EU and Australia in the Asia-Pacific region have been reflected in a number of specific instances of cooperation. First, this has been evident with regard to Asia-Pacific regional organisations such the Association of Southeast Asian Nations Regional Forum (ARF). Through the ARF, former Australian foreign minister Alexander Downer (1996) noted the key role of Australia and the EU in supporting the development of a 'new Asia Pacific security structure'. Second, the EU and Australia have supported a number of bilateral initiatives such as the Jakarta Centre for Law Enforcement

Cooperation, which is aimed at assisting Indonesia in being 'better able to detect, prevent and investigate serious transnational crime' (EU Delegation Indonesia, 2004). Third, an agreement has been signed whereby Australia could implement some aid projects on behalf of the EU and the EU could implement some aid projects on behalf of Australia (EU Delegation Australia, 2009). This agreement, the first of its kind signed by the EU has resulted in Australia implementing EU aid in Fiji and the EU implementing Australia aid in South Sudan. Agreements of this nature then serve to illustrate the strength of EU–Australia cooperation on Asia-Pacific issues.

Trade in the first instance may not seem to be an important aspect of EU–Australia cooperation given past disputes over the Common Agricultural Policy (CAP) and the asymmetrical nature of economic relations. With regard to trade asymmetry, the EU has a substantial trade surplus with Australia of €19.37 billion, and while the EU is Australia's second largest trading partner and represents 13.2 per cent of total Australian, Australia is only the EU's fifteenth largest trading partner representing only 1.4 per cent of total EU trade (European Commission, 2013a).[2] Irrespective of these facts, however, the EU shares with Australia many similar objectives with regard to international trade. This was first espoused officially in 1997 as part of a Joint Declaration, which noted shared interests with respect to 'trade liberalisation, greater transparency and the implementation of the World Trade Organisation (WTO) and Organization for Economic Cooperation and Development (OECD) principles concerning both trade in goods and services and investment' (EU Delegation Australia, 1997). The Joint Declaration equally significantly, contributed to the signing of a Mutual Recognition Agreement (MRA) in 1998.[3] This agreement was then followed by another comprehensive bilateral agreement in the form the 2002 Agenda for Cooperation. A particular focus of cooperation between the EU and Australia, however, has been on economic issues with respect to the Asia-Pacific region. This cooperation has involved efforts to effectively engage 'with Asian countries in order to promote broader principles about level playing fields, investment, openness … all these concepts that we both embrace' (EEAS official 2, 2012). The extent of cooperation on trade matters then serves to reinforce the extent to which the modern EU–Australia relationship has become broad-based in its nature.

A new irritant emerges? The Eurozone crisis as a source of public disagreement between the EU and Australia

The EU–Australia relationship, particularly since the implementation of substantial CAP reforms in the early 1990s, has experienced very few bilateral disagreements. Consequently, the emergence of the Eurozone crisis as a source of disagreement runs counter to the general trend of bilateral relations. Indeed, early interactions between the EU and Australia surrounding the crisis were mostly of a positive or a supportive nature. In the first instance this was due to the fact that the Eurozone crisis was perceived to be directly associated with the start of the global financial crisis in 2008. Former Australian foreign minister Stephen

Smith noted 'the need for a global response to the international financial crisis' (2008), instead of specifically criticising the EU. The intensification of the Eurozone crisis in 2009/10, however, saw the approach of an Australian government change. This was evident in former minister for trade Simon Crean's (2009) criticism of the supposed protectionist measures implemented by the EU. As the Eurozone crisis came to be seen as distinct from the global financial crisis, the Australian government's explicit criticism of the EU would become increasingly evident.

The shift from criticism of the EU in the context of the global financial crisis to criticising the EU in isolation has been a gradual process. This is evident in former Australian treasurer Wayne Swan's statement: 'I accept that they face a European crisis, for Europeans to solve ... but Europe must also recognize that there is a weight of responsibility to all other economies of the world to do this' (Uren and Norington, 2011). Swan's criticism indicates the beginning of the Australian government shifting from seeking to support EU attempts to solve the Eurozone crisis to outright criticism of the EU itself. For instance, the perceived failure of the EU to address the crisis was seen by an interviewed Department of Foreign Affairs and Trade (DFAT) official as 'reenergising Euroscepticism in Australia' (DFAT official 2, 2013). And such a view can also be associated with the recently elected government, given Prime Minister Tony Abbott's statements prior to the 2013 Australian election. Abbott (2013), while criticising Australia's linking of its Emissions Trading Scheme with the EU, argued sarcastically that the Rudd government had 'subcontracted out an important element of Australian economic policy' to 'the bureaucrats of Brussels. The people who have been so good at managing the economies of Europe over the last few years'.

The rhetoric of Abbott, while obviously intended for a domestic audience, demonstrates clearly the scepticism with which certain Australian political elites have come to view the EU as a consequence of the Eurozone crisis.

Given Australia's criticism of the EU's management of the Eurozone crisis, it is to be expected that the EU would begin take issue with some of the rhetoric directed its way. This was evident with regard to successive Australian governments transitioning from criticising the EU's handling of the economic crisis to criticising the EU directly. Specifically, the EU's frustration with Australian political elites was evident when former Australian Prime Minister Julia Gillard stated 'we acknowledge that every country faces its own unique circumstances; but we do believe there are some lessons for the world in the Australian way' (ABC News, 2012). In response to Gillard's criticism, *The Australian* reported that EU officials had argued that 'Ms Gillard's suggestions for Europe were only repeating what some European leaders had already been suggesting, and contained no "new ideas"' (Shanahan, 2012). Indeed, an interviewed EEAS official posed the question as to whether criticism is 'coming because of a genuine concern about how this will affect the Australian economy or is this part of reaffirming a view that the European project is wrong' (EEAS official 3, 2012)? Nevertheless this sense of frustration underlines the extent to which the extent to which the Eurozone crisis, whether EU officials like it or not, is being used to sustain external criticism of the EU itself.

As a consequence of the continuation of Australian criticism of the management of the Eurozone crisis, it is perhaps unsurprising that the EU has begun to more explicitly show its frustration with such an approach. An interviewed European External Action Service (EEAS) official noted that 'singling out the Europeans last year, we might have been willing to take the stick, but this year, I think as our political public begins to have a more mature sense of all this, there will be a greater sense of impatience regarding too much criticism' (EEAS official 1, 2012). A similar perspective was expressed by former Commission President Barroso who noted at the G20 summit in 2012 that 'frankly, we are not coming here (G20 Summit) to receive lessons in terms of democracy or in terms of how to handle the economy' (Wintour, Traynor and Smith, 2012). Nevertheless, the growing weariness of EU officials regarding external criticism then suggests that they are, at the very least, aware of the need to address damage caused by the Eurozone crisis to perceptions of the EU. A Council of the European Union official acknowledged this fact when commenting that:

> Australia is extremely worried, so whenever an Australian minister comes to Brussels the first thing they ask about is the crisis. Fortunately Barroso and Van Rompuy have rehearsed their responses very well because Australia is not the only ones asking questions. So they have their responses ready and they always explain things very clearly and honestly to the Australians.
>
> (Council official 1, 2012)

From this perspective therefore the growing willingness of EU officials to directly address the issue of the Eurozone crisis, suggests that there is a growing understanding of the need to engage with third countries, regardless of the validity of the their criticisms of the EU.

Perception versus reality: the limited tangible impact of the Eurozone crisis on EU external relations

Business as usual? The likely future impact of the Eurozone crisis on EU–Australia relations

The Eurozone crisis has undeniably contributed to an exchange of rhetoric not seen in the EU–Australia relationship for over twenty years. As a result it is not surprising that it has had some impact on relations at the political level. A DFAT official noted, in the context of Australian government criticism of the EU, that 'you'd always like these things not to have been said rather than to have been said (DFAT official 3, 2013). Irrespective of this fact, it is important to examine the impact on the Eurozone crisis on the functioning of the broader bilateral relationship between the EU and Australia. As a Commission official noted, while there have been calls from 'Australia to the EU to act in a responsible way … this has not impacted on the everyday relationship' (Directorate General (DG) Agriculture official 1, 2012). A feature of Australian criticism not impacting on the broader bilateral relationship may be the fact that there has been a clear distinction made between political rhetoric and cooperation between EU and Australian officials. This notion was reflected on by a DFAT official who noted that the Eurozone crisis 'is something that has been used for domestic politics in Australia. European diplomats and I'm guessing most of their politicians, to the extent that they are aware the remarks have been made, will understand that the remarks have been made for domestic politics purposes' (DFAT official 3, 2013). Statements of this nature then indicate the need potentially for a distinction to be made between what might be termed the 'headline' aspects of the EU–Australia relationship and the actual cooperation that is 'occurring on the ground'.

A key observation made by a number of interviewed EU and Australian officials, has been the extent to which the Eurozone crisis has, thus far, not altered the main dynamics of the EU–Australia relationship. This is best surmised by a Commission official who argued that while the Eurozone crisis 'does have an impact … I don't feel that it has an impact that really changes the overall relationship' (DG Trade official 1, 2012). An EEAS official also noted that 'there is a difference between political rhetoric and reality' (EEAS official 4, 2013). Similar sentiments were expressed by a DFAT official who further added that the 'relationship is broad-based enough so as to mean that one particular issue cannot have a significant impact. Australian criticism of the EU is reflective of an honest relationship' (DFAT official 1, 2012). Whether Australian criticism of the EU indicates an 'honest' or 'strong' relationship may be subjective but it does suggest that EU–Australian relations are sufficiently durable so as to withstand a dispute over an issue such as the Eurozone crisis. Similarly to there being suggestions that EU officials and politicians are aware of criticism of the EU for Australian domestic purposes, there have been suggestions from EU officials that Australian officials and politicians are aware of the need to not necessarily believe simplistic depictions of the Eurozone crisis. A Council official remarked on this fact by noting that 'the Australian Mission (to the EU in Brussels) are very much aware that what the chapters say is not the whole truth and that we still, by far, have the largest economy in the world and we are still one of your largest trade partners' (Council official 1, 2012). Once again, sentiments such as these illustrate the inability, thus far, of the Eurozone crisis to significantly disrupt cooperation between the EU and Australia.

While the Eurozone crisis as an issue in itself has not a tangible impact on EU–Australia relations to this point in time, it is important to investigate the likelihood a similar trend continuing into the future. Specifically, in an economic context a Commission official noted that the EU is 'a natural ally with Australia' and that 'we are on the same side as Australia in almost all trade discussions' (DG Trade official 2, 2012). With such commonalities between the EU and Australia present, it would appear the continuation of the Eurozone crisis would not pose a significant threat to future bilateral cooperation. From an Australian perspective, however, such premonitions might be premature. Evidence of this fact can be found in the comments of a DFAT official who noted that 'the real problem that we are going to run into is that the Eurozone crisis has made Europe even more inward looking for perfectly logical, sensible, understandable reasons. The problem already existed that negotiating with Europe was hard because of the difficulty of getting them to reach an agreement' (DFAT official 3, 2013). These comments then are an obvious warning of the potential ramifications of the Eurozone crisis on EU–Australia should it continue long-term into the future. Despite this fact, it is important to note that the continued strength of the EU and the Euro is of great importance to third countries such as Australia. As a DFAT official remarked, 'it is in our interest to help the EU to get out of the mess that it's in' (DFAT official 3, 2013). This comment more broadly reflects the reality that regardless of the EU's perceived mismanagement of the Eurozone crisis, the EU as international actor remains of great importance to a country such as Australia.

Broader implications for EU external relations

An undeniable feature of the Eurozone crisis is that it has had a negative impact on external perceptions of the EU. The extent to which it has impacted in a substantive way on the EU's relations with third countries, however, is something that is yet to be proven. In the context of Australian perceptions of the EU, a DFAT official noted that 'we'd like Europe to get its house in order'. These comments nevertheless were tempered by the fact that the same official noted that the Eurozone crisis had not meant that Australia is 'less interested in Europe. Business is not less interested' (DFAT official 4, 2013). Similar observations regarding the continuing importance of the EU as an international actor have also been made in the context of the relations with other third countries. Fägersten (2012) has argued that 'while the euro-crisis could lead to both more balanced and slightly more asymmetrical partnerships – depending on the partner – it will not necessarily diminish the value of having Europe as partner'. This observation suggests that the financial implications of the Eurozone crisis could contribute to the shifting of dynamics in relations with third countries. This scenario has been specifically linked to the EU-China relationship whereby China has been seen to be assuming a more prominent stance due to their significant purchase of EU member states debt. Nevertheless the extent of this investment does not necessarily mean that the EU itself is becoming a less important partner for China. This is evident by the fact that in 2012 the EU invested six billion dollars in China, and that the EU remains China's largest trading partner and import market (European Commission, 2013). Consequently, even with regard to relations with China, the EU still remains an important international partner.

Despite the likelihood of the Eurozone crisis not altering substantially the importance of the EU for significant international actors such as China, there is potential for it to negatively influence relations with developing countries. A Commission official commented on this fact while noting that the Eurozone was not likely to have a substantial impact on:

> partners like Australia but it may have implications for our developing partners simply because of the economic crisis and the whole debate about the

> budget means that we might have more constraints than in the past in financial terms.
>
> (DG Development official 1, 2012)

As noted previously, questions have been raised regarding the EU's likely expenditure on external relations in the current budget. Attempts were made to address these concerns, however, with the Commission report on the 2013 budget stating that funding for overseas aid would increase by 1.9 per cent compared to that of 2012. Nevertheless, it has been suggested that any potential financial constraints as a result of the Eurozone crisis could contribute to closer cooperation with developed countries. A DFAT official remarked on this fact by noting that the 'crisis is forcing the EU to do more with less money, meaning that closer cooperation with Australia is in its interests' (DFAT official 1, 2012). A specific example of closer cooperation can already be found in the previously mentioned delegated aid delivery agreement signed between the EU and Australia. This agreement, while not specifically aimed at addressing EU budget constraints, could nevertheless serve as a potential future example of bilateral cooperation being facilitated by the Eurozone crisis.

A key example of the limited impact of the crisis, thus far, has been the decision of third countries to continue to actively pursue bilateral agreements with the EU. Among the most notable of these agreements has been the EU–Canada Free Trade Area (FTA) known as the Comprehensive Economic and Trade Agreement (CETA). CETA is noteworthy because it represents, in terms of agreements thus far signed by the EU, the largest agreement completed with a developed country. From Canada's perspective the EU remains 'a massive market – its members have a combined economy of more than $17 trillion, which is larger than the US market. Freer access to that market opens up significant opportunities for Canadian companies' (Goldfarb, 2012). Following CETA, 2013 saw the beginning of negotiations for an EU–US FTA, formally known as the Transatlantic Trade and Investment Partnership (TTIP). Such an agreement would aim 'to liberalise trade and investment between the two blocs, which together make up 40 per cent of global economic output' (European Commission, 2013). In the case of Australia, there have also been recent proposals for an FTA at the G20 Summit hosted in Brisbane, Australia (Abbott, 2014). While such an FTA would not be as significant as those signed between Canada and the US in terms of world trade, they nevertheless symbolise the EU's ongoing desirability as an international economic actor for third countries.

Conclusion

As an issue, the Eurozone crisis is having a significant impact in negatively influencing external perceptions of the EU as an international actor. As Arne Niemann and Charlotte Bretherton (2013) argue, the Eurozone crisis has 'consumed the energies of policymakers internally and generated perceptions of disunity and incompetence externally'. Second, the case study of this chapter, the

EU–Australia relationship, has similarly demonstrated that the Eurozone crisis has damaged perceptions of the EU. Specifically, criticism has focused on the perceived inability of the EU to effectively implement measures to directly address the crisis. As a DFAT official remarked, the inability of the EU to address the Eurozone crisis effectively is having a direct impact on the perceived 'ability of European countries both individually and collectively to be global players' (DFAT official 3, 2013). These sentiments help to a significant extent to illustrate how the Eurozone crisis has come to dominate, and influence negatively, external perceptions of the EU.

Despite the Eurozone crisis facilitating negative perceptions of the EU, a clear distinction must be drawn between such perceptions and their actual impact on the EU's relations with third countries. As Fägersten (2012) argues, 'there are so far no unequivocal indications of any broad foreign policy implications arising out of the euro-crisis'. The EU–Australia relationship is a key example of this fact given that the Eurozone crisis has failed to disrupt, in any substantive way, bilateral cooperation. From a third country's perspective, the Eurozone crisis has not detracted from the EU's continued status as an important international actor. In the case of Australia, there remains the perception that the 'EU is a fabulous entity to work with. If they are on board then they can make a real difference and this has been shown time and again regarding a huge range of international settings' (DFAT official 3, 2013). Statements of this nature help to demonstrate how the EU remains an important international actor for third countries such as Australia. Thus, while the duration of the Eurozone crisis may serve an irritant with regard to the EU's relations with third countries, it is unlikely to substantially alter the extent to which the EU itself is perceived to be an important international actor.

Notes

1 Twenty-six EU officials and 16 Australian officials have been interviewed as part of an ongoing PhD research project. All references and quotes from these interviews are listed only with the date on which they were conducted, owing to the need for anonymity.
2 In 2012 EU imports to Australia totalled €14.45 billion compared to exports of €33.85 billion.
3 The MRA is an agreement which allows for 'conformity assessment (testing, inspection and certification) of products traded between Europe and Australia to be undertaken in the exporting country, rather than have to be carried out on arrival in the importing country' (European Commission, 2009a).

References

Abbott, T. (2013) Address to Liberal National Party State Convention, Brisbane, 20 July. Available at: http://foreignaffairs.co.nz/2013/07/20/tony-abbott-transcript-address-to-lnp-state-convention-brisbane/ (accessed 3 December 2014).

Abbott, T. (2014) Joint press conference with Francois Hollande, 19 November. Available at: www.liberal.org.au/latest-news/2014/11/19/prime-minister-joint-press-conference-president-hollande-parliament-house (accessed 2 December 2014).

ABC News (2012) 'Learn from us on economy, Gillard tells world leaders,' 18 June. Available at: www.abc.net.au/news/2012-06-18/learn-from-us-on-economy-gillard-tells-world-leaders/4076000 (accessed 3 December 2014)..

Ashton, C. (2011) 'A world built on co-operation, sovereignty, democracy and stability,' speech at Corvinus University, Budapest 25 February. Available at: http://europa.eu/rapid/press-release_SPEECH-11-126_en.htm (accessed 3 December 2014).

Barroso, J. M. (2011) 'Shared futures: Europe and Australia in the twenty-first century,' EU delegation to Australia, 6 September. Available at: http://eeas.europa.eu/delegations/australia/documents/press_corner/20111005_03_en.pdf (accessed 3 December 2014).

Cameron, F. (2013) *The EU as a Global Actor in Times of Crisis*. Sankt Augustin: Konrad Adenauer Stiftung.

Chaban, N. and M. Holland (2013) 'Assuming superpower status? Evolving Asian perceptions of the EU,' *L'Espace Politique* 19(1). Available at: http://espacepolitique.revues.org/2573 (accessed 3 December 2014).

Crean, S. (2009) 'ABARE Outlook 2009: A Changing Climate for Agriculture,' 4 March, Office of Minister of Trade, Australia. Available at: www.trademinister.gov.au/speeches/2009/090303_abare.html (accessed 3 December 2014).

Downer, A. (1996) 'Asia Pacific Security: Practical Cooperation in an Asian Context,' address to the International Institute for Strategic Studies, London, 18 September. Office of Minister of Foreign Affairs, Australia. Available at: www.foreignminister.gov.au/speeches/1996/iiss_asi.html (accessed 3 December 2014).

Duke, S. (2012) *The Euro Crisis, the Other Crisis and the Need for Global Thinking*. Maastricht: European Institute of Public Administration.

Economides, S. (2013) 'How to build a foreign policy for introvert Europe?', *Open Democracy*, 5 March. Available at: www.opendemocracy.net/spyros-economides/how-to-build-foreign-policy-for-introvert-europe-0(accessed 3 December 2014).

Emerson, M. (2012) *Implications of the Eurozone Crisis for EU Foreign Policy: Costs and Opportunities*. Brussels: Centre for European Policy Studies.

EU Delegation Australia (1997) 'Joint Declaration on Relations between the European Union and Australia,' 26 June, Delegation of the European Commission to Australia and New Zealand. Available at: http://eeas.europa.eu/australia/docs/australia_joint_declaration_en.pdf (accessed 4 December 2014).

EU Delegation Australia (2009) 'Union–Australia Partnership Framework: A Strategic Partnership Built on Shared Values and Common Ambition,' Delegation of the European Union to Australia, October. Available at: http://eeas.europa.eu/delegations/australia/documents/eu_australia/partnership_framework2009eu_en.pdf (accessed 3 December 2014).

EU Delegation Indonesia (2004) 'Rule of Law and Security,' Delegation of the European Union to Indonesia. Available at: http://eeas.europa.eu/delegations/indonesia/documents/eu_indonesia/law_en.pdf (accessed 3 December 2014).

European Commission (2009a) 'Press Release: EU and Australia boost bilateral trade, call for Doha deal,' 23 June. Available at posted at http://europa.eu/rapid/press-release_IP-09-984_en.htm (accessed 3 December 2014).

European Commission (2009b). 'EU and Australia boost bilateral trade: call for Doha deal,' 23 June. Available at posted at http://europa.eu/rapid/press-release_IP-09-984_en.htm?locale=EN (accessed 3 December 2014).

European Commission (2013a) 'European Union, trade in goods with Australia,' Directorate General for Trade, November. Available at: http://ec.europa.eu/trade/policy/countries-and-regions/countries/australia/ (accessed 3 December 2014).

European Commission (2013b) 'China'. Available at: http://ec.europa.eu/trade/policy/countries-and-regions/countries/china/ (accessed 3 December 2014).

European Commission (2013c) 'EU and US conclude second round of TTIP negotiations in Brussels,' 15 November. Available at: http://europa.eu/rapid/press-release_IP-13-1091_en.htm(accessed 3 December 2014).

European Commission (2013d) 'EU position in world trade,' 1 July. Available at: http://ec.europa.eu/trade/policy/eu-position-in-world-trade/ (accessed 3 December 2014).

European Union (2009) 'Global Europe: competing in the world,' *Europa*, 20 May. Available at: http://europa.eu/legislation_summaries/external_trade/r11022_en.htm (accessed 3 December 2014).

Fägersten, B. (2012) *European Foreign Policy and the Eurozone Crisis: A Swedish Perspective.* Stockholm: The Swedish Institute of International Affairs.

Goldfarb, D. (2012) 'Canada–EU trade agreement: A big deal,' Conference Board of Canada, 18 December. Available at: www.conferenceboard.ca/economics/hot_eco_topics/default/12-12-18/canada-eu_trade_agreement_a_big_deal.aspx (accessed 3 December 2014).

Hill, C. (1993) 'The capability-expectations gap, or conceptualizing Europe's international role,' *Journal of Common Market Studies* 31(3): 305–328.

Mehta, P. B. (2013) 'The Indian Perspective – Europe: A Continent without a Strategy,' in *Europe's Strategic Future: Implications of the Eurozone Crisis.* Washington, DC: The Atlantic Council.

Mirtchev, A. (2013) 'How Will the Ongoing Crisis in Europe Shape its Future Geopolitical Role?,' in *Europe's Strategic Future: Implications of the Eurozone Crisis.* Washington, DC: The Atlantic Council.

Nicoletti, B. (2013) *'Crisis upon Decline': Foreign Policy Perspectives on the EU beyond the Eurozone Crisis.* Milan: ISPI.

Niemann, A. and C. Bretherton (2013) 'EU external policy at the crossroads: the challenge of actorness and effectiveness,' *International Relations* 27(3): 261–275.

Shanahan, D. (2012) 'Europe won't be "lectured" by Julia Gillard, EC chief Jose Manuel Barroso has said,' *The Australian*, 19 June.

Smith, S. (2008) 'Press Conference: Launch of the Australia–EU Partnership Framework,' 29 October. Australian Minister for Foreign Affairs. Available at: www.foreignminister.gov.au/transcripts/2008/081029_pc.html (accessed 3 December 2014).

Uren, D. and Norington, B. (2011) 'Wayne Swan lays into inertia in Europe as world economy risks "stagnation",' *The Australian*, 27 September.

Wintour, P., I. Traynor and H. Smith (2012) 'G20 summit: Barroso blames eurozone crisis on US banks,' *The Guardian*, 19 June.

Youngs, R. (2011) 'European Foreign Policy and the Economic Crisis: What Impact and How to Respond,' Working Paper, FRIDE, Madrid.

List of interviews

Council of the European Union official 1 interviewed by the author in Brussels, 23 November 2012.

Department of Foreign Affairs and Trade (DFAT) official 1 interviewed by the author in Brussels, 20 November 2012.

Department of Foreign Affairs and Trade (DFAT) official 2 interviewed by the author in Canberra, 7 August 2013.

Department of Foreign Affairs and Trade (DFAT) official 3 interviewed by the author in Melbourne, 24 July 2013.
Department of Foreign Affairs and Trade (DFAT) official 4 interviewed by the author in Brussels, 12 November 2013.
European Commission, Directorate General Agriculture, official 1 interviewed by the author in Brussels, 28 November 2012.
European Commission, Directorate General Trade official 1 interviewed by the author in Brussels, 20 November 2012.
European Commission, Directorate General Trade official 2 interviewed by the author in Brussels, 28 November 2012.
European Commission, Directorate General Development official 1 interviewed by the author in Brussels, 26 November 2012.
European External Action Service (EEAS) official 1 interviewed by the author in Brussels, 23 November 2012.
European External Action Service (EEAS) official 2 interviewed by the author in Brussels, 22 November 2012
European External Action Service (EEAS) official 3 interviewed by the author in Brussels, 23 November 2012.
European External Action Service (EEAS) official 4 interviewed by the author in Brussels, 13 November 2013.
MEP 1 interviewed by the author in Brussels, 28 November 2012.

20 Core–periphery relations in the European Union

Some conclusions

Brigid Laffan, Christian Schweiger and José M. Magone

Core–periphery relations play an important role within nation states, across continents and at the global level. Throughout history and in the contemporary world there has been a pronounced tendency towards the formation of cores of strength, areas that are economically more advanced, more urbanised and more intensely interconnected than areas that are proximate but peripheral. To be peripheral implies being on the margins or fringes of a state or world region and dependent on the core. Political order and economic well-being are moulded by the way in which relations between core and periphery are played out through time and space (for a thorough historical review of core–periphery relations in the capitalist world economy, see Wallerstein, 2014).

The central focus of this volume is on core–periphery relations within the EU and the implications for European integration. The volume combines theoretical, comparative and empirical perspectives focussing on core–periphery dynamics from the standpoint of the core member states and those classified as peripheral. The volume's geographical reach includes the heartlands of the EU, its southern and eastern peripheries, and specific member states. The global dimension also receives attention. Although the objective of the volume is not to focus exclusively on the troubled countries in the Eurozone, the volume acknowledges the critical role that the emergence of creditors and debtors has played in the development of the Eurozone crisis and its mediation.

In drawing conclusions from the rich and varied perspectives in this volume, four questions stand out. First, what is the nature and sources of the core–periphery divide in the EU. Second, has the cleavage become more severe during the financial and sovereign debt crisis? Third, what are the effects of a deepening core–periphery divide for the governance of the EU, its influence in the world and its legitimacy vis-à-vis its citizens and fourth what was the impact on Europe's global policies.

The nature and sources of the core–periphery divide in the EU

The iterative process of EU enlargement from six to 28 states greatly increased the heterogeneity of the Union. Thus managing diversity and divergence is a key challenge for the Union and the process of integration. In the EU of six, the only serious core–periphery divide was the north–south divide within Italy. Successive enlargements have changed this dramatically leading to a Union with a core of highly developed economies forming a golden triangle, and a southern and eastern periphery with a number of countries between core and periphery.

The Union did not set out to become a 'Transfer Union' despite a core–periphery divide within its borders. Cohesion policy was therefore an important means for Europeanisation, changing previous administrative cultures into one contributing positively to market building, predominantly in the peripheral economies. Unfortunately, as a recent Bertelsmann report on the twentieth anniversary of the internal market highlights, the core countries Germany, Denmark, the Benelux and Austria were the ones that profited most from the integrated market, while the southern, central and eastern periphery benefited less (Bertelsmann, 2014). In spite of the cohesion funds, the divide remained more or less the same.

The character of the core–periphery divide in the Union is multi-layered and multi-faceted. However, at the centre is the fact that the EU is a 'dualist economy', which is evident in multiple socio-economic indicators (see Chapter 1). The national economies of the member states are quite heterogenous and diverse in terms of GDP per capita, strength of the welfare state, nature of flexicurity, and quality of the democratic political system. One could also add that there are substantially varieties in economic market culture. This is valid not only for the Eurozone countries but also for the European Union at large. While core countries are generally better governed and have a stronger economy, the peripheral countries are under considerable pressure to perform similarly, otherwise socioeconomic divergence to the EU average may increase rapidly.

Has the cleavage become more severe during the financial and sovereign debt crisis?

The Eurozone crisis that evolved in 2009 from the global financial crisis greatly exacerbated the core–periphery divide within the Union. The crisis exposed deep fissures in the design of EMU as the crisis impacted very differently on Eurozone member states. Four countries, Greece (2010), Ireland (2010), Portugal (2011) and Cyprus (2012) having lost access to the financial markets became programme countries. Put simply they exchanged the interdependence of EU membership for dependence on their partners and the IMF. Spain avoided a full bailout but had to succumb to a programme for its banks and to commit to wide-ranging reforms albeit without a Troika presence (2012). Although Italy remained a creditor country, its economy also suffered severely during the financial crisis and the financial markets placed a high premium on its capacity to borrow at the height of the crisis. The key objective in relation to Italy, the country that was seen as too big to bail and too big to fail, was to maintain market access. Italy did however experience acute pressures of contagion.

All programme countries became dependent on their partners for the funding to maintain public expenditure and financial systems. Becoming a programme country carried with it a series of consequences and costs. Each programme country had to negotiate the terms of a deal, sign multiple Memorandums of

Understanding (MoUs), and enter the world of Troika monitoring and surveillance. The 'troika', consisting of the European Commission, the ECB and the IMF became part and parcel of governance within these states (see Chapter 1 by authors). Conditionality, which was developed as a governance tool for candidate countries of the Union, became an instrument of domestic EU policy (see Chapter 1). Europeanisation, long regarded as an important external scaffolding, a *vincolo esterno,* was experienced as 'coercive Europeanisation' according to Magone (Chapter 6) or the 'domination of the periphery by the centre' (Sepos, Chapter 3).

As already described above, by the end of 2009 the financial crisis had pushed individual Eurozone economies towards a profound sovereign debt crisis. The Lisbon Treaty did not provide institutional solutions to the sovereign debt crisis. Therefore, parallel to the bailout programmes based on 'coercive Europeanisation', new ad hoc measures had to be undertaken to secure the stability of the Eurozone. However, instead of a proactive role of the EU institutions, it was the so-called directorate of France and Germany represented by German chancellor Angela Merkel and French president Nicolás Sarkozy (the so-called 'Merkozy') that took over the initiative. The frantic policy developments that followed under Germany's reluctant leadership have created a complex and multi-layered policy architecture predominantly aimed to instilling fiscal and macroeconomic stability in the Eurozone. Ultimately, the various new policy mechanisms and structures blur the division between the euro core and the outsiders. This explains why in the traditionally Eurosceptic United Kingdom calls for the renegotiation of the existing treaty structure with the aim of implementing clear safeguards for countries outside the Eurozone against deeper political integration have grown louder. The resulting call of a public referendum on the future of British membership of the EU by 2016/17 on the basis of the renegotiation of the UK's membership terms leaves the future of the third largest member state hanging in the balance. The British exit from the EU would substantially shake up the EU's internal power balance and profoundly affect the dynamics of the Single Market (Schweiger, chapter 4). Most of all it would almost certainly accelerate the process of the euro core moving towards a political union with the potential for tax harmonisation and the implementation of joint budgetary resources.

No further enlargement could result in the increasing encapsulation of the euro core, especially if the UK's demands for the renegotiation of the EU's treaty structure should result in the clear division between economic and political cooperation inside and outside of the Eurozone. However, the insider–outsider cleavage between the Eurozone and rest of the Single Market cannot conceal the deepening divisions inside the euro core itself.

What are the effects of a deepening core–periphery cleavage for the governance of the European Union or its legitimacy vis-à-vis its citizens?

Up to 2008 there was evidence of significant convergence, which according to the World Bank was unmatched outside East Asia, but the crisis had a major impact on the process of convergence (Galgoczi, chapter 9). The crisis policy response was predominantly downward adjustment of wages and public expenditure in the weaker countries, with high social and economic costs. The crisis exposed the limits of Europeanisation, particularly in southern Europe, leading Magone (Chapter 6) to conclude that Europeanisation has been superficial and that the key challenge is to reform the southern European model of capitalism. The accumulated problems in the structures of southern economies have barely been addressed in the heat of the crisis. The contrast with the Eastern periphery of the EU is marked. In comparison with most CEE countries, the shares of exports, FDI and particularly green-field FDI is much lower in the southern periphery (Galgoczi, Chapter 9). Paradoxically, the high levels of conditionality that accompanied the Big Bang enlargement in 2004, with a strong focus on institution building, may have prepared the eastern periphery for engagement with the single market in a much more effective manner than the relatively short enlargement processes that integrated the southern periphery into the Union. The objective of EU policy must be to strengthen the capacity of its peripheries to compete in the single market, but deep structural reform is largely the responsibility of the member states; external prodding matters but is no substitute for domestic responsibility for modernisation.

The Eurozone crisis was and remains a critical juncture for European governance and integration. The EU evolved as a highly fragmented, sector-driven system of public policy-making with multiple access points and a high level of consensus. Because of the nature and depth of the Eurozone crisis and the absence of EU level policy instruments to address it, policy-making in the crisis was hierarchical, driven by the Eurogroup meeting at both heads of state and government and finance ministers. The European Council became the epicentre of the crisis response. The EU system tends to obfuscate and fragment power but this was not the case during the Eurozone crisis. The crisis brought underlying power relationships sharply into focus. The geometry of leadership changed (Schweiger, chapter 4). Germany emerged as the dominant power in responding to the crisis and Chancellor Merkel became the face of the creditors. Germany effectively had a veto on the development of the policy toolkit; its domestic economic policy paradigm led it to place primary emphasis on fiscal retrenchment and the further tightening of economic policy rules in the form of the Six Pact, Two Pact and Fiscal Compact. Germany did not seek this leadership imperative and it involved a costly deployment of political capital to get German parliamentary endorsement of expensive bailouts. In the early phase of the crisis, the Franco-German couple, in the form of Merkozy, publically played a central role. This however disguised the asymmetry of the relationship between France and Germany, particularly in the economic sphere. The weak performance of the French economy and the strength of German preferences meant that France could only influence German policy on the margins. During this period, it became apparent that France and Germany, the motor of integration, could not act as the driver of integration at this juncture. Moreover, Chancellor Merkel's leadership style was extremely cautious at a time that might have called for robust leadership. The United Kingdom, as a non-euro member state, was at the margins of the crisis. The objective of the UK was to try to insulate its domestic economy from the crisis fall-out. In the UK, the crisis emboldened Eurosceptics within the governing Conservative party and UKIP. This led Prime Minister Cameron in January 2013 to pledge that if he won the next UK election, achieved in May 2015, he would renegotiate the terms of UK membership and offer the UK electorate an 'in–out' referendum. This adds additional uncertainty to the EU at a fragile time in its evolution and increases the functional and political pressures for differentiated integration (Schweiger, Chapter 4; Auer, Chapter 5).

The Eurozone crisis has left the EU with a low trust regime; electorates in the creditor countries feel that they have taken risks to support the countries in trouble and are beginning to realise that they may not get all their money back. The core–periphery economic divide has been matched by a less pronounced but no less important political divide. Eurosceptic parties of the right have had a strong electoral performance in the creditor countries whereas parties of the radical left have done better in the Mediterranean countries, especially Greece where SYRIZA achieved power and Spain where Podemos has done well in local and regional elections. This raises the question of whether or not a bottom-up pan-European social movement could alter the core policy paradigms of the Eurozone and create Europe from below (Sepos, Chapter 3). The experience of SYRIZA in power suggests that their radical policies have little traction elsewhere in Europe apart from Spain. Even in Spain, the two main parties lost a considerable share of the vote – in the European parliamentary election 2014 and regional elections 2015 – but not their central position in the political system.

The crisis has led to 'more Europe' in the form of additional policy instruments to safeguard the euro and banking union but these developments are a limited form of functional federalism. In a number of chapters, authors have called for a deepening of integration and much more ambition in the direction of 'a fully fledged, symmetrical, cooperative EU federal model, rather than more differentiated integration' (Sepos, Chapter 3). The elements of such an EU federal model involve more political and institutional integration in addition to greater fiscal federalism. Given the political and economic cost of the crisis within states and in relations between states, there appears little appetite for a fundamental reform of the EU. Paradoxically, the experience of the crisis makes it more not less difficult to enhance solidarity within the Union and increase its public finance capacity. Enhanced transfers requires trust and trust is a scarce commodity in the EU.

The international dimension

The crisis has taken an extraordinary toll on the Union's institutions, political actors, legal and policy-making systems. It has turned attention inwards and had a negative impact on perceptions of the EU in the international system. Endless meetings, muddling through and last-minute reprieve have brought the Union's weakness of political authority sharply into focus. As the Union came to terms with the first acute phase of the crisis, it was starkly reminded that geo-politics were back. Secure within a continent that was essentially prosperous and pacifist, the Union was reminded that history had not ended as the Arab Spring turned into the Arab winter and Russian president Vladimir Putin flexed his considerable power in Ukraine. Europe's 'ring of friends' was transformed into a 'ring of fire' (Rüger, chapter 18). Europe has a limited ability to influence its neighbourhood, particularly to the south given the complexities of what is happening in the greater Middle East. It can and has used sanctions against Russia, but maintaining them will be a severe test. For Europe, the boundaries between its internal world and the world outside have become increasingly blurred and very risky. European Muslims are going to the Middle East to fight with ISIS and the threat of terrorism is present on the European continent. To this must be added the severe pressure of migration across the Mediterranean. The EU and its member states face critical challenges in managing the Eurozone crisis and its centre–periphery dynamics, but it also faces a range of external challenges that will mould just what kind of European Union enters the third decade of the twenty-first century.

Conclusions: learning to understand Europe as a 'dualist economy'

The main aim of this book is to heuristically analyse the main aspects of core–periphery relations in the European Union. The sovereign debt and Eurocrises showed how vulnerable the European Union still is economically. An important major factor is the still existing between a core and periphery Europe. It is important that European leaders recognise the dualist nature of the European political economy, because then can the strategy of economic integration adjust better to the reality of the individual member states. It will be always a challenge for the European Union to deal with this heterogeneity and diversity, but by recognising it, a renewed European integration project based on past achievements may move forward with more solidarity and cohesiveness that has been the case until today. Although Germany's stability culture is a valuable element uploaded to the European level, a compromise has to be found with elements of flexibility and heterogeneity within a realistic and clear framework of rules but also principal Single Market values beyond pure liberalisation, which all member-states can adhere to without reducing too much the quality of life of its citizens. The model of a 'social market economy' as enshrined in the Treaty of Lisbon could be a re-balancing of the till now dominance of the neo-liberal agenda. Efforts in this direction are being undertaken within and outside the Eurozone; however, only the future will tell if a new compromise between stability and flexibility will emerge and in the long run bear fruit.

References

Bertelsmann Foundation (2014) '20 Jahre Binnenmarkt. Wachstumseffekte der zunehmenden europäischen Integration'. Available at: www.gedproject.de/uploads/tx_uandiproducts/files/20JBinnenmarkt_2014_final.pdf (accessed 23 December 2014).

European Economic Community (EEC) (1957) 'Preamble, Treaty Establishing the European Economic Community, EEC Treaty'. Available at: http://europa.eu/legislation_summaries/institutional_affairs/treaties/treaties_eec_en.htm (accessed 30 June 2015).
Wallerstein, Immanuel (2011–2014) *The Modern World System*, 4 vols. Berkeley and Los Angeles: University of California Press.

Index

For Product Safety Concerns and Information please contact our EU representative GPSR@taylorandfrancis.com
Taylor & Francis Verlag GmbH, Kaufingerstraße 24, 80331 München, Germany

www.ingramcontent.com/pod-product-compliance
Ingram Content Group UK Ltd.
Pitfield, Milton Keynes, MK11 3LW, UK
UKHW020020200926
475702UK00014B/1976

9781138487314